T0271129

The Federal Reserve's Role in the Global Economy

The importance of international considerations in the US Federal Reserve System's deliberations has grown over time as global financial crises and events create ever stronger repercussions in the US economy. This book critically evaluates the role of the Federal Reserve System as a player in the international monetary system over the past 100 years, starting with its initial responsibility under the gold standard and looking ahead to the challenges it will face in the twenty-first century under the fiat standard. The book is based on a conference of the same name held at the Federal Reserve Bank of Dallas in September 2014, as part of the Federal Reserve System's centennial, and contributors include many of the most highly regarded financial historians and policymakers.

Michael D. Bordo is Board of Governors Professor of Economics at Rutgers University. He is also a research associate of the NBER and a distinguished visiting fellow at the Hoover Institution, Stanford University. He has published widely in monetary economics and economic history with 15 books and over 200 journal articles and chapter contributions.

Mark A. Wynne is a vice president at the Federal Reserve Bank of Dallas, Associate Director of Research for International Economics, and the founding Director of the Bank's Globalization and Monetary Policy Institute. In the latter role, Wynne is responsible for developing and leading the Bank's research program on globalization and understanding its implications for the conduct of US monetary policy.

STUDIES IN MACROECONOMIC HISTORY

Series Editor: Michael D. Bordo, *Rutgers University*

Editors
Owen F. Humpage, *Federal Reserve Bank of Cleveland*
Chris Meissner, *University of California, Davis*
Kris James Mitchener, *Santa Clara University*
David C. Wheelock, *Federal Reserve Bank of St. Louis*

The titles in this series investigate themes of interest to economists and economic historians in the rapidly developing field of macroeconomic history. The four areas covered include the application of monetary and finance theory, international economics, and quantitative methods to historical problems; the historical application of growth and development theory and theories of business fluctuations; the history of domestic and international monetary, financial, and other macroeconomic institutions; and the history of international monetary and financial systems. The series amalgamates the former Cambridge University Press series *Studies in Monetary and Financial History* and *Studies in Quantitative Economic History.*

Other books in the series

Owen Humpage, Editor, *Current Federal Reserve Policy Under the Lens of Economic History,* 2015
Michael D. Bordo and William Roberds, Editors, *The Origins, History, and Future of the Federal Reserve,* 2013
Michael D. Bordo and Ronald MacDonald, Editors, *Credibility and the International Monetary Regime,* 2012
Robert L. Hetzel, *The Great Recession,* 2012
Tobias Straumann, *Fixed Ideas of Money, Small States and Exchange Rate Regimes in Twentieth-Century Europe,* 2010
Forrest Capie, *The Bank of England: 1950s to 1979,* 2010
Aldo Musacchio, *Experiments in Financial Democracy: Corporate Governance and Financial Development in Brazil, 1882–1950,* 2009
Claudio Borio, Gianni Toniolo, and Piet Clement, Editors, *The Past and Future of Central Bank Cooperation,* 2008
Robert L. Hetzel, *The Monetary Policy of the Federal Reserve: A History,* 2008
Caroline Fohlin, *Finance Capitalism and Germany's Rise to Industrial Power,* 2007
John H. Wood, *A History of Central Banking in Great Britain and the United States,* 2005
Gianni Toniolo (with the assistance of Piet Clement), *Central Bank Cooperation at the Bank for International Settlements, 1930–1973,* 2005
Richard Burdekin and Pierre Siklos, Editors, *Deflation: Current and Historical Perspectives,* 2004
Pierre Siklos, *The Changing Face of Central Banking: Evolutionary Trends since World War II,* 2002

(continued after index)

The Federal Reserve's Role in the Global Economy

A Historical Perspective

Edited by

MICHAEL D. BORDO

Rutgers University, New Jersey

MARK A. WYNNE

Federal Reserve Bank of Dallas

CAMBRIDGE
UNIVERSITY PRESS

CAMBRIDGE
UNIVERSITY PRESS

32 Avenue of the Americas, New York, NY 10013

Cambridge University Press is part of the University of Cambridge.

It furthers the University's mission by disseminating knowledge in the pursuit of education, learning, and research at the highest international levels of excellence.

www.cambridge.org
Information on this title: www.cambridge.org/9781107141445

First published 2016

A catalog record for this publication is available from the British Library.

Library of Congress Cataloging in Publication Data
Names: Bordo, Michael D., editor. | Wynne, Mark A., editor.
Title: The Federal Reserve's role in the global economy : a historical
perspective / edited by Michael D. Bordo, Mark A. Wynne.
Description: New York : Cambridge University Press, 2016. |
Series: Studies in macroeconomic history |
Includes bibliographical references and index.
Identifiers: LCCN 2015043517 | ISBN 9781107141445 (hardback)
Subjects: LCSH: Federal Reserve Banks. | Monetary policy – United States. |
Financial crises – United States. | United States – Economic policy – 2009– |
BISAC: BUSINESS & ECONOMICS / Economics / Macroeconomics.
Classification: LCC HG2563.F463 2016 | DDC 332/.042–dc23
LC record available at http://lccn.loc.gov/2015043517

ISBN 978-1-107-14144-5 Hardback

Contents

Contributor Biographies

Charles Bean served as deputy governor for monetary policy at the Bank of England, a position he held from 2008 until June 2014. Prior to that, he held positions as executive director and chief economist at the Bank. Bean has served in a variety of other public policy roles, including as a consultant to HM Treasury; special adviser to both the Treasury Committee of the House of Commons and to the Economic and Monetary Affairs Committee of the European Parliament; and as special adviser to the House of Lords inquiry into the European Central Bank. Other previous posts include roles in HM Treasury; professor and department chair at the London School of Economics; and visiting professor at Stanford University. He has published widely, in both professional journals and more popular media, on monetary policy, European unemployment, and macroeconomics, generally. He has served on the boards of several academic journals and was managing editor of the *Review of Economic Studies*. Bean was named president of the Royal Economic Society in 2013 and knighted in June 2014. He earned a BA in economics and mathematics from Emmanuel College, Cambridge, and a PhD from Massachusetts Institute of Technology.

Michael D. Bordo is Board of Governors Professor of Economics and director of the Center for Monetary and Financial History at Rutgers University. He has held previous academic positions at the University of South Carolina and Carleton University in Ottawa, Canada. Bordo has been a visiting professor at the University of California, Los Angeles; Carnegie Mellon University; Princeton University; Harvard University; and Cambridge University, where he was Pitt Professor of American History and Institutions. He is currently a distinguished visiting fellow at the Hoover Institution at Stanford University. Bordo has been a visiting scholar at the International Monetary Fund; Federal Reserve Banks of St.

Louis, Cleveland, and Dallas; Federal Reserve Board of Governors; Bank of Canada; Bank of England; and the Bank for International Settlements. He is a research associate of the National Bureau of Economic Research. He is also a member of the Shadow Open Market Committee. He has published many articles in leading journals and thirteen books on monetary economics and monetary history. He is editor of a series of books for Cambridge University Press titled *Studies in Macroeconomic History*. Bordo has a BA from McGill University, an MSc from the London School of Economics, and a PhD from the University of Chicago.

James M. Boughton is a senior fellow at the Center for International Governance Innovation (CIGI). Prior to joining CIGI, he held a number of positions at the International Monetary Fund, serving as historian, assistant director in the Strategy, Policy, and Review Department, and in various positions in the Research Department. He also was a professor of economics at Indiana University and an economist in the Monetary Division at the Organization for Economic Cooperation and Development in Paris. Boughton is the author of two volumes of IMF history: *Silent Revolution: The International Monetary Fund 1979–1989* and *Tearing Down Walls: The International Monetary Fund 1990–1999*. His other publications include a textbook on money and banking, a book on the US federal funds market, three books on IMF topics that he coedited, and articles in professional journals on international finance, monetary theory and policy, international policy coordination, and the history of economic thought. Boughton earned a BA in economics from Duke University, an MA in economics from the University of Michigan, and a PhD in economics from Duke University.

Mark A. Carlson is a senior economist in the Division of Monetary Affairs at the Federal Reserve Board of Governors. In addition to contributing to staff efforts supporting monetary policy at the Federal Reserve, he has worked on issues related to financial stability and to developments in the commercial banking sector. His research focuses on understanding financial crises, particularly historical episodes such as the banking crises of the 1930s and the panics of the National Banking Era, and on understanding the impact of such crises on financial intermediation. Dr. Carlson's work has been published in the *Journal of Political Economy*; the *Journal of Money, Credit and Banking*; the *Berkeley Economic Journal of Economic Analysis and Policy*; and *Explorations in Economic History*. He received his PhD from the University of California, Berkeley.

Stephen G. Cecchetti is academic dean and a professor of international economics at Brandeis International Business School. Prior to rejoining Brandeis in January 2014, he completed a five-year term as economic adviser and head of the Monetary and Economic Department at the Bank for International Settlements in Basel, Switzerland. While there, Cecchetti participated in numerous postcrisis global regulatory reform initiatives, including involvement with both the Basel Committee on Banking Supervision and the Financial Stability Board in establishing new international standards. Cecchetti's academic appointments include serving on the faculties of the Stern School of Business at New York University and the Department of Economics at the Ohio State University. He has also served as executive vice president and director of research at the Federal Reserve Bank of New York; editor of *Journal of Money, Credit and Banking*; research associate at the National Bureau of Economic Research; and as research fellow at the Center for Economic Policy Research. Cecchetti received a PhD in economics from the University of California, Berkeley.

Richard H. Clarida is the C. Lowell Harriss Professor of Economics and International Affairs at Columbia University, where he has taught since 1988. From February 2002 until May 2003, he served as assistant secretary of the Treasury for economic policy, working as chief economic adviser to the Treasury secretary. Other positions have included chairman of the economics department at Columbia University, professor at Yale University, and senior staff economist with the Reagan administration's Council of Economic Advisers. Clarida's work on monetary policy, exchange rates, interest rates, and international capital flows has appeared in academic journals. He has been a global strategic adviser with PIMCO since 2006. Clarida is a member of the Council on Foreign Relations and the National Bureau of Economic Research. With NBER, he has served as director of the project on and editor of *G7 Current Account Imbalances: Sustainability and Adjustment* (University of Chicago Press, 2007). Since 2004, he has served as coeditor of the *NBER International Macroeconomics Annual* and since 2009 as co-managing editor of the *Journal of Applied Financial Economics*. Clarida received his BS from the University of Illinois and his MA and PhD from Harvard University.

Michael P. Dooley has served as professor of economics at the University of California, Santa Cruz since 1992, after holding positions at the Board of Governors of the Federal Reserve System and in the Research Department of the International Monetary Fund. He is a partner at Cabezon Investment

Group and Drobny Global Advisors. His research includes issues in open-economy macroeconomics, including Bretton Woods II, crises in emerging markets, debt management, capital controls, capital flight, and liberalization of financial markets. Dooley is also a research associate at the National Bureau of Economic Research and an international research fellow with the Kiel Institute for the World Economy. He is an editor with the *International Journal of Finance and Economics*. Dooley earned a BS in economics from Duquesne University, an MA in economics from the University of Delaware, and a PhD in economics from Pennsylvania State University.

Barry Eichengreen is the George C. Pardee and Helen N. Pardee Professor of Economics and Professor of Political Science at the University of California, Berkeley, where he has taught since 1987. He is also a research associate of the National Bureau of Economic Research, research fellow of the Center for Economic Policy Research, and a fellow of the American Academy of Arts and Sciences. Eichengreen is the convener of the Bellagio Group of academics and economic officials and chair of the Peterson Institute of International Economics' academic advisory committee. He has served as senior policy adviser at the International Monetary Fund, has held Guggenheim and Fulbright fellowships, and has been a fellow of the Center for Advanced Study in the Behavioral Sciences at Stanford University and of the Institute for Advanced Study in Berlin. Eichengreen's recent books are *From Miracle to Maturity: The Growth of the Korean Economy*, with Dwight H. Perkins and Kwanho Shin, and *Exorbitant Privilege: The Rise and Fall of the Dollar and the Future of the International Monetary System*. He is also a regular monthly columnist for *Project Syndicate*. Eichengreen earned a PhD in economics from Yale University.

Richard W. Fisher was president and CEO of the Federal Reserve Bank of Dallas from 2005 to 2015. Fisher served as a member of the Federal Open Market Committee, the Federal Reserve's principal monetary policymaking group. He is a former vice chairman of Kissinger McLarty Associates and was founder of Fisher Capital Management and Fisher Ewing Partners. He served as assistant to the secretary of the Treasury during the Carter administration. As deputy US trade representative from 1997 to 2001, Fisher oversaw the implementation of NAFTA and various agreements with Vietnam, Korea, Japan, Chile, and Singapore. He was a senior member of the team that negotiated the bilateral accords for China and Taiwan's accession to the World Trade Organization. Throughout his career, Fisher has served on numerous for-profit and not-for-profit boards, taught graduate courses, and served on several university boards. He also serves on

Harvard University's Board of Overseers, one of the university's two governing boards. Fisher was a Weatherhead Fellow at Harvard in 2001, is an honorary fellow of Hertford College at Oxford University, and is a fellow of the American Academy of Arts and Sciences. He is a recipient of the Service to Democracy Award and Dwight D. Eisenhower Medal for Public Service from the American Assembly and a Dallas Business Hall of Fame inductee. Fisher attended the US Naval Academy, earned a degree in economics from Harvard University, read Latin American politics at Oxford, and received an MBA from Stanford University.

Owen F. Humpage is a senior economic advisor specializing in international economics in the Research Department of the Federal Reserve Bank of Cleveland. His research focuses on the international aspects of central-bank policies and has appeared in the *International Journal of Central Banking*, the *International Journal of Finance and Economics,* and the *Journal of Money, Credit and Banking.* Humpage has taught at Case Western Reserve University, Oberlin College, Cleveland State University, and Baldwin-Wallace College. He holds a BA in economics from the University of Dayton, an MA in economics from Miami University, and a PhD in economics from Case Western Reserve University.

Harold James, who studies economic and financial history and modern German history, is the Claude and Lore Kelly Professor in European Studies, a professor of history and international affairs, and director of the Contemporary European Politics and Society program at Princeton University. He is also a Marie Curie Visiting Professor at the European University Institute. Before joining Princeton in 1986, he was a fellow of Peterhouse at Cambridge University for eight years. James has authored a number of books, including *International Monetary Cooperation since Bretton Woods, The End of Globalization,* and *Making the European Monetary Union.* He is a past recipient of the Helmut Schmidt Prize in German–American Economic History and the Ludwig Erhard Prize for writing about economics. As coauthor of *The Deutsche Bank, 1870–1995,* he won the Financial Times Global Business Book Award in 1996. James holds a PhD from Cambridge University.

Steven B. Kamin is director of the International Finance Division at the Board of Governors of the Federal Reserve System. His fields of interest are open-economy macroeconomics and international finance. Kamin has held a number of positions at the Board, including serving as chief of the international development section and as senior economist. He has also worked as a visiting economist at the Bank for International Settlements, senior economist with the Council of Economic Advisers, and as research consultant at the World Bank. Kamin's most recent work has been published in the *Journal of International Economics, Journal of Money, Credit and Banking,* and *Journal of International Money and Finance.* Kamin earned a BA in economics and history from the University of California, Berkeley and a PhD in economics from the Massachusetts Institute of Technology.

Donald Kohn is Robert S. Kerr Senior Fellow in the Economic Studies Program at the Brookings Institution. He is also a member of the Financial Policy Committee at the Bank of England. A former vice chairman of the Federal Reserve, he is an expert on monetary policy, financial regulation, and macroeconomics. He advised former Federal Reserve Chairman Ben Bernanke throughout the 2008–09 financial crisis and was a key adviser to former Fed Chairman Alan Greenspan. Kohn is a forty-year veteran of the Federal Reserve System. He has served as an adviser to the Board for monetary policy, secretary of the Federal Open Market Committee, director of the Division of Monetary Affairs, and in a number of other staff positions at the Board of Governors. He was appointed to the Board in 2002 and as vice chair in 2006. He also served as chairman of the Committee on the Global Financial System, a central bank panel that monitors and examines broad issues related to financial markets and systems. Kohn has written extensively on issues related to monetary policy and financial stability. He holds a PhD in economics from the University of Michigan.

Frederic S. Mishkin is the Alfred Lerner Professor of Banking and Financial Institutions at the Graduate School of Business at Columbia University and a research associate at the National Bureau of Economic Research. His research focuses on monetary policy and its impact on financial markets and the aggregate economy. Mishkin is a former member of the Board of Governors of the Federal Reserve System, and he previously served as senior fellow at the FDIC Center for Banking Research, president of the Eastern Economic Association, executive vice president and director of research at the Federal Reserve Bank of New York, and associate economist of the Federal Open Market Committee. Mishkin has taught at the University of Chicago, Northwestern University, Princeton University, and Columbia. He has authored more than 20 books, including *The Economics of Money, Banking and Financial Markets,* and *Financial Markets and Institutions,* and he has published over 200 articles in professional journals and books. Mishkin has served as editor and on the editorial board for numerous academic journals. He has been a consultant to the Federal

Reserve Board, the World Bank, the Inter-American Development Bank, and the International Monetary Fund, as well as to central banks throughout the world. He was also a member of the International Advisory Board to the Financial Supervisory Service of South Korea and an adviser to the Institute for Monetary and Economic Research at the Bank of Korea. Mishkin received his PhD in economics from the Massachusetts Institute of Technology.

Guillermo Ortiz is chairman of Grupo Financiero Banorte–IXE. He was governor of the Banco de México from 1998 to 2009. He served as secretary of Mexico's Finance Ministry from 1994 to 1997 and undersecretary from 1988 to 1994. He is a member of the Group of Thirty. He chairs the Per Jacobsson Foundation and is on the board of the Center for Financial Stability, the advisory council of the SWIFT Institute, and the advisory board of the Globalization and Monetary Policy Institute at the Federal Reserve Bank of Dallas. Ortiz is also director and member of other international organizations and serves on the board of several companies. His previous posts include executive director at the International Monetary Fund and manager in the Economic Research Department of the Banco de México. He served as chairman of the board of the Bank for International Settlements, where he also chaired the Central Bank Governance Forum. Ortiz also was a member of the Committee to Study Sustainable Long-Term Financing of the IMF and on the Committee on IMF Governance Reform. While at the IMF, he chaired the External Panel for the Review of the Fund's Risk Management Framework. Ortiz has taught at universities in Mexico and the United States. He has written and published two books and numerous papers on economics and finance in specialized journals in Mexico and abroad and has received several honors and awards. He graduated from the National Autonomous University of Mexico (UNAM) and earned master's and doctoral degrees in economics from Stanford University.

Gary Richardson joined the Federal Reserve System as historian in 2012. The position was established in connection with the centennial of the Federal Reserve, which marked its hundredth anniversary in December 2013. As the Fed's historian, Richardson collaborates with experts at the Federal Reserve and other organizations to identify, preserve, and make accessible the Fed's historical materials. At the time of his appointment at the Fed, Richardson was an economics professor at the University of California, Irvine and served as a faculty research associate at the National Bureau of Economic Research. He has lectured and written numerous articles on banking, monetary policy, and the Fed. Richardson conducts his work as the Fed's historian as a member of the Federal Reserve Bank of Richmond's Research Department. Richardson earned a BA in political science from the University of Chicago and a PhD in economics from the University of California, Berkeley.

John B. Taylor is the Mary and Robert Raymond Professor of Economics at Stanford University and the director of the Introductory Economics Center. He is also the George P. Shultz Senior Fellow in Economics at the Hoover Institution and a senior fellow of the Stanford Institute for Economic Policy Research. Taylor's academic fields of expertise are macroeconomics, monetary economics, and international economics. His research on the foundations of modern monetary theory and policy has been applied by central banks and financial market analysts around the world. He has been on the President's Council of Economic Advisers, the Congressional Budget Office's Panel of Economic Advisers, and the California Governor's Council of Economic Advisors. Taylor served as Undersecretary of Treasury for International Affairs from 2001 to 2005. He is the author of *Global Financial Warriors: The Untold Story of International Finance in the Post-9/11 World*; *Getting Off Track: How Government Actions and Interventions Caused, Prolonged and Worsened the Financial Crisis*; and *First Principles: Five Keys to Restoring America's Prosperity*, for which he was awarded the Hayek Prize. Among other awards, he received the Treasury Distinguished Service Award and the Medal of the Republic of Uruguay. Taylor is a Guggenheim Fellow and a fellow of the American Academy of Arts and Sciences and the Econometric Society. He formerly served as professor of economics at Princeton University and Columbia University. Taylor received a BA in economics from Princeton and a PhD in economics from Stanford.

Edwin M. Truman, joined the Peterson Institute for International Economics as a senior fellow in 2001, and has been a nonresident senior fellow since 2013. Previously he served as Assistant Secretary of the US Treasury for International Affairs from December 1998 to January 2001 and returned as counselor to the secretary in 2009. He also served as director of the Division of International Finance of the Board of Governors of the Federal Reserve System and was one of three economists on the staff of the Federal Open Market Committee. Truman has been a member of numerous international groups working on economic and financial issues. He has also been a visiting economics lecturer at Amherst College and a visiting economics professor at Williams College. He has published on international monetary economics, international debt problems, economic development, and European economic integration. He is the author, coauthor or editor of

Sovereign Wealth Funds: Threat or Salvation? (2010), *Reforming the IMF for the 21st Century* (2006), *A Strategy for IMF Reform* (2006), *Chasing Dirty Money: The Fight Against Money Laundering* (2004), and *Inflation Targeting in the World Economy* (2003). Truman has a BA from Amherst College and a PhD in economics from Yale University.

Paul A. Volcker launched the Volcker Alliance in 2013 to address the challenge of effective execution of public policies and to help rebuild trust in government. Volcker worked in the US federal government for almost thirty years, culminating in two terms as chairman of the Board of Governors of the Federal Reserve System from 1979 to 1987. For ten years, he served as chairman of Wolfensohn & Co., as well as professor emeritus of International Economic Policy at Princeton University. From 1996 to 1999, he was chairman of a committee to determine existing dormant accounts and other assets in Swiss banks of victims of Nazi persecution. From 2000 to 2005, he served as chairman of the board of trustees of the International Accounting Standards Committee. In April 2004, he was asked by UN Secretary-General Kofi Annan to chair an inquiry into the United Nations' Oil-for-Food Program. In 2007, he was asked by the president of the World Bank to chair a panel of experts to review the operations of the bank's Department of Institutional Integrity. From November 2008 to 2011, he served as chairman of the President's Economic Recovery Advisory Board. Volcker was educated at Princeton, Harvard, and the London School of Economics.

David C. Wheelock, who joined the Federal Reserve Bank of St. Louis in 1993, is vice president and deputy director of the Research Division. He serves as an adviser to the Bank president on monetary policy and conducts policy-related economic research. Before joining the St. Louis Fed, Wheelock was a faculty member of the Department of Economics at the University of Texas at Austin. He has written numerous articles on banking and monetary policy topics for professional journals and Federal Reserve publications. Wheelock is the author of *The Strategy and Consistency of Federal Reserve Monetary Policy, 1924–1933*. Wheelock received a BS from Iowa State University and an MS and PhD from the University of Illinois at Urbana-Champaign.

Eugene N. White is Distinguished Professor of Economics at Rutgers University and a research associate of the National Bureau of Economic Research. He has written extensively on stock market and real estate booms and crashes, conflicts of interest, deposit insurance, banking supervision, the microstructure of securities markets, and war finance. He testified before the Congressional Oversight Panel for the Troubled Asset Relief Program and served on the Federal Reserve's Centennial Advisory Council. He is currently at work on studies of the evolution of bank supervision in the United States and of central banking in Europe. On sabbatical this year, he is a visiting scholar at the Banque de France and a visiting professor at the École des Hautes Études en Sciences Sociales in Paris. White earned an AB in history from Harvard University, a BA in history and economics from Oxford University, and an MA and PhD in economics from the University of Illinois Urbana–Champaign.

Mark A. Wynne is a vice president, associate director of research, and director of the Globalization and Monetary Policy Institute at the Federal Reserve Bank of Dallas. He is responsible for developing and leading the Bank's research program on globalization and understanding its implications for the conduct of US monetary policy. Since joining the Dallas Fed in 1989, Wynne has had a variety of responsibilities, including briefing the Bank's president on national and international economic conditions prior to meetings of the Federal Open Market Committee, providing updates on key economic issues to the Bank's board of directors, and conducting research on such topics as the effects of fiscal policy, understanding business cycles, inflation measurement, and the workings of monetary unions. His research has appeared in academic journals and in Federal Reserve publications. He holds a BA and MA from the National University of Ireland–University College, Dublin, and an MA and PhD in economics from the University of Rochester.

Acknowledgments

The chapters in this book were prepared for a conference on "The Federal Reserve's Role in the Global Economy: A Historical Perspective" that was hosted by the Federal Reserve Bank of Dallas on September 18–19, 2014, as part of the Federal Reserve System's centennial observances. We would like to thank Richard Fisher, former president and chief executive officer of the Federal Reserve Bank of Dallas, and Harvey Rosenblum, former executive vice president and director of Research at the Federal Reserve Bank of Dallas, for their support for the conference. We would also like to thank Kay Gribbin, Laurel Brewster, Jenae Golden, and Magda Salazar for logistical support during the conference, and especially Valerie Grossman for her outstanding assistance with the preparation of this book.

Introduction

Michael D. Bordo and Mark A. Wynne

This book critically evaluates the role of the Federal Reserve System as a player in the international monetary system over the past 100 years, starting with its initial responsibility under the gold standard and looking forward to the challenges it will face under the twenty-first century fiat standard. The book is based on a conference of the same name held at the Federal Reserve Bank of Dallas on September 18–19, 2014, as part of the Federal Reserve System's centennial observances.

The Federal Reserve Act was signed into law by President Woodrow Wilson on December 23, 1913. The cities that would host the twelve individual reserve banks were announced on April 2, 1914, and then the banks opened for business on November 16, 1914. In this chapter, we will highlight some of the salient themes addressed by the contributors to this book and how these themes have repeated over the years. The Fed both influences and is influenced by the global economy, but the strength of that influence has varied over the past century. We can usefully divide the Fed's history into four distinct eras. (1) From 1914 to the mid-1930s, Federal Reserve policy was dictated by the rules of the gold standard, and the Fed occasionally took actions to support foreign central banks. (2) During the Great Depression, all countries eventually abandoned the gold standard, but gold inflows from Europe during the latter half of the 1930s complicated life for Fed policymakers. With the outbreak of war, monetary policy became subservient to fiscal policy. (3) The Fed-Treasury Accord of 1951 ushered in the modern era of an independent Fed, and during the following two decades monetary policy was conducted in the context of the Bretton Woods system. That system collapsed in 1971 and was followed by decades of turmoil. (4) But by 2014, the Fed had become the closest thing the world has to a global central bank. In the absence of a major reversal of the trend in recent decades toward greater globalization, the importance of international factors will likely only grow over time.

The Federal Reserve Act was signed in 1913, the peak year for the age of globalization that existed prior to World War I. From about 1870 to 1914, the global economy was integrated to an extent that was not to be seen again until the latter decades of the twentieth century. The center of the global financial system was of course London, and some believed that the absence of a US central bank had a detrimental effect on the competitiveness of US exports. In particular, the German-American banker Paul Warburg, who was a leading architect of the Federal Reserve System (Bordo and Wheelock, 2013), argued that an American central bank could help develop a market in international trade acceptances and promote the international use of the US dollar (Broz, 1997). This view was also shared by Benjamin Strong, who was the first governor of the Federal Reserve Bank of New York. Underpinning this first era of globalization was the classical gold standard, under which the currencies of the world's major economies were fully convertible into gold. The rule-like gold standard regime was associated with a high degree of price stability and exchange rate stability. The United States had resumed convertibility after the Civil War in 1879 and the Gold Standard Act of 1900 cemented the gold-based nature of the US monetary system. The Federal Reserve Act required that member banks pay in their capital in gold or gold certificates. The reserve banks were required to maintain gold reserves equal to at least 40 percent of their outstanding notes and 35 percent of their outstanding deposits. Maintenance of adequate gold coverage was thus a pivotal consideration in the Fed's policy during the first two decades of its existence. Capital inflows and outflows (or "external drains") were of particular importance for districts such as New York that were more intimately linked to the international economy than, say, districts such as Dallas.

When the Federal Reserve System opened for business in 1914, gold convertibility had been suspended by most countries for what was expected at the time to be a relatively brief conflict between the major European powers. After the cessation of hostilities in 1918, restoration of something resembling the prewar international monetary order was a major priority for the world's leading central bankers. The actions of the Federal Reserve Bank of New York – which played an outsized role in the System at that time – were not infrequently influenced by a desire to ease Britain's transition back onto gold. As of 1924, sterling was still trading at a discount relative to its 1914 parity: the Bank of England simply lacked the gold reserves to restore the prewar parity. Under the leadership of the New York Fed, the reserve banks reduced discount rates from 4.5 percent in early 1923 to a range of 3–4 percent by the middle of 1924. The predecessor of the Federal Open Market Committee (FOMC) – the Open Market Investment Committee – authorized the New York Fed to purchase $300 million in US Treasuries to push down yields in the United States and encourage gold flows to the United Kingdom. The New York Fed also extended a $200 million line of credit to the Bank of England in exchange for an equivalent amount of sterling. The United Kingdom returned to gold in 1925 but had a difficult time maintaining convertibility. In 1927, Benjamin Strong orchestrated a reduction in the discount rate again to encourage gold flows toward London. But only eight reserve banks did so voluntarily. For the first time in the history of the System, the Board imposed the rate cut on the dissenting banks.

The United States remained on the gold standard until the onset of the Great Depression, when the Roosevelt administration suspended convertibility in 1933 and then devalued the dollar by 40 percent against gold in 1934 as part of its efforts to end the Depression. The Gold Reserve Act of 1934 authorized the Treasury to intervene in gold and foreign exchange markets, and created the Exchange Stabilization Fund, which was capitalized using gold transferred from the Fed to the Treasury. The Roosevelt administration also reorganized the structure of the Federal Reserve System with the Banking Act of 1935, effectively shifting the locus of power from New York to Washington. Both Acts reduced the Fed's autonomy, especially as regards international monetary arrangements and policy. International concerns took something of a back seat for the duration of the 1930s and 1940s, although during the latter half of the 1930s the scale of gold inflows from Europe left the Fed with less scope to use open market operations to respond to macroeconomic conditions. For the duration of World War II and for several years thereafter, the primary concern of the Fed was to support the Treasury in financing the war effort and managing the legacy of debt that was accumulated over the course of that conflict. By the later 1940s and early 1950s, tensions were beginning to set in between the need for the Fed to promote full employment and price stability, while at the same time pegging long-term interest rates. The result was the famous Fed-Treasury Accord of 1951 that marks the beginning of the modern era of a Federal Reserve that is independent within the structure of government.

The subsequent decade of the 1950s was something of a golden era for Federal Reserve policymakers. Freed of the constraints to peg long-term interest rates and with international considerations playing a minor role in policy deliberations, the FOMC focused primarily on domestic

macroeconomic objectives and relied heavily on changes in reserve requirements to respond to expected inflation. While World War II was still in
progress, representatives of the Allied powers met in Bretton Woods, New
Hampshire to devise a new international monetary architecture that would
avoid the problems of the interwar years. The new system would effectively
have the dollar at its core, but the United States committed to converting
dollars into gold at the request of foreign central banks (Bordo, 1993). At
the end of World War II, the United States held 71 percent of the world's
stock of monetary gold. Under the new system, the United States pegged the
dollar to gold at $35 an ounce, whereas the other major developed countries
pegged their currencies to the dollar. Exchange rates between the major
currencies were fixed but adjustable, the expectation being that adjustments
would be rare. For most of the 1950s the system operated without too much
difficulty, as most currencies were not fully convertible. The United States
had the world's largest economy, while Europe and Japan were focused on
postwar reconstruction.

The Bretton Woods era began in earnest in late 1958 as the currencies
of the major European countries became fully convertible. It was not long
before the inherent contradictions in the system became obvious. The essential idea of the Bretton Woods system was to try to circumvent some of the
problems associated with the gold standard by having the dollar function
as a currency to facilitate global commerce. But the very act of providing
dollar liquidity to accommodate the need for foreign exchange reserves as
global commerce expanded threatened the viability of the system. This is
often referred to as the Triffin dilemma. Once the stock of outstanding dollar liabilities exceeded the US gold stock, the United States would no longer
be able to make good on its promise to convert dollars into gold (Triffin,
1960). By August 1960, the total outstanding dollar liabilities of the United
States exceeded the US gold stock. By the end of 1965, US liabilities to foreign official institutions also exceeded the US gold stock.

In the early 1960s, the Treasury and the Fed began a series of stopgap
measures to keep the system afloat by intervening in foreign exchange markets. It was at this time that the Fed established its first swap line with a
foreign central bank (the Bank of France in 1962), and the swap network
eventually grew to include fourteen central banks (and the BIS) by the
1970s. Through the 1960s, the FOMC frequently worried about balance
of payments developments, gold loss, and exchange rate movements, but
these factors were never the main drivers of policy. An exception was the
sterling crisis of 1968, when the Fed temporarily tightened policy with the
objective of boosting the dollar and stanching gold losses. With primary

responsibility for international economic policy resting with the Treasury, the Fed did not have to give as much weight to international factors in its deliberations. Some have argued that because of this, it was easier for the Fed to pursue the inflationary policies that ultimately led to the demise of the Bretton Woods system in 1971 (Bordo, 1993; Meltzer, 2009a, 2009b). A credible commitment to price stability by the Fed was the *sine qua non* of any fixed exchange rate system relying on the US dollar as its key international reserve and vehicle currency, and from the mid-1960s onward, the Fed was to fail significantly in this regard.

The demise of the Bretton Woods system ushered in a decade (or, arguably, decades) of international monetary turmoil that has since been labeled the Great Inflation (Bordo and Orphanides, 2013). World inflation more than tripled from less than 5 percent in 1969 to 16.4 percent in 1974. Further peaks were attained in 1990 (26.9 percent) and 1994 (27.1 percent) before the more benign recent decade and a half where the world inflation rate has once again fallen below 5 percent. Contrary to the expectations of some, the transition to floating as opposed to fixed exchange rates did not free the Fed to focus exclusively on the domestic economy because it was also during this period that the United States was becoming more integrated into the global economy. Exports as a share of US GDP doubled from 5 percent in 1970 to 10 percent by 2000. Imports nearly tripled, from 5 percent in 1970 to 14 percent in 2000. The United States also became more financially integrated with the rest of the world: foreign assets as a share of GDP tripled from 20 percent in 1970 to 60 percent in 2000. The growth of syndicated bank lending to sovereign governments during the 1970s laid the groundwork for the Emerging Market debt crises of the 1980s and 1990s, starting with Mexico in 1982. The success of Paul Volcker's attempts to tame inflation in the United States was followed by a dramatic appreciation of the US dollar, which by 1985 was deemed to be excessive. The 1985 Plaza Accord sought to drive down the value of the dollar, while the 1986 Louvre Accord sought to stabilize the dollar that had dropped in value precipitously. All through this period, the Fed actively intervened in foreign exchange markets, mainly against the German Mark, but that came to an end in 1995. Since then the United States has only intervened in foreign exchange markets twice, in 1998 with a substantial purchase of yen, and in September 2000 with a substantial purchase of euros.

By the beginning of the twenty-first century, the Fed had evolved into being the closest thing the world has to a global central bank. Figure 1.1 shows the policy rates of the major central banks since the beginning of the twenty-first century. Policy rates have been at their effective lower bound

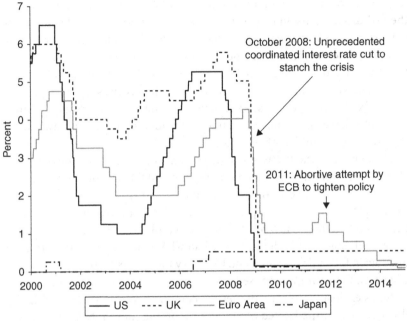

Figure 1.1. Policy rates of the major central banks.
Note: The chart plots the federal funds target rate for the United States, the main refinancing operation rate for the euro area, the uncollateralized overnight call rate for Japan, and the base rate for the United Kingdom. Policy rates have been reported as ranges in the United States since December 16, 2008, and in Japan since October 5, 2010. The chart plots average rates for these countries. On April 4, 2013, the main operating target for Japan changed to the monetary base.
Source: Haver Analytics.

for seven years at the time of writing. Two features of this figure are of interest, namely the coordinated reduction in interest rates that took place in October 2008 and the abortive tightening of policy by the European Central Bank (ECB) in 2011. The rate cut in 2008 included more central banks than the big four shown here. Specifically, the central banks of Canada, Sweden, and Switzerland also acted the same day, and several other central banks took actions along similar lines within days. This chart is suggestive of the leader–follower relationship that some argue exists between the Fed and central banks in the rest of the world (see, for example, Belke and Gros, 2005).

Some empirical evidence shows that foreign central banks do indeed respond to the level of interest rates set by the Fed when making their own decisions. Estimates of policy rules for foreign central banks show that they

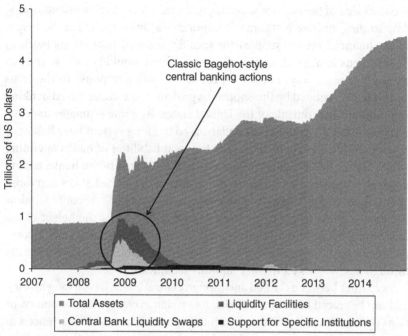

Figure 1.2. The balance sheet of the Federal Reserve.
Note: Liquidity Facilities = term auction credit, loans, net portfolio holdings of commercial paper funding facility, net portfolio holdings of TALF LLC. Support for Specific Institutions = net portfolio holdings of Maiden Lane LLC, Maiden Lane II LLC, Maiden Lane III LLC, preferred interests in AIA Aurora LLC & Alico Holdings LLC.
Source: Haver Analytics.

do seem to respond to the level of interest rates set by the Fed, independently of domestic economic developments. And this creates the potential for a multiplier effect when the Fed pursues an excessively loose monetary policy, as some have argued it has been doing for some time now. The way this works is simple. The Fed adopts a looser policy stance, foreign central banks cut rates in response, the Fed cuts rates in response to that action, foreign central banks cut again, and so on ad infinitum until we end up with a much lower level of interest rates everywhere than originally intended. That is, financial globalization creates a multiplier effect that amplifies actions on the part of the Fed. If the Fed gets it wrong – if it behaves in a less systematic or excessively accommodative manner – this spills over to the rest of the world.

Figure 1.2 shows the growth in the Fed's balance sheet since the onset of the global financial crisis. The figure highlights three sub-components of the asset side of the balance sheet: liquidity facilities (such as discount window lending and the plethora of temporary facilities created at the height of the financial crisis), support for specific financial institutions (such as Bear Stearns and AIG), and finally central bank liquidity swaps. The latter were in some ways a novel aspect of the policy response to the crisis and were necessitated by the enormous growth of the dollar-based banking system that exists outside of the United States. By some estimates the entities that make up the external dollar-based banking system have liabilities of about $15 trillion, which exceeds the total liabilities of banks operating within the United States. However, a key difference between banks issuing dollar-denominated liabilities operating within the United States and those operating overseas is that the former can access the Fed's discount window in times of stress whereas the latter cannot. Note that at the height of the crisis the volume of lending through these swap facilities was of a comparable order of magnitude to what the Fed was lending out domestically through our various temporary liquidity facilities.

Swap lines between the Fed and foreign central banks have a long history, and can be traced back to the 1960s. As foreign exchange market interventions become less frequent, and with the consolidation of the currencies of several of the European central banks under the euro, all of the swap lines were discontinued in 1998 except those with the Banco de México and the Bank of Canada. And there things remained until the global financial crisis, when lines were created in December 2007 with the ECB and the Swiss National Bank to allow them to supply dollar liquidity to commercial banks in their jurisdictions. These swap lines were increased numerous times during the crisis and were eventually made unlimited.

As the crisis abated, the swap lines were pared back and by the beginning of 2010, we were back to the pre-crisis situation where the Fed only had lines with the Mexicans and the Canadians. But with the onset of the euro area debt crisis in the spring of 2010, dollar swap lines with the ECB, Bank of England, Swiss National Bank, Bank of Japan, and Bank of Canada were re-established, and they were made semi-permanent ("until further notice") in 2013. Importantly, these arrangements entail not just a commitment by the Fed to supply dollars overseas, but by these banks to swap their domestic currencies with each other. To date, there have been no substantive drawings on any of these lines. The swap lines are one of the permanent legacies of the policy response to the crisis, and are further testimony to how enmeshed the financial systems of the world have become. They are the international equivalent of the liquidity support the Fed provides domestically at times of maximum stress. But because financial globalization has pushed currency use beyond national borders, traditional liquidity provision is not sufficient to deal with financial crises. Bagehot has gone global.

The Federal Reserve has never been immune to international developments, but the importance of international factors has varied over the years. One of the key arguments made in support of the creation of the Fed at the beginning of the twentieth century was that it would help foster the internationalization of the US dollar. Well, if that was the plan, it has been wildly successful, maybe too much so. The dollar is now the world's main international currency. Does the experience of the Fed's first century teach us anything about how best to prepare for the next century? The first issue is the perennial question of what monetary constitution – or in the language of modern economics, what rule – is best. The Federal Reserve was conceived in a world where the backing of money by gold or some other commodity was held to be the foundation upon which stable money rested. That system never worked as well as many still believe, and the last vestiges disappeared at the beginning of the 1970s. Indeed, it was the absence of a rule for US monetary policy under the Bretton Woods standard that hastened the disappearance of gold from the international monetary system. We now understand the importance of rules-based policy. Critics of the Fed argue that the deviation of the FOMC from rule-like behavior in the run up to the crisis contributed in a significant way to the excesses that led to the crisis, and also to the sluggish pace of the recovery (see, e.g., Taylor, 2009; Ohanian, Taylor, and Wright, 2012). Given the global impact of the Fed's decisions, errors here spill over to the rest of the world and get amplified. Should the Fed adhere to a rigid rule like the so-called Taylor Rule, which prescribes settings for the Fed's policy rate based on the deviation of output from potential output and the deviation of inflation from some target level (see Taylor, 1993), or is the "constrained discretion" provided by a rule-like policy framework such as inflation targeting adequate? An even bigger question is whether strict rules – if adopted – should respond to external indicators such as the exchange rate or foreign growth. Policy in smaller countries does indeed frequently respond to external factors. Would it ever be appropriate for the Fed to do the same? And finally there is a whole set of new issues raised by the development of a dollar-based banking system outside the United States and the need for the Fed to provide liquidity to this system in times of stress (even with a purely domestic mandate). As with domestic liquidity provision in times of stress, there is a moral hazard problem associated with the existence of such facilities. Mere knowledge of their existence may encourage banks to take greater risks than they otherwise would. Of course, the Fed can limit that risk-taking domestically through its supervision of US banks. But how best to deal with this problem outside of the US remains an open question.

The remaining chapters in the book delve into these issues in greater detail.

Chapter 2 by Barry Eichengreen describes the doctrinal, or conceptual, foundations of Federal Reserve policy from its founding through the early 1930s. Eichengreen identifies the role of international factors in those doctrines and conceptions and shows that international considerations were at most just part of the constellation of factors shaping the Federal Reserve's outlook and policies even during the gold standard era that ended in 1933. Which is not to say that the influence of international factors were absent, or negligible, or that the Fed's policies were without consequences for the rest of the world. Having described the doctrinal foundations of the Fed's policies, Eichengreen then analyzes how they influenced the Fed's actions on a number of key occasions during the first two decades of the System's history, focusing on episodes where the international economy and the rest of the world played an important role.

Chapter 3 by Mark Carlson and David Wheelock examines the evolution of Federal Reserve monetary policy from the mid-1930s through the 1950s in an effort to understand better the apparent success of policy in the 1950s. Whereas others have debated whether the Fed had a sophisticated understanding of how to implement policy, Carlson and Wheelock's focus is on how the constraints on the Fed changed over time. The Roosevelt administration's gold policies and New Deal legislation limited the Fed's ability to conduct an independent monetary policy. The Fed was forced to cooperate with the Treasury in the 1930s, and fully ceded monetary policy to Treasury financing requirements during World War II. Nonetheless, the Fed retained a policy tool in the form of reserve requirements, and from the mid-1930s to 1951, changes in required reserve ratios were the primary means by which the Fed responded to expected inflation. The inability of the Fed to maintain a credible commitment to low interest rates in the face of increased government spending and rising inflation led to the Fed-Treasury Accord of March 1951. Following the Accord, the external pressures on the Fed diminished significantly, which enabled the Fed to focus primarily on macroeconomic objectives. Carlson and Wheelock conclude that successful economic outcomes require not only a good understanding of how to conduct policy, but also a conducive environment in which to operate.

Michael Bordo and Owen Humpage examine the Fed's behavior under the Bretton Woods system from 1960 to 1973 in Chapter 4. During this period, Federal Reserve policymakers often mentioned balance-of-payments concerns in their deliberations and in their statements of policy actions. They did sometimes – especially in crisis situations – adjust policy slightly or temporarily because of international developments. Overall, however, US monetary policy focused primarily on economic growth at potential and full employment, even at the cost of inflation. Federal Reserve policymakers typically treated balance-of-payments objectives as superfluous to the domestic designs of monetary policy or simply mentioned and ignored them. This attitude was possible because the Federal Reserve viewed expanding capital constraints, efforts at international cooperation, and sterilized foreign-exchange operations as relieving monetary policy of responsibility for international developments and shifting accountability for international events to the US Treasury. These nonmonetary policies were often successful in the short term. Ironically, however, by eliminating the balance of payments as a constraint on US monetary policy, they allowed the Federal Reserve to create the accelerating and entrenched inflation that doomed Bretton Woods. They ultimately made the outcome worse.

Chapter 5 by Ted Truman traces the evolution of the Federal Reserve and its engagement with the global economy over the last three decades of the twentieth century. Truman's chapter examines the Fed's role in international economic and financial policy and in international economic analysis covering four areas: the emergence and taming of the Great Inflation, developments in US external accounts, foreign exchange analysis and activities, and external financial crises. By the year 2000, the international role of the US dollar was more significant than it had been within the narrow confines of official currency arrangements that characterized the Bretton Woods period due to the extraordinary globalization of financial markets that had taken place in the interim. Other currencies, including the nascent euro, the waning yen, and the yet to be internationalized Chinese renminbi, were acquiring roles in the international financial system alongside a large number of currencies of smaller economies. But the international financial system had become so large and integrated that even as the US dollar's share of international financial flows and stocks declined somewhat, the dollar's absolute importance, and with it the responsibilities of the Federal Reserve, expanded. Truman concludes that during this period the US central bank emerged to become the de facto central bank to the entire world.

John Taylor addresses the Fed's recent performance from a global perspective in Chapter 6. Taylor starts with a series of theoretical and historical observations on the benefits of rules-based policy and tries to answer the question posed by Paul Volcker in a speech in 2014, namely "What is the approach (or presumably combination of approaches) that can better reconcile reasonably free and open markets with independent national policies, maintaining in the process the stability in markets and economies that is in the common interest?" Taylor starts by explaining the basic theoretical framework, its policy implications, and its historical relevance. He then reviews the empirical evidence on the size of the international spillovers caused by deviations from rules-based monetary policy, and explores the many ways in which these spillovers affect and interfere with policy decisions globally. Finally, he considers ways in which individual monetary authorities and the world monetary system as a whole could adhere better to rules-based policies in the future and whether this would be enough to achieve the goal of stability in the globalized world economy.

Chapter 7 by Frederic Mishkin and Eugene White reviews how central banks have historically responded to financial crises, looking at the experience of the United Kingdom, France, and the United States, from the Overend-Gurney panic of 1866 to the collapse of LTCM in 1998. Mishkin and White document that "unprecedented" actions by central banks are the norm rather than the exception. The reason for this lies in the necessity of reconciling central banks' mandates for price stability and financial stability. As Mishkin and White note, under both fixed and flexible exchange rate regimes, price stability requires a rule that can be easily monitored so that central banks, and the political authorities who delegate policy responsibility to them, will be induced to follow credible policies that avoid time-inconsistency problems. The nature of financial crises is such that addressing them almost invariably requires a temporary violation of a price stability. Attempts to set a policy rule for financial stability by following Bagehot's recommendations accept that the policy will not seek to forestall a crisis but only respond when a financial crisis has hit, taking remedial action to assist solvent institutions but allowing the shock from the crisis to percolate through the whole economy. However, as Mishkin and White document, in most episodes, central banks have acted preemptively to manage failures of large financial institutions and buffer the economy from the shocks emanating from the crisis. While the reactive approach risks a recession or a deeper recession, the preemptive approach creates incentives for moral hazard. For the latter approach to be successful, two elements are essential. First, the conditions when the price stability rule will be temporarily violated must be well understood so that it becomes a contingent rule and there will be no market penalty. Second, in order to ensure that the preemptive approach does not set the stage for the next crisis, actions must be taken to mitigate moral hazard.

The book concludes with Chapter 9 summarizing remarks made at a panel by a group of eminent former policymakers (Charles Bean of the Bank of England, Stephen Cecchetti of the Bank for International Settlements, Donald Kohn of the Federal Reserve, and Guillermo Ortiz of the Bank of Mexico) critically evaluating the Fed's actions in the recent global financial crisis, along with some remarks made by Paul Volcker at the close of the conference.

References

Belke, Ansgar and Daniel Gros, 2005. "Asymmetries in the Trans-Atlantic Monetary Policy Relationship: Does the ECB Follow the Fed?" CESIfo Working Paper 1428.

Bordo, Michael D., 1993. "The Bretton Woods International Monetary System: A Historical Overview" in Michael D. Bordo and Barry Eichengreen (eds.), *A Retrospective on the Bretton Woods System: Lessons for International Monetary Reform*. Chicago, IL: University of Chicago Press.

Bordo, Michael D. and Athanasios Orphanides, 2013. *The Great Inflation: The Rebirth of Modern Central Banking*. Chicago, IL: University of Chicago Press.

Bordo, Michael D. and David C. Wheelock, 2013. "The Promise and Performance of the Federal Reserve as Lender of Last Resort 1914–1933" in Michael D. Bordo and Will Roberds (eds.), *The Origins, History, and Future of the Federal Reserve: A Return to Jekyll Island*. Cambridge: Cambridge University Press.

Broz, J. Lawrence, 1997. *International Origins of the Federal Reserve System*. Ithaca, NY: Cornell University Press.

Meltzer, Allan H., 2009a. *A History of the Federal Reserve, Volume 2, Book 1, 1951–1969*. Chicago, IL: University of Chicago Press.

2009b. *A History of the Federal Reserve, Volume 2, Book 2, 1970–1985*. Chicago, IL: University of Chicago Press.

Ohanian, Lee E., John B. Taylor, and Ian Wright, 2012. *Government Policies and the Delayed Economic Recovery*. Palo Alto, CA: Hoover Institution Press.

Taylor, John B., 1993. "Discretion versus Policy Rules in Practice." *Carnegie-Rochester Conference Series on Public Policy* 39: 195–214.

2009. *Getting Off Track: How Government Actions and Interventions Caused, Prolonged, and Worsened the Financial Crisis*. Palo Alto, CA: Hoover Institution Press.

Triffin, Robert, 1960. *Gold and the Dollar Crisis: The Future of Convertibility*. New Haven, CT: Yale University Press.

2

Doctrinal Determinants, Domestic and International, of Federal Reserve Policy 1914–1933

Barry Eichengreen

2.1 Introduction

In this chapter, I expand on the role of the Federal Reserve System in the international economy from its founding to the early 1930s, and I revisit the themes in my earlier book on the gold standard and the Great Depression.[1] Books are not always improved by second editions; sometimes they are best left to speak for themselves. In addition, I have recently written elsewhere on the role of international factors in shaping Federal Reserve policy.[2]

For these reasons I will take a somewhat different approach to the mission with which I have been tasked. I will describe the doctrinal foundations of Federal Reserve policy from the establishment of the institution through the early 1930s, focusing on the role of international factors in those doctrines and conceptions. My conclusion is that international considerations were at most part of the constellation of factors shaping the Federal Reserve's outlook and policies even in the high gold standard era that ended in 1933. However, neither was the influence of international factors absent, much less negligible. Nor were the Fed's policies without consequences for the rest of the world. Having described the doctrinal foundations of Federal Reserve policy, I will then analyze how the doctrines in question influenced the central bank's actions and shaped the impact of monetary policy on a number of key occasions, focusing in

[1] The earlier work in question being Eichengreen (1992).
[2] In Eichengreen (2013).

Prepared for the Federal Reserve Bank of Dallas conference on "The Federal Reserve's Role in the Global Economy: A Historical Perspective," Dallas, September 18–19, 2014. I thank the conference organizers, Michael Bordo and Mark Wynne, my discussant Harold James, and conference participants including Michael Dooley and Ted Truman for helpful conversations.

particular on episodes where the international economy and the rest of the world played an important role.

The doctrinal foundations of Federal Reserve policy were disputed, of course, from the institution's very creation, and in some sense even before. And those doctrinal foundations have continued to be disputed by observers of the central bank, both contemporary observers, including some within the Federal Reserve System, and historians. Different monetary policymakers have always conceived of their task differently. Their different conceptions have not always been consistent; indeed they have sometimes clashed openly. Understanding the role of these different doctrines thus entails analyzing their interplay. It means critically evaluating the work of monetary historians who may have exaggerated the influence of some doctrines relative to others. And it requires examining the role of those competing doctrines or conceptual frameworks in instances when policymakers made consequential decisions.

The approach taken here has several advantages for the task at hand. It highlights the role of ideas in the formulation and execution of policy. Ideas are not everything; in central banking as in other spheres of public policy, outcomes are shaped also by interests, by institutions, and by other factors.[3] But ideas were especially important, I would argue, in this early period when initial conceptualization of the appropriate conduct of Federal Reserve policy was taking place.

In addition, the approach taken here emphasizes the role of individuals as the carriers of ideas. Doctrine influences policy only when individuals involved in the policymaking process make a compelling case that the principles or framework in question provide useful guidance and answers to the questions at hand. Doctrines need advocates in order to influence policy. Proponents of a particular doctrinal point of view need to be able to convince their colleagues of the merits of their way of viewing the policy problem. Emphasizing the importance of doctrine in informing the actions of the Federal Reserve thus directs attention to the role of persuasion, personnel, and personality in the making of monetary policy.

The approach here also serves to usefully highlight the fact that no single doctrine has served to inform and guide Federal Reserve policy. The appropriate doctrinal foundations of US monetary policy were (and are) disputed. The influence of competing doctrines has waxed and waned with circumstance, personnel, and personality. Some will argue that this is

---

[3] For reviews of some of the relevant literature in political science, see Goldstein (1994) and Hay (2004).

always the case; I would argue that it was especially true in the US central bank's formative years.

Finally, this approach focusing on the doctrinal foundations of Federal Reserve policy highlights how the decentralized structure of the early System provided an especially fertile seedbed for competing central banking doctrines. Different doctrines could develop and dominate in different parts of the system. At several key junctures this gave rise to disagreements among reserve banks. Unchecked, it threatened the coherence of monetary policy.

A final clarification before proceeding: in this discussion of the role of international factors in the conduct of Federal Reserve policy, it will be important to distinguish several different senses in which international considerations could have influenced decisionmaking. First, the Fed could have organized policy around an international target or external economic indicator. It could have adopted an exchange rate target (as it did in this period by pegging the dollar price of gold and maintaining a minimum statutory ratio of gold reserves to monetary liabilities) and adapted policy accordingly (something that will have to be established). Second, the Fed could have adjusted its policies so as to influence economic and financial conditions in other countries, because developments abroad had a significant impact on the American economy and thereby affected the Fed's ability to meet its domestic, or internal, objectives.[4] Third, the Fed could have adjusted its policies with problems in other countries in mind because it cared about the problems of those other economies, independently of any immediate impact on the US economy. Finally, the Fed could have adjusted its policies with international considerations in mind because it was concerned with the stability of the international monetary and financial system as a whole.

In what follows I will argue that international considerations, in all four of these senses, played a role in the formulation of Federal Reserve policy at some point in the course of the central bank's first two decades.

2.2 Doctrinal Foundations

Federal Reserve policy between 1914 and 1933 was informed not by one doctrine but by several. In this section I lay out those competing doctrines and describe the contexts in which they arose.

---

[4] Modern observers refer to these as the "spillover" and "spillback" effects of monetary policy.

2.2.1 Gold Standard Doctrine

When the Federal Reserve System was created, the United States was on the gold standard. Specie resumption, following its suspension during the Civil War, was completed in 1879. The Gold Standard Act of 1900 then cemented the gold-based nature of the country's monetary circulation.[5] Gold coinage was free, gold could be held by individuals and financial institutions, and paper currency was convertible into gold coin. Member banks were required by the Federal Reserve Act, signed into law in December 1913, to pay in their capital subscriptions in gold or gold certificates (US Treasury certificates previously issued to the public that were 100 percent secured by gold in the Treasury). Federal Reserve banks were required, in turn, to hold gold as backing for their liabilities. Specifically, they were required to maintain gold reserves equal to at least 40 percent of their outstanding notes and 35 percent of their deposit liabilities. Those gold reserves were then used to settle payments between Federal Reserve districts arising out of check clearings and other transactions, via transfers from the account of one reserve bank to another through the Interdistrict Settlement Fund.[6]

The maintenance of an adequate gold cover for the central bank's liabilities was thus a foundation of policy from the point in time when the US central bank opened its doors in 1914 to the suspension of gold convertibility in 1933. Backing in the amount of 35 to 40 percent of liabilities, a proportion not atypical of contemporary central banks, was seen as important for confidence and for what academics and officials today refer to as the credibility of policy. It followed that the conventions of the gold standard ("rules," the term favored by Keynes in 1925, is too strong) were important for shaping the outlook of Federal Reserve officials and the policies of the system.[7] Losses of gold were seen as signaling the need to raise discount rates to prevent reserves from falling further (since discounting bills was a way of injecting notes into circulation and, indirectly, of influencing deposits). Increases in reserves indicated that circumstances were propitious for cutting rates and making credit more freely and cheaply available through the discount window. Capital inflows and outflows (external drains) were of particular importance for reserve districts such as New York closely connected to international markets.

---

[5] The 1900 Act unambiguously fixed the value of the dollar at 25 8/10ths grains of gold of 90 percent purity (equivalent to $20.67 per troy ounce), effectively demonetizing silver.

[6] See Eichengreen, Chitu, Mehl, and Richardson (2014).

[7] The phrase used by Keynes in *The Economic Consequences of Mr. Churchill* (1925).

This said, the Federal Reserve Act mandated only maintenance of a minimum reserve ratio, not the continuous maintenance of a specific reserve ratio. From the outset, the reserve banks and the system as a whole had more gold than required courtesy of member bank subscriptions.[8] During World War I, large inflows from embattled Europe then pushed the ratio of gold reserves to note liabilities to more than 84 percent (in March 1917). That ratio declined when the United States entered the war but still stood at nearly 50 percent at the conclusion of hostilities. The same was true for much of the 1920s, with a few exceptions highlighted below.

All this provided scope for creative interpretation of the conventions of the gold standard. It allowed the Federal Reserve System to sterilize gold movements when it so chose. Meltzer (2003), focusing on the period 1923–29, shows that there were instances where the central bank sterilized both inflows and outflows in the short run, although it did not ignore the gold standard rules in the long run.[9] His analysis, like that of Hardy (1932), points to stricter adherence to the gold standard rules before 1925 than after.

But, irrespective of whether or not the minimum reserve ratios of the gold standard bound, gold standard doctrine still influenced policy. The gold standard was not simply a set of constraints on the operation of monetary policy; it came packaged with a set of priorities and a mind frame for central bankers.[10] Maintenance of the gold parity was paramount. If a minimum gold ratio was required for a minimum of confidence, then accumulating and maintaining additional gold over and above the minimum was useful for gaining additional confidence. Changes in the domestic price of gold – external devaluation – could fatally undermine that self-same confidence; instead, internal devaluation (reductions in wages and prices) was required in response to adverse shocks. Although the central bank could not remain passive in the event of such shocks, the burden of adjustment fell mainly on other parties and markets.

2.2.2 Real Bills Doctrine

The real bills doctrine – the idea that the central bank should provide just as much money and credit as needed to accommodate the legitimate needs of

---

[8] These excess reserves came to some $138 million (or 7 percent of the country's monetary gold) as of December 31, 1914, when the first round of capital subscriptions was complete.

[9] Meltzer (2003, p. 172).

[10] Peter Temin and I (2000) refer to this as the gold standard mentalité.

commerce but not finance speculative activity – long predated the founding of the Fed. The central ideas are in the work of John Law (1705), writing in the aftermath of the founding of another important central bank, the Bank of England. They were echoed in Adam Smith's *Wealth of Nations*.[11] They were championed by members of the Banking School in the mid-nineteenth century. Importantly, they were central to the thinking of such late-nineteenth and early-twentieth century American banking and monetary reformers as Charles Conant, J. Laurence Laughlin, and H. Parker Willis.

They were therefore enshrined in the Federal Reserve Act. The act's preamble spoke of the desirability of an "elastic currency" that expanded and contracted as needed to accommodate production and trade.[12] The act instructed reserve banks to extend credit by rediscounting the short-term, self-liquidating paper presented to them by commercial banks. Limiting its discounts to such eligible paper ensured that the new central bank would be providing support for wholesome activities like trade and production while not encouraging unhealthy financial speculation. Tying the extension of central bank credit to trade and production was a way of anchoring policy in a period when the constraints of the gold standard did not bind. The practice of discounting real as opposed to fictitious bills was seen as ensuring that the central bank did not abuse its ample monetary powers by providing dangerously large amounts of credit for speculative financial purposes. And discounting only self-liquidating bills meant that there was no danger of chronic credit expansion and inflation.

Some contemporary monetary experts were aware that adherence to the real bills doctrine could lend a dangerously procyclical cast to monetary policy. A. Piatt Andrew, assistant professor of economics at Harvard University at the time (and later assistant to the National Monetary Commission and Assistant Secretary of the Treasury), emphasized the point in 1905.[13]

Nonetheless, the real bills doctrine found a ready reception within the Federal Reserve System. As Humphrey (2001) describes, economists on the Federal Reserve Board such as Adolph Miller (a student of Laughlin and subsequently professor of economics at the University of California, Berkeley) and influential reserve bank governors such as George Norris of Philadelphia and James McDougal of Chicago initially advanced a relatively pure and unvarnished version of the doctrine. They explained how the real bills doctrine could be implemented through the central bank's

---

[11] As analyzed by Laidler (1981).
[12] It spoke of the importance of "accommodating [the needs of] commerce and business."
[13] See Andrew (1905).

rediscounting function and, eventually, open market operations. These ideas pointed to member bank borrowing (via rediscounts) and market interest rates (as influenced by open market operations) as indicators of whether the Fed was succeeding in providing an elastic currency. These adherents to the real bills doctrine, who dominated both the Board and the reserve banks, grew increasingly influential in the course of the 1920s and especially following the death in 1928 of Benjamin Strong, the powerful governor of the Federal Reserve Bank of New York, who held rather different views.[14]

2.2.3 Riefler–Burgess Doctrine

Closely related to the real bills doctrine was the Riefler–Burgess Doctrine, a term coined by Brunner and Meltzer (1968). This arose out of observations on the part of W. Randolph Burgess, publications head of the statistics department of the Federal Reserve Bank of New York, and Winfield Riefler, an economist at the Board, concerning the interaction of discount-window borrowing and open market operations. Riefler and Burgess discovered the tendency for changes in discount-window borrowing and open market operations to offset one another. They showed that when the Fed provided the banks with more cash via open market purchases of securities, they had less need to turn to the discount window, and vice versa. And when the Fed purchased securities or rediscounted on behalf of one reserve bank, other reserve banks had less occasion to apply to the discount window, since credit could flow between Federal Reserve districts via the interbank market.

The discovery was inadvertent; it occurred in 1922 when the reserve banks first purchased government securities not to manage money and credit conditions but simply to augment their earning assets. Nonetheless, the implications were profound. As Burgess (1964) described the lessons, "First, as fast as the Reserve Banks bought Government securities in the market, the member banks paid off more of their borrowings; and, as a result, earning assets and earnings of the Reserve Bank remained unchanged. Second, they all discovered that the country's pool of credit is all one pool and money flows like water throughout the country."

It followed that neither the quantity of discounts nor the extent of open market operations was an adequate gauge of policy, since the two instruments were near-perfect substitutes from the point of view of credit creation.

---

[14] This is the conclusion of both Friedman and Schwartz (1963) and Timberlake (2005). For more on Strong, see below.

Neither was the expansion and contraction of commercial bank balance sheets in a particular Federal Reserve district, New York for example, especially informative since balance sheets in the different centers were linked by inter-district flows. The only statistic adequate for capturing the stance of policy was the level of interest rates prevailing in the market. When market interest rates were high, rediscounting and credit injected via open market operations were insufficient to meet the needs of business and commerce, and conversely when market rates were low. Riefler, Burgess, and their followers placed particular emphasis on short-term interest rates, given that rediscounting by banks was the incremental source of credit on the margin and the bills so rediscounted were short-term and self-liquidating.

The close connection between this emphasis on short-term market inter-est rates as a measure of the stance of policy in the Riefler–Burgess Doctrine and the central implication of the real bills doctrine will be clear. Also evi-dent is a certain ambiguity about what is meant by market interest rates and the potential for confusion between real and nominal rates, as is the poten-tial for a procyclical bias in monetary policy. The main difference from the real bills doctrine was that Riefler and Burgess acknowledged the role for activist policy – the central bank could actively influence credit conditions if it so chose through open market operations – rather than limiting its operations to passively rediscounting real bills.

2.2.4 Warburg Doctrine

Paul Warburg was a German-American banker, tireless campaigner for a US central bank, and frequent interlocutor of the National Monetary Commission. He was a member of the Federal Reserve Board from its founding in 1914 and vice governor from 1916 until his resignation in 1918. He continued to advise the System as a member of the Federal Advisory Council in the 1920s. Warburg was conversant with monetary arrange-ments in Europe, and he saw the creation of a central bank to backstop a market in bankers' acceptances as enhancing the efficiency of US credit markets and boosting the competitiveness of the American economy. A market in trade acceptances generated in the course of international transactions would be especially advantageous, in his view, for the com-petitiveness of US exports (Warburg having started out in the business of financing exports in Germany).[15]

---

[15] Warburg's interest in developing a market in trade acceptances, and how his initiatives were received, are described more fully by Broz (1997).

Thus, Warburg saw an important role for the Fed as promoting the development of this missing market in trade acceptances and fostering international use of the US dollar. Starting in 1914, the Guarantee Trust Company of New York began originating trade acceptances, and other US banks, notably National City Bank, quickly followed. These banks preferred, as banks do, to take their commission and sell the resulting asset on to other investors, the problem being that domestic demand for this still relatively unfamiliar asset was narrow (and in the circumstances of World War I, European demand could not be tapped). This made the price of these instruments relatively volatile, which only reinforced the narrowness and underdevelopment of the market.

Hence the role for the Fed as market maker. It purchased trade acceptances when private demand was weak and their prices showed signs of falling below prevailing levels, or (equivalently) when interest rates on dollar trade credit showed signs of rising relative to interest rates on alternative sources (the principal alternative source being sterling trade credit in London). Between 1917 and 1919 and for much of the 1920s, the Federal Reserve banks regularly bought and held as much as two-thirds of total outstanding acceptances (less in 1929 and the early 1930s when private demand for these relatively safe assets was strong, more in other periods like 1917 and 1927 when private demand was weak).[16]

Warburg's view that the Federal Reserve should serve as market maker in order to foster financial development, and dollar internationalization in particular, was widely shared. It was shared, specifically, by Benjamin Strong, governor of the Federal Reserve Bank of New York. Strong subscribed to Warburg's arguments about the connections between a liquid market in trade acceptances and the competitiveness of US exports. He also appreciated that the existence of a market in trade acceptances in London provided the Bank of England with a convenient lever for managing credit conditions.[17]

And what Strong believed, a majority on the Federal Reserve Board also believed (not for the last time). Thus, the Board quickly authorized the reserve banks to purchase trade acceptances for their own account, initially restricting the maturity of the bills in question (so that the transactions would be self-liquidating) but eventually giving the reserve banks discretion over maturities. While this idea that the Fed should act as market

---

[16] Details are from Eichengreen and Flandreau (2012).
[17] See Chandler (1958, pp. 86–91).

maker and currency internationalizer never dominated other priorities, it was a significant aspect of US central bank doctrine in the 1920s.[18]

Not everyone views the resulting policies in a favorable light. Rothbard argues that this policy of "unconditional support" for the acceptance market prevented the Federal Reserve from stemming the expansion of credit in the late 1920s, ultimately with disastrous consequences.[19] Others like Hardy reject the accusation, concluding that Federal Reserve support for the acceptance market never achieved levels where it seriously distorted policy.[20]

2.2.5 Strong Doctrine

Friedman and Schwartz (1963) argue that Federal Reserve policy through 1928 was shaped by the influential views of Benjamin Strong. Strong's views are not easily summarized. He believed in the desirability of fostering the market in trade acceptances, as we have seen, through System operations as acceptance buyer of last resort. He was sensitive to the role of the central bank in managing the financial system, situated as he was at the epicenter of US financial markets and having been involved in managing the last major financial crises in 1907 and 1914. Strong was advised by Irving Fisher and other economists who emphasized price-level targeting (price-level stabilization in contemporary parlance) as a goal of policy.[21] He was also close to foreign central bankers like Bank of England Governor Montagu Norman, attuning him to the role of the US central bank in helping to manage the gold standard system. Along with the sympathy he felt for foreign central banks, Strong understood that the United States depended increasingly on international trade and finance, and that the stable exchange rates of the gold standard worked to the advantage of the country by encouraging commodity exports and foreign lending.

Having embraced these myriad goals, it followed that Strong was no rigid adherent of the real bills doctrine. Rather than looking exclusively at the level of interest rates, he looked also at money and credit aggregates when gauging the stance of policy and at price-level changes when evaluating the effects. He was a believer in discretionary policy: he opposed formal rules for targeting stable prices and specifically came out against Congressional

---

[18] Nor did it necessarily dominate Benjamin Strong's own other priorities, as we will see below.

[19] Rothbard (2011, p. 723).

[20] See Hardy (1932, chapter 12).

[21] Hetzel (1985, pp. 7–8).

legislation to this effect.[22] He was comfortable with using the Fed's discretionary powers to sterilize gold inflows in violation of conventional gold standard doctrine if doing so was necessary to achieve other targets, such as a stable price level.

This, of course, also created a tension with Strong's desire to support a stable international monetary system, since the sterilization of gold inflows could lead to chronic gold losses for other countries. On other occasions like 1924 and 1927 when Strong prioritized these international considerations, his policies might downplay the implications for domestic price and financial stability. These conflicts point to the fundamental shortcoming of the Strong Doctrine, namely, that it sought to pursue multiple objectives with limited instruments.

2.2.6 Harrison Doctrine

George Harrison succeeded Benjamin Strong as governor of the Federal Reserve Bank of New York on Strong's death in November 1928 and occupied that position in the late stages of the Wall Street boom, during the Crash and through the depths of the Great Depression. It is therefore interesting to ask whether there was such a thing as a Harrison Doctrine as distinct from the Strong Doctrine.

Friedman and Schwartz argue that Fed policy changed with Strong's succession by Harrison; it became more restrictive in the late stages of the expansion and less accommodating in the slump.[23] Others like Wheelock (1991) and Meltzer (2003) see continuity where Friedman and Schwartz see change. If there was a change, it was not in doctrine, in their view, but rather in the ability of the head of the New York Fed to build the consensus needed to implement his policies. Where Strong was willful and assertive, Harrison was thoughtful and reflective; in the turbulent circumstances of the early 1930s, he was unable to unify his colleagues behind his policies. The difference, in this view, was one of temperament, not of doctrine.

Such a conclusion is not surprising, since Harrison served as Strong's deputy for the better part of nine years. Harrison shared Strong's view of the desirability of maintaining the gold standard. He shared his predecessor's view that the Federal Reserve had an important role in the maintenance of financial stability. The statement might seem peculiar given the three banking crises occurring on his watch, but it is no less accurate for the fact.

[22] Timberlake (2005, p. 212).
[23] Friedman and Schwartz (1963, pp. 411–17).

Harrison moved aggressively to rein in what he perceived as excesses on Wall Street by raising the cost of brokers loans, and following the Crash in October 1929 he acted, without the express permission of the Board, to flood financial markets with liquidity. Like Strong, Harrison appreciated the role of the Federal Reserve in providing the global public good of international monetary stability. He was sympathetic to Reichsbank President Hans Luther's application for an emergency loan in the summer of 1931 but lacked the gumption to move ahead without the cooperation of the Bank of England and Bank of France, which was not forthcoming.

If there was a doctrinal difference between Harrison and Strong, it was one of shading. Harrison was perhaps less attuned to the role of the central bank in the maintenance of price stability and more inclined to the Riefler–Burgess Doctrine. Harrison was not as close to Irving Fisher and other members of the Stable Money Association. Less experienced than Strong in technical aspects of money and finance, he was more inclined to defer to other Federal Reserve officials when they interpreted events in terms of the Riefler–Burgess Doctrine. Thus, he was prepared to conclude from the fact that interest rates were low after 1929 that monetary policy was accommodating. Although Harrison occasionally advocated open market purchases, he did so on other, very specific grounds – that they would help to stabilize the international system, that they would address specific risks to financial stability, and that they were needed to fend off political threats to the integrity of the central bank – and not because he was worried by deflation or believed that monetary policy was insufficiently accommodating of the needs of the economy.

2.2.7 Glass–Steagall Doctrine

The Glass–Steagall Act of 1932 relaxed collateral requirements on Federal Reserve notes. In doing so it was a move away from gold standard doctrine. By expanding the range of securities against which the central bank could lend, it also constituted a rejection of the real bills doctrine (something of which the bill's reluctant co-sponsor, Carter Glass, was painfully aware). It was an acknowledgment that the central bank should have the flexibility required to pursue other goals such as price stability, economic stability, and financial stability. As such it was a transition in thinking from earlier conceptual frameworks to the monetary views of Franklin Delano Roosevelt and his Brains Trust.

But the Glass–Steagall Act was initially conceived as a temporary measure set to expire after one year. Thus, to characterize it as a new monetary doctrine is a stretch. The act was drafted by Treasury and Federal Reserve Board staff and sponsored by Glass and Henry Steagall, chairmen of the Senate and House Banking Committees. It reflected concerns on the part of Harrison and Eugene Meyer, chairman of the Federal Reserve Board, that eligible securities were growing increasingly scarce as the Depression deepened. As securities on the reserve banks' balance sheets matured but more were not offered for discount (regardless of the rate), reserve banks were forced to substitute gold, where they had it, for other backing for their note issue and to take steps to actively contract the note issue (through open market sales of government securities), where they lacked additional, or "free," gold.[24]

In principle, there was a third alternative, namely abandoning the gold standard. Treasury Secretary Ogden Mills warned President Hoover in early 1932 that the Federal Reserve, short of free gold but reluctant to further restrict the money supply, might be forced to contemplate this step.[25] Reflecting the continuing influence of gold standard doctrine, all involved quickly concluded that it was better to modify the provisions making for gold backing of Federal Reserve notes rather than abandoning them entirely.

Under the Glass–Steagall Act passed on February 27, 1932, government securities were made eligible as collateral for the note issue. Reserve banks were authorized in addition to lend on previously ineligible commercial paper, broadening the range of assets against which member banks could borrow.[26] This initiative reflected a shift in prevailing monetary-policy thinking away from the rules of the gold standard and the real bills doctrine toward the more discretionary approach favored by, inter alia, Benjamin Strong. What was initially seen as a temporary expedient then became permanent policy, partly because the circumstances of February 1933, when the act was set to expire, were so extreme, but also because the explosion of inflation and financial speculation feared by critics of the act failed to materialize. That experience in turn informed the belief, developed by FDR and his advisors in the course of 1933, that monetary policy should be enlisted in the pursuit of price stability and economic recovery.

---

[24] Those sales of securities would have forced member banks to borrow at the discount window, furnishing the Fed with additional eligible paper to count as collateral, as noted by Board of Governors (1933).

[25] Hoover (1952, pp. 115–16).

[26] Initially, eligibility had been limited to notes bearing on their face evidence that they grew out of specific commercial transactions or carrying a stamp certifying that the borrower had filed with the rediscounting bank a sworn financial statement indicating that the discounted paper was self-liquidating. The sworn-statement provision was eliminated subsequently, but other restrictions remained.

2.2.8 Roosevelt Doctrine

If characterizing Glass–Steagall as monetary doctrine is a stretch, then describing FDR's monetary policies as being informed by an explicit monetary doctrine would be an absurdity. Roosevelt was an experimentalist; he was more inclined to try out a policy on an ad hoc basis and see whether it worked than to allow his actions to be dictated by a particular doctrinal framework.

Reflecting this, the president was counseled by several different groups of advisors with different views of policy, and he was inclined, as in other contexts, to adopt elements of the advice given by each group even when contradictory. In one camp was William Woodin, FDR's first Treasury secretary and staunch believer in the gold standard. Several members of the delegation that Roosevelt sent to the World Economic Conference in mid-1933 were similarly predisposed toward maintenance of that system.[27]

At the other end of the doctrinal spectrum were George Warren and his fellow inflationists. An agricultural economist at Cornell University, Warren had served on the Agricultural Advisory Commission set up by then New York Governor Roosevelt to investigate farm problems, and he continued to advise FDR during the transition and after. Warren detected in the data a correlation between the dollar price of gold and the dollar price of agricultural commodities, leading him to advocate higher gold prices as a solution to farm problems and then to the problems of the economy as a whole. His arguments were lent a veneer of academic respectability by Yale University economists James Harvey Rogers, an expert on the gold standard but also a believer that the system could be managed, and Irving Fisher, by this time something of a celebrity owing to his theory of the compensated dollar.[28]

How these contradictory positions might be reconciled was never clear; Roosevelt's response was to embrace them all and ignore the conflict. He allowed his Treasury secretary to assert that the suspension of the gold standard in March was temporary. When the Thomas Amendment to the Agricultural Adjustment Act in April then authorized the president to raise

---

[27] Delegates so inclined included James Cox, former governor of Ohio, and arguably Cordell Hull.

[28] Fisher was precluded from serving as a formal advisor to the president by his advocacy of eugenics, status as a prohibitionist, and notorious "high plateau" argument made of the stock market in 1929, but he still had extensive contacts with FDR and his circle (as described by Barber (1996)). On the compensated dollar plan, see de Boyer des Roches and Betancourt (2012).

the dollar price of gold by as much as 50 percent, he took no action. He allowed his delegates to the World Economic Conference to negotiate an agreement implying an eventual return to the gold standard but then blew it and them out of the water with his bombshell message in July. His gold buying program starting in October pushed up the dollar price of gold, consistent with the views of the inflationists of the importance of restoring commodity prices to pre-Depression levels, but he then rejected their counsel, and that of John Maynard Keynes, by pegging the price of gold at $35 an ounce in January 1934, thereby restoring select elements of the earlier gold standard. This may have been the reflationary monetary policy the economy needed, but it was not a policy informed by a consistent doctrine.

If there was a Roosevelt Doctrine, it was that monetary policy was best made by an entity other than the central bank until the latter was reorganized, with guidance from Roosevelt's hand-picked reformers, and got its act together, as it were.

2.3 Episodes

In this section I describe a number of key episodes in Federal Reserve policy in the 1920s and 1930s, focusing on cases where international considerations played a role, and analyze how the doctrines described above interacted to shape policy.

2.3.1 The Downturn of 1920–1921

The 1920–21 recession was the first major downturn on the new central bank's watch. As is the case of most recessions, a combination of factors contributed to the cyclical swing; the task is to prioritize them. And among those priorities, modern scholars argue, were monetary policies dictated by gold standard doctrine.

US prices had risen sharply during World War I.[29] Gold standard doctrine now pointed to the desirability, and indeed the necessity if the statutory gold price of $20.67 was to be maintained, of pushing them back toward prewar levels. Internal devaluation, in the form of the requisite wage and price adjustments, was seen as the appropriate adjustment mechanism by adherents to this doctrine.

---

[29] Inflation as measured by the GDP deflator ran at 17 percent in 1917, 19 percent in 1918, and 14 percent in 1919.

Once-high US gold ratios began falling following the armistice, from 48.3 percent of the note issue at the end of the war to just 43.5 percent in December 1919, alarmingly close to the statutory minimum. The New York Fed, particularly exposed to international financial pressures, saw its reserves fall to an even lower 40.2 percent. System-wide, the reserve ratio then fell further, to an alarmingly low 40.9 percent, in May 1920.

How had a once impregnable reserve position fallen to such worrisome levels? First, the United States removed its wartime embargo on gold exports in June 1919, making it an obvious source of gold for other countries seeking to replenish their reserves. Second, the reserve banks and the Board were precluded from more aggressively raising discount rates in 1919, so as to halt inflation and stem gold exports, by their role in supporting placement of the Victory Loan (the successor to wartime Liberty Loans), as needed to fund the Treasury's ongoing deficits (which were not easily eliminated, given constraints on the pace of postwar demobilization), and then in aiding Treasury efforts to roll over its short-term debt. The situation was not unlike that following World War II, when efforts by the Federal Reserve to peg the interest rates on US Treasury obligations led to several sharp bursts of inflation.

This combination of low discount rates, inflation, and the end of the export embargo made gold losses inevitable. Gold standard doctrine counseled increases in the rediscount rate to stem those losses and accelerate internal adjustment.[30] Discussion of this option became increasingly urgent once the Victory Loan was successfully placed.

The objection to this explanation for the decision to raise discount rates in 1919–20 is the observation that the Federal Reserve, in principle, could have temporarily suspended reserve requirements. This alternative is emphasized by critics of the present interpretation such as Kuehn (2011). But the gold standard mentalité militated against such unconventional action. And had the Fed temporarily suspended its gold-backing requirements in order to avoid raising the discount rate, it is not clear what other mechanism would have prevented reserve ratios from falling further and gold reserves from being exhausted.

On November 3, 1919, the directors of the New York Fed, aware of the precarious position of their bank, voted to raise discount rates for various categories of paper by 0.25–0.75 percentage points from prevailing levels of 4.0 percent. Quickly four other reserve banks followed. With the gold reserve ratio continuing to fall, New York then raised the rate it charged

---

[30] So argue Friedman and Schwartz (1963, p. 234).

for discounting government paper to 5 percent in April and 5½ percent in July. It raised its discount rate for commercial paper even more sharply, to 7 percent by mid-1920. Again, other reserve banks followed. These increases in policy rates now succeeded in inducing the sharp fall in prices prescribed by gold standard doctrine. That in turn led to a reversal in the direction of gold flows and an increase in reserve ratios system-wide and at the New York Fed in particular.

Along with gold standard doctrine, the real bills and Strong doctrines played a role in these decisions. The Annual Report of the Board of Governors for 1920 pointed to the tendency for banks to extend credit to finance "speculation in corporate stocks and securities [and]… unsold goods in storage" (commodity speculation of a non-self-liquidating sort) as opposed to the legitimate business transactions privileged by the real bills doctrine, and invoked this as an argument for raising rates.[31] Strong's correspondence documents the importance he attached in this period, in addition, to restoring the international gold standard, starting in the United States but extending to Europe, as the basis for domestic and international prosperity.[32] Interest rate increases might be painful in the short run, but they were necessary for achieving the longer-run goals to which Strong, and others who shared his view, attached priority.

Moreover, not everyone subscribed to the view that there would be pain in the short run. The Annual Report of the Board of Governors for 1920 rejected the notion that Federal Reserve policy precipitated the recession. The most policy did, the Board argued, was to "slow down the immediate tendency toward expansion."[33] Indeed, the short time span between the first interest rate increases at the end of 1919 and the onset of recession in January 1920 (according to the NBER business cycle date) suggests that this objection was not baseless; the early date of the onset of recession suggests that other factors were also at work. Those other factors plausibly included postwar reductions in government contracting and spending (federal spending fell by nearly two-thirds between fiscal years 1919 and 1920) and increased union militancy and strike activity, leading to increases in labor costs.

But if Federal Reserve policy, and the gold standard, real bills, and Strong doctrines informing it, did not bring on the recession, they at least played a role by amplifying and extending it. In addition, the fact that the economy bounced back sharply from the 1920 to 1921 recession rendered Federal

[31] Board of Governors (1921, p. 12).
[32] See, for example, Chandler (1958, pp. 122–24, 173–74).
[33] Board of Governors (1921, p. 14).

Reserve officials, and New York Fed officials in particular, favorably disposed toward increases in rates in the late stage of a financial boom on the next occasion one developed, at the end of the 1920s.

2.3.2 Policy in 1924 and 1927

The Fed's expansionary policy actions in 1924 and 1927 are widely seen as two further instances when international considerations played a consequential role in decision making. These episodes are controversial. They are portrayed as having been shaped by Benjamin Strong and as disproportionately informed by the Strong Doctrine. They are criticized for subordinating domestic conditions to international factors and therefore as feeding domestic instabilities. Out of consensus, there are also those who challenge the notion that the 1924 and 1927 policy actions were in fact motivated by international considerations.

As of 1924, reconstruction of the international gold standard was still far from complete. The pound sterling, the second linchpin of the international system, was still trading at a discount relative to 1914 levels, and the Bank of England lacked gold reserves sufficient to restore convertibility at the prewar parity. For Strong, who saw reconstruction of the international gold standard as a US priority, this was a problem for the Federal Reserve Bank of New York and the System to address. With leadership from New York, the reserve banks reduced their discount rates from the 4½ percent levels prevailing since early 1923 to 3–4 percent between May and October of 1924. In addition, the Open Market Investment Committee authorized the New York Fed to purchase $300 million of Treasury bonds, pushing down yields and encouraging capital and gold to flow across the Atlantic to the United Kingdom, in order to help the Bank of England replenish its reserves. Finally, the Federal Reserve Bank of New York provided a $200 million line of credit to the Bank of England in exchange for an equivalent amount of sterling deposit credit.[34]

None of this was secret. In a 1924 statement prepared for the House of Representatives Committee on Banking and Currency, Strong cited international considerations as a rationale for lower discount rates and expansionary open market operations. These initiatives were designed "to render what assistance was possible by our market policy toward the recovery of sterling and resumption of gold payment by Great Britain."[35]

---

[34] With J. P. Morgan & Co. providing a supplementary $100 million credit.
[35] 69th Congress, 1st session, Stabilization, Hearings on H.R. 7895 before Committee on Banking and Currency, part 1, p. 336.

The question is whether international considerations were the main explanation for the central bank's accommodating stance. Commercial and industrial activity was relatively weak. The Board, in its Annual Report for 1924, noted that the industrial sector was in mild recession from mid-1923 to mid-1924, although trade volumes and farm incomes were both rising strongly.[36] It could be that Fed officials were influenced by this industrial weakness, although none of the doctrines informing policy necessarily privileged the industrial sector or saw it as the Fed's responsibility to stabilize industrial production.

Since 1924 saw gold inflows, gold standard doctrine also counseled ease, special concerns with the Bank of England notwithstanding. The 1924 Annual Report cites gold inflows as "the most important single influence affecting the volume of Federal Reserve bank credit in use" during the year.[37] There is also a clear statement of the Riefler–Burgess Doctrine, pointing to the need to look to the level of short-term market rates as a measure of monetary conditions, given the tendency for open market operations and member bank rediscounts to move in offsetting directions. And commercial paper rates stayed stubbornly high (rising further in the third quarter of 1923), despite the weakness of industrial conditions. Finally, the Annual Report justified open market purchases in terms of the real bills doctrine, noting that "there was no evidence of the growth of speculation."[38]

My reading is that the impetus for discount rate reductions in May–October 1924 came mainly from the international side, since domestic weakness that might have motivated action was limited to industry and was largely over by the time policymakers moved. It helped that their decisions did not egregiously violate other prevailing policy doctrines.

The 1927 episode is even more controversial. Having returned to gold in April 1925, the Bank of England was struggling to stay there. A high exchange rate made for problems of trade competitiveness. Industrial unrest culminating in a coalminers' strike disrupted exports. Revenues from service exports continued to disappoint. And starting in 1926, the Reichsbank and Bank of France, having accumulated sterling claims, sought to convert them into gold.

Strong, in continuous contact with his friend and pen pal Montagu Norman, was aware of the latter's problems. In July 1927, at Norman's instigation, he convened a meeting with Hjalmar Schacht of the Reichsbank,

---

[36] Board of Governors (1925, p. 1).
[37] Board of Governors (1925, p. 8).
[38] Board of Governors (1925, p. 12).

and Charles Rist of the Bank of France, along of course with Norman himself, at the Long Island estate of Treasury Undersecretary Ogden Mills. Strong came away convinced of the need to cut rates in order to induce gold to flow toward London and relieve the pressure on the Bank of England. He saw to it that Norman, Schacht, and Rist continued on to New York and Washington to meet with chairman of the New York Fed, and with the Board of Governors. Their meetings had the desired effect. Eight reserve banks, starting with Kansas City, voted to cut rates. The decision was then imposed on the dissenting reserve banks by the Board for the first time in the history of the System. In addition, the System undertook some $80 million of open market purchases over the course of the summer.

With benefit of 20/20 hindsight, Strong's critics dismissed the policy as counterproductive. The reduction in policy rates gave an additional fillip to speculation in a period when financial markets were already frothy. It subsidized the provision of brokers' loans. In the words of Adolph Miller, Strong's leading critic on the Board, the decision gave "a further great and dangerous impetus to an already overexpanded credit situation, notably to the volume of credit used on the stock exchanges."[39] The Board's Annual Report for 1927 noted the disquieting growth of security loans by commercial banks, a phenomenon not obviously compatible with the real bills doctrine, but did not comment further on the conflict.[40]

Once more, however, there were other factors pointing in the direction of a more expansionary policy, again raising the question of whether it was really the Strong Doctrine that carried the day. The United States was on the receiving end of gold inflows in the first part of the year, which dictated some relaxation of policy according to conventional gold standard logic regardless of the situation of the Bank of England. However, those gold inflows had clearly ended by June – that is, in advance of the reduction in policy rates. The United States experienced a coal strike starting in April and then weakness in manufacturing production as Henry Ford closed down his assembly lines to retool from the Model T to the Model A. As a result, industrial production was weak in the second half of the year. In justifying its discount rate reductions, the Board of Governors pointed to the "recession in business in the United States" that became evident around the middle of the year. It pointed to "the tendency toward firmer conditions in the money market," consistent with the focus of the Riefler–Burgess Doctrine on short-term market rates. But it wrote most extensively about

[39] Miller (1935, p. 449).
[40] Board of Governors (1928, pp. 5–6).

the international situation.[41] Clarke (1967) concludes on this basis and from the minutes of the Open Market Investment Committee that "external considerations probably weighed more heavily than domestic ones."[42]

2.3.3 The Crash and Its Aftermath

Its response to the Great Crash is widely cited as demonstrating that the Fed was capable of committing egregious policy errors without any role for international considerations. This statement is half right. It is right in that international factors played little role in the policy decisions of late 1929 and 1930. The Board in its Annual Report for 1929 did seek to deflect attention from its policy of direct pressure and from increases in the discount rate of the Federal Reserve Bank of New York as factors in the stock market crash by citing the role of an "important failure of a finance company in England [the Hatry Scandal]," which resulted in a loss of confidence by British investors and some withdrawals of foreign funds from the New York market. It pointed to the 100 basis point discount rate increase by the Bank of England on September 26 as creating stringency in New York.[43] It noted also that gold inflows reversed direction starting in October. After rising by some $250 million in the previous ten months, the monetary gold stock fell by $100 million in November and December, as foreigners previously attracted by high interest rates and a soaring stock market repatriated their funds.

Conventional gold standard doctrine dictated tightening. In fact, this is contrary to how the Fed responded. Informed by the Strong and Harrison Doctrines, it instead neutralized the impact of gold outflows with expansionary open market operations. In the last week of October, reserve banks purchased $150 million of government securities, purchases that continued into November and December. The Federal Reserve Bank of New York took

---

[41] "During this period it also became evident that there was a serious credit stringency in European countries generally, and it was felt that easy money in this country would help foreign countries to meet their autumn demand for credit and exchange without unduly depressing their exchanges or increasing the cost of credit to trade and industry. Easier credit conditions abroad would also facilitate the financing of our exports and would thus be of benefit to American producers. By purchasing securities at that time the Federal Reserve banks were in fact successful in easing the condition of the money market and in exerting a favorable influence on the international financial situation." Board of Governors (1928, p. 10).

[42] Clarke (1967, p. 125).

[43] "This series of events," it went on, "culminated in the last week in October in a break of unprecedented severity in stock prices..." Board of Governors (1930, p. 9).

the lead, purchasing securities for its own account; after a short dispute over with whom the authority to authorize purchases ultimately rested, the Board endorsed the policy.[44] Cumulative open market purchases in the eight months ending in June 1930 were $400 million. Charles Hardy, a contemporary observer of the central bank, characterized these purchases as "enormous," not our retrospective evaluation perhaps but an indication of how they looked at the time.[45]

These actions were intended to prevent distress among member banks "taking over in large volume loans previously carried by nonbanking lenders."[46] This quick action by a central bank that understood how to respond to financial stringency caused by stock-market problems, like those of 1907 and 1914, averted a wave of bank failures in New York. It prevented stringency in money markets and a spike in money-market rates. In other words, the commonplace characterization that the Fed stood by while the financial system was crashing down is not an accurate portrayal of its actions in 1929.

But having provided emergency liquidity sufficient to prevent a wave of bank failures, Federal Reserve officials concluded that their work was done. The real bills doctrine pointed to the discount rate and level of discounts as indicating whether further loosening of policy was warranted. The Federal Reserve Bank of New York was able to reduce its discount rate from 6 to 5 percent on November 1 and 4½ percent on November 15. Six more reserve banks followed suit by January 1930. Rates were then reduced further, to 2 percent in New York, 2½ percent in Boston, and 3 percent in Cleveland, Atlanta, Chicago, St. Louis, and San Francisco, and 3½ percent in Philadelphia, Richmond, Minneapolis, Kansas City, and Dallas over the course of 1930.[47] None of this resulted in the reserve banks being flooded with speculative discounts, reassuring adherents to the real bills doctrine. The Riefler–Burgess Doctrine pointed to the level of short-term market interest rates as a measure of the stance of policy, and these too declined in the wake of the Crash.

But in this, a period when the price level was falling (wholesale prices declined by more than 10 percent in the course of 1930), it became apparent that Federal Reserve doctrine drew no distinction between real and nominal interest rates. Insofar as officials were aware that the price level was falling, they rejected the claim that price-level stabilization was a legitimate

---

[44] Meltzer (2003, p. 236).
[45] Hardy (1932, p. 56).
[46] Board of Governors (1930, p. 10).
[47] Including the first days of 1931.

goal of policy. They warned that efforts to stabilize prices might be interpreted as a mandate to fix the prices of specific commodities, farm products for example. They objected that pursuing stable prices could conflict with other legitimate goals of policy, such as preventing the excessive use of central bank credit for speculative purposes. They asserted that the central bank lacked the capacity to stabilize prices, anticipating arguments about pushing on a string in liquidity-trap-like conditions.[48]

Modern scholarship has answers to all these objections. Making the central bank strongly independent and giving it an explicit price-level mandate can allow it to pursue a price-stability goal without succumbing to lobbying by specific commodity producers. If pursuit of price stability threatens financial stability, then the central bank should develop other instruments – what we would call "macroprudential" tools – to contain those risks.[49] Even if there was no demand for Federal Reserve credit at prevailing low interest rates, then the Fed still could have influenced price-level developments through additional open market or gold market purchases (quantitative easing) and statements of intent designed to shape expectations (forward guidance), as was done in 1933, although these steps were not obviously compatible with gold standard doctrine (just as their implementation in 1933 required first suspending the gold standard).[50]

Be this as it may, Federal Reserve policy in 1930 was informed not by modern scholarship but by the real bills, Riefler–Burgess, and gold standard doctrines.

2.3.4 1931

The period from May through December 1931 was a clear instance where international considerations dominated decision making. As the Board of Governors put it, "Throughout the year unfavorable developments abroad were an important factor in business and credit conditions in the United States."[51] The Strong Doctrine attached great importance to a stable

---

[48] The list of objections goes on; the complete set is enumerated in Hardy (1932, chapter 10).

[49] Naturally, the Fed's recent failed experiment with such a policy, "direct pressure" in 1929, did not incline it toward this view.

[50] The Fed had been able to ignore its $100 million of gold losses when purchasing $150 million of government securities in the final months of 1929 because those losses were small and it had excess reserves given large gold inflows earlier in the year. Whether it would have been able to maintain the statutory cover ratio in the face of the much larger counterfactual open market purchases needed to stabilize prices in 1930 is an entirely different question.

[51] Board of Governors (1932, p. 2).

international monetary system, which now began to unravel with the crises in Austria and Germany.

Much like Strong in 1924, Harrison took the lead in mobilizing the resources of the Federal Reserve System to support other embattled countries. In mid-May, he requested approval from the Board to contribute up to $3 million to an emergency loan to Austria, which the Board quickly approved.[52] In late June, the crisis having spread to Germany, Harrison obtained the approval of the Board to extend a much larger credit, up to $50 million, to the Reichsbank. In the end, with the Bank for International Settlements, the Bank of England, and the Bank of France participating, the US share of the $100 million requested by German officials was limited to $25 million. But even the full $100 million was small relative to the liabilities of the German banking system, liabilities that now continued to hemorrhage out of the country. There is an obvious analogy with the dollar swap lines extended by the Federal Reserve to the ECB, the Swiss National Bank, and the central banks of four emerging markets in the 2008–09 crisis.

The next stage developed less positively. To stay on the gold standard, the Reichsbank needed a second credit. Efforts to organize this foundered over French unhappiness with the German government's failure to comply with the terms of the Versailles Treaty. Paris saw the currency crisis as an opportunity to force Berlin into line and made impossible demands on the German government.[53] In addition, Harrison and others feared that their loans were simply financing capital flight. Flight by foreign banks could be halted or at least slowed by a standstill agreement like that negotiated by Austria with its foreign creditors. But Harrison worried that much of the capital flight in question was in fact the transfer abroad of funds by Germans unsettled by the country's tumultuous politics. This could only be halted by shutting down the German banking system, something that was inconsistent with the Strong Doctrine of supporting international transactions.

In the end, efforts to organize a second German loan were unsuccessful; Germany was forced to impose controls, and the crisis leapfrogged to London. Harrison understood that sterling was a key international currency, and that the survival of the gold standard system turned on its fate.

---

[52] With the Austrian crisis quick to spill over to Hungary, a similar loan was arranged for the National Bank of Hungary, again with Fed participation.

[53] The French government demanded that Germany drop its customs union proposal, commit to full resumption of reparations payments, and renounce rearmament spending as a precondition for further assistance. This was impossible for Chancellor Brüning, who had staked himself politically to an aggressive foreign policy.

He hoped that the Fed could work with other central banks and the private banking community to assemble an overwhelming show of force. The central banks would provide credits to the Bank of England, while other banks would extend a loan to the British government. In the event, shock and awe proved infeasible. The central bankers wanted the British government (governments, actually, since one replaced another in August) to implement a domestic policy package, budgetary economies mainly, to support the currency, which was easier said than done. The private bankers were reluctant to participate on any terms.

As a result, the emergency aid dribbled out. In July, with laborious negotiations underway, the New York Fed purchased some $10 million of sterling on the foreign exchange market. On July 30 the directors of the New York Fed and the Board of Governors finally approved a $125 million credit to the Bank of England – a much smaller amount than requested and less than the United Kingdom ultimately required.[54] It then took another month for Harrison to arrange a $200 million loan to the British government by a consortium of US banks headed by J. P. Morgan. Although these resources were an order of magnitude larger than those previously provided to Austria, they were again too little, too late.

The story of the United Kingdom's suspension of gold convertibility has been told elsewhere. What matters for present purposes is the Fed's response. Sterling's depreciation created a demand for liquidity which foreigners obtained by repatriating funds from New York. It excited fears that the dollar might be devalued, making for gold losses for the New York Fed in particular. Although the gold reserves of the System still substantially exceeded the 40 percent minimum, the argument that the central bank needed to signal its commitment to maintenance of the gold standard was compelling against this unsettled backdrop.[55]

Consistent with gold standard doctrine, the New York Fed raised its rate from 1½ to 2½ percent on October 8 and then to 3½ percent on October 16. This was the largest increase in a reserve bank discount rate in a two-week period in the history of the System. By mid-November that 3½ percent

---

[54] The Bank of France provided a matching $125 million credit and similarly intervened to support sterling on the foreign exchange market.

[55] Friedman and Schwartz (1963) agree. As they write (p. 382) of this episode, "The sharp rises in discount rates were widely supported not only within the System but also outside. The maintenance of the gold standard was accepted as an objective in support of which men of a broad range of view were ready to rally. The drain of gold was a dramatic event for which there were many precedents. Thus both the problem and its solution seemed clear and straightforward."

level had been matched by the other reserve banks.[56] Rather than sterilizing gold outflows to prevent the money supply and prices from falling further, the Federal Reserve allowed its holdings of government securities to fall by $15 million between mid-September and the end of the year. All this was done, recall, in the depths of the Depression, when prices and output were collapsing. There is no question about which doctrine carried the day. Even those like George Harrison with other concerns now subordinated them to defense of the gold standard, an objective that had similarly been prioritized by his mentor Benjamin Strong.

2.3.5 After Glass–Steagall

As gold continued flowing out of the country in the final months of 1931, the free gold constraint increasingly looked ready to bind. This led to passage in February 1932 of the Glass–Steagall Act loosening collateral requirements for Federal Reserve notes, as described above. By allowing the Federal Reserve banks to back their liabilities with government bonds above the 40 percent gold minimum, it gave the System, with gold reserves of 70 percent of liabilities, room to engage in expansionary open market operations.

It also represented a doctrinal shift, among the Fed's critics if not necessarily also officials of the Federal Reserve themselves. Pre-Glass–Steagall restrictions on what assets were eligible as backing for Federal Reserve notes reflected the sway of the real bills doctrine. The Fed, those restrictions indicated, should discount and purchase only high-quality commercial paper generated in the course of normal business transactions. By removing this restriction and adding government bonds to the list of eligible assets, this new legislation generated in the Treasury and the White House and passed overwhelmingly by the Congress sent the Fed a clear signal that the central bank should contemplate broader objectives. As Meltzer puts it, "The System could not ignore the message in this action."[57]

Nor was the message limited to Glass–Steagall. Representative Thomas Goldsborough, Democrat from Maryland, was campaigning for a bill that would have required the Federal Reserve to take steps to raise prices to 1926 levels. Senator Elmer Thomas, Democrat of Oklahoma, had begun lobbying for a bill that would have required the Federal Reserve to print

---

[56] Richmond and Dallas went up to 4 percent.
[57] Meltzer (2003, p. 357).

an additional $2.4 billion of essentially uncollateralized notes.[58] Other prospective legislation foresaw early payment of the World War I Veterans Bonus to be financed by issuance of Federal Reserve notes.

Federal Reserve officials saw these initiatives as unsound. They were inflationary. They were a threat to the gold standard. They endangered financial stability. They were at odds, in other words, with the doctrinal foundations of Federal Reserve policy, regardless of where that doctrinal basis was found. They also represented a threat to the independent conduct of monetary policy, such as it was. If there was going to be unsound monetary policy, better there should be a little than a lot, Federal Reserve officials were led to conclude. Better it should be implemented by the central bank's in-house experts rather than populist politicians.

Between March and May, the Fed thus engaged in a sustained program of expansionary open market operations, purchasing $1 billion of government debt, sufficient to offset roughly 20 percent of the cumulative decline in M1 from its peak in 1929 to its winter of 1932 trough.

In July the central bank then halted its open market operations. Why the Fed halted them is easier to explain on doctrinal grounds than why it initiated them in March.[59] Interest rates, having spiked in late 1931 and early 1932, had now begun falling again and were below the levels reached prior to the United Kingdom's devaluation.[60] Member bank borrowing from the System had declined; any Riefler–Burgess-based arguments for easing that might have prevailed at the beginning of 1932 no longer held. Bank liquidity had continued to rise, further agitating real bills advocates who worried about a burst of speculative lending. The Federal Reserve System had experienced steady gold losses in the spring and early summer.[61] Those gold losses were particularly heavy in May and June. Conventional gold standard doctrine dictated monetary tightening in response.

By the end of June the gold reserve ratio of the Federal Reserve Bank of New York, in particular, had fallen to barely 50 percent and was headed lower, creating concerns for Harrison and his Board.[62] Other reserve banks with bigger fish to fry (the Chicago Fed was faced with the possible failure

[58] A campaign that, in a sense, came to fruition with the Thomas Amendment to the Agricultural Adjustment Act in 1933.

[59] The decision to initiate them in March, I have argued, is easier to explain on political than doctrinal grounds.

[60] Friedman and Schwartz (1963, p. 323) provide additional detail.

[61] Those gold losses of more than $400 million offset nearly half of the open market expansion.

[62] The reserve ratio of the System as a whole was still 56 percent. On the concerns of Harrison and the directors of the New York Fed, see Meltzer (2003, p. 369).

of the Dawes Bank and other metropolitan banks to which it was linked and was therefore anxious to husband its reserves) were reluctant to continue participating in the open market program, suggesting that were it to continue a disproportionate share of purchases would have to be undertaken by New York.[63] Bordo, Choudhri, and Schwartz (2002) and Hsieh and Romer (2006) reject the argument that those gold losses raised the specter of an imminent gold standard crisis and that it was in response to such a crisis that the Fed drew back in July. This, in my view, is not the point. What mattered was not the specter of an imminent crisis but gold standard doctrine broadly defined – the gold standard mentalité that suggested tightening when gold flowed out and loosening when it flowed in. That plus the fact that the Congress adjourned for the summer on July 16, removing the pressure for reflation and allowing other doctrinal imperatives to carry the day.

2.4 Conclusion

The era from 1914 to 1933 was one in which the fledgling Federal Reserve System, like a child learning to walk, struggled to find its policymaking feet. There were also notable lapses in this period, mainly after 1929, when the Fed, like an infant taking its first tentative steps, failed to maintain its footing.

Policy in this period was guided by different monetary policy frameworks, some of which, like the real bills doctrine, placed little weight on international considerations, but others of which, like gold standard doctrine, attached to them the highest priority. The Warburg Doctrine emphasizing the desirability of internationalizing the dollar and the Strong Doctrine prioritizing reconstruction of the international gold standard similarly directed officials to external and international dimensions of the new central bank's policies. In contrast, the Riefler–Burgess and Glass–Steagall Doctrines, while otherwise having little in common, downplayed international factors in favor of domestic market conditions.

In the same way a young child just beginning to walk has not yet learned how to put one foot in front of the other, officials within the Federal Reserve System had not yet figured out on which of these doctrines to lean when

---

[63] Epstein and Ferguson (1984) explain the conflict between Chicago and New York differently, arguing that banks in the Chicago district were heavily invested in short-term government bonds, while banks in New York had portfolios heavy on long-term bonds. Coelho and Santoni (1991) question their interpretation.

formulating policy. The influence of different doctrinal foundations waxed and waned as a function of personnel and personality. Their influence varied with circumstance: gold standard doctrine was more likely to be influential when the Fed's gold cover ratio was low relative to statutory requirements than when it was high; and the Strong Doctrine emphasizing the importance of a stable international monetary system was more likely to influence central bank policy when that system was perceived to be at risk. On other occasions, international considerations faded into the background. There were also clear differences of opinion about the importance of international considerations in different parts of the Federal Reserve System – differences that manifested themselves in conflicts between New York and other reserve banks.

Finally, what does modern central banking doctrine say about the role of international considerations in the conduct of policy in this period? It suggests that the Fed was right not to ignore conditions in the rest of the world. US policy could and did have a first-order impact on other countries, such as the United Kingdom and Germany. And what happened in the United Kingdom and Germany didn't stay in the United Kingdom and Germany; rather, the spillback effects of developments there could be considerable. The same is true of threats to the stability of the international monetary and financial system as distinct from individual countries. When the stability of the system was threatened in 1931, the impact on the US economy was considerable; these were not developments that a prudent central bank could neglect.

That said, Federal Reserve officials could have dealt more wisely with the international aspects of policy. Attempting to reconstruct an international gold standard along prewar lines in social, political, and economic circumstances that were now radically changed was not the wisest decision. But once that decision was taken, the Fed should have either supported the resulting system wholeheartedly or else acknowledged that the experiment was a failure and abandoned it. The half-measures taken in 1931 to support Austria, Germany, and the United Kingdom solved nothing. The sharp increases in Federal Reserve discount rates taken in the wake of these European crises, with the goal of defending what remained of the gold standard, only further weakened the US economy and the banks while again solving nothing. At this late date the Fed's response only delayed the inevitable, namely the suspension of dollar convertibility.

The other lesson of this period is that even a central bank with good reason to worry about economic and financial conditions in the rest of the world will achieve nothing if it fails to attend to the health and stability of its own economy. This was true of the Fed in the 1920s and 1930s. The same is true today when we hear calls for the Federal Reserve to abandon policies tailored to the needs of domestic stability in order to address problems in the rest of the world.

References

Andrew, Piatt, 1905. "Credit and the Value of Money." *Publications of the American Economic Association* 6: 95–115.

Barber, William, 1996. *Designs within Disorder: Franklin D. Roosevelt, the Economists, and the Shaping of American Economic Policy, 1933–1945*. New York, NY: Cambridge University Press.

Board of Governors of the Federal Reserve System, 1921. *Seventh Annual Report of the Federal Reserve Board*. Washington, DC: Government Printing Office.

1925. *Eleventh Annual Report of the Federal Reserve Board*. Washington, DC: Government Printing Office.

1928. *Thirteenth Annual Report of the Federal Reserve Board*. Washington, DC: Government Printing Office.

1930. *Fifteenth Annual Report of the Federal Reserve Board*. Washington, DC: Government Printing Office.

1932. *Seventeenth Annual Report of the Federal Reserve Board*. Washington, DC: Government Printing Office.

1933. *Eighteenth Annual Report of the Federal Reserve Board*. Washington, DC: Government Printing Office.

Bordo, Michael, Ehsan Choudhri, and Anna Schwartz, 2002. "Was Expansionary Monetary Policy Possible During the Great Contraction? An Examination of the Gold Standard Constraint." *Explorations in Economic History* 39: 1–28.

Broz, Lawrence, 1997. *The International Origins of the Federal Reserve System*. Ithaca, NY: Cornell University Press.

Brunner, Karl and Allan Meltzer, 1968. "What Did We Learn from the Monetary Experience of the United States in the Great Depression?" *Canadian Journal of Economics* 2: 334–48.

Burgess, W. Randolph, 1964. "Reflections on the Early Development of Open Market Policy." *Federal Reserve Bank of New York Monthly Review* 36: 219–26.

Chandler, Lester, 1958. *Benjamin Strong, Central Banker*. Washington, DC: Brookings Institution Press.

Clarke, Stephen, 1967. *Central Bank Cooperation 1924–31*. New York, NY: Federal Reserve Bank of New York.

Coelho, Philip and Gary Santoni, 1991. "Regulatory Capture and the Monetary Contraction of 1932: A Comment on Epstein and Ferguson." *Journal of Economic History* 51: 182–89.

De Boyer des Roches, Jerome and Rebeca Gomez Betancourt, 2012. "Origins and Development of Irving Fisher's Compensated Dollar Plan." Unpublished manuscript, Paris Dauphine and University of Lumiere Lyon.

Eccles, Marriner and Sydney Hyman, 1951. *Beckoning Frontiers: Public and Personal Recollections*. New York, NY: Alfred A. Knopf.

Eggertsson, Gauti, 2008. "Great Expectations and the End of the Depression." *American Economic Review* 98: 1476–516.

Eichengreen, Barry, 1992. *Golden Fetters: The Gold Standard and the Great Depression, 1919–1939*. New York, NY: Oxford University Press.

2013. "Does the Federal Reserve Care About the Rest of the World?" *Journal of Economic Perspectives* 27: 87–104.

Eichengreen, Barry, Livia Chitu, Arnaud Mehl, and Gary Richardson, 2014. "Mutual Assistance between Federal Reserve Banks 1913–1960 as Prolegomena to the TARGET2 Debate." NBER Working Paper No. 20267 (June).

Eichengreen, Barry and Marc Flandreau, 2012. "The Federal Reserve, the Bank of England, and the Rise of the Dollar as an International Currency, 1914–39." *Open Economies Review* 23: 57–87.

Eichengreen, Barry and Peter Temin, 2000. "The Gold Standard and the Great Depression." *Contemporary European History* 9: 183–207.

Epstein, Gerald and Thomas Ferguson, 1984. "Monetary Policy, Loan Liquidation, and Industrial Conflict: The Federal Reserve and the Open Market Operations of 1932." *Journal of Economic History* 44: 957–83.

Fishback, Price, 2010. "U.S. Monetary and Fiscal Policy in the 1930s." *Oxford Review of Economic Policy* 26: 385–413.

Friedman, Milton and Anna Schwartz, 1963. *A Monetary History of the United States 1867–1960*. Princeton, NJ: Princeton University Press.

Goldstein, Judith, 1994. *Ideas, Interests and American Trade Policy*. Ithaca, NY: Cornell University Press.

Hardy, Charles, 1932. *Credit Policies of the Federal Reserve System*. Washington, DC: Brookings Institution.

Hay, Colin, 2004. "Ideas, Interests and Institutions in the Comparative Political Economy of Great Transformations." *Review of International Political Economy* 11: 204–26.

Hetzel, Robert, 1985. "The Rules versus Discretion Debate over Monetary Policy in the 1920s." *Federal Reserve Bank of Richmond Economic Review* 71: 3–14.

Hoover, Herbert, 1952. *Memoirs, Volume 3: The Great Depression, 1929–41*. New York, NY: Macmillan.

Hsieh, Chang-Tai and Christina Romer, 2006. "Was the Federal Reserve Constrained by the Gold Standard During the Great Depression? Evidence from the 1932 Open Market Purchase Program." *Journal of Economic History* 66: 140–76.

Humphrey, Thomas, 1982. "The Real Bills Doctrine." *Federal Reserve Bank of Richmond Economic Quarterly* 68: 3–13.

2001. "The Choice of a Monetary Policy Framework: Lessons from the 1920s." *Cato Journal* 21: 285–313.

Hyman, Sidney and George Bach, 1976. *Marriner S. Eccles: Private Entrepreneur and Public Servant*. Stanford, CA: Graduate School of Business Press.

Keynes, John Maynard, 1925. *The Economic Consequences of Mr. Churchill*. London: Macmillan.

Kuehn, Daniel, 2011. "A Critique of Powell, Murphy and Woods on the 1920–21 Depression." *Review of Austrian Economics* 24: 273–91.

Laidler, David, 1981. "Adam Smith as a Monetary Economist." *Canadian Journal of Economics* 14: 185–200.

Law, John, 1705. *Money and Trade Considered.* Edinburgh: Heirs and Successors of Andrew Anderson.

Meltzer, Allan, 2003. *A History of the Federal Reserve, Volume 1: 1913–1951.* Chicago, IL: University of Chicago Press.

Miller, Adolph, 1935. "Responsibility for Federal Reserve Policies 1927–29." *American Economic Review* 25: 442–57.

Patinkin, Don, 1993. "Irving Fisher and His Compensated Dollar Plan." *Federal Reserve Bank of Richmond Economic Quarterly* 79: 1–34.

Rothbard, Murray, 2011. *Economic Controversies.* Auburn, AL: Ludwig von Mises Institute.

Steiner, William, 1922. *The Mechanism of Commercial Credit: Terms of Sale and Trade Acceptances.* New York, NY: Appleton & Co.

Timberlake, Richard, 2005. "Gold Standards and the Real Bills Doctrine in U.S. Monetary Policy." *Economic Journal Watch* 2: 196–233.

Warburg, Paul, 1914. *Essays on Banking Reform in the United States.* New York, NY: Academy of Political Science.

Wheelock, David, 1991. *The Strategy and Consistency of Federal Reserve Monetary Policy 1924–1933.* Cambridge: Cambridge University Press.

Comments on Barry Eichengreen, "Doctrinal Determinants, Domestic and International, of Federal Reserve Policy 1914–1933"

Harold James

Barry Eichengreen has presented a very helpful overview of the early stages of the development of the Federal Reserve System: the overriding analogy is that of the development of a child, which needs a prop or support as it learns to move and eventually walk and even run (and then it doesn't need the support anymore). The props are conceptual: as Eichengreen defines them, "doctrines" which then explain the policy response to shocks or "events." There look as if there are a good many of these competing doctrines, and not all of them are clearly defined alternatives: in the order that Eichengreen presents them, they are the gold standard doctrine, the real bills doctrine, Riefler–Burgess, Warburg, Strong, Harrison, Glass–Steagall, and Roosevelt Doctrines.

These "doctrines" probably should not be defined as equal in weight. In particular, the gold standard is more than a set of beliefs, but is rather the international framework within which monetary policy operated until 1933. A number of constraints – maybe they can be seen as props, but maybe also as obstacles – followed necessarily from the gold standard environment. Indeed it is important to remember that the gold standard does not require the existence of an institution such as a central bank for its operation, and that many countries operated in the classical gold standard without a central bank (as obviously the United States did until 1914).

The gold standard constraints are well known. They can be expressed in a series of trilemmas, or impossible trinities, of which by far the best known is the inability simultaneously to maintain fixed exchange rates, capital flows, and autonomous monetary policy.

In addition to this, there are others: Eichengreen himself has often emphasized the constraint first formulated by Karl Polanyi, and recast in the form of another trilemma by Dani Rodrik: that the gold standard required adjustments that became harder or even impossible with a political representation of workers who were hit by monetary policy induced economic slowdowns. In the form of a trilemma, this looks like the impossibility of fixed exchange rates, capital flows, and democratization, and can be thought of as a political economy trilemma.[1]

But there are other similar patterns of restraint, concerning financial stability: fixed exchange rates, capital flows, and financial stability are hard to reconcile with each other.

Finally, a fourth trilemma occurs with respect to the geopolitics of the gold standard regime. This is an aspect of the debates about monetary reform in the early twentieth century that is not often presented in the literature about the origins of the Federal Reserve System. But both the third and fourth trilemmas appear very sharply in the argumentation of Paul Warburg.

Why was Warburg so influential? Above all because he appeared after the major financial crisis of October 1907 as the Cassandra figure who had accurately predicted the panic. His initial contribution, "Defects and Needs of Our Banking System," came out in the *New York Times* Annual Financial Review on January 6, 1907; its main message was about the need to learn from continental Europe. Warburg started with a complaint that "The United States is in fact at about the same point that had been reached by Europe at the time of the Medicis, and by Asia, in all likelihood, at the time of Hammurabi. [...] Our immense national resources have enabled us to live and prosper in spite of our present system, but so long as it is not thoroughly reformed it will prevent us from ever becoming the financial center of the world. As it is, our wealth makes us an important but dangerous factor in the world's financial community."[2] The Cassandra warning about the danger posed by the American financial system would make Warburg look like a true prophet after a renewed period of tension after October 1907. The panic, the need for a response coordinated by J. P. Morgan, and the debate about whether Morgan had profited unduly from his role as lender-of-last resort is one of the most celebrated incidents in US financial history. By 1910, Warburg had firmly established himself as the preeminent banking expert on reform of the monetary system.

---

[1] See Barry Eichengreen, *Golden Fetters: The Gold Standard and the Great Depression, 1919–39*, Oxford: Oxford University Press, 1992; http://rodrik.typepad.com/dani_rodriks_weblog/2007/06/the-inescapable.html; Michael Bordo and Harold James, "The European Crisis in the Context of the History of Previous Financial Crises," NBER Working Paper no. 19112, June 2013.

[2] Paul Warburg, "Defects and Needs of Our Banking System," *New York Times*, January 6, 1907.

The problem of the American system in his eyes was that it relied on single signature promissory notes: when confidence evaporated in a crisis, the value of these became questionable and banks would refuse to deal with them. Warburg proposed to emulate the trade finance mechanism of the London City, where the merchant banks (acceptance houses) established a third signature or endorsement on the bill, a guarantee that they would stand behind the payment; the addition of this guarantee provided a basis on which a particular bank favored by a banking privilege conferred by law, the Bank of England, would rediscount the bill, that is, pay out cash.[3] The second element of the Warburg plan was fundamentally a state bank, an innovation that recalled the early experimentation of Alexander Hamilton but also the controversies about the charter renewals of the First and the Second Bank of the United States.

Warburg was also very mindful of the international politics of the response to the 1907 crisis. The most mature economy and the financial center of the world was the United Kingdom, but it was growing more slowly than the larger challengers: the United States, and in Europe the heavily export-oriented German Empire. The language of Warburg's public appeals made analogies to armies and defense: "Under present conditions in the United States ... instead of sending an army, we send each soldier to fight alone." His proposed reform would "create a new and most powerful medium of international exchange – a new defense against gold shipments."[4] The experience of US financial crises in the past, in 1893 and in 1907, where there was a dependence on gold shipments from Europe indicated a profound fragility. Building up a domestic pool of credit that could be used as the basis for issuing money was a way of obviating the dependence. The reform project involved the search for a safe asset, not dependent on the vagaries and political interferences of the international gold market.

In the tense debates about the design of the new institution, Warburg consistently presented the issue in terms of a need to increase American security in the face of substantial vulnerability. As Warburg presented it, the term chosen in the original Aldrich Plan, as well as the eventual name of the new central bank, brought a clear analogy with military or naval reserves. "The word 'reserve' has been embodied in all these varying names, and this

---

[3] Paul Warburg, "A Plan for a Modified Central Bank," *Proceedings of the Academy of Political Science in the City of New York*, No. 4, Essays on Banking Reform in the United States, July 1914, originally 1907.

[4] Warburg, "Defects and Needs."

is significant because the adoption of the principle of co-operative reserves is the characteristic feature of each of these plans. There are all kinds of reserves. There are military and naval reserves. We speak of reserves in dealing with water supply, with food, raw materials, rolling stock, electric power, and what not. In each case its meaning depends upon the requirements of the organization maintaining the reserve."[5]

It follows from the character of the trilemmas that the new institutional arrangement did not have sufficient tools to deal with all the policy challenges that arose from a very turbulent international setting. The Fed began its operations just after the outbreak of the European War that became World War I. Eichengreen correctly emphasizes how the international (gold standard) constraints played a major role in the tragedy of 1931, when gold outflows set off a new wave of US bank failures (the third wave of bank failures, in the chronology of Friedman and Schwartz). With that the economic downturn really became the Great Depression.

The framework of Eichengreen's paper also implicitly asks whether policymaking became easier in the absence of the gold standard constraint. There were clearly big policy mistakes – in the case of the Federal Reserve relating to the imposition of increased bank reserves – that triggered the violent recession of 1937. The learning process continued, and it was subject – as it was in the Great Depression – to destructive interactions with inappropriate fiscal policy.

---

[5] September 29, 1916 – The Reserve Problem and the Future of the Federal Reserve System, Address of Hon. Paul M. Warburg before the Convention of the American Bankers Association, Kansas City, Mo; available at http://fraser.stlouisfed.org/docs/historical/federal%20reserve%20history/bog_members_statements/Warburg_19160929.pdf

3

Navigating Constraints

The Evolution of Federal Reserve Monetary Policy, 1935–1959

Mark A. Carlson and David C. Wheelock

3.1 Introduction

Efforts to understand the "Great Inflation" of the 1960s and 1970s have noted that economic outcomes in the 1950s were good by comparison, perhaps because of well-executed monetary policy. Romer and Romer (2002, 2004) argue that the Fed ran a "sophisticated" monetary policy in the 1950s that responded aggressively to expected inflation and contributed to the decade's good economic performance. Similarly, Hetzel (2008, pp. 55, 58) contends that in the 1950s, Federal Reserve Chairman William McChesney Martin, Jr., "laid the foundation of modern central banking," and "had views on monetary policy that foreshadowed those of [Paul] Volcker and [Alan] Greenspan." Other studies have been more critical of the Fed's execution of monetary policy in the 1950s (e.g., Brunner and Meltzer, 1964; Meltzer, 2009); nonetheless, inflation was low and output growth was relatively stable during the 1950s in contrast with many other decades of the Fed's first century.

Considerable research has sought to explain the apparent change in monetary policy between the 1950s and mid-1960s when inflation began to take hold.[1] However, rather than comparing monetary policy in the 1950s with later periods, in this chapter we begin with the 1950s and look back to

[1] Recent examples include Bordo and Orphanides (2013) and the papers noted therein.

This chapter was presented at the Federal Reserve Bank of Dallas conference, The Federal Reserve's Role in the Global Economy: A Historical Perspective, September 18–19, 2014. The authors thank Michael Bordo and Gary Richardson for comments on a previous version of this chapter, and Ed Atkinson and Peter McCrory for research assistance. Views expressed herein are not necessarily official positions of the Board of Governors of the Federal Reserve System or the Federal Reserve Bank of St. Louis.

the preceding years from the mid-1930s through the 1940s in an effort to better understand the evolution of monetary policy from the failures of the Great Depression to the apparent successes of the 1950s. We argue that an important part of the Fed's success in the 1950s was the absence of political and international pressures that had constrained policy in earlier years.

The Great Depression resulted in major changes to the regulation of the US banking and financial system, the international monetary system, and the structure and authority of the Federal Reserve System. Two acts were especially important for the Federal Reserve. First, the Gold Reserve Act of 1934 authorized the Treasury to intervene in gold and foreign exchange markets, and to negotiate international monetary agreements. The act created the Exchange Stabilization Fund (ESF), capitalized using a $2 billion "profit" on gold transferred from the Fed to the Treasury (as required by the act), and then revalued from $20.67 to $35 per ounce. The ESF rivaled the Fed's government securities portfolio in size. An internal Fed memorandum concluded that the ESF enabled the Treasury Secretary "to assume complete control of general credit conditions and to negate any credit policies that the Federal Reserve might adopt."[2] In the words of Meltzer (2003), the ESF and other powers granted to the Treasury Secretary relegated the Fed to a "backseat" position for monetary policymaking.

The second important piece of legislation was the Banking Act of 1935. That act created the Fed's Board of Governors and reconstituted the FOMC to consist of the seven governors and five reserve bank presidents. The act specified that the chairman of the Board of Governors also chair the FOMC.[3] The act reduced the authority and independence of the reserve banks, and placed responsibility for monetary policy largely in the hands of politically appointed officials who, presumably, would be more responsive to the public will as expressed by Congress and the administration.[4]

Although the Fed's autonomy was reduced, particularly with regard to international monetary arrangements and policy, the Fed was also handed

---

[2]   Quoted in Meltzer (2003, p. 457).
[3]   The Board of Governors replaced the Federal Reserve Board. However, throughout this paper, we use Board of Governors and Federal Reserve Board interchangeably. The Banking Act of 1935 also changed the title of the chief executive officers of Federal Reserve banks from governor to president, and assigned the title of governor to all members of the Board of Governors.
[4]   Prior to the Banking Act of 1935, the Secretary of the Treasury and Comptroller of the Currency had been members of the Federal Reserve Board (the Treasury Secretary was, in fact, chairman of the Board). The Banking Act of 1935 removed the Treasury Secretary and Comptroller from the Federal Reserve Board. However, given other New Deal changes, the ability of the Treasury Secretary to pressure the Fed likely became greater after 1933 than it had been before.

some new responsibilities and tools. For example, the Banking Act of 1933 authorized the Fed to set maximum rates that banks could pay on deposits; the Securities Exchange Act of 1934 authorized the Fed to set margin requirements for loans used to purchase or hold securities; and the Banking Act of 1935 permitted the Board of Governors to adjust required reserve ratios imposed on member banks. Thus, a new era began for the Fed in the mid-1930s involving both new constraints on policy, but also new policy instruments.

Our period of study includes World War II. Shortly after Pearl Harbor, the Fed announced that it would cooperate fully with the Treasury Department to finance the war effort. The Fed used open market operations to peg the yields on short- and medium-term Treasury securities and to enforce a 2.5 percent ceiling on the long-term government bond yield. The yields on shorter-term securities were permitted to rise somewhat in the late 1940s, but the ceiling on the long-bond yield remained in place until the Fed-Treasury Accord of March 1951. The war and its effects severely constrained the Fed's ability to direct monetary policy toward controlling inflation or stabilizing output.

By contrast, in the 1950s, the Fed was relatively unconstrained by political pressures or international monetary forces. Unlike the 1930s, when large gold inflows swamped the Fed's ability to use open market operations or increases in its discount rate to absorb banking system reserves, or the 1940s, when monetary policy was focused on maintaining low interest rates for the Treasury, in the 1950s, the Fed was largely free to pursue macroeconomic policy objectives. With fewer political and international constraints, the Fed was able to focus more on expected inflation and fluctuations in economic activity in the 1950s than it had during 1935–50.

This chapter documents the evolution of Federal Reserve monetary policy from the mid-1930s through the 1950s. We begin by showing empirically that the response of monetary policy to macroeconomic variables in the 1950s did not hold in the 1930s or 1940s. Although concerned about inflation and output, prior to the Fed-Treasury Accord of 1951, political constraints and (in the 1930s) international capital movements seriously limited the Fed's ability to respond to macroeconomic conditions, especially with open market operations and discount rate changes. Drawing on both published reports and meeting transcripts, we then describe how Fed officials sought to achieve macroeconomic objectives using its newly acquired tools – especially changes in reserve requirements and credit controls – when its traditional monetary policy tools were either ineffective or dedicated to alternative uses by political realities.

We focus much of our narrative description on the Fed's use of reserve requirements. Changes in required reserve ratios were an important component of the Fed's policy strategy throughout the 1930s–50s. Fed officials did not change reserve requirements lightly. They recognized that changes could have large impacts on financial institutions and officials believed that changing requirements too often would be destabilizing. Each recommended change was discussed and debated at length, and those discussions are revealing about the policy views of Fed officials at the time.

The chapter is organized as follows: Section 3.2 provides an overview of how monetary policy responded to macroeconomic conditions over the entire period from 1935 to 1959, and in particular presents evidence that the Fed changed required reserve ratios in response to economic developments. We then consider the 1930s, 1940s, and 1950s separately and, using Taylor-style regressions, estimate the responsiveness of policy to inflation and output gaps during each period; we find that policy was most responsive during the 1950s. Section 3.3 delves into the narrative evidence to understand why the policy reaction functions differ in our three periods. We document how Fed policymakers used their tools to try to balance domestic economic performance objectives with objectives resulting from political or economic pressures. Section 3.4 offers conclusions. Overall we conclude that, during the 1950s, for the first time since the 1920s, neither international forces nor political pressures constrained the Fed. The resulting environment helped produce one of the most successful eras of the Fed's first 100 years.

3.2 An Empirical Description of Monetary Policy, 1935–1959

Following Romer and Romer (2002), we begin by examining the responsiveness of monetary policy to macroeconomic conditions, specifically expected inflation and the output gap. Figures 3.1 and 3.2, respectively, plot the inflation rate (year-over-year percentage change in the CPI) and the output gap (calculated as the deviation of the log of an index of industrial production, IP, from trend).[5] Both figures also identify dates between 1935 and 1959 when the Fed changed required reserve ratios imposed on member banks (solid vertical lines identify dates when increases in reserve requirements took effect and dashed vertical lines indicate dates when

---

[5] The trend is calculated using a Hodrick-Prescott filter applied to monthly industrial production data for 1919–2006. See the appendix for data source information.

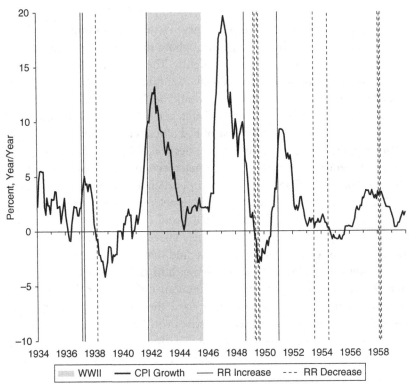

Figure 3.1. Inflation and changes in required reserve ratios, 1935–59.

reductions took effect).[6] Table 3.1 lists the required reserve ratios specified by the Federal Reserve Act and all subsequent changes in the ratios through 1959. Required reserve ratios were generally higher for central reserve city banks, that is, member banks in New York City and Chicago, than for banks in other reserve cities, which in turn were higher than those for country banks. Ratios were also higher for demand deposits than for time deposits.[7]

---

[6]   The dates shown in the figures are for changes in requirements applied to reserve city banks, which are listed in Table 3.1.

[7]   Under the National Bank Act of 1863, all national banks were required to hold reserves equal to 25 percent of their notes and deposits. Banks located in central reserve cities were required to hold their required reserves in the form of gold or "lawful" money, whereas banks in reserve cities and country banks were permitted to hold a portion of their reserves in the form of deposits with national banks in central reserve cities or, in the case of country banks, reserve cities. Under the Federal Reserve Act, member banks were required to hold their required reserves in the form of deposits with Federal Reserve banks or lawful money (vault cash). In 1917, an amendment to the Federal Reserve Act

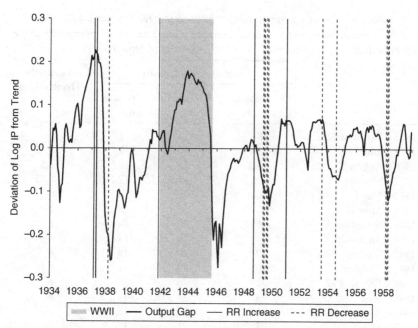

Figure 3.2. Output gap and changes in required reserve ratios, 1934–59.

Changes in reserve requirements were a prominent component of the Fed's monetary policy strategy from the mid-1930s through the 1950s. Originally, reserve requirements were imposed mainly to ensure the liquidity of individual banks.[8] However, by the 1930s, the Fed recognized that "it is no longer the primary function of legal reserve requirements to assure or preserve the liquidity of individual member banks. Rather, the two main functions ... are, first, to operate in the direction of sound credit conditions by exerting an influence on changes in the volume of bank credit, and, secondly, to provide the Federal Reserve banks with sufficient resources to enable them to pursue an effective banking and credit policy."[9]

As shown in the figures, throughout the period, increases in required reserve ratios tended to occur when either inflation was rising or the output

lowered required reserve ratios but specified that only deposits with reserve banks could be used to satisfy reserve requirements. In 1959, the Act was amended to once again allow vault cash to count toward a member bank's required reserves.

[8] See Carlson (2015) on the use of reserve requirements to ensure the liquidity of individual banks.

[9] "Member Bank Reserves – Report of the Committee on Bank Reserves of the Federal Reserve System." *Federal Reserve Board Annual Report*, 1932, pp. 260–61.

Table 3.1. *Federal Reserve member bank reserve requirements, 1913–59*

Effective date[a]	(Percent of deposits)			
	Net demand deposits			Time deposits (all bank classes)
	Central Reserve City banks	Reserve City banks	Country banks	
1913 – December 23	18	15	12	5
1917 – June 21	13	10	7	3
1936 – August 16	19.5	15	10.5	4.5
1937 – March 1	22.75	17.5	12.25	5.25
1937 – May 1	26	20	14	6
1938 – April 16	22.75	17.5	12	5
1941 – November 1	26	20	14	6
1942 – August 20	24	20	14	6
1942 – September 14	22	20	14	6
1942 – October 3	20	20	14	6
1948 – February 27	22	20	14	6
1948 – June 11	24	20	14	6
1948 – September 24, 16	26	22	16	7.5
1949 – May 5, 1	24	21	15	7
1949 – June 30, July 1	24	20	14	6
1949 – August 1	24	20	13	6
1949 – August 11, 16	23.5	19.5	12	5
1949 – August 18	23	19	12	5
1949 – August 25	22.5	18.5	12	5
1949 – September 1	22	18	12	5
1951 – January 11, 16	23	19	13	6
1951 – January 25, February 1	24	20	14	6
1953 – July 9, 1	22	19	13	6
1954 – June 24, 16	21	19	13	5
1954 – July 29, August 1	20	18	12	5
1958 – February 27, March 1	19.5	17.5	11.5	5
1958 – March 20, April 1	19	17	11	5
1958 – April 17	18.5	17	11	5
1958 – April 24	18	16.5	11	5

[a] When two dates are listed, the first applies to the change at central reserve city or reserve city banks and the second applies to country banks.
Source: Board of Governors of the Federal Reserve System (1971), table 10.4.

gap was positive, and decreases tended to occur when inflation was falling or the output gap was negative. This correlation suggests that the Fed used changes in reserve requirements to "meet fundamental changes in the economy and the financial situation" (FOMC Executive Committee Minutes, August 5, 1949). However, some changes in required reserve ratios did not line up with inflation or the output gap. Some of these deviations from "normal" policy may have reflected special factors affecting measured inflation and output, such as the removal of price controls and conversion of factories from defense to civilian uses after World War II. However, as we discuss below, before the Fed-Treasury Accord of 1951, changes in required reserve ratios were the Fed's primary tool for responding to inflation and the business cycle. Without the ability to change reserve requirements, the Fed would have had considerable difficulty responding to inflation or output gaps.[10] During 1935–41, the scale of gold inflows meant that the Fed had less scope for using open market operations to respond to macroeconomic conditions, and during 1941–51, political considerations dictated the use of open market operations primarily to monetize government debt.

We test formally whether changes in reserve requirements responded to macroeconomic conditions. First, we simply consider whether ratios were increased or decreased. Thus our measure for the response of reserve requirements can take on three values: 1 if requirements were increased in the current quarter relative to the previous quarter, −1 if requirements were lowered from one quarter to the next, and 0 if there was no change.[11] Given the discrete and ordered nature of our dependent variable, we estimate an ordered-logit regression.

Second, to account for differences in the magnitude of changes in reserve requirements, as well as the fact that required reserve ratios differed both across classes of member banks (i.e., central reserve city, reserve city, and country) and between demand and time deposits, we estimate a regression that uses changes in the "required reserve step index" (RSI) of Haslag and Hein (1995) as the dependent variable. The RSI measures the amount of bank reserves liberated (reduced) by any decrease (increase) in required reserve ratios, but not by flows of deposits between classes of banks or

---

[10] We are not claiming that the Fed was particularly successful in controlling inflation or stabilizing output, just that given the economic and political constraints, changing reserve requirements was the only feasible tool the Fed had for attempting to control inflation or close gaps.

[11] Specifically, the value of the dependent variable is non-zero in quarters in which the required reserve ratio on demand deposits for reserve city or central reserve city banks was changed.

between demand and time deposits. An increase in required reserve ratios lowers the RSI, whereas a reduction in ratios increases the RSI.

Both regressions relate changes in reserve requirements to measures of inflation and output. For inflation, we use the change in the consumer price index measured as the percentage change from the last month in one quarter to the last month in the next. Our measure of the output gap is the deviation of log IP from trend shown in Figure 3.2. We use the gap value for the last month in a quarter. A positive gap indicates that the economy is performing above trend. Because policymakers have limited access to real-time data when formulating policy, we follow Clarida, Galí, and Gertler (2000) and Romer and Romer (2002) in using measures of expected inflation and the output gap that are the predicted values derived from regressions of current values on three lagged values of inflation and one lagged value of the output gap.[12]

For the ordered-logit regression, we anticipate positive coefficients on predicted inflation and the output gap, indicating that required reserve ratios were increased in response to higher forecast inflation or output gap. However, because an increase in required reserve ratios lowers the RSI, we expect negative coefficients on predicted inflation and the output gap for the regression that uses the change in RSI as the dependent variable. The results for both regressions, shown in Table 3.2, are consistent with the idea that the Federal Reserve raised required reserve ratios in response to increases in predicted inflation and output gaps.[13]

3.2.1 Comparisons of Fed Reaction Functions across Different Eras

The regressions reported in Table 3.2 suggest that the Fed responded to macroeconomic conditions. However, in changing required reserve ratios, the Fed's proximate objectives were to adjust bank reserve positions and influence credit conditions, which policymakers saw as the mechanism

---

[12] We omit the years around World War II (specifically, 1941Q4–1946Q4) for both our first-stage prediction regressions and the second stage regressions. We also allow for separate constants during the three periods of interest: 1930s, the postwar period until shortly after the Accord was signed (1951Q4), and from that point until the end of 1959.

[13] Because estimates of trend output used to construct a measure of the output gap are sensitive to starting and ending points and de-trending method, we estimated an alternative set of regressions in which we replace the predicted output gap with the predicted growth rate of output (industrial production). The coefficient on output growth in this regression is also positive (in the ordered-logit regression) and statistically significant, indicating that reserve requirements were increased in response to increases in predicted output growth.

Table 3.2. *Response of reserve requirements to macroeconomic conditions*

	Ordered-logit	Change in RSI
Predicted output gap	18.05***	−2.14**
	(5.41)	(0.91)
Predicted rate of inflation	0.56***	−0.05*
	(0.18)	(0.03)
Constant1	−1.34	0.13
	(0.49)	(0.08)
Constant2	4.32	n/a
	(0.86)	
Observations	78	78
LR χ^2	43.69	n/a
Pseudo R^2	0.34	0.14

Notes: Robust standard errors are in parentheses; ***, **, and * indicate statistical significance at the 1, 5, and 10 percent levels, respectively. The two constants in the ordered-logit regression are a result of having three possible outcome values. The first constant indicates the log-odds of having the lowest outcome rather than the two higher outcomes while the second constant indicates the log-odds of having one of the two lowest outcomes rather than the highest outcome.

by which they could achieve their ultimate macroeconomic objectives. Thus, we next examine whether the proximate targets or indicators of monetary policy evolved in a manner consistent with a response of policy to macroeconomic conditions. Further, we are interested in whether this responsiveness varied across three periods: 1935Q1–1941Q3; 1947Q1–1951Q4; and 1952Q1–1959Q3.[14] For this comparison, we conduct an exercise similar to Romer and Romer (2002) in that we regress indicators of monetary policy on macroeconomic variables to see whether they were systematically related to macroeconomic conditions.

Romer and Romer (2002) argue that the Fed targeted short-term interest rates in the 1950s, and they use the federal funds rate as the dependent

[14] We end the first period in the quarter before the United States entered World War II. We exclude 1946 in part as it may have taken some time to convert to a more peacetime economy and as the peg on short-term Treasury Bills, which ended in early 1947, would distort some of these results. We classify all of 1951 as part of the second period as it was some months after the Accord before the Federal Reserve was fully implementing monetary policy. Our results for the response of policy to inflation are weaker if we include all of 1959 in our estimation period. Romer and Romer (2002) report a similar result, which they attribute to a tightening of policy in response to an increase in expected inflation that failed to materialize. As with the ordered-logit regression, we use predicted inflation and the predicted output gap. As described in footnote 12, when estimating these first-stage regressions we use only the years included in the three regime periods (so that the World War II years are excluded).

variable in a forward-looking Taylor rule for that decade. However, data on the federal funds rate are not available before the 1950s, when the funds market reawakened after being moribund from the latter part of the 1930s through the 1940s. Instead, we use the average market rate on 4–6-month commercial paper as one indicator of the stance of monetary policy.[15]

We also use the level of net free reserves, that is, total member bank reserves in excess of legal requirements less borrowed reserves, as a second indicator of policy. The Fed began to interpret the level of borrowed reserves as a meaningful guide to the stance of monetary policy in the 1920s, and then watched free reserves closely in the 1930s when banks began to hold substantial excess reserves and borrowed reserves declined to negligible levels. In the 1950s, FOMC deliberations often included discussion of the level of free reserves that would most likely be consistent with the Committee's desired policy objectives, and open market operations often targeted a specific range for free reserves (Brunner and Meltzer, 1964; Calomiris and Wheelock, 1998; Meltzer, 2009). We regress the two policy indicators on measures of predicted inflation and output gap as described above.

Tables 3.3 and 3.4 report our regression estimates. The models in Table 3.3 use free reserves as the policy variable, whereas those in Table 3.4 use the commercial paper interest rate. Similar to Romer and Romer (2002), we find that in the 1950s, monetary policy tended to tighten (indicated by a reduction in free reserves or an increase in interest rates) when expected output exceeded trend or inflation rose. However, we find no evidence that either free reserves or the interest rate responded to inflation or the output gap in the earlier periods. Of course, the short sample periods make estimating reliable relationships difficult, but the evidence is consistent with the idea that monetary policy, as reflected in short-term interest rates and free reserves, did not respond systematically to inflation or the output gap during 1935–41 or 1946–51 (let alone during the war years, 1941–45).[16]

---

[15] Although data on short-term Treasury security yields are also available for the entire period, because the Fed pegged the rate on those securities during and for several years after the war, they exhibit little variation over time and are unrelated to economic activity or inflation over much of our sample period.

[16] Typically, Taylor-type interest rate rules such as those shown in Table 3.4 have coefficients on inflation that are fairly close to 1, whereas our coefficients are notably smaller. We find that the coefficient estimates for inflation are sensitive to the specific measure of the output gap and method of adjusting for serial correlation. For instance, using the unemployment rate in the 1950s rather than the industrial production based output gap, we obtain a coefficient on inflation that is just more than 1 (quarterly data on the unemployment rate are not available for the entire period). However, whereas the magnitudes of the coefficients are sensitive to model specification, qualitatively the relative responsiveness of

Table 3.3. *Response of free reserves to macroeconomic conditions*

	Period 1 1935Q1 to 1941Q3	Period 2 1947Q1 to 1951Q4	Period 3 1952Q1 to 1959Q3
Predicted output	−1246.2	506.7	−4641.9*
gap	(2492.9)	(917.7)	(1735.2)
Predicated rate of	25.9	−5.19	−194.2*
inflation	(104.8)	(12.79)	(104.3)
Constant	3519.4**	650.5***	280.3**
	(1508.1)	(76.31)	(128.2)
Observations	27	20	31
F-statistic	0.19	0.19	10.5
Adjusted R^2	-	−0.08	0.41

Notes: Robust standard errors are in parentheses; ***, **, and * indicate statistical significance at the 1, 5, and 10 percent levels, respectively. The regressions control for serial correlation using the Prais–Winsten method.

Table 3.4. *Response of commercial paper rate to macroeconomic conditions*

	Period 1 1935Q1 to 1941Q3	Period 2 1947Q1 to 1951Q4	Period 3 1952Q1 to 1959Q3
Predicted output	0.04	0.19	6.39*
gap	(0.27)	(0.86)	(3.41)
Predicated rate of	−0.01	−0.00	0.18
inflation	(0.01)	(0.02)	(0.15)
Constant	0.74***	1.58***	2.38***
	(0.11)	(0.50)	(0.42)
Observations	27	20	31
F-statistic	0.94	0.03	3.33
Adjusted R^2	0.40	-	0.26

Notes: Robust standard errors are in parentheses; ***, **, and * indicate statistical significance at the 1, 5, and 10 percent levels, respectively. The regressions control for serial correlation using the Prais–Winsten method.

Our failure to detect a response of monetary policy indicators to macroeconomic conditions during the late 1930s or the late 1940s might reflect the fairly short sample periods, which makes precise estimation difficult. It

monetary policy to macroeconomic conditions is not. The finding that monetary policy was more responsive in the 1950s than in earlier years is quite robust. Thus, we are less concerned here with the absolute size of the coefficients than with the relative size and significance of the relationships with macroeconomic variables across time periods.

could also be that policymakers simply had incorrect models of the economy and thus were not responding appropriately. However, the monetary authorities were probably considerably more constrained in their ability to respond to economic developments during 1935–51 than they were after the Accord. We next delve into the historical record to discern better how the Fed's objectives and policy constraints evolved over time.

3.3 The Historical Record

The information in the previous section suggests that during 1935–51, the Fed adjusted reserve requirements in response to economic conditions, but that broader measures of policy – free reserves and short-term interest rates – did not respond to inflation or output gaps before 1951. The following sections draw on Federal Reserve records and other sources to understand better how the Fed used its various tools, especially reserve requirements, to implement policy during the prewar period (1935–41), wartime and early postwar period (1941–51), and after the Fed-Treasury Accord (1951–59).

3.3.1 The "Backseat" Era, 1935–1941

Histories of the Federal Reserve focus primarily on the Fed's understanding of the role of monetary policy in the economy and its willingness to take actions to smooth the business cycle or maintain price stability. In particular, the Fed's failure to respond aggressively to banking panics, deflation, or the severe decline in output during the contraction phase of the Great Depression has been the subject of much study (e.g., Friedman and Schwartz, 1963; Wicker, 1966; Meltzer, 2003). Whether the Fed had a better understanding of the role of monetary policy or had become more willing to respond to economic activity by the second half of the 1930s remains an open question, but is not the primary concern of our study. Instead, we focus on how the Fed's actions were shaped by changes in the constraints on the Fed's ability to carry out monetary policy.

From the mid-1930s until US entry into World War II, monetary policy was dominated by two competing considerations that limited the Fed's ability to use open market operations and the discount rate to achieve macroeconomic policy objectives. On the one hand, large gold inflows gorged the banking system with reserves, many of which accumulated as excess reserves. Fed officials grew increasingly concerned that the growth in excess reserves could lead to an inflationary expansion of credit. By June 1935, the excess reserves held by member banks exceeded the size of the Fed's holdings of government securities and were continuing to grow. As excess reserves rose, the proportion that the Fed could eliminate through open market sales became smaller. Consequently, the Fed turned to its newly acquired authority to increase required reserve ratios to convert a portion of excess reserves into required reserves.

Pressure from the Treasury Department further constrained the Fed in its desire to control inflation. Treasury officials desired to avoid increases in government security yields, which would raise the cost of financing federal deficits. FOMC transcripts and other documentary evidence described below illustrate some of the political pressures on the Fed in this era.

Whereas gold outflows had contributed to monetary contraction and deflation during 1930–33, beginning in 1934, gold inflows added considerably to the stock of high-powered money and were the primary driver of changes in the money supply during 1934–41 (Friedman and Schwartz, 1963; Romer, 1992; Hanes, 2006). The Fed's concern with gold inflows and the growth of reserves in the mid-1930s is clear from Federal Reserve reports, meeting transcripts, and histories of the Fed (e.g., Friedman and Schwartz, 1963; Meltzer, 2003). Officials were particularly concerned about the growth of reserves in excess of requirements, and the potential for rapid growth in bank lending and inflation (Carpenter, 1940). To reduce excess reserves, the Board increased reserve requirements in three steps during 1936–37 that in sum doubled all required reserve ratios and brought them to the maximums allowed by law. The first increase was announced in July 1936. The Board's *Annual Report for 1936* outlined the case: "Excess reserves by the summer of 1936 amounted to more than $3 billion. On the basis of these excess reserves and the legal reserve ratios then in effect, bank credit could have been expanded to twice the volume in use at the peak of business activity in 1929; and the gold inflow was still in progress" (p. 1).

In December 1936, the Treasury Department began to sterilize gold inflows to prevent them from further increasing bank reserves. According to Meltzer (2003, pp. 504–07), Treasury Department staff proposed sterilization as an alternative to a Fed plan to conduct open market sales or increase reserve requirements further. The Fed subsequently agreed not to sell securities but went ahead with the second and third hikes in reserve requirements in early 1937.

The Fed stressed that the increases in reserve requirements (and gold sterilization) "did not reflect changes in Federal Reserve credit policy, which continued to be directed toward monetary ease. They were adopted with a view to reducing redundant reserves created by the gold movement and did not affect the existing volume of currency and bank deposits which had been built up in recent years" (*Annual Report for 1936*, p. 2). The Board asserted that "member banks had large amounts of unused reserves, and ... the demand for credit for business purposes was relatively small" (ibid., p. 2). The Board went on to argue that "The part of excess reserves thus eliminated [by the increase in reserve requirements] was superfluous for prospective needs of commerce, industry, and agriculture, and, if permitted to become the basis of a multiple expansion of bank credit, might have resulted in an injurious credit expansion" (ibid., p. 14).

The Board noted that even after the doubling of reserve requirements, "Banks continue to have a substantial amount of excess reserves on which to expand credit and can obtain additional reserves by recourse to Federal Reserve Banks" (ibid., p. 2). Further, "The existing volume of bank deposits ... was not reduced by the increase in requirements, and these deposits, if actively utilized, would be sufficient to finance a volume of business far greater than was transacted in 1936" (ibid., p. 2).

One of the Fed's goals in raising reserve requirements was to make it feasible for the System's other tools, chiefly open market operations and the discount rate, to influence bank reserves and credit conditions: "The necessity of calling Federal Reserve credit into use would once again make the banking system more directly responsive to Federal Reserve policy" (ibid., p. 2). The Board went on to argue that "The Federal Reserve System is again placed in a position where such reduction or expansion of member bank reserves as may be deemed in the public interest may be effected through open market operations" (ibid., p. 15).

Figure 3.3 plots the monetary gold stock, the total reserves of Federal Reserve member banks, and the ratio of excess-to-total reserves of member banks during 1934–41. Vertical lines identify the dates when the three increases in reserve requirements of 1936–37 took effect, and April 16, 1938 when reserve requirements were lowered. As the figure shows, during 1934–36 the growth in total reserves and increase in the ratio of excess-to-total reserves reflected growth of the monetary gold stock. The figure also shows the impact of the increases in reserve requirements on the excess-to-total reserves ratio, and of the gold sterilization program on the growth of total reserves.

Further evidence of the importance of gold flows on bank reserves during the 1930s (but not in later years) is shown by regressions presented in Table 3.5. Here we use monthly data to estimate the impacts of Fed policy actions, as reflected by open market operations, reserve requirements, and changes in the discount rate, and gold flows on the free reserves of Fed

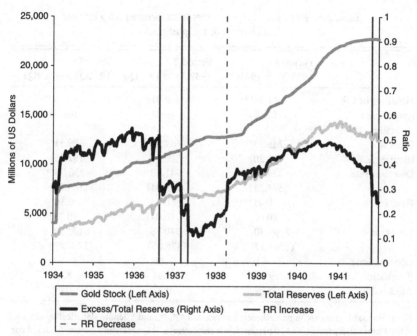

Figure 3.3. Monetary gold stock, bank reserves, and changes in required reserve ratios, 1934–41.

member banks. Increases in the Fed's holdings of government securities add reserves to the banking system, as do gold inflows, whereas increases in required reserve ratios reduce free reserves by reducing the amount of reserves held by banks in excess of requirements. Increases in the Fed's discount rate tend to increase free reserves by discouraging discount window borrowing. As the estimates show, gold inflows had a strong positive impact on free reserves during the 1930s, but not in later years. In addition to gold flows, during the 1930s, free reserves also reflected changes in the Fed's holdings of government securities and changes in reserve requirements.[17] Free reserves were not systematically related to the Fed's discount rate, which was changed infrequently during this period. Of course, the regressions in Table 3.5 should be viewed with considerable caution, as they omit other sources and uses of reserves besides Fed actions and gold flows. Nonetheless, they are consistent with other evidence that gold flows were an important source of the growth of reserves during the 1930s (but not

---

[17] Reserve requirements are measured here as the unweighted average of the required reserve ratio applied to demand deposits in central reserve city and reserve city banks.

Table 3.5. *Response of free reserves to monetary policy actions*
and changes in the gold stock

	Period 1 1935Q1 to 1941Q3	Period 2 1947Q1 to 1951Q4	Period 3 1952Q1 to 1959Q3
Holdings of US government securities	1.48*** (0.50)	0.01 (0.03)	0.15** (0.06)
Reserve requirements	−245.33*** (32.20)	−69.25** (28.34)	−29.11 (82.35)
Discount rate	328.91 (394.21)	−41.60 (69.94)	−256.06** (104.19)
Gold stock	0.41*** (0.07)	0.04 (0.04)	0.16 (0.16)
Constant	−2400.80 (1869.77)	980.75 (876.25)	−6133.92 (3707.89)
Observations	81	60	93
F-statistic	19.82	6.44	3.18
Adjusted R^2	0.49	0.27	0.09

Notes: Standard errors are in parentheses. The symbols ***, **, and * denote statistical significance at the 1 percent, 5 percent, and 10 percent levels respectively. The regressions control for serial correlation using the Prais–Winsten method.

in later years) and, taken with the results in Table 3.3 showing no clear response of free reserves to predicted inflation or the output gap, suggest that gold flows were a predominant focus of policy in this period.

3.3.2 Pressure from the Treasury Secretary

The initial hike in reserve requirements, which took effect in August 1936, elicited almost no reaction in financial markets. However, interest rates increased somewhat following the subsequent hikes in March and May 1937. Yields on long-term government bonds rose from 2.25 percent in February to 2.75 percent in early April 1937. Figure 3.4 plots the long-term Treasury bond yield and three-month Treasury bill yield alongside the dates of changes in required reserve ratios to illustrate the behavior of interest rates around dates when the Fed changed required reserve ratios. The increase in yields following the March 1937 increase in ratios displeased Treasury Secretary Morgenthau. At a meeting of the FOMC Executive Committee on March 13, Chairman Eccles reported that Morgenthau had informed him that the Treasury stood ready to end gold sterilization or to use the resources of the Exchange Stabilization Fund to lift government

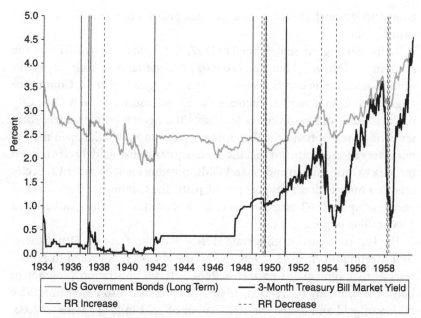

Figure 3.4. Government security yields and changes in required reserve ratios, 1934–59.

bond prices (FOMC, *Memorandum of Discussion*, March 13, 1937). FOMC members subsequently met with Morgenthau and assured him of their desire to maintain an "orderly" market for government securities. At its meeting on March 15, the FOMC voted to make open market purchases to preempt action by the Treasury (FOMC, March 15, 1937, p. 7).

Perhaps because of further pressure from Morgenthau, Eccles began to argue for open market purchases of government securities, the prices of which he viewed as "quite out of line" (FOMC Executive Committee, March 23, 1937). At an FOMC meeting on April 3, Eccles proposed that the Fed engage in open market purchases because "it would take the banks some time to accustom themselves to operating with a smaller amount of excess reserves" (FOMC, April 3, 1937, p. 7). Eccles went on to argue that open market purchases were justified because the hikes in reserve requirements had "disturbed" the government securities market.

Morgenthau continued to press the Fed to prevent government secu-rity yields from rising. Nonetheless, the Board decided to implement the planned third and final hike in reserve requirements on May 1. Prior to the increase, however, the FOMC agreed to use open market purchases to expand member bank excess reserves by as much as $250 million. In this instance, both the Fed and the Treasury appear to have perceived a need to support government securities prices when the Treasury was issuing debt.

By its meeting on September 11, 1937, the FOMC recognized that the economy had slowed.[18] Further, Fed staff forecast that New York City banks would soon have no excess reserves and they suggested that the Committee might wish to take steps to increase the excess reserves of New York City banks to $250 million in order to maintain a neutral policy stance. After reviewing their options, the Committee agreed to undertake open market purchases and recommend that the Treasury desterilize gold. Eccles relayed the idea to Morgenthau and, at an FOMC meeting on September 12, Eccles reported Morgenthau's support for the plan. The Committee then voted to purchase up to $300 million of securities while the Treasury desterilized $300 million of gold.

The Fed continued to cooperate closely with the Treasury Department. At a meeting on April 15, 1938, the Board of Governors voted to reduce reserve requirements as part of a Roosevelt administration program to boost the economy (Carpenter, 1940). The program also desterilized $1.4 billion of gold and ended the sterilization of gold inflows (Meltzer, 2003, p. 531). The Board explained that "Although there had been excess reserves in amounts considered ample to meet all probable needs of agriculture, commerce, and business, the volume of business activity had declined with such rapidity as to produce injurious deflationary effects upon commodity prices, the capital market, and industry generally. In these circumstances ... the Board decided that a reduction in reserve requirements of member banks might be helpful ... by assuring the continued availability of ample funds for meeting business requirements and thereby preventing injurious credit contraction" (*Annual Report*, 1938, pp. 73–74).

---

[18] The contribution of the doubling of reserve requirements in 1936–37 to the subsequent recession has been debated. Friedman and Schwartz (1963) argue that the action was an important cause of the recession. They contend that banks held excess reserves as a precaution against bank runs, and reduced credit supply in an effort to rebuild their excess reserves after reserve requirements were raised. Subsequent research, however, suggests that the hikes were more benign. Calomiris, Mason, and Wheelock (2011) estimate a forecasting model of member bank reserve ratios (both reserves/assets and reserves/deposits) using December 1935 data for individual banks. The study finds that the actual reserve ratios of member banks after the increases in reserve requirements were no higher, and often lower, than predicted by the model, suggesting that the hikes were not contractionary, at least not in the way argued by Friedman and Schwartz (1963). Other studies, such as Velde (2009), find that the hikes may have contributed but were not the only cause of the recession.

3.3.3 World War II to the Accord

Inflationary pressures began to build as the economy recovered from the 1937 to 1938 recession. Although gold inflows ended in mid-1941, inflation did not abate. On November 1, 1941, the Fed responded by lifting required reserve ratios to their legal maximums.

World War II changed the environment for the Fed. Gold inflows ceased. During the war, the Fed directed its open market operations entirely to assisting in the goal of funding war expenditures at low interest rates. Price controls and rationing were imposed to limit inflation and allocate scarce resources (Sproul, 1951). The Fed made one change in reserve requirements during the war – a reduction affecting only central reserve city banks.

The Fed's close cooperation with the Treasury grew stronger after Pearl Harbor. The Fed pledged to peg the existing structure of yields on shorter-term securities and enforce a ceiling of 2.5 percent on the yield for long-term government bonds.[19] At the short end of the yield curve, the Fed capped the rate on the ninety-day Treasury bill at 3/8 percent. Moreover, the Fed guaranteed that a seller of bills to the Fed could buy back securities of a like amount and maturity at the same rate of discount. For banks, this policy effectively made Treasury bills the equivalent of cash; in essence, they were excess reserves that drew interest (Friedman and Schwartz, 1963; Sproul, 1951; Walker, 1954). The bill rate was below 3/8 percent when the cap was established, but rates soon rose to that level and the Fed was forced to purchase a growing amount of bills to maintain the cap. This gave the Treasury even greater ability to influence monetary policy. Simply by increasing the amount of bills it issued, the Treasury put upward pressure on money markets and forced the Fed into additional purchases that increased the supply of bank reserves.

During 1942, the Fed's holdings of government securities rose by $3.9 billion. Although the purchases added to the stock of reserves, higher reserve requirements as well as increased demand for currency reduced member banks' excess reserves by $1.1 billion. Because New York City and Chicago banks experienced especially heavy reserve outflows, the Board reduced reserve requirements on demand deposits in central reserve city banks from 26 to 20 percent in three equal-size cuts in August, September, and October 1942. The cuts left the required reserve ratio on demand deposits for central reserve city and reserve city banks identical, while the ratio for

---

[19] See Wicker (1969) for a detailed discussion of the negotiations between the Treasury and the Fed on implementing the ceiling.

country member banks remained 14 percent. According to Meltzer (2003, p. 600), the Board was reluctant to lower reserve requirements for central reserve city banks but did so at the request of the Treasury. The Board made clear in its annual report for 1942 that the cut in the required reserve ratio was intended to support the government securities market: "The smooth functioning of the money market and the success of the war finance program required the participation of central reserve city banks, and it was therefore necessary to supply these banks with the reserves required for such participation. Banks elsewhere, on the other hand, had large amounts of unused reserves and were constantly gaining funds. For those reasons the reductions in reserve requirements were made applicable solely to central reserve city banks" (*Annual Report for 1942*, p. 20).

No further changes were made to required reserve ratios during the war. However, in 1943, Congress passed legislation exempting government war loan deposit accounts from reserve requirements and deposit insurance assessments. The legislation, which the Fed had recommended, facilitated the placement of new Treasury debt issues by increasing temporarily the amount of excess reserves in the banking system.

3.3.4 After the War

The end of the war left the external environment for the Fed largely unchanged. Capital controls remained in place for many countries and, for the most part, gold flows and the balance of payments were of little concern to the Fed over the remainder of the 1940s and most of the 1950s. As shown by the regression estimates in Table 3.5, gold flows had little impact on the level of free reserves in this period.

The absence of pressures from gold flows or the balance of payments did not mean that the Fed was free to use monetary policy to control inflation or smooth the business cycle. The Fed remained committed to low and stable interest rates on government securities, including enforcement of a ceiling on the long-term bond yield. Low long-term bond yields were important for containing government borrowing costs when the ratio of government debt to GDP was exceptionally high, and they were a priority of the Truman administration. Moreover, a substantial amount of government debt was owned by commercial banks, which would have had sizable mark-to-market losses if interest rates rose (Wallich and Keir, 1979). However, with the lifting of price controls and rationing, and expiration of some credit regulations, inflation once again became a concern. Thus the Fed had two potentially conflicting goals. With open market operations used primarily to enforce the 2.5 percent ceiling on the long-term government bond yield and otherwise support Treasury funding operations, the Fed again turned to reserve requirements and credit controls to regulate the growth of private credit in an attempt to control inflation.

For a time, the postwar regime worked reasonably well. Inflation spiked when price controls were lifted, but then subsided. The Board of Governors considered raising required reserve ratios for central reserve city banks in 1946, but dropped the idea when the New York Fed president expressed opposition (Meltzer, 2003, pp. 604–41). Treasury bond yields remained below 2.5 percent. Eichengreen and Garber (1991) interpret the immediate postwar environment in terms of target zones, arguing that the Fed had an explicit target zone for interest rates and an implicit target zone for inflation. In the absence of large real shocks, the Fed's commitment to preventing sustained inflation was credible, which kept the yields on long-term government securities from rising above the 2.5 percent ceiling. Moreover, the yields on short-term government securities were gradually allowed to rise and the Federal Government budget was in balance, both of which helped keep inflation expectations in check.[20]

Shortly after the war ended, the Fed's official statements began to make a case for allowing greater flexibility in the market yields on Treasury securities. For example, the Board's *Annual Report for 1946* states that "In view of the large public debt outstanding, it is desirable to maintain at the existing low levels the rate at which the Government can borrow on its long-term obligations." However, "the relationship between rates for various types of market issues might be permitted to become more responsive to demand … A readjustment of short-term rates and the introduction of some flexibility would provide some check to further … credit expansion" (p. 6).

In 1947, the Fed and Treasury agreed to let the yields on shorter-term government securities rise, but retained the ceiling of 2.5 percent on long-term bonds. The Treasury ran a budget surplus in 1948, which further eased pressure on the Fed to monetize government debt.

The Fed was unwilling, or perhaps unable, to step further away from supporting the Treasury's debt financing operations. The Fed's 1947 *Annual Report* expressed concerns both about the stability of the government securities market and the likely effect of even a gradual relaxation of the ceiling on long-term government bond yields: "Constant Federal Reserve operations are essential for the maintenance of an orderly market and reasonable

---

[20] Including both on- and off-budget accounts, the Federal budget swung from a deficit of $16 billion in 1946 to surpluses in 1947–49.

stability of prices ... To permit a gradual decline in prices of government securities, moreover, might result in heavy liquidation of investor holdings" (p. 7).[21]

Its unwillingness (or inability) to withdraw further from supporting the government securities market led the Fed to ask Congress for additional tools to control the growth of private credit. Those tools included additional authority to raise reserve requirements and to impose them on nonmember banks: "Strengthening of monetary policy to regulate overall bank credit expansion in accordance with the economy's needs could be accomplished by legislation extending authority to increase the statutory reserve requirements of member banks and to require nonmember banks to hold additional reserves in an amount corresponding to the increase for member banks." Further, the Fed suggested a secondary reserve requirement that banks could satisfy by holding short-term Treasury securities: "Under this measure banks would be restricted as to the amount and types of securities they could sell to obtain additional reserves but would not have to reduce their total holdings of securities in order to meet the requirement." This "would make it possible for the Federal Open Market Committee to require banks to immobilize a portion of their greatly expanded holdings of Government securities instead of permitting them to treat these holdings as excess reserves, which can be used at will to expand loans" (*Annual Report for 1947*, p. 9). The proposed requirement was designed to increase the demand for Treasury securities, and thereby hold down the cost of Treasury financing, while enhancing the Fed's ability to control the growth of private credit. In short, the Fed was asking for a new tool that would help it achieve two goals – low Treasury funding costs and control of inflation – that increasingly were in conflict with one another.

In addition to enhanced authority to set reserve requirements and impose a secondary requirement, the Fed sought expanded authority to regulate specific types of private credit. The Securities Exchange Act of 1934 had authorized the Fed to set margin requirements on loans used to purchase stocks and other securities. In September 1941, President Roosevelt had issued an executive order authorizing the Fed to also regulate installment and other forms of credit, but Congress terminated that authority on November 1, 1947. The Fed asked Congress to reestablish that authority,

---

[21] Moreover, Sproul (1951) noted that, with large government debt outstanding and ongoing adjustment to a peacetime economy, significant action by the Fed at that time would have had "a cost in fiscal and financial disorder, and in terms of reduced production and employment which few would have wanted to contemplate" (p. 315).

which the Board argued would "help curb prevailing inflationary credit tendencies" (*Annual Report for 1947*, p. 10).

Congress did not act on the Fed's proposals to extend reserve requirements to nonmember banks or to authorize a secondary reserve requirement. However, in August 1948, Congress granted temporary authority to the Board to increase reserve requirements on member banks and to reinstate controls on consumer installment credit. Earlier in 1948 the Fed had increased reserve requirements on central reserve city banks. In September, the Board raised requirements on all classes of member banks to equal or exceed their highest rates since the establishment of the Federal Reserve System (see Table 3.1).[22] The Board also reimposed regulations on consumer installment credit and maintained high margin requirements on loans for purchasing and carrying securities, all in an effort to slow the growth of private-sector credit.

Discussions at the September 8, 1948, meeting of the FOMC Executive Committee provide an illuminating example of the challenges the Fed faced in coordinating its various tools to meet multiple objectives. At that time, the FOMC desired tighter monetary conditions to counter rising credit demand and inflation. However, the Executive Committee knew that raising shorter-term interest rates would make maintaining the ceiling on the long-term bond yield more difficult. Chairman McCabe noted that "the Federal Reserve System probably would be called upon to continue substantial purchases of Government securities from nonbank investors which would supply banks with additional reserves which, in turn, would permit further credit expansion. He proposed an increase in reserve requirements, noting that they would absorb the reserves which would be supplied by Reserve System purchases from nonbank investors" (FOMC Minutes of the Executive Committee, September 8, 1948, p. 3). However, others expressed concern that an increase in reserve requirements would be ineffective. Chicago Fed President Young, for example, argued that raising reserve requirements would not achieve the Fed's intended objective of controlling inflation because the Fed would likely be forced to purchase Treasury securities, and thereby increase total reserves, in order to prevent market yields from rising as banks sold securities to adjust to an increase

---

[22] The tightening of conditions resulted in some conflict between the Federal Reserve and the Treasury. Minutes of the FOMC Executive Committee for August 11, 1948, suggest that the FOMC believed that the Treasury was seeking power to approve or disapprove any change in reserve requirements, which prompted a letter from the Federal Reserve stating its prerogative to change reserve requirements as necessary to meet its responsibilities in the field of monetary policy.

in reserve requirements. That is, the Fed's commitment to keep Treasury security yields from rising meant that it would end up using open market purchases to nullify the tightening effects of any increase in reserve requirements (Meltzer, 2003, p. 666; FOMC Minutes of the Executive Committee, September 8, 1948).

Pressures on the Fed diminished in 1949 as the economy slipped into recession. Loans to businesses and other forms of private credit declined in the first half of the year. The Fed responded to the slackening pace of economic activity by reducing margin requirements in March, easing regulations on consumer installment credit in March and April, and reducing reserve requirements in May and again in August. The Fed also sold short-term government securities, however, "in order to prevent a disorderly decline in short-term yields" in the face of strong demand (*Annual Report for 1949*, p. 7). Thus, the Fed's use of reserve requirements in the pursuit of general macroeconomic goals again conflicted somewhat with the objective of maintaining orderly conditions in the government securities market.

Interestingly, international concerns may have prompted a stronger Federal Reserve response to this recession. With most of the international economy still recovering from the war, at least some Fed policymakers were concerned that a US recession would prompt even greater difficulties abroad "...because of the importance of the American economy in the world picture and the danger to the rest of the world of a serious depression in this country, every effort should be made to prevent such a condition from concurring" (FOMC Executive Committee Minutes, August 5, 1949).

Rising inflation once again became a problem for the Fed in 1950. International issues also played a role as the outbreak of the Korean War brought increased government spending. Economic activity also picked up. The Fed was again faced with two pressing, and conflicting, objectives: controlling inflation and supporting the Treasury's funding operations by maintaining the ceiling on the long-term bond yield and ensuring that the Treasury's issuance of new debt was successful. In an effort to slow the growth of credit, in August the Fed increased reserve bank discount rates and engaged in small open market sales. However, the Fed soon reversed course and bought government securities, "principally for the purpose of assuring the successful refunding of maturing securities and ... to maintain a stable market for long-term bonds" (*Annual Report for 1950*, pp. 2–3). The Fed then resorted to using reserve requirements and other regulations in an effort to slow the growth of private credit. The Defense Production Act of September 1950 gave the Fed new powers to regulate consumer and real estate credit markets. The Fed immediately tightened existing regulations on consumer installment lending and issued new regulations on construction and real estate lending. On December 29, the Fed also announced increases in reserve requirements to take effect in January 1951.

The Fed's commitment to the Treasury meant that it was largely unable to use open market sales to slow the growth of bank reserves, so the Fed resorted to raising reserve requirements (and imposing credit controls) in an effort to contain the growth of private credit without increasing the cost of credit for the Treasury. This effort was at best only partly successful, and ultimately broke down when the Korean War brought increased government expenditures. Inflation expectations rose and the Fed's commitment to preventing the yield on Treasury bonds from rising above 2.5 percent became untenable. As Eichengreen and Garber (1991, p. 195) write, "The cap on interest rates was rendered inconsistent with foreign policy imperatives and their fiscal implications." The Fed and Treasury were forced to compromise, and in March 1951 they reached an accord that freed the Fed from its commitment to prevent increases in government bond yields.

3.3.5 Post-Accord Policy

The story of the conflict and negotiations leading to the Accord is well known (e.g., see Meltzer, 2003). The Accord came about because the Fed found itself in an untenable position: "As the year [1951] opened, business and consumer psychology reflected the impact of the Chinese intervention in Korea ... Buying activity was intense, and upward pressure on prices was strong and was supported by active use of credit" (*Annual Report for 1951*, p. 1). Despite the imposition of additional credit controls and higher reserve requirements, "inflationary pressures in the private sector of the economy continued and extension of bank credit ... proceeded at an unusually rapid rate. In the light of these developments it became increasingly clear that anti-inflationary credit and monetary measures could not be made effective – in fact that credit and monetary developments would tend to be inflationary – as long as Government securities were given a 'monetary quality' by support of their prices" (ibid., pp. 3–4).

After several rounds of discussion, and an awkward meeting of the Board of Governors with President Truman at the White House, the Treasury Department agreed to release the Fed from its commitment to hold the yield on long-term government bonds at or below 2.5 percent and to allow market forces to determine the yields on Treasury securities. In return, the Fed acknowledged that the "successful financing of the Government's

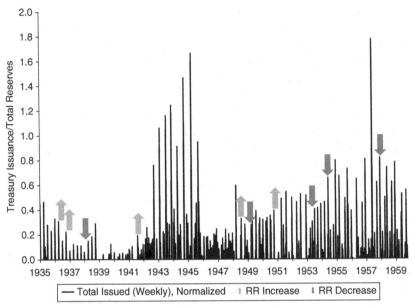

Figure 3.5. Treasury issuance to total bank reserves and changes in required reserve ratios, 1935–59.

requirements" remained an important goal of debt management and monetary policies (ibid., p. 4).

The Accord removed the formal constraint on Fed policy associated with pegging interest rates. Nevertheless, the Fed still felt obligated to provide support for Treasury issuance, and for some time, the Fed assisted the Treasury without ceding control of monetary policy. Figure 3.5 shows the dollar amount of securities issued by the Treasury Department during 1935–59. We include securities issued for cash as well as securities issued in exchange for outstanding issues, and we divide the amount issued by total member bank reserves to show the volume of securities issued relative to a measure of the capacity of the banking system to absorb them. As shown in Figure 3.5, Treasury issuance resumed in the early 1950s after having been negligible in the late 1940s. At the time, Treasury securities were offered by subscription rather than at auctions (Garbade, 2012). The Treasury would announce the amount, price, and coupon rate that they intended to sell about a week before an offering closed. This procedure risked having an offering fail if market interest rates rose before the closing. Part of the Fed's support was to refrain from actions that might be interpreted as a change in monetary policy near dates of Treasury financings – so-called even-keel policy (Wallich and Keir, 1979; Humpage, 2014). Additionally, also shown in Figure 3.5, the timing of some changes in reserve requirements and open market operations was geared toward ensuring that the banking system had sufficient reserves to absorb the securities sold by the Treasury. On a few occasions the Fed purchased securities to ensure that a funding operation did not fail. For example, the Fed purchased a significant amount of newly issued one-year Treasury certificates after a sharp increase in interest rates risked the failure of a Treasury offering in July 1958 (see Garbade, 2012).

However, the Federal Reserve also took a number of steps to ensure its monetary policy independence. For example, in the early 1950s, the Federal Reserve adopted a policy of purchasing only Treasury bills (the so-called bills only policy) to avoid pressure to support the prices of long-term government securities (Humpage, 2014). Moreover, Meulendyke (1998) reports that even though Fed officials saw interest rates as the primary channel by which monetary policy affects the economy, FOMC members thought it unwise to target a particular interest rate in order to break firmly from the pre-Accord regime of pegging rates at the behest of the Treasury.

In its *Annual Report for 1951*, the Fed claimed that the Accord had an immediate positive impact: "Withdrawal of Federal Reserve support of the Government securities market following the Treasury-Federal Reserve accord was an important factor in changing inflationary psychology ... As a result of this change in climate, expectations of further depreciation of the value of the dollar were widely revised [and] search for various hedges against inflation was moderated ... Foreign appraisal of prospects for the dollar also improved and this was a factor in the subsequent cessation of gold outflow from the United States" (ibid., p. 2). The subsequent absence of foreign pressures is again consistent with our results in Table 3.5 showing that gold flows had little impact on free reserves during 1952–59.

The Accord enabled the Fed to redirect open market policy away from full-time support of the government securities market toward controlling inflation and limiting fluctuations in economic activity. Nonetheless, changes in reserve requirements and credit regulation remained components of the Fed's policy throughout the 1950s. The Fed also considered changing how it set reserve requirements and continued to seek Congressional approval to extend reserve requirements to nonmember banks.[23] The Fed

---

[23] For example, at a meeting on March 6, 1951, the Board considered a plan that would relate reserve requirements directly to changes in the volume of private-sector loans and investments on the books of commercial banks. "Under the plan the Board would be authorized to require any bank whose loan assets rose ... to hold a supplementary reserve requirement of up to a maximum of 50 percent of the increase in loan assets." The plan

was unable to persuade Congress, however, until 1980 when the Monetary Control Act subjected nonmember banks and other depository institutions to the reserve requirements imposed on Federal Reserve member banks.

3.3.6 The Fed's Operating Procedures

Following the Accord, the Fed adopted an operating framework that closely resembled the framework it had first used in the 1920s, which the Fed acknowledged in its *Annual Report for 1957* (p. 9).[24] That framework presumed that member banks are reluctant to borrow from the Fed, and when conditions force them to borrow, banks will respond by tightening credit in an effort to reduce their indebtedness to the Fed. Thus, when the Fed wanted to tighten policy, it would use open market operations to reduce the supply of nonborrowed reserves in the banking system, which initially would cause banks to borrow more from the Fed but subsequently reduce the supply of credit in an effort to repay their borrowing. For example, in 1952 "the Federal Reserve System followed a policy of restraining the pace of credit expansion by making it necessary for member banks to borrow in order to obtain reserves. This put them under pressure to restrict expansion of their loans and investments. Thus discount operations at the Reserve Banks again became an effective instrument of credit policy, … [which was a] realization of the purposes envisaged by the Treasury-Federal Reserve accord of March 1951" (*Annual Report for 1952*, p. 1).

Changes in reserve requirements remained a component of the Fed's policy strategy after the Accord. The Fed reduced requirements in 1954, primarily "to make sure that banks would be supplied with reserves in amounts sufficient to encourage them to seek uses for their funds and thus to foster credit and monetary expansion" (*Annual Report for 1954*, p. 8). However, the Fed partly sterilized the reduction in reserve requirements by engaging in offsetting open market sales in order "to absorb reserve funds not needed until the fall period of active currency and credit demand" (p. 7). Thus, open market operations were used to "fine tune" the impact of changes in reserve requirements on bank reserve positions.

The Fed reduced reserve requirements again in 1958 as part of an effort to stimulate the economy during a recession. The cut reduced required

---

was intended to apply to both member and nonmember banks (Minutes of the Board of Governors, March 6, 1951, p. 2).

[24] Meltzer (2009) refers to the policy framework developed in the 1920s as the "Riefler-Burgess" doctrine, after Fed officials Winfield Riefler and W. Randolph Burgess. During the 1950s, Riefler was a special assistant to the Board of Governors.

reserves by $1.5 billion. In addition, the Fed added $2 billion of reserves via open market purchases and cut Federal Reserve bank discount rates by nearly 2 percentage points (*Annual Report for 1958*, p. 3). The decrease in reserve requirements was seen as a valuable part of the Fed's strategy due to the publicity surrounding it. The announcement of a change in reserve requirements "receives wide attention and is public evidence of efforts of the Federal Reserve System to use its monetary tools to encourage business recovery. Open market operations, on the other hand, receive far less attention and are understood by relatively few persons" (Minutes of the Board of Governors, May 20, 1958).

As shown in Table 3.5, after the Accord, changes in reserve requirements did not systematically affect the level of free reserves as they had in earlier years when reserve requirements were the primary tool of monetary policy. Of course, the regressions in Table 3.5 should be viewed with considerable caution. The time periods are short and the regressions omit other sources and uses of reserves besides Fed policy actions. However, the regressions are consistent with evidence from other sources suggesting that after the Accord, the Fed turned more toward open market operations and discount rate changes to implement policy, and sometimes used offsetting open market operations to blunt the impact of changes in reserve requirements on bank reserve positions. Nonetheless, the Fed's statements do make clear that changes in reserve requirements remained an important component of policy, even as open market operations and discount rate changes became the principal tools for implementing policy.

3.4 Conclusion

International considerations reemerged as a policy concern in 1958. The Board's *Annual Report for 1958* noted that "Gold movements and the underlying developments in international trade and payments are … constantly under review in the determination of monetary policy" (p. 16). The *Report* noted further that during the first half of 1958, gold outflows drained some $1.5 billion of reserves from the banking system, thus running against the Fed's efforts to promote monetary expansion and counter the economic recession (p. 17). Significantly, the *Report* also drew attention to the Fed's own reserve requirement, noting that the "ratio of gold certificate reserves of the Federal Reserve Banks to their note and deposit liabilities dropped from 46.3 to 42.1 percent, but it remained well above the statutory minimum of 25 percent" (p. 17). The Fed's *Annual Report for 1959* also highlighted gold outflows as having had a large impact on bank reserves in that year. The report notes that the United States experienced net gold outflows of $1.1 billion in 1959, and that the deficit in the balance of payments was nearly $4 billion.

The reemergence of balance of payments deficits and gold flows as policy concerns marked the end of an era in which the absence of significant external pressures allowed the Fed to direct monetary policy primarily toward controlling inflation and smoothing the business cycle. Unlike the 1930s, when gold inflows had a considerable impact on short-term rates and free reserves, and were viewed by the Fed as a serious inflation threat, throughout most of the 1950s, gold flows and other international considerations had almost no impact on domestic monetary conditions or policy. Similarly, after the Fed-Treasury Accord, political pressures on the Fed diminished, although the Fed was careful to maintain an even-keel policy during periods of Treasury funding operations.

Bordo and Eichengreen (2013) argue that concern about balance of payments deficits and gold outflows led the Fed to pursue a tighter monetary policy during the early 1960s than was warranted by domestic considerations alone. Further, as the decade continued, the Fed came under considerable political pressure to keep interest rates from rising despite increased government spending and rising inflation. Our findings suggest that the absence of such concerns and pressures in the 1950s enabled the Fed to be responsive to the domestic economy in that decade. Of course, a lack of external constraints and pressure does not guarantee a responsive policy, and that the Fed was responsive to inflation and the business cycle in the 1950s suggests a level of sophistication in the Fed's "lean against the wind" policies. Still, a lesson of the 1950s is that it requires both enlightened policymakers and a conducive environment to assure a successful outcome.

References

Board of Governors of the Federal Reserve System, 1943. *Banking and Monetary Statistics, 1914–41*. Washington, DC: Board of Governors of the Federal Reserve System.

1971. *Banking and Monetary Statistics, 1941–70*. Washington, DC: Board of Governors of the Federal Reserve System.

Bordo, Michael D. and Barry Eichengreen, 2013. "Bretton Woods and the Great Inflation" in Michael D. Bordo and Athanasios Orphanides (eds.), *The Great Inflation: The Rebirth of Modern Central Banking*. Chicago, IL: University of Chicago Press, 449–96.

Bordo, Michael D. and Athanasios Orphanides, eds., 2013. *The Great Inflation: The Rebirth of Modern Central Banking*. Chicago, IL: University of Chicago Press.

Brunner, Karl and Allan H. Meltzer, 1964. "The Fed's Attachment to the Free Reserves Concept." Subcommittee on Domestic Finance, Committee on Banking and Currency. Washington: United States House of Representatives. 88th Congress, 2nd Session.

Calomiris, Charles W., Joseph Mason, and David C. Wheelock, 2011. "Did Doubling Reserve Requirements Cause the Recession of 1936–1938? A Microeconomic Approach." NBER Working Paper No. 16688.

Calomiris, Charles W. and David C. Wheelock, 1998. "Was the Great Depression a Watershed for American Monetary Policy?" in Michael D. Bordo, Claudia Goldin, and Eugene N. White (eds.), The Defining Moment: The Great Depression and the American Economy in the Twentieth Century. Chicago, IL: University of Chicago Press, 23–65.

Carlson, Mark, 2015. "Lessons from the Historical Use of Reserve Requirements in the United States to Promote Bank Liquidity." International Journal of Central Banking 11: 191–224.

Carpenter, Samuel R., 1940. "Development of the Open Market Function of the Federal Reserve System." Dissertation submitted at the Graduate School of Banking at Rutgers University.

Clarida, Richard, Jordi Galí, and Mark Gertler, 2000. "Monetary Policy Rules and Macroeconomic Stability: Evidence and Some Theory." Quarterly Journal of Economics 115: 147–80.

Eichengreen, Barry and Peter M. Garber, 1991. "Before the Accord: U.S. Monetary-Financial Policy, 1945–51" in R. Glenn Hubbard, (ed.), Financial Markets and Financial Crises. Chicago, IL: University of Chicago Press, 175–205.

Federal Open Market Committee, 1948. Minutes of the Executive Committee of the Federal Open Market Committee, September 8, 1948.

Friedman, Milton and Anna J. Schwartz, 1963. A Monetary History of the United States, 1867–1960. Princeton, NJ: Princeton University Press.

Garbade, Kenneth, 2012. Birth of a Market. Cambridge, MA: MIT Press.

Hanes, Christopher, 2006. "The Liquidity Trap and U.S. Interest Rates in the 1930s." Journal of Money, Credit, and Banking 38: 163–94.

Haslag, Joseph H. and Scott E. Hein, 1995. "Measuring the Policy Effects of Changes in Reserve Requirement Ratios." Federal Reserve Bank of Dallas Economic Review, 2–15.

Hetzel, Robert L., 2008. The Monetary Policy of the Federal Reserve: A History. Cambridge: Cambridge University Press.

Humpage, Owen, 2014. "Independent within – Not of – Government: The Emergency of the Federal Reserve as a Modern Central Bank." Federal Reserve Bank of Cleveland Working Paper 14-02.

Meltzer, Allan H., 2003. A History of the Federal Reserve Volume 1, 1913–1951. Chicago, IL: University of Chicago Press.

2009. A History of the Federal Reserve Volume 2, Book 1, 1951–1969. Chicago, IL: University of Chicago Press.

Meulendyke, Ann-Marie, 1998. U.S. Monetary Policy and Financial Markets. New York, NY: Federal Reserve Bank of New York.

Romer, Christina D., 1992. "What Ended the Great Depression?" Journal of Economic History 52: 757–84.

Romer, Christina D. and David H. Romer, 2002. "A Rehabilitation of Monetary Policy in the 1950's." *American Economic Review Papers and Proceedings* 92: 121–27.
2004. "Choosing the Federal Reserve Chair: Lessons from History." *Journal of Economic Perspectives* 18: 129–62.
Sproul, Allan, 1951. "Changing Concepts of Central Banking," in *Money, Trade, and Economic Growth*. New York, NY: MacMillan Company.
Velde, Francois R., 2009. "The Recession of 1937 – A Cautionary Tale." Federal Reserve Bank of Chicago. *Economic Perspectives* 33(4): 16–37.
Wallich, Henry and Peter Keir, 1979. "The Role of Operating Guides in U.S. Monetary Policy: A Historical Review." *Federal Reserve Bulletin* 65(9): 679–91.
Walker, Charles, 1954. "Federal Reserve Policy and the Structure of Interest Rates on Government Securities." *Quarterly Journal of Economics* 68: 19–42.
Wicker, Elmus, 1966. *Federal Reserve Monetary Policy 1917–1933*. New York, NY: Random House.
1969. "The World War II Policy of Fixing A Pattern of Interest Rates." *Journal of Finance* 24: 447–58.

Appendix Data Sources

Consumer Price Index: Bureau of Labor Statistics (seasonally adjusted, Haver Analytics).

Discount Rate, Federal Reserve Bank of New York: Board of Governors of the Federal Reserve System (1943), table 115, and Board of Governors of the Federal Reserve System (1971), table 12.1.

Industrial Production: Board of Governors of the Federal Reserve System, Release G.17 (seasonally adjusted, Haver Analytics).

Interest Rate on 4–6-Month Commercial Paper: Board of Governors of the Federal Reserve System (1943), table 120, and Board of Governors of the Federal Reserve System (1971), table 12.5.

Federal Reserve Holdings of US Government Securities: Board of Governors of the Federal Reserve System (1943), table 101, and Board of Governors of the Federal Reserve System (1971), table 10.1.

Free Reserves (Reserves in excess of legal requirements minus reserves borrowed from Federal Reserve Banks): Board of Governors of the Federal Reserve System (1943), table 101, and Board of Governors of the Federal Reserve System (1971), table 10.1.

Gold Stock: Board of Governors of the Federal Reserve System (1943), table 101, and Board of Governors of the Federal Reserve System (1971), table 10.1.

Required Reserve Step Index: Haslag and Hein (1995).

Required Reserve Ratios: Board of Governors of the Federal Reserve System (1971), table 10.4.

Treasury Issuance (Sum of securities issued for cash or in exchange for other securities): *Treasury Bulletin*, various issues.

Yield on Three-Month Treasury Bills: Board of Governors of the Federal Reserve System (1943), table 123, and Board of Governors of the Federal Reserve System (1971), table 12.7.B.

Yield on Long-Term US Government Bonds: Board of Governors of the Federal Reserve System (1943), table 129, and Board of Governors of the Federal Reserve System (1971), table 12.12.B.

Comments on Mark A. Carlson and David C. Wheelock,
"Navigating Constraints: The Evolution of Federal Reserve
Monetary Policy, 1935–1959"

Gary Richardson

Commentators should tell readers what they need to know about a chapter and what information, inferences, and conclusions could be questioned. Readers should realize that this chapter, as a whole, is thoughtful and accurate. I agree with almost everything in it. I make a few minor methodological suggestions (and I've made suggestions in the past that have been incorporated in the final draft). But, these suggestions should not distract readers from the main point: you can learn a lot by reading this chapter.

What do the authors do in this chapter? First, they document the evolution of Federal Reserve policy from the 1930s through the 1950s. This evolution includes the introduction of new policy tools and the imposition of new constraints. The former came during the New Deal of the 1930s. The latter came also during the New Deal and also due to the exigencies of World War II. Then, the authors explain why the Fed's policies were good during the 1950s and bad during the 1930s. By good, I mean contributed toward economic expansion and stable prices. By bad, I mean the opposite. The authors present narrative and statistical evidence to support their arguments. The key argument is that factors limited the Fed's ability to conduct an independent monetary policy in the 1930s and 1940s. These factors included the Roosevelt administration's gold policies, New Deal legislation, and World War II. These constraints prevented the Fed from reacting appropriately to expected inflation and economic fluctuations, particularly during the 1930s, leading to bad policies and outcomes in the 1930s and during wartime expansion and demobilization.

What were the new policy tools? Most of these tools came during the 1930s. The tools included the power to set margin requirements, which

Views expressed herein are those of the author and not necessarily those of the Federal Reserve Bank of Richmond or the Federal Reserve System.

the Federal Reserve Board received from the Securities Exchange Act. The tools included the power to set reserve requirements as well as rates on deposits, particularly demand deposits in commercial banks. These tools also included the expansion of powers to conduct open market operations as well as discount, industrial, and emergency lending.

This New Deal legislation eased constraints on Federal Reserve policymakers, providing powers to take actions which policymakers could not take before. The proposals underlying much of legislation predate the New Deal. Politicians and policymakers debated many of these initiatives during the 1910s, and proposed many of these initiatives during the early 1930s, but the legislation failed to pass Congress until events such as the Banking Holiday provided an impetus for reform. Most of these proposals expanded the Fed's powers to conduct countercyclical operations and relaxed constraints against expansionary policies embedded either in the policies of the Federal Reserve System, the mindset of its leaders, or the original Federal Reserve Act. New Deal changes in the structure of the System set the foundation for independent monetary policy in the 1950s and later.

Before 1932, for example, the Federal Reserve was required to back the high-powered money (that is, currency plus deposits at the Fed) with gold and short-term commercial paper. This requirement came from the original Federal Reserve Act, which imposed two strict constraints. One was that currency plus deposits at the Fed had to be backed by at least 40 percent gold. The other was that currency plus deposits at the Fed had to be backed to 100 percent by gold and eligible paper, which were short-term bank loans backed by commodities in the process of production, distribution, or sale.

Banking Acts in 1932 and afterwards changed the way that the Fed backed money. By the end of the Roosevelt administration, the Fed backed high-powered money with a combination of gold, other assets, and Treasury debt; it had taken large steps toward the way in which we back our money supply today.

The other foundation for modern policy that came about during the New Deal was the creation of the FOMC's modern structure in the Banking Act of 1935. That act removed the Secretary of Treasury and Comptroller of Currency from the Federal Reserve Board. Then, to the FOMC, it added the Board of Governor's chair, vice chair, and other members.

The FOMC was created in 1933 to replace a previous structure for making open market decisions, which included the bank governors (the CEOs now called presidents), and excluded members of the Federal Reserve Board. The Banking Act of 1935, in short, put the Board of Governors in the driver's seat at the FOMC.

Marriner Eccles, who supervised the writing of the original draft for Title 2 of the Banking Act of 1935, wanted to make a different change. Some recent news articles claim that Marriner Eccles was the author of the Banking Act of 1935 and created the Fed's modern monetary independence. Those accounts are misleading. The draft that Marriner Eccles originally submitted to Congress and which passed the House of Representatives would have created an FOMC of five members. Three of them would have been the Governor of the Fed, the Secretary of Treasury, and the Comptroller of Currency. All of these individuals would have served at the pleasure of the president. The FOMC would also have included two reserve bank CEOs, who in the Eccles plan, could have been replaced by the president at frequent intervals. The FOMC, in other words, would have been an extension of the executive branch. It would not have been independent. Carter Glass objected to this proposal and held prolonged hearings in the Senate in 1935. His committee rewrote portions of the act pertaining to the FOMC. His amendments passed the Senate, survived the conference committee, and appeared in the version of the bill signed by the president. Carter Glass clearly wanted the FOMC to be independent of the president and the executive branch of the federal government.

I think the chapter does an excellent job of using statistical evidence to support its argument and narrative evidence. I have a few minor quibbles about the coefficients and the statistical functions. For instance, Table 3.2 examines changes in reserve requirements, and how those changes correlated with macroeconomic conditions. The ordered-logit specification that they employ ignores much of the information in this table. They have detailed data on the magnitude of these reserve requirement changes. They condense that information into a simple indicator variable, up or down. This may bias the standard errors of their estimates as well as the coefficients. Minor adjustments to these regressions (which the authors have now added to the essay) could increase the accuracy of their estimates and strengthen their arguments.

My biggest questions in the statistical part come from the way they create the variable, the output gap, which goes into their regressions. They plot the output gap in Figure 3.2. When you look at it, you'll notice something odd. The most expansionary period for industrial production comes in 1936. In that year, unemployment exceeded 10 percent, with a substantial share of the labor force excluded from the calculation because they either participated in government jobs programs or had left the labor force. Industrial production in many industries fell below the level before the Great Depression. Yet, their measure of the output gap indicates that economic activity in this year was substantially over trend.

There is something intriguing about the way that they create this measure of the output gap. Like all economists, they are filtering data on industrial production to create deviations from trend. In this case, their filter judges much of the Great Depression to be a change in trend rather than a deviation from trend. Changing the filter will change this result. Linear, HP, and Baxter-King filters, for example, find different peaks in the output gap. Some turn the 1936 gap from positive to negative. If you change the filtering technique, it can change the time series for the output gap. That would change the regression coefficient substantially and actually could make it go to zero or go to negative. The one thing I've really encouraged them to do is do some more work on that issue. Although, I note that every paper about the macroeconomics of the Great Depression runs into this problem; do you want to explain deviations from trend, changes from trend, or both?

One way to resolve this issue is to make the regression more consistent with the rhetoric of the chapter. The chapter and David's presentation discuss the way the trend is changing. Both talk about the acceleration and de-acceleration of industrial production. That language appears throughout their narrative and in the written records. This language suggests using the second moment of industrial production – not its level or deviation from trend but the change in industrial production or the change of the output gap. I think if their regressions focus on these measures, they will provide stronger statistical support for their arguments (note that the authors later incorporated these ideas into a series of robustness checks and confirmed this supposition).

Readers may ask, what do these regressions tell us? The Fed used some policy tools consistently from the 1930s to the late 1950s. By consistently, we mean that in circumstance X, the Fed responded with policy Y. Which tools did they use consistently? They used reserve requirements consistently. But, many other tools were used inconsistently. In particular, the Fed moved interest rates much less in response to expected inflation above trend or industrial production below trend in the 1930s than they did in the 1950s.

I want to point out that this pattern arose because the Fed refused to respond to deflation during the late 1920s and early 1930s. The Fed's leaders did not want to respond aggressively to the decline in industrial output in the early 1930s. They did not believe that they should (or could) respond to this situation.

Now, the chapter tries to explain the coefficients on these regressions by saying, "It's the constraints that the Roosevelt administration placed on the Fed that mute the Fed's reaction; the New Deal tied the Fed's hands."

I'm not actually sure that the authors believe this. In previous writings, they discuss the reasons that the Fed reacted insufficiently to the contraction in the early 1930s. They're also aware that the Treasury took control of monetary policy in 1933 in order to force the Fed to pursue reflationary and expansionary policies. Their chapter does not discuss these issues, in part, I believe, because the conference organizers charged them with examining the Fed's policies from the mid-1930s through the mid-1950s. This edit moved the authors away from talking about the reasons that the Fed did not respond to deflation and Depression in the 1920s and 1930s. The Fed's failure did not stem from the New Deal, Roosevelt, or World War II, because the problem preceded those events by five or ten years.

The Fed's problems here stem from the institutional constraints that Barry Eichengreen talked about in the last paper on the gold standard rules and from the legal limits on open market operations and discount lending contained in the original Federal Reserve Act. These institutions and laws tied the hands of the Fed. Sometimes the tie was due to the legal constraint; the Fed approached or feared approaching legal bounds on backing dollars with gold and other eligible assets. On many occasions, the ties were intellectual constraints. The system's leaders did not want to respond or did not think that they should respond to these problems.

Andrew Mellon may be the most infamous liquidationist in this period. He was the chairman of the Federal Reserve Board during the Roaring Twenties through 1932. President Herbert Hoover wrote in discussions with Mellon that Mellon argued that the Fed should not act. "What we want is to liquidate stock, liquidate bonds, and liquidate companies. We want the contractionary phase of the Depression to be as sharp and as quick as it can so we can get back to an expansionary phase of the business cycle and begin the economic recovery."

I think that the reason the Fed did not respond to the obvious deflation and output gap in the early 1930s was that the leaders of the system intellectually did not want to take action. When the authors of this chapter argue, "what's the difference between the 1950s and the 1930s?" I'm not sure that the answer is constraints on actions imposed by the New Deal, but rather constraints which were mental. Policy differences between the 1930s and 1950s, in other words, appear to be due in large part to the intellectual outlook of the leaders in those decades, rather than changes in legal powers or constraints between the two periods.

4

Federal Reserve Policy and Bretton Woods

Michael D. Bordo and Owen F. Humpage

In a fundamental sense, a country's external payments cannot be in satisfactory equilibrium unless the domestic economy is in reasonable balance and its basic national and international objectives are being met.

Economic Report of the President 1966, p. 160

4.1 Introduction

The Bretton Woods system looked to correct perceived problems of the interwar gold-exchange standard – competitive devaluation, protectionism, deflation, unemployment – by establishing institutions that might credibly maintain a set of parity values for national currencies, while still allowing countries to independently pursue domestic economic objectives and, if necessary to that end, adjust those parity values. It offered a compromise between those who wanted greater exchange-rate flexibility and those who wanted a return to the gold standard. In a world of imperfect wage and price flexibility and incomplete factor mobility, however, Bretton Woods arguably attempted an improbable task. In such a world, monetary-policy independence and fixed exchange rates will not always remain compatible, a situation then requiring the use of significant restraints on capital flows. The latter, however, are disruptive and wholly incompatible with efficiency in a market economy. Moreover, as applied to parity values, credible and adjustable are antithetical attributes.

Consequently, the system that emerged – far from its planners' vision – confronted persistent problems with macroeconomic adjustment, exchange-rate credibility, and adequate liquidity. Within that imperfect system, the US dollar quickly became the key international reserve and vehicle currency, making a credible US commitment to price stability the central necessary condition for the sustainability of the system.

That commitment, of course, was not fulfilled. Before 1959, when most advanced currencies were not widely convertible and when trade and financial restraints proliferated, Bretton Woods and a US monetary policy largely focused on price stability seemed well suited. Persistent US balance-of-payments deficits supplied the world with the dollar and gold reserves that countries needed to maintain their parities in a growing economy. Still, the world did not accept the dollar as gold's equivalent, and by 1960, just as Bretton Woods was becoming fully functional, concerns about the dollar's convertibility raised serious questions about Bretton Woods' viability and elicited criticisms of the dollar's privileged place in that system. Confidence in Bretton Woods was shaken. The changed environment would henceforth require US policymakers to weigh external objectives more carefully in formulating US macroeconomic policies, but with memories of the Great Depression still fresh, no US administration would sacrifice growth and employment to exchange-rate – or even price – stability during the late-1960s and 1970s.

This chapter investigates how, in this environment, international considerations may have affected US monetary policy. Between 1960 and 1973, Federal Reserve policymakers often mentioned balance-of-payments concerns in their deliberations and in their statements of policy actions. They did sometimes – especially in crisis situations – adjust policy slightly or temporarily because of international developments. Overall, however, US monetary policy focused primarily on economic growth at potential and full employment. Federal Reserve policymakers typically treated balance-of-payments objectives as superfluous to the domestic designs of monetary policy or simply mentioned and ignored them. This attitude was possible because the Federal Reserve viewed expanding capital constraints, efforts at international cooperation, and sterilized foreign-exchange operations as relieving monetary policy of responsibility for international developments and shifting accountability for international events to the US Treasury. These nonmonetary policies were often successful in the short term. Ironically, however, by eliminating the balance of payments as a constraint on US monetary policy, they allowed the Federal Reserve to create the accelerating and entrenched inflation that doomed Bretton Woods. They ultimately made the outcome worse.

4.2 Fixed Exchange Rates and Full Employment

The designers of the Bretton Woods system envisioned a cooperative international monetary arrangement that would foster exchange-rate stability,

but would still allow countries to pursue key domestic economic objectives, notably, full employment.[1] The agreement reflected a fundamental
lesson from the interwar years: as desirable as fixed exchange rates might
be for promoting international commerce, countries would not long maintain parities at the expense of full employment, economic growth, or price
stability. Domestic economic stability had now become a prerequisite for
international cooperation and exchange-rate fixity (Kenen, 2008).

In the United States, this ordering of policy preferences found expres-
sion in the Employment Act of 1946, which required the federal government "to use all practical means ... for the purposes of creating and
maintaining ... conditions under which there will be afforded useful
employment opportunities ... for those able, willing and seeking to work"
(Pub. L. 79–304 – 70th Congress, Ch. 33 – 2d, S. 380, Sec. 2). This statute
referred only obliquely to price stability (Economic Report of the President
(ERP), 1966, pp. 176–77) and did not mention the balance-of-payments or
exchange-rate objectives. The Employment Act, of course, did not preclude
US policymakers from considering price stability and external economic
goals, but it clearly stated US policy preferences for the Bretton Woods era.

The basic structure of the Bretton Woods system also attempted to rem-
edy potential conflicts between internal and external equilibrium among
its member nations. Under Bretton Woods, countries established fixed parity values for their currencies. The United States pegged the dollar to gold
and pledged to buy and sell the metal freely at $35 per ounce with foreign
monetary authorities. The other major developed nations pegged their currencies to the dollar, promising to keep their exchange rates within a 1 percent band around that central rate by intervening in dollars. When faced
with transitory balance-of-payments problems, countries with insufficient
reserves could borrow from the newly created International Monetary
Fund (IMF) and could impose capital restraints instead of quickly institut-
ing deflationary macroeconomic policies or prematurely altering their par
values. If, however, the balance-of-payments difficulties persisted, countries were to make appropriate adjustments to their monetary and fiscal
policies. If ultimately faced with a "fundamental disequilibrium" in their
balance of payments, countries could adjust their parities. Although the

---

[1] Bordo (1993) and James (1996) provide surveys of Bretton Woods. Meltzer (2003, 2009a,
2009b) offers a detailed, contextually rich discussion of Federal Reserve policy under
Bretton Woods. Meltzer (1991) contains a narrower focus. Eichengreen (2000, 2013) has
also recently discussed Federal Reserve policy during Bretton Woods. Pauls (1990) offers
a more Federal Reserve centric view of the period. Coombs (1976) and Solomon (1982)
are valuable discussions from former Federal Reserve officials.

IMF never clearly defined the concept of fundamental disequilibrium, it seemed to center on an inability to simultaneously maintain internal and external equilibrium at the existing parity (Kenen, 2008, p. 4). In the limit, then, the Bretton Woods system allowed nations to solve any fundamental conflict between internal and external equilibrium in favor of the former.[2]

4.3 From Dollar Shortage to Triffin's Paradox

World War II severely damaged economic capacity throughout Europe and in Japan. The war-torn countries looked to the United States, which at the time produced over one-half of the world's manufacturing, for their needed consumption and investment goods (Yeager, 1966, p. 335). This created a demand for dollars, but the war had also depleted most of the belligerents' reserves. Gold had flown into the United States before and during the war, and by the war's end the United States held 71 percent of the world's stock of monetary gold (ERP, 1963, p. 69). Moreover, with the official gold price set at its prewar value, subsequent inflation drove the real price of gold too low to induce a sufficient supply (Meltzer, 1991; Bordo, 1993; James, 1996).

To meet the reserve shortage, the United States channeled dollars into Europe, Japan, and – eventually – developing countries, through various grant and loan programs, most notably the Marshall Plan. These government grants and loans, together with private capital outflows, shifted the US balance of payments into deficit by 1950, where it would remain, with a few yearly exceptions under some definitions, throughout the Bretton Woods era. To further aid foreign countries' acquisition of dollar reserves, the United States tolerated European and Japanese trade policies that discriminated against it. The United States, nevertheless, generally ran a trade surplus during the Bretton Woods period, but not enough to compensate for its financial outflows. All in all, the United States lost $382 million worth of gold reserves on average each year from 1949 through 1958 and increased its liquid dollar liabilities to foreigners at an average annual $1.1 billion over the same period. Still, until 1958, US officials generally viewed the balance-of-payments deficits and gold losses as a necessary and desirable step toward global adjustment.

Foreign productivity and competitiveness improved faster after World War II than many observers anticipated (Yeager, 1966, pp. 458–63). By

---

[2] Under this arrangement, deficit countries felt pressures to adjust their exchange rates more immediately than surplus countries. Bretton Woods maintained a scarce currency clause, but it was never invoked.

1958, major European countries had acquired sufficient foreign-exchange reserves to make their currencies fully convertible for current-account transactions.[3] Countries also loosened some of their capital controls. With the full convertibility of the key currencies, Bretton Woods had finally become fully functional.

Despite the economic progress made in Europe and Japan, the US balance of payments worsened and did so in a particularly unsettling manner. The overall balance-of-payments deficit (liquidity basis) had averaged $326 million per year between 1946 and 1957, but from 1958 through 1969, the overall deficit averaged $3.1 billion per year. All of the deterioration was attributable to capital flows; the average trade surplus was little changed. US direct investment outflows increased from an annual average of $913 million between 1946 and 1957 to $2.2 billion between 1958 and 1969. Other long-term capital outflows likewise increased from $255 million to $1.2 billion over the same period. Most startling, however, was a sharp increase in short-term capital outflows – particularly in the early 1960s. Short-term capital – including unrecorded transactions – had generally flown into the United States averaging $261 million per year between 1946 and 1958. In 1960, $2.5 billion in short-term capital flowed out of the United States, as interest-rate margins favoring foreign investments widened. The administration attributed this widening to cyclical patterns creating tighter monetary policies in Europe and Japan than in the United States (ERP, 1961, pp. 33–34). Between 1960 and 1969, the average annual outflow of short-term capital equaled $2.0 billion. The dollar shortage was becoming a dollar glut.

Confidence in the Bretton Woods system – specifically the dollar price of gold – began to fade shortly after the European currencies became fully convertible. Since the inception of the Bretton Woods system, the United States had provided needed dollar liquidity through its balance-of-payments deficits. Triffin (1960, pp. 8–9) understood the dilemma that this situation created: the very act of providing dollar liquidity to accommodate the need for reserves as global commerce expanded threatened the viability of the Bretton Woods system, because once the stock of outstanding dollar liabilities exceeded the US gold stock, the United States could not fulfill its commitment to freely convert dollars to gold. The official dollar price of gold would then lose credibility. In August 1960, total outstanding dollar liabilities began to exceed the US gold stock (Figure 4.1).[4] By

---

[3] The Japanese yen became convertible for current-account transactions in 1964.

[4] Congress required the Federal Reserve to hold gold reserves equal to 25 percent of its note and deposit liabilities. In 1958, the London gold market understood the limits that the

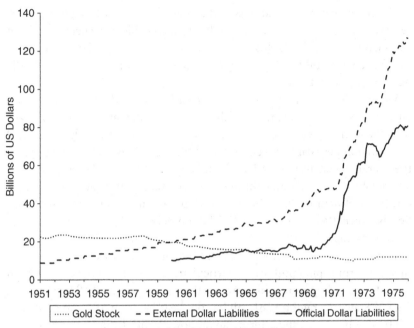

Figure 4.1. Gold and external dollar liabilities.
Source: Board of Governors (1976), tables 14.1 and 15.1.

December 1965, outstanding dollar liabilities to official institutions, which could directly exchange them, exceeded the US gold stock.

As if anticipating the situation, the drain on the US gold stock accelerated in early 1958. Some central banks "unwilling to embarrass the U.S. authorities" bought the metal in the London gold market instead of directly from the US Treasury (Samuel Montagu & Co. Ltd, 1961, p. 11). In August 1960, however, private "hot money" demand for gold firmed and began driving prices well above the $35.0875 that the US Treasury then offered foreign central banks. In October 1960, "there was now widespread private enquiry for gold arising from the apprehension of belief that the recurring heavy withdrawals of gold from the U.S. Treasury would soon force an increase in the official U.S. dollar price of gold" (Samuel Montagu & Co. Ltd, 1961, p. 7). Concerns that the Kennedy administration, which pledged to get the economy moving again, might follow Roosevelt's precedent and devalue the dollar upon taking office heightened this "apprehension." Central banks

required gold reserves implied (see Samuel Montagu & Co. Ltd., 1959, p. 10). On March 3, 1965, Congress ended the reserve requirement on deposit liabilities, and on March 18, 1968, Congress dropped the reserve requirement on notes.

then backed out of the London market. On October 20, 1960, the London gold price rose well above $35 per ounce. It briefly reached $40.50 (offer) per ounce. On October 27, 1960, the Bank of England with US assistance began supplying gold to the market. Gold prices fluctuated between $35.35 and $36.50 for the remainder of the year, above the US gold export point of $35.20.[5] They remained above the gold export point through January and February 1961.

McKinnon (1993, pp. 15–26) and others have argued that the threat posed by Triffin's paradox resulted because the Federal Reserve did not credibly commit to maintain price stability. If US monetary policy had anchored the dollar's purchasing power, then foreign countries' demands for international liquidity would have determined their reserve accumulation. Their reserve holdings would not then have represented a threat to the US gold stock. Be that as it may, inflation in the United States accelerated after 1965. By 1970, foreign central banks, in defense of their parities, began accumulating massive amounts of US dollars. US official dollar liabilities, which had increased by $5.5 billion during the 1960s, increased $55.4 billion just between December 1969 and March 1973. US inflation made the corrosive situation that Triffin described much worse.[6]

4.4 Temporary Solutions to Temporary Problems and Permanent Consequences

The Eisenhower and Kennedy administrations and many observers attributed the worsening US balance-of-payments position between 1957 and 1962, by and large, to transitory factors stemming from US military and economic-aid commitments, recent cyclical developments, and the reemergence of Western Europe and Japan as global competitors. They did not see the external imbalance as "fundamental," requiring a real dollar depreciation of some type. Indeed, a 1962 Brookings Institute study supported this view (Solomon, 1982, p. 58). The study suggested that the US balance-of-payments position would shift to a $1.9 billion surplus by 1968, even

---

[5] Data on the London gold market in 1960 are from Samuel Montagu and Co. Ltd. (1961). Coombs (1976, p. 47) estimates the US gold export price at $35.20 per ounce.

[6] Another factor contributing to Triffin's paradox arose because of the slow pace with which cross exchange rates adjusted under Bretton Woods. Deficit countries defended their currencies by selling dollars whereas surplus countries did so by buying dollars. When dollars flowed from deficit to surplus countries, they left a country that needed them and entered a country that often held too many. This cross-rate adjustment problem increased the likelihood that the surplus country would seek to exchange the dollars for gold.

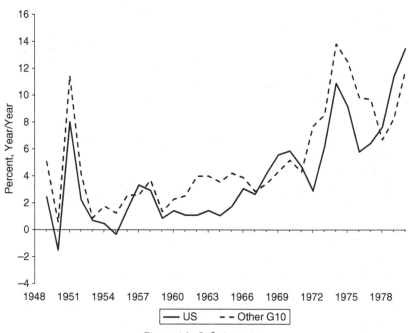

Figure 4.2. Inflation rates.
Sources: US Bureau of Labor Statistics; IMF (various issues).

assuming that the economy grew at potential, that is 4 to 4½ percent growth with a 4 percent unemployment rate (ERP, 1964, pp. 130–31). The surplus resulted because the study anticipated greater price stability in the United States than abroad. Inflation in the United States had, with the exception of 1957, remained below that of the other G10 countries from 1948 through 1968 (Figure 4.2). Under slightly less favorable assumptions, the Brookings study anticipated a small $600 million basic-balance deficit (ERP, 1964, pp. 130–31). Under these expectations, little of a "fundamental" nature needed to be done.

US policymakers also appreciated that with the maturation of the Bretton Woods system – economic recovery abroad, growing currency convertibility, and an adequate pool of liquidity – short-term financial flows could henceforth be more sensitive to international interest-rate differentials and exchange-rate uncertainty. They seemed to believe, however, that once the transitory adjustments to the US trade and long-term financial accounts were complete, credibility in the dollar would strengthen. Renewed credibility in the dollar would lessen the problem of short-term financial flows.

In response to the turmoil in the London gold market and the underlying balance-of-payments shortfall, the United States undertook a series of stop-gap policy initiatives designed to strengthen confidence in the dollar and, thereby, Bretton Woods until the Brookings prediction unfolded. Some of the measures relied on international cooperation and looked to improve the operations of the international financial system, and others hoped to hasten adjustment in the US balance of payments. Despite the decidedly "nonfundamental" nature of these policies, they created – as we will see – an atmosphere in which the Federal Reserve could focus monetary policy on full employment and economic growth instead of on price stability and external equilibrium. These stopgap measures then provided the environment in which the FOMC formulated the monetary-policy decisions that ultimately led to the demise of Bretton Woods.

4.4.1 Improving Bretton Woods: Gold Pool and GAB

Of the policies intended to strengthen confidence in Bretton Woods, the gold pool was arguably the most important. In October 1961, the United States, Belgium, France, Italy, the Netherlands, Switzerland, West Germany, and the United Kingdom formed the gold pool. Initially, the pool functioned as a gold-sales consortium, but in early 1962, gold prices began to fall, and the pool started purchasing gold.[7] Thereafter, through 1964, the gold pool generally functioned as a successful stabilizing speculator, but in 1965, the situation changed.[8] International tensions, stemming primarily from uncertainty about the British pound's parity, France's accelerated conversions of dollar reserves into gold, and that country's public criticisms of the Bretton Woods system, resulted in reoccurring bouts of very heavy speculative demand for gold. The gold pool found its resources dwindling as it struggled to keep the gold price below $35.20, and the pool collapsed in March 1968, following the British pound's devaluation. A segregated two-tier, official and private, gold market followed. Countries pledged not to transact in the private gold market. Dollars or Special Drawing Rights (SDRs) would have to satisfy future increases in reserve needs.

Likewise, the waning confidence in the dollar pointed to a problem with the IMF's borrowing facilities. Should the United States need to borrow other key currencies from the IMF to defend the dollar, the fund might be unable to fulfill the request. Given the US quota, which determined

---

[7] This section draws on Bank of England (1964) and *Bulletin* (1961–67).
[8] On the collapse of the Gold Pool, see: Coombs (1976, pp. 152–73).

its borrowing allotment, the United States – and other large developed countries – could potentially request more key currencies than the IMF had on hand (ERP, 1962, pp. 15–16; Solomon, 1982, p. 93). To increase emergency liquidity to key industrialized countries – especially the United States – the ten largest countries, the G10, initiated the General Arrangements to Borrow (GAB) in October 1962.[9] Accordingly, the G10 would lend the IMF up to $6 billion worth of their currencies (ERP, 1962, p. 16; ERP, 1963, pp. 127–28).

4.4.2 Improving the Balance of Payments: Capital Restraints

With European countries now better able to compete in global markets, the Eisenhower and Kennedy administrations pressed for the removal of discriminatory trade practices that foreign countries had levied primarily against the United States. The Kennedy administration also took steps to encourage exports and reduce the duty free allowances of US tourists. Both administrations also attributed much of the US balance-of-payments shortfall to the United States' military-assistance and economic-development programs. Given the Cold War atmosphere, cutting such aid was not feasible, so the Eisenhower and Kennedy administrations – sometimes under a threat of troop redeployment – increasingly tied such aid to purchases of US goods and services (Gavin, 2004).

The Kennedy and Johnson administrations also promoted three key policy changes designed, respectively, to restrain portfolio outflows, bank lending to foreigners, and direct investment abroad.[10] The first set of controls assessed a tax designed to offset the interest-rate advantage that foreigners gained by issuing bonds and stocks in the United States instead of in Europe. On July 19, 1963, the Kennedy administration proposed an Interest Equalization Tax (IET), which levied a 1–15 percent excise on foreign debts – depending on their maturity – and a 15 percent excise on foreign stocks (Public Law 88–563, September 2, 1964).[11]

Of course, once one type of borrowing was blocked, "other types of capital flows accelerated, offsetting much or all of the gains from the IET" (ERP,

---

[9] The G10 consisted of Belgium, Canada, France, Germany, Italy, Japan, the Netherlands, Sweden, the United Kingdom, and the United States. Switzerland joined in 1964 bringing the number to eleven, but G10 stuck.

[10] Bordo and Eichengreen (2013, pp. 479–81) provide a summary of these controls and related actions. Meltzer (2009b, pp. 693–704) discusses the imposition of controls after 1964.

[11] The IET did not apply to developing countries and allowed broad exemptions to Canada.

1966, p. 165). Consequently, on February 10, 1965, the Johnson administration renewed and expanded the IET, and introduced a second program focused on financial institutions' lending to foreigners. The Federal Reserve asked banks to voluntarily limit the overall growth of their foreign lending, while giving priority to foreign loans that promoted US exports and helped developing countries. Similar guidelines applied to nonbank financial institutions. In addition, the Commerce Department asked nonfinancial corporations to reduce their individual net international balances. The objective was to reduce capital outflows, increase net exports, and encourage the remittance of earnings held abroad (ERP, 1968, pp. 173–74), but, by and large, to voluntarily trim their direct foreign investment.

All of these capital controls were subsequently strengthened.[12] Congress allowed the administration to raise the IET rates by 50 percent in 1967. On January 1, 1968, the president tightened the Commerce Department's direct-foreign-investment program and made it mandatory (ERP, 1968, pp. 173–74). The president also gave the Federal Reserve authority to make its voluntary guidelines mandatory, but the threat worked well enough, and the Federal Reserve kept them "voluntary." The Federal Reserve did, however, issue revised and "substantially more restrictive guidelines for banks and other financial institutions" (AR, 1969, p. 9). With banks now required to reduce foreign lending, especially short-term lending, the "new guidelines, covering both banks and other financial institutions, represent a major tightening of the program begun in 1965" (ERP, 1968, p. 174).[13]

4.4.3 Federal Reserve Foreign-Exchange Intervention

Perhaps the most important, certainly the longest-lasting, and ultimately the most controversial of the stopgap measures that the US Treasury and Federal Reserve adopted in the early 1960s to postpone US gold losses and maintain confidence in the dollar were their foreign-exchange operations. The Federal Reserve, always acting in concert with the Treasury, engaged in many different types of transactions, but its main operations attempted to stem US gold losses through the use of foreign-exchange swaps. Because the Federal Reserve routinely sterilized these transactions, swap operations did not impinge on the designs of monetary policy (MacLaury, 1969). Like capital constraints and other administration programs, these foreign-exchange

---

[12] These restraints seem to have had little effect (Eichengreen, 2000).
[13] On April 4, 1969, President Nixon indicated his desire to eliminate capital controls and began relaxing restrictions on direct investment. The IET was abolished in January 1974.

operations – to the extent that they were effective – gave monetary policy more leeway to pursue domestic objectives.

In March 1961, the US Treasury's Exchange Stabilization Fund (ESF), with the Federal Reserve Bank of New York acting as its agent, began to intervene in the foreign-exchange market for the first time since 1939. The Treasury's initial operations consisted primarily of forward sales of German marks, Swiss francs, Dutch guilder, and Italian lira designed to reduce the forward premiums on these currencies against the dollar.[14] Forward premiums were barometers of market confidence in the dollar, and they provided a strong incentive for financial flows when they exceeded levels consistent with existing interest-rate differentials.

The Treasury's operations were successful and profitable (FOMC, September 12, 1961, p. 44), but a lack of resources severely limited the ability of the ESF to mount a broader dollar defense. Consequently, the Treasury encouraged the Federal Reserve's participation in foreign-exchange operations. Whereas the ESF's budget was ultimately subject to Congressional appropriations, the Federal Reserve had a seemingly unlimited capacity to acquire foreign exchange. On February 13, 1962, after a lengthy debate about its legal authority for such actions, the FOMC authorized intervention in the foreign-exchange market.[15]

The FOMC saw its foreign-exchange operations as *temporary* measures designed to prevent sudden and reversible losses of gold and, thereby, maintain confidence in the dollar. They were not to delay or prevent necessary market corrections, since doing so might only make the inevitable adjustment more disruptive (FOMC, September 12, 1961, p. 55). Moreover, prolonged interventions could undermine the willingness of private traders to make a market in foreign exchange (FOMC, December 5, 1961, p. 60). The primary mechanism for Federal Reserve exchange-market operations, the Reciprocal Currency Arrangements, or swap network, reflected the FOMC's operational philosophy, but distinguishing a priori between temporary and permanent market disturbances proved impossible to do.

In a typical swap transaction, the Federal Reserve and a foreign central bank undertook simultaneous and offsetting spot and forward foreign-exchange transactions typically at the same exchange rates and equal interest rates. Repayment terminated the drawing, but not the credit

---

[14] The Treasury also undertook some limited spot transactions, and engaged in some gold swaps (Bordo, Humpage, and Schwartz, 2015).

[15] On the debate about the Federal Reserve's legal authority for intervention, see Todd (1992), Hetzel (1996) and Bordo, Humpage, and Schwartz (2015).

line, which central banks renewed annually. Swap drawings initially had a term of three months, but could be renewed once. Central banks were not to seek a second renewal, nor were they to continuously draw on a line for more than a year. Also, central banks in the swap network did not apply conditions, such as the adoption of macroeconomic policies or the application for an IMF loan, to their use.[16]

In March 1962, the Federal Reserve established its first swap line with the Bank of France. By the end of that year, the Federal Reserve had set up lines with central banks in nine key countries: Austria, Belgium, Canada, France, Germany, Italy, the Netherlands, Switzerland, and the United Kingdom. Altogether, the lines provided up to $900 million equivalent in foreign exchange. The network continued to grow, and it evolved from a small, very short-term credit facility in 1962 to a large, intermediate-term facility by the closing of the US gold window in August 1971. By then, the swap network totaled $11.2 billion equivalent in foreign exchange and involved fourteen central banks, having picked up the central banks of Denmark, Japan, Mexico, Norway, and Sweden over the intervening years.[17] The Federal Reserve also acquired two swap lines with the Bank for International Settlements, one in Swiss francs and one in other key European currencies. Over the years, the term of a typical swap drawing also increased from the original three months to six months. The expansion of the swap lines was a natural consequence of both the mounting threat to the US gold stock and the growing volume of international transactions, but the increasing length of swap drawings and the frequent tendency to renew them suggested that the underlying disequilibrium had more of a fundamental, than a temporary, nature.

The Federal Reserve used its swap network to provide cover to central banks temporarily holding unwanted dollar balances. Between 1962 and the closing of the US gold window in 1971, the Federal Reserve borrowed $11.5 billion worth of foreign exchange through swaps primarily for this purpose. The Federal Reserve then sold the newly acquired foreign exchange back to the same central bank for the unwanted dollars. This set of transactions – the swap drawing plus dollar acquisition – left the foreign central bank holding exactly the same amount of dollars as it did before the swap operation. Now, however, the dollars it held were covered against

---

[16] As Bordo, Humpage, and Schwartz (2015) explain, conditionality in the late 1970s encouraged the Federal Reserve to acquire a large portfolio of German marks and Japanese yen in the early 1980s, and to end the use of swaps for intervention.

[17] The FOMC denied applications from Ireland and Venezuela.

foreign-exchange risk, since the Federal Reserve contracted to buy them back via the forward leg of the swap at a known exchange rate.

Because swap drawings matured in three months, the Federal Reserve quickly looked for opportunities to fund their repayment.[18] The FOMC, however, precluded the foreign-exchange desk from buying foreign exchange in the market if it was trading above par. When the Federal Reserve could not acquire the foreign exchange in the market, it had three options: the FOMC might buy more time by rolling the swap drawing over. Alternatively, the desk might buy the needed funds off-market from a central bank that was willing to acquire additional dollars in exchange. If these options failed, the Federal Reserve could buy foreign exchange from the US Treasury, which had promised in 1961 to backstop the Federal Reserve's swap operations. If the Treasury did not presently hold the necessary foreign exchange, it would sell special certificates – later Roosa bonds – or gold to acquire the needed funds, or borrow them from the IMF.[19]

All in all, the Federal Reserve's swap lines often succeeded in preventing countries from converting temporary inflows of unwanted dollar reserves into US monetary gold, especially prior to 1970. Thereafter, however, through the closing of the gold window, the Treasury financed most of the Federal Reserve's swap repayments through asset sales (Bordo, Humpage, and Schwartz, 2015). In any event, the operations failed to clearly distinguish between temporary dollar movements and those reflecting fundamental US balance-of-payments imbalances. As a consequence, they did not preclude – and arguably worsened – the ultimate adjustment.

The Federal Reserve's swap lines were reciprocal, meaning that foreign central banks could initiate a drawing if they needed a temporary increase in their dollar reserves. As such, swap lines served to augment countries' foreign-exchange reserves. Between 1962 and 1971, foreign central banks initiated $15.3 billion worth of swap drawings, with the Bank of England undertaking more than half of the total. Swaps offered an often useful short-term palliative.

---

[18] Hopefully, the source of the unwanted dollar balances at a specific central bank had also dissipated by the time the swap matured.

[19] Roosa bonds, named after Treasury Undersecretary for Monetary Affairs, Robert Roosa, who designed them, were non-marketable, medium-term, foreign-currency-denominated bonds that the US Treasury issued to foreign central banks. They differ from foreign-currency-denominated Carter bonds of the 1970s in that the latter were sold in Swiss and German capital markets, not directly to central banks.

4.5 Federal Reserve Monetary Policy, 1951–1972

During most of the 1950s, exchange-market and balance-of-payments developments had virtually no influence on US monetary-policy decisions (Bordo, 1993; Eichengreen, 2013; Carlson and Wheelock, 2014). US policy-makers viewed the persistent balance-of-payments deficits and gold losses during the "dollar-shortage" years as a natural process that fostered global economic recovery and the Bretton Woods system.

During this period, US monetary policy focused on domestic objectives, notably price stability. According to Romer and Romer (2002a, pp. 122–23; 2002b, p. 18), the FOMC believed that inflation ultimately damaged economic growth and that the negative economic consequences of inflation could begin at relatively low rates and build quickly, even if the economy were experiencing some unemployment. The Eisenhower administration advocated balanced budgets and price stability. Moreover, and like the Eisenhower administration, Chairman William McChesney Martin and some other FOMC participants – notably Alfred Hayes, president of the Federal Reserve Bank of New York – maintained that domestic price stability was necessary to maintain the gold peg under Bretton Woods, which they all strongly supported (Bordo and Eichengreen, 2013, p. 454).

The insignificance of international considerations as well as the prominence of price stability in monetary-policy decisions began to change after 1958. The Kennedy administration took office in 1961 believing that the economy had slipped below its potential growth path in 1956. Recessions in 1957–58 and 1960–61 pushed the economy further below potential where it had remained. In 1961, the unemployment rate was near 8 percent – 4 percentage points above a level consistent with the administration's estimate of full employment (ERP, 1962, p. 46). The Kennedy administration put the current output gap at about 8 percent of potential and believed that the gap would persist through mid-1963 under the best-case scenario (ERP, 1962, p. 52). This initial estimate proved too optimistic, and the Kennedy and Johnson administrations continued to project output gaps until 1965 (ERP, 1966, p. 41). They would focus economic policy primarily on achieving full employment, which the Employment Act of 1946 set as "the keystone of national economic policy," and growth at potential.

Nevertheless, President Kennedy "used to tell his advisers that the two things which scared him most were nuclear war and the payments deficit" (Schlesinger, 1965, p. 654). Besides the policies mentioned in section four, Kennedy sometimes undertook domestically orientated macroeconomic policies in a manner that accommodated – or at least did not worsen – the balance-of-payments situation. The most important of such operations teamed the Treasury with the Federal Reserve in a plan to twist the yield curve.

4.5.1 Operation Twist, 1960–1964

Under the prevailing macroeconomic orthodoxy of the Kennedy and Johnson administrations, fiscal policy was the chief instrument of demand management. Monetary policy was to accommodate fiscal policy by keeping interest rates low, thereby fostering investment and other types of interest-sensitive spending or, more generally, "accommodating an expansion of demand" (ERP, 1965, p. 66). Both the Kennedy and early Johnson administrations, however, recognized that the existing international situation compromised the Federal Reserve's efforts to foster internal balance: "If low interest rates encouraged foreign borrowing in the United States and a large outflow of funds seeking higher yields abroad, monetary policy may have to be more restrictive than domestic economic objectives alone would dictate" (ERP, 1962, p. 86). Relatively low US interest rates would worsen the US balance-of-payments position and promote greater gold losses.

Hoping to support domestic economic expansion and simultaneously reduce the outflow of funds to foreign money markets, the Federal Reserve looked to "twist" the yield curve. Monetary policy attempted to raise short-term interest rates to a level consistent with rates abroad, thereby reducing capital outflows, while simultaneously preventing a cyclical rise in long-term interest rates, thereby encouraging domestic investment. At the program's start on October 23, 1960, during the turmoil in the London gold market, the FOMC modified its controversial "bills only" operating procedure by buying securities other than Treasury bills, but still remained at the relatively short end of the yield curve. At the time, the committee only wanted to avoid downward pressure on three-month Treasury yields, which seemed unduly low. The committee stressed, however, that domestic objectives of monetary policy took precedence over the external objectives of policy (AR, 1961, p. 69).

On February 2, 1961, President Kennedy "announced that the Federal Reserve and Treasury were developing techniques to help keep long-term rates down while holding short-term rates at internationally competitive levels" (ERP, 1962, p. 88, table 8). The timing of this announcement suggests that Chairman Martin sought the administration's endorsement before he got the FOMC's official approval. At its February 7, 1961, meeting, the FOMC approved open-market operations in longer-term Treasury securities, a policy that would eventually become known as Operation Twist (AR, 1962, pp. 39–43). The desk would start buying Treasuries in the 1 to 5½ year maturity range and, after the market became accustomed to the operations, extend purchases to the 5½ to 10 year maturity range. The FOMC authorized outright purchases within a limit, at the time, of $1 billion, but also allowed "offsetting purchases and sales of securities for the purpose of altering the maturity pattern of the System portfolio" (AR, 1962, p. 41). The Fed was also quick to point out that the objective of the operation was not to "seek a given fixed rate for Government securities of any maturity" (AR, 1962, p. 40). That is, Operation Twist was not a reversion to pre-Accord Federal Reserve debt-management policy of pegging specific Treasury yields.

Governor J. L. Robertson offered a lengthy dissention from the new policy that centered on four concerns (AR, 1962, pp. 42–43): first, Robertson believed that Operation Twist – unlike "bills only" – was predicated on an untested theory of the term structure and was not likely to succeed. Second, the change unjustly suggested that the FOMC had "pursued incorrect operations practices" in following "bills only" since 1953. Third, Operation Twist would disrupt the market for Treasuries by creating confusion about where on the term structure the desk might choose to operate. Such uncertainty could drive private participants from the market. Fourth, the FOMC was giving too much discretion to the Manager of the Open Market Account. The FOMC had designed "bills only" to take that discretion from the Manager and to assure the market that the post-Accord Fed did not intend to maintain any specific Treasury yields (Meltzer, 2009a). The president of the Federal Reserve Bank of Chicago, Carl E. Allen, also dissented on the same grounds as Governor Robertson.[20] Other FOMC participants, who continuously supported Operation Twist, frequently objected to purchases of long-term bonds, preferring instead to remain in the intermediate range of the yield curve. Like Robertson and Allen, they feared that operations at the long end suggested that the Federal Reserve was pegging a bond rate and might disrupt private participation in the market.[21]

Consequently, the Federal Reserve never bought a substantial amount of Treasuries at the longest end of the yield curve but preferred instead to remain in the short-to-intermediate range (Table 4.1). The FOMC's acquisition of short-term Treasury securities, for example, accounted for 27 percent of its total purchases of Treasuries between 1960 and 1964. Consistent with

[20] Allen was not a voting member of the FOMC until the March 28, 1961, meeting.
[21] See, for example, AR, 1962, pp. 73, 76, and 98.

Table 4.1. *Average annual change in Federal Reserve holdings of Treasury securities*

	Total	Less than one year	Between 1 and 5 years	Greater than five years
Millions of dollars:				
1951–59:	356	450	178	−272
1960–64:	2079	558	1396	124
1965–66:	3636	7010	−3024	−350
Percent of total change:				
1951–59:	100	126	50	−76
1960–64:	100	27	67	6
1965–66:	100	193	−83	−10

Source: Board of Governors (1976), table 9.5.

the broad objective of Operation Twist, this percentage was, indeed, much smaller than that found either between 1951 and 1959 or between 1965 and 1966. Instead, the FOMC's acquisition of Treasury securities in the 1–5-year maturity range accounted for 67 percent of all Treasury securities purchased between 1960 and 1964 – a share substantially greater than over either the previous eight years or the subsequent two years. The Federal Reserve's acquisitions of Treasuries at the long end of the yield curve, however, were very small. Securities with a maturity of more than five years equaled only 6 percent of the total acquisitions.[22] Between 1951 and 1959 and again in 1965 and 1966, the Federal Reserve reduced its holdings of longer-term Treasury securities. Consequently, the Federal Reserve, at best, exerted a small "twist" effect on the very long end of the yield curve, if it indeed had any effect.[23]

For its part, the US Treasury would purchase securities maturing in more than ten years for various government investment and trust accounts and would begin to concentrate new offerings in relatively short maturities to exert upward pressure on short-term yields. "Open market and debt management operations added substantially to the supply of U.S. Government securities maturing within 1 year" during 1961 (ERP, 1962, pp. 88–89). The

---

[22] The Federal Reserve reduced its holding of Treasury bonds with maturities greater than ten years.

[23] Swanson (2011) using high-frequency, event-study techniques finds that Operation Twist announcements in February, March, and April 1961 had a significant, but small impact on long-term bond yields consistent with the objectives of the program. Modigliani and Sutch (1966b) find at most weak evidence for Operation Twist effects. These were largely concentrated in the 1–5-year portion of the yield curve. Their initial study attributed modest term-structure effects only to changes in Regulation Q (Modigliani and Sutch, 1966a).

Treasury would continue complimentary debt-management operations through 1964. "In each of the past four years [1961 through 1964], the volume of bills issued by the Treasury accounted for half or more of the total increase in the marketable debt. In addition, the Treasury used refunding operations to counteract the tendency for the passage of time to shorten the maturity of the Federal debt (ERP, 1965, p. 69).

In 1962, the Fed began undertaking other monetary-policy measures to augment the twin objectives of Operation Twist.[24] In January 1962, July 1963, and November 1964, the Fed raised Regulation Q limits, permitting commercial banks to pay higher interest rates on time and savings deposits. US monetary authorities thought that loosening Regulation Q would allow domestic commercial banks to compete for funds more effectively against foreign banks and that doing so would keep pressure off long-term rates because commercial banks would channel any new deposits into mortgages, state and local securities, and similar long-term instruments (ERP, 1963, p. 59). In addition, loosening Regulation Q would encourage banks to offer more negotiable time certificates, which effectively added to the supply of short-term securities, thereby pushing short-term yields higher (ERP, 1964, p. 47). The Federal Reserve usually undertook increases in Regulation Q ceilings in tandem with hikes in the discount rate. On July 17, 1963, the Fed increased the discount rate from 3 to 3½ percent "largely to reinforce efforts to raise short-term interest rates for balance of payments reasons" (ERP, 1964, p. 47) (Figure 4.3). The Fed took the action in response to increases in foreign interest rates (Solomon, 1982, p. 47). The Fed again raised the discount rate to 4 percent on November 24, 1964, for balance-of-payments purposes, following a hike in the Bank of England's bank rate. The Fed also lowered reserve requirements on time and savings deposits, thereby releasing reserves to encourage domestic expansion without undertaking open-market operations (ERP, 1963, p. 59).[25]

Operation Twist continued through 1964, and although the FOMC focused primarily on supporting the expansion of aggregate demand, international considerations did seem to modify monetary policy somewhat. During these years, the Federal Reserve increased its total holdings of US Treasury securities by nearly $2 billion on average per year, substantially more than the average increase over the previous eight years. Net free reserves – a then common gauge of monetary policy – became positive in

---

[24] Also see the discussion of policy in Bordo and Eichengreen (2013, pp. 459–63).
[25] The Fed allowed member banks to count vault cash as required reserves and lowered reserve requirements in August 1960 for the same reason.

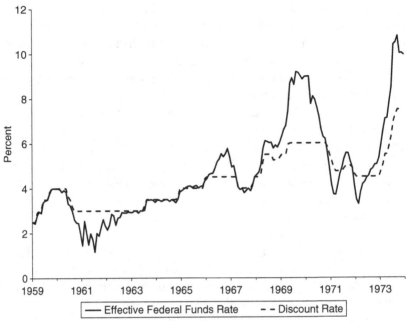

Figure 4.3. Federal Reserve policy rates.
Source: Haver Analytics.

mid-1960, suggesting stimulus (Figure 4.4). Free reserves peaked in January 1961, but remained positive until early 1965. Nevertheless, from 1960:Q4 through 1961:Q2 and from 1962:Q4 though 1965:Q4, the federal funds rate often remained higher than a standard Taylor rule might predict; that is, monetary policy remained somewhat tighter than domestic economic objectives alone warranted (Figure 4.5).[26] Moreover, the operations of the Federal Reserve and Treasury resulted in a yield curve broadly consistent with the aims of the program (Figure 4.6). Short-term interest rates rose after 1961, and although longer-term yields did not fall, they remained – in contrast to previous postwar cyclical experiences – "steadily resistant to upward pressure during the expansion" (ERP, 1965, p. 69).

Operation Twist, however, did not help the balance of payments. Although the overall balance-of-payments position improved somewhat

---

[26] Following Taylor (1999), we estimated a Taylor Rule with real-time data from the Federal Reserve Bank of Philadelphia. Our inflation target is two percent, and we define the GDP gap relative to trend as calculated using a Hodrick-Prescott filter. Rule 2 gives twice as much weight to the output gap as rule 1.

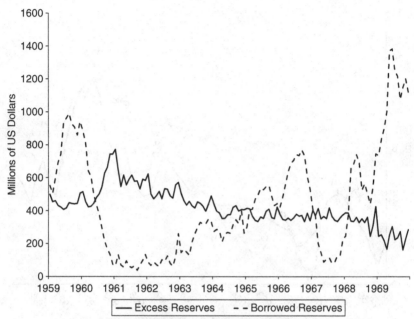

Figure 4.4. Net free reserves.
Note: Net free reserves equal excess reserves less borrowed reserves.
Source: Board of Governors (1976), table 10.2.

between 1960 and 1964, it was all attributable to trade. Capital flows, at best, demonstrated some improvements in some years.

4.5.2 Compatible Objectives, 1965–1969

From 1965 through 1969, any influence that international objectives exerted on Federal Reserve monetary-policy decisions seemed to wane. Operation Twist ended after 1964 because the United States did not need a bifurcated interest-rate policy to handle the emerging domestic economic problem, inflation, and the persistent balance-of-payments concern, gold losses. Tighter monetary policy and higher interest rates addressed both problems simultaneously, so even if FOMC participants still worried about balance-of-payments shortfalls, their concerns hid comfortably behind a focus on inflation (AR, 1966, p. 101). FOMC participants would differ primarily over the relative importance of inflation and full employment goals in policy decisions. Of course, those interested in a tighter, inflation-focused monetary policy often cited balance-of-payments criterion to bolster their case.

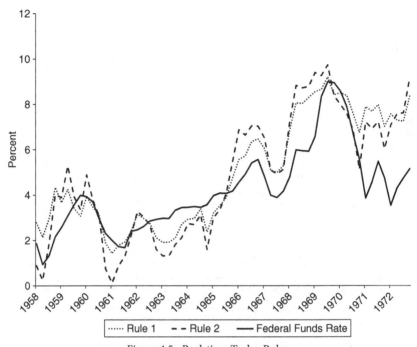

Figure 4.5. Real-time Taylor Rules.
Sources: Haver Analytics, authors' calculations, see endnote #26.

Also contributing importantly to this diminution of external objectives in Federal Reserve policy was – in conjunction with the array of other policies in place – the administration's February 10, 1965, and January 1, 1968, extensions and tightening of restraints on cross-border capital flows.[27] In a fixed-exchange-rate regime, rigid controls on capital flows give a domestically orientated monetary policy more leeway. Capital constraints and foreign-exchange interventions continued to receive the Federal Reserve's full participation, but these actions also shifted responsibility for the nation's balance-of-payments problems increasingly to the administration, giving the Federal Reserve added leeway to focus on domestic-policy concerns (Bordo and Eichengreen, 2013; Eichengreen, 2013). The existence of capital

[27] "It seemed to me that there were other and better techniques than a tight money policy to alter the balance of payments. An attempt by the Federal Reserve to offset speculative international capital flows by raising interest rates was a misuse of monetary policy. Taxes and the existing voluntary program to control such flows would be far better" (Maisel, 1973, p. 73).

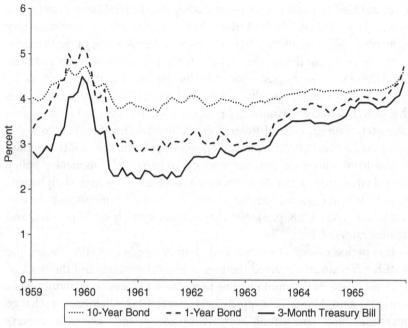

Figure 4.6. Treasury yields.
Source: Haver Analytics.

restraints and the implied shift in responsibility for the balance of payments would strongly influence monetary policy until the end of Bretton Woods.

In 1965, the FOMC increasingly cited inflationary pressures as the justification for its actions (AR, 1966, p. 18). Economic activity was "unusually vigorous," particularly in the second half of the year (AR, 1966, p. 3). By the end of the year, the output gap had virtually disappeared and the unemployment rate was close to the administration's 4 percent goal. Defense spending rose sharply and business investment accelerated, promising continued economic growth. Credit demand strengthened and interest rates firmed. With the requirements of the Employment Act of 1946 fulfilled, the FOMC initially looked to "attain somewhat firmer conditions in money markets," and free reserves turned negative by March (AR, 1966, p. 15). Inflation pressures, however, continued to build throughout the year, and on December 6, 1965, in the face of strong resistance from the Johnson administration, the Federal Reserve raised the discount rate from 4 to 4½ percent and raised Regulation Q limits (Figure 4.3).

Although the discount-rate hike seemed a clear signal of the FOMC's intention to tighten further (ERP, 1967, p. 55), the monetary tightening in

1965 and 1966 was relatively modest. Perhaps the Federal Reserve hesitancy reflected the Johnson administration's and Congress' criticisms of monetary tightening (Meltzer, 2009a). Net free reserves remained negative throughout these years, but the nominal federal funds rate increased only 150 basis points, and the real (ex post) federal funds rate fell by sixty basis points. By late 1966, the FOMC arguably undertook the first of the stop-go operations that would characterize monetary policy during the Great Inflation era and ultimately damage Federal Reserve credibility. In October 1966, as tightening credit conditions threatened economic growth, the FOMC adopted a "less firm" stance for monetary policy. In early 1967, monetary policy moved vigorously to ease domestic credit conditions "through complementary changes in open market operations, reserve requirements, and the discount rate" (AR, 1968, p. 3). Net free reserves again became positive, and interest rates fell.

This period of monetary ease ended on November 18, 1967, when the British government devalued the pound by 14.3 percent, and the Bank of England raised its discount rate to 8 percent – its highest level in fifty-eight years (Bulletin, March 1968, pp. 273–74). Since 1962, US foreign-exchange operations had lent strong support to the pound. US policymakers feared that other countries would quickly follow the pound's devaluation. Speculative pressure might then focus on the dollar and seriously undermine – possibly destroy – credibility in the Bretton Woods system. To minimize the potential spillover effects onto the dollar, the Federal Reserve increased the discount rate back to 4½ percent on November 19, 1967, and tightened reserve requirements on December 27, 1967. Net free reserves began to shrink and the federal funds rate increased.

In 1968, inflation accelerated and "an inflationary psychology was becoming embedded in decision-making for key sectors of the economy" (AR, 1969, p. 6). This included the traded-goods sector. In 1968, US inflation exceeded that of the ten largest US trading partners by nearly a full percentage point. Generally, since World War II, US inflation remained below inflation in the other key developed countries (Figure 4.2). The differential had recently been narrowing, especially since 1965, the year in which the US trade surplus began shrinking. In 1968, the United States posted a $1.8 billion trade surplus, down from $4.6 billion in the previous year and a recent high of $8.5 billion in 1964. Inflation impacted the balance of trade, the key positive component in the US balance of payments. With inflation rising and weakening the trade balance, monetary policy did not face a conflict between its domestic and international policy objectives.

On March 17, 1968, the gold pool suspended operations. Since the devaluation of the British pound, the gold pool had lost $3 billion worth of gold

(FOMC Minutes, April 2, 1968, p. 4). The Federal Reserve increased the discount rate on March 14, 1968, from 4½ to 5 percent both in response to the gold pool and the rising inflation rate. The Fed increased the discount rate again in April, and open-market operations became decidedly more restrictive, primarily as a response to rising inflation. On June 28, 1968, Congress approved the administration's long-delayed package of fiscal constraints including a 10 percent surtax on personal and corporate income and limitations on federal spending. Many FOMC participants saw tighter fiscal policy as important in reducing excessively stimulative fiscal pressures (Maisel, 1973). The tighter fiscal policy and a concern of slowing economic activity led the FOMC to ease monetary policy somewhat in the summer.[28] The Federal Reserve cut the discount rate as market rates declined. Free reserves, however, remained negative.

This half-hearted, stop-go concern for economic softness was brief. "During 1969, the Federal Reserve moved to a very restrictive monetary policy in an effort ... to dissipate deeply rooted expectations of continuing inflation" (AR, 1970, p. 3). By mid-year net free reserves became dramatically more negative and the real federal funds rose sharply (Figure 4.7). The Federal Reserve increased the discount rate on April 4, 1969, to 6½ percent and hiked reserve requirements. In any event, inflation accelerated during 1969 and was running just above 6 percent at year's end.

The Federal Reserve's anti-inflation policy – and hence its legitimate contribution to the country's external economic problems – from 1965 through 1969 was an obvious failure because the FOMC did not stick to it for long enough.[29] The inflation rate rose from around 1 percent in early 1965 to 6 percent by the end of 1969. After 1965:Q3, the federal funds rate remained persistently below the level that a Taylor rule would prescribe as consistent with domestic economic objectives (Figure 4.5). The overall balance-of-payments deficit did not improve; the United States lost $3.6 billion worth of gold, and liquid dollar liabilities expanded by $16.4 billion.

4.5.3 Benign Neglect, 1970–1972

After 1969, the internal and external objectives of monetary policy again came into conflict. Over the previous four years, the US economy had generally operated at, or somewhat above, its potential, suggesting – under the

---

[28] Meltzer (2009a) contends that the Congressional delay in passing the tax surcharge explains why the FOMC did not tighten monetary policy sooner.
[29] Meltzer (2009a) discusses many reasons for this failure.

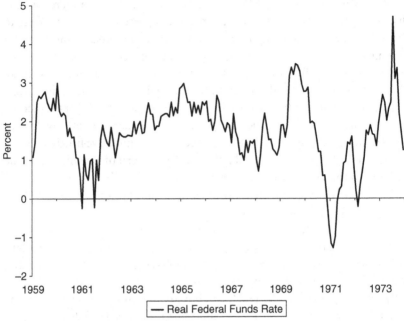

Figure 4.7. Real federal funds rate.
Note: The real federal funds rate equals the nominal federal funds rate less the year-over-year percent change in the CPI.
Source: Haver Analytics.

then prevailing paradigm – that the accompanying rise in inflation was primarily of the demand-pull variety.[30] In such an environment, aggregate demand was excessive, and monetary policy needed to tighten, especially if fiscal policy failed to do so. In these circumstances, a tighter policy was consistent with the Employment Act of 1946; unemployment was well below 4 percent in 1969. Moreover, a tighter policy had the additional benefit of fostering the nation's balance-of-payments objectives.

Late in 1969, however, economic activity peaked. The United States then operated below potential, at least until early 1972, but inflation remained relatively high. According to the then-predominant distinction between demand-pull and cost-push inflations, if the economy were below potential, aggregate demand was deficient, and any persistent price pressure was of the cost-push variety. Conventional monetary and fiscal policies could do little to prevent cost-push inflation without forcing the economy into

[30] Hetzel (2008) discusses how the demand-pull, cost-push view of inflation affected monetary policy during the Great Inflation.

a protracted recession. Their proper role was to keep economic growth at potential, while incomes policy dealt with cost-push inflation. Capital restraints could handle balance-of-payments concerns. Burns adhered to this view of policy.

The seemingly hard-stop monetary policy of 1969 shifted decidedly to "go" in 1970, as the economy experienced a recession that lasted from January through November. "To help stimulate economic activity while at the same time guarding against fueling inflation, monetary policy during 1970 shifted from a posture of restraint that had prevailed during much of 1969 to a posture designed to assure adequate expansion in monetary and credit aggregates and an easing in over-all credit conditions" (AR, 1971, p. 7).[31] Open-market operations brought the nominal federal funds rate from nearly 9 percent in January 1970 to 4.9 percent by year's end (Figure 4.3). The real federal funds rate dropped from 2.8 percent to a negative 0.7 percent over this same time frame (Figure 4.7). The Federal Reserve cut the discount rate from 6 to 5¾ percent on November 16, 1970, and to 5½ percent on December 4, 1970. Short-term interest rates fell relative to those abroad, intensifying the capital outflows. The money stock (M2) grew 3.7 percent faster than output, and inflation remained around 5½ percent at year's end.

Although the economy grew in 1971, it remained below potential. Inflation continued to moderate, but reached only 3.3 percent at year's end. The FOMC seemed to absolve itself from responsibility: "Developments over the first 7 months of the year [1971] brought increasingly into question whether conventional monetary and fiscal policies alone were adequate to combat the cost-push inflation and deterioration in the US balance of payments, while at the same time continuing to promote more vigorous recovery in the domestic economy" (AR, 1971, p. 7). The FOMC opted for economic growth, and in "1971 monetary policy encouraged further substantial growth in bank reserves, money [supply], and bank credit in helping to stimulate economic recovery from the mild recession of 1969–70" (AR, 1972, p. 3). The Federal Reserve lowered the discount rate twice in January to 5 percent, and again to 4¾ in mid-February. Money growth grew at double-digit rates and exceeded real economic growth by more than 8 percentage points on average over the year. The real federal funds rate remained below 1 percent (and often negative) through August 1971.

By the summer of 1971, speculators were moving funds out of dollars into US gold. The Federal Reserve raised the discount rate from 4¾

---

[31] The 10 percent tax surcharge also expired in 1970.

to 5 percent on July 16, and the federal funds rate increased. On August 15, 1971, President Nixon closed the gold window. He also imposed a ninety-day US wage and price freeze, which then led to wage and price controls, and a 10 percent surcharge on all dutiable US imports. In the near crisis atmosphere that prevailed, capital restraints began to emerge. Initially the Federal Reserve seemed to maintain the somewhat firmer monetary policy tone that it adopted in July, but eased again in October. The Federal Reserve then lowered its discount rate to 4¾ percent in November 1971 and again to 4½ percent in December 1971. Apparently, the president's actions loosened external constraints on monetary policy.

At the Smithsonian meeting on December 17–18, 1971, the United States devalued the dollar against gold by approximately 8½ percent to $38 per ounce. Other countries also revalued their currencies relative to the dollar, bringing the overall dollar depreciation to 10.7 percent against the key foreign currencies (de Vries, 1976, p. 555). But, the Smithsonian Agreement did little to restore confidence in Bretton Woods. During 1972, speculators, who saw the devaluation as too small, pushed many European currencies to the tops of their permissible – and now wider – exchange-rate bands. Reflecting the continued uncertainty, gold prices reached $60 per ounce by mid-1972, well above the new official price.

US monetary policy did little to build confidence in Bretton Woods after the devaluation as it continued its stop-go behavior. Although it firmed slightly immediately following the Smithsonian Agreement, US monetary policy eased again in September 1972. The real federal funds rate, however, remained below 2 percent throughout the year. The money stock continued to grow at double-digit rates or 4 percentage points faster than output growth each quarter through 1973: Q1.

In 1972, foreign central banks accumulated large amounts of unwanted dollars, as they defended their currencies' parity values. In doing so they stoked home inflationary pressures. Price levels in foreign G10 nations rose 7.7 percent on average for the year. US inflation, although lower than the foreign G10 average, began rising sharply. Foreign central banks' attempts to tighten monetary policies only encouraged capital inflows. Many countries increasingly attempted to adopt or strengthen their capital restraints. On February 12, 1973, with exchange markets in Europe and Japan closed and gold prices hovering around $90 per ounce, the United States devalued the dollar by an additional 10 percent to $42 per ounce. When markets reopened speculation against the dollar became rampant, as those holding dollars did not want to again be caught off guard (FOMC, March 7, 1973, p. 3). Within a month nearly all major currencies were floating against the dollar. The Bretton Woods system ended. Economic growth, full employment, and price stability now took precedence over exchange-rate fixity.

4.6 Conclusion

During the Bretton Woods era, the FOMC frequently mentioned balance-of-payments developments, fears of gold loss, and exchange-rate concerns in its deliberations and in its explanations of policy actions, but these international considerations carried little overall weight in the committee's decisions – even after 1958, when such issues became critical for Bretton Woods' survival. After 1960, US monetary policy focused instead on domestic economic objectives, chiefly full employment and growth at potential. International crises, such as the British pound's devaluation, did sometimes prompt the Federal Reserve to temporarily tighten monetary policy in hopes of bolstering the dollar and forestalling gold losses, and sometimes international considerations shaped the contours – if not the overall thrust – of US monetary policy, as during Operation Twist. In addition, international factors sometimes helped recommend and support monetary action taken for domestic objectives, as when policy tightened in 1968 and 1969. These instances, however, were clearly the exception; Federal Reserve policy preferences normally conformed to the Employment Act of 1946.

Federal Reserve policymakers could largely disregard international considerations, especially after 1965, because the US Treasury instituted, and by then strengthened, a number of stopgap devices – the gold pool, the General Arrangements to Borrow, capital restraints, sterilized foreign-exchange operations – to shore up the dollar and Bretton Woods. These not only gave monetary policy the latitude with which to focus on domestic-policy objectives, but also shifted responsibility for international developments from the FOMC to the Treasury. Often these devices were successful in forestalling US gold losses, and, given the circumstances, they arguably prolonged the life of Bretton Woods. Ultimately, however, they were destructive.

By removing the pressure of international considerations from FOMC policy decisions, these devices made it easier for the FOMC to pursue the inflationary policies that ultimately destroyed Bretton Woods. A credible commitment to price stability by the Federal Reserve was the *sine qua non* of any fixed-exchange-rate system relying on the US dollar as its key international reserve and vehicle currency, and after 1965, the Federal Reserve failed in this regard.

Removing the international constraints on monetary policy was a sufficient – not a necessary – condition for the Great Inflation that followed, but it may have added the spark to the abundant theoretical tinder already available.[32] At the time, mainstream economists and policymakers downplayed the importance of money in the inflation process, emphasizing instead the ability of fiscal policy to control inflation. Monetary policy was to help keep aggregate demand at potential. This required reliable measurement, but policymakers at the time consistently underestimated the natural rate of unemployment and overestimated potential output. Such errors would lead policymakers to pursue a monetary policy that was excessively easy. A failure to distinguish between nominal and real interest rates may also have biased policy toward too much ease. Other policymakers believed that inflation was not as socially disruptive as unemployment and, accepting a permanent Phillips Curve tradeoff, they were willing to trade higher inflation for a lower unemployment rate. Often they pressured the Federal Reserve to ease monetary policy.

In any event, monetary policy eventually created the Great Inflation, and to the extent that stopgap policies removed international constraints on monetary policy, they ultimately contributed to the collapse of Bretton Woods – the system they sought to maintain.

References

Bank of England, 1964. "The London Gold Market." *Quarterly Review* 4: 16–21.

[AR] Board of Governors of the Federal Reserve System. various issues. *Annual Report of the Federal Reserve System*. Washington, DC: Board of Governors of the Federal Reserve System.

Board of Governors of the Federal Reserve System, 1976. *Banking and Monetary Statistics, 1941–1970*. Washington, DC: Board of Governors of the Federal Reserve System.

Bordo, Michael D., 1993. "The Bretton Woods International Monetary System: A Historical Overview" in Michael D. Bordo and Barry Eichengreen (eds.), *A Retrospective on the Bretton Woods System, Lessons for International Monetary Reform*. Chicago, IL: The University of Chicago Press.

Bordo, Michael D. and Barry Eichengreen, 2013. "Bretton Woods and the Great Inflation" in Michael D. Bordo and Athanasios Orphanides (eds.) *The Great Inflation, Rebirth of Modern Central Banking*. Chicago, IL: Chicago University Press.

Bordo, Michael D., Owen F. Humpage, and Anna J. Schwartz, 2015. *Strained Relations: U.S. Foreign-Exchange Operations and Monetary Policy in the Twentieth Century*. Chicago, IL: University of Chicago Press.

---

[32] Bordo and Orphanides (2013) provide a survey of work on the Great Inflation.

Bordo, Michael D. and Athanasios Orphanides, 2013. "Introduction" in Michael D. Bordo and Athanasios Orphanides (eds.), *The Great Inflation, Rebirth of Modern Central Banking*. Chicago, IL: Chicago University Press.

[Bulletin] Board of Governors of the Federal Reserve System. various issues. "Treasury and Federal Reserve Foreign Exchange Operations" *Federal Reserve Bulletin*. Washington, DC: Board of Governors of the Federal Reserve System.

Carlson, Mark and David Wheelock, 2014. "Navigating Constraints: The Evolution of Federal Reserve Monetary Policy, 1935–1959."

Coombs, Charles A., 1976. *The Arena of International Finance*. New York, NY: John Wiley & Sons.

de Vries, Margaret Garritsen, 1976. *The International Monetary Fund 1966–1971, The System under Stress*, vol. 1. Washington, DC: International Monetary Fund.

1985. *The International Monetary Fund 1972–1978, Cooperation on Trial*, vol. 1. Washington, DC: International Monetary Fund.

[ERP] Economic Report of the President. various issues. Washington, DC: Government Printing Office.

Eichengreen, Barry, 2000. "From Benign Neglect to Malignant Preoccupation: U.S. Balance of Payments Policy in the 1960s" in George Perry and James Tobin (eds.), *Economic Events, Ideas and Policies: The 1960s and After*. Washington, DC: Brookings Institution.

2013. "Does the Federal Reserve Care about the Rest of the World?" *Journal of Economic Perspectives* 27: 87–104.

[FOMC] Federal Open Market Committee. various issues. *Minutes of the Federal Open Market Committee*. Washington, DC: Board of Governors of the Federal Reserve System.

Gavin, Francis J., 2004. *Gold, Dollars, and Power, The Politics of International Monetary Relations, 1958–1971*. Chapel Hill, NC: The University of North Carolina Press.

Hetzel, Robert L., 1996. "Sterilized Foreign-Exchange Intervention: The Fed Debate in the 1960s." Federal Reserve Bank of Richmond. *Economic Quarterly* 82: 21–46.

2008. *The Monetary Policy of the Federal Reserve, A History*. New York, NY: Cambridge University Press.

[IMF] International Monetary Fund. various issues. *International Financial Statistics*.

James, Harold, 1996. *International Monetary Cooperation Since Bretton Woods*. New York, NY: Oxford University Press.

Kenen, Peter B., 2008. "Bretton Woods System" in Steven N. Durlauf and Larry E. Blume (eds.), *The New Palgrave Dictionary of Economics*, 2nd ed., online: Palgrave Macmillan.

MacLaury, Bruce K., 1969. "Discussion of Questions Raised by Governor Maisel Concerning System Foreign Currency Operations." Unpublished Board of Governors of the Federal Reserve System memorandum, January 30.

Maisel, Sherman J., 1973. *Managing the Dollar*. New York, NY: W.W. Norton.

McKinnon, Ronald I., 1993. "The Rules of the Game: International Money in Historical Perspective." *Journal of Economic Literature* 31: 1–44.

Meltzer, Allan H., 1991. "U.S. Policy in the Bretton Woods Era." Federal Reserve Bank of St. Louis. *Economic Review* 73: 54–83.

2003. *A History of the Federal Reserve, vol.1, 1913–1951*. Chicago, IL: University of Chicago Press.

2009a. *A History of the Federal Reserve vol. 2, book one, 1951–1969*. Chicago, IL: University of Chicago Press.

2009b. *A History of the Federal Reserve vol. 2, book two, 1970–1986*. Chicago, IL: University of Chicago Press.

Modigliani, Franco and Richard Sutch, 1966a. "Debt Management and the Term Structure of Interest Rates: An Empirical Analysis of Recent Experience." *Journal of Political Economy* 75: 569–89.

1966b. "Innovations in Interest Rate Policy." *American Economic Review* 56: 178–97.

Pauls, B. Dianne, 1990. "U.S. Exchange-Rate Policy: Bretton Woods to Present." *Federal Reserve Bulletin* 76: 891–908.

Romer, Christina D. and David H. Romer, 2002a. "A Rehabilitation of Monetary Policy in the 1950s." *American Economic Review* 92: 121–27.

2002b. "The Evolution of Economic Understanding and Postwar Stabilization Policy" in *Rethinking Stabilization Policy*. Kansas City, KS: Federal Reserve Bank of Kansas City.

Samuel Montagu & Co. Ltd. various issues. *Annual Bullion Review*.

Schlesinger, Arthur M., 1965. *A Thousand Days, John F. Kennedy in the White House*. Boston, MA: Houghton, Mifflin Co.

Solomon, Robert, 1971. "Use of Swap Network." Unpublished Board of Governors of the Federal Reserve System memorandum, August 13.

1982. *The International Monetary System: 1945–81*. New York, NY: Harper and Row.

Swanson, Eric T., 2011. "Let's Twist Again: A High-Frequency Even-Study Analysis of Operation Twist and Its Implications for QE2." *Brookings Papers on Economic Activity* Spring: 151–207.

[Task Force] Task Force on System Foreign Currency Operations, 1990. "Reciprocal Currency Arrangements (The 'Swap' Network)." Paper #9, January 24, unpublished Board of Governors of the Federal Reserve System report.

[Task Force] Task Force on System Foreign Currency Operations, 1990. "Profits and Losses in U.S. Foreign-Currency Operations." Paper #10, January 8, unpublished Board of Governors of the Federal Reserve System report.

Taylor, John B., 1999. "A Historical Analysis of Monetary Policy Rules" in John B. Taylor, (ed.), *Monetary Policy Rules*. Chicago, IL: University of Chicago Press.

Todd, Walker F., 1992. "Disorderly Markets: The Law, History, and Economics of the Exchange Stabilization Fund and U.S. Foreign-Exchange Market Intervention" in George G. Kaufman (ed.), *Research in Financial Services: Private and Public Policy*, vol. 4, Greenwich, CT: JAI Press, 111–79.

Triffin, Robert, 1960. *Gold and the Dollar Crisis, The Future of Convertibility*. New Haven, CT: Yale University Press.

Yeager, Leland B. 1966. *International Monetary Relations: Theory, History, and Policy*. New York, NY: Harper & Row Publishers.

Comments on Michael D. Bordo and Owen Humpage, "Federal Reserve Policy and Bretton Woods"

James M. Boughton

Mike Bordo and Owen Humpage offer us a very nicely reasoned analysis of how the Federal Reserve conducted monetary policy during the years that the Bretton Woods system of fixed but adjustable exchange rates was in effect (1946–73). Their basic story line is that the Bretton Woods system aimed to achieve international financial stability – currency convertibility with credibly pegged exchange rates – while providing room for national authorities to pursue independent macroeconomic policies aimed at achieving full employment. Judged by that standard, the system obviously failed. The abandonment of the system in the early 1970s was the inevitable consequence of its internal contradictions ("credible and adjustable are antithetical attributes") and – more importantly – the failure of the Federal Reserve and the US government to adopt the necessary supporting macroeconomic policies.

This line of reasoning has a long intellectual pedigree, and it is consistent with the conventional wisdom about the early postwar years. I would not wish to suggest that it is wrong, but I would like to make the case for an alternative historical perspective that portrays the Bretton Woods system in a more favorable light.

The fundamental purpose of the Bretton Woods system, as it was envisaged by its founders in the early 1940s, was not to re-enable fixed exchange rates. The par-value exchange-rate system was an *instrument* to further broader objectives. The fundamental purpose was not even to recreate monetary stability on an international scale. That was an *intermediate* goal. The fundamental purpose was to create the preconditions for economic prosperity and the preservation of world peace.

As expressed in Article I of the IMF Articles of Agreement, one of the purposes of the agreement was "To facilitate the expansion and balanced growth of international trade, and to contribute thereby to the promotion

121

and maintenance of high levels of employment and real income and to the development of the productive resources of all members as *primary object-ives* of economic policy" (emphasis added). That was a pretty ambitious goal – high employment and economic growth –, but the rhetoric at the Bretton Woods conference was even loftier. The delegates from forty-five countries had spent all of their adult lives enduring the Great War, the cha-otic aftermath of the war, the Great Depression, and World War II. Their goal was to put all of those memories behind them forever. John Maynard Keynes, in his closing address to the conference, expressed the ambition most clearly: If "we can so continue [to work together], this nightmare, in which most of us present have spent too much of our lives, will be over. The brotherhood of man will have become more than a phrase."

Bretton Woods should be judged not by whether it succeeded at estab-lishing an enduring system of pegged exchange rates underpinned by gold and the US dollar, but by whether it succeeded in promoting high employ-ment, economic growth, and a more peaceful world. That last point, of course, is the most controversial. The proposition that trade and other eco-nomic interactions will ensure peaceful relations has a reasonable theoreti-cal foundation, and it most certainly is to be hoped. The evidence, however, is mixed. Perhaps if the Soviet Union had joined the IMF and the World Bank, and if it had committed itself to cooperating with the West, the rec-ord would have tilted more toward global peace. Even so, a world in which many countries grow economically but at widely differing rates is bound to engender conflicts that offset much of the benefit.[1]

The *economic* effects of the system were more clearly positive and pro-vide much greater justification for the optimism that prevailed at Bretton Woods. When the system became operational in 1946, one country had a fully convertible currency; one country held nearly three-quarters of the world's stock of monetary gold; and one country accounted for at least a third of the world's exports. Without that country's commitment to restore multilateral trade and finance, as expressed in the Bretton Woods agree-ments, the potential for a continuation of the autarky, mercantilism, and financial chaos of the interwar period would have been close to a certainty. The world economy over the next quarter century, the Bretton Woods era, developed far more positively than anyone expected at the outset.

Aggregating world data for the Bretton Woods era is fraught with com-plications, but the big picture is unambiguous. International trade and world GDP both grew at rapid rates throughout the period, and the growth

---

[1]   For an analysis see Ala'i, Broude, and Picker (2006), including remarks by this author.

of trade led and outpaced output growth. After collapsing in the period from 1914 through the end of World War II, the ratio of exports to GDP rose steadily in the Bretton Woods era. From 1960 – when current-account convertibility was largely restored – through 1972, world GDP in real terms grew by more than 5 percent a year, broadly based and led by export growth. Bretton Woods was an era of prosperity and of rising and spreading aspirations. Then it collapsed, and over the next forty years world output growth slowed to 3 percent a year. Was this a failure, or an inevitable result of the earlier success?

One measure of the success of the Bretton Woods system is that by 1972, the number of countries with net creditor positions in the IMF had risen from one to seventeen. Even more indicative of the spread of prosperity and the shifting balance of economic power is that the system was no longer dependent on the US role as the premier creditor. In fact, the seventeen creditor countries in 1972 did not include the United States. It did include eleven European countries, four from the Americas, and one each from Asia and the Middle East.[2] The weaknesses and inconsistencies of US macroeconomic policies – including those of the Federal Reserve chronicled in this chapter – were a major catalyst for the end of the Bretton Woods system, but it is a stretch to argue that they were the root cause. At the risk of oversimplifying a complex situation, the root cause was the fact that economic growth in, and rising international trade among, a highly diversified group of countries had made the maintenance of fixed exchange rates both undesirable and a practical impossibility. The world is not a common currency area.

A second theme of the chapter is the relationship between the Federal Reserve and the US Treasury in coping with international stresses during the Bretton Woods era. The system itself was designed largely by the US and British Treasuries, with inputs from other countries also working mainly through finance officials. The Federal Reserve was, however, well represented at the Bretton Woods conference, with about a dozen officials led by the Chairman of the Board of Governors, Marriner Eccles. Their role was not decisive, but they clearly had a strong interest in the outcome.

Bordo and Humpage recount how the US Treasury and the Federal Reserve reacted to the increasing instability of the international financial system as the Bretton Woods years ticked away, especially after 1960. As they note, much of the burden was shouldered by the Treasury rather than

---

[2] Austria, Belgium, Brazil, Canada, Finland, France, Germany, Ireland, Italy, Japan, Kuwait, Mexico, Netherlands, Norway, Spain, Sweden, and Venezuela.

the Fed, through such measures as negotiated tariff reductions, controls on capital outflows, participation in the General Arrangements to Borrow (from 1962),[3] and the Interest Equalization Tax (1963–74).

More generally, as discussed also by Mark Carlson and David Wheelock in Chapter 3, the Treasury administered the Exchange Stabilization Fund. The ESF had been established in January 1934 as part of the Roosevelt administration's program to stabilize the value of the US dollar in the wake of the devaluation against gold. The establishing legislation gave the Secretary of the Treasury broad discretion to use the fund for this general purpose, and successive administrations proved to be inventive in devising new methods.[4] In the Bretton Woods era, the Treasury used the ESF primarily to conduct forward swaps in several currencies.

The Federal Reserve got involved in attempts to stabilize the dollar in part because, as Bordo and Humpage note, the central bank's financial resources were less tightly constrained than those of the Treasury. This advantage induced the Fed to undertake swap operations and other forms of exchange-market intervention; to participate in the Gold Pool with other central banks; and to implement Operation Twist from 1960 to 1964. In the early 1960s, selective policy actions such as discount rate increases and a loosening of Regulation Q, while aimed primarily at domestic goals, may also have helped stabilize the dollar. Overall, however, the Federal Reserve was secondary to the Treasury as an agent for international stability.

Another key part of the United States' effort to stabilize the dollar and preserve the Bretton Woods system was the Treasury's use of its reserve assets in the International Monetary Fund (IMF). In 1963, the United States engaged in a stand-by arrangement with the IMF, on which it drew on several occasions in 1964 and 1965 to use its gold tranche position to combat downward pressure on the dollar.[5] For that and other related reasons, the IMF's holdings of US dollars rose from 51 percent of quota in August 1961 to 94 percent at the end of 1966, nearly exhausting the US creditor position.

The Treasury also participated actively in the creation of SDRs in 1968 as a supplement to existing reserve assets, and in the use of SDRs from

---

[3] The original participants in the GAB – generally described as the Group of Ten or G10 – comprised eight governments and two central banks (those of Germany and Sweden).

[4] See www.treasury.gov/resource-center/international/ESF/Pages/esf-index.aspx and Henning (1999).

[5] In that era, stand-by arrangements were used as a window for accessing a member country's own contributions to the IMF, then known as the member's "gold tranche." After the gold tranche was replaced by the "reserve tranche" in 1978, each member had an automatic right to draw on it, and the use of stand-by arrangements for this purpose was abandoned.

1970. As originally defined, the SDR was equivalent to the gold value of the US dollar. (In 1974, after the end of the system of fixed exchange rates, the SDR was redefined as a currency basket.) Every participating country, including the United States, received an allocation of SDRs starting in 1970. Those allocations were (and still are) in effect a line of credit that monetary authorities can draw upon and that are liquid enough to serve as official reserves alongside gold and convertible currencies. At the outset (and again for the last thirty years), the United States was a net holder of SDRs as other countries drew on their credit lines and then swapped the SDRs for US dollars. But from the end of 1970 through 1982, the United States was almost always a net user of SDRs.

The essence of this story is that, much like the efforts to preserve the euro area since 2009, a lot of effort – by the Federal Reserve, the Treasury, and agencies in other countries – went into trying to save the Bretton Woods system in the late 1960s and early 1970s. In this case at least, all of these measures ultimately proved to be too little and too late to save the Bretton Woods system. But should we lament its death? Eventually, every system ends and is succeeded by another. Should we consider this demise a systemic failure, or should we be grateful that the collapse of the system enabled economic growth to continue unconstrained in subsequent years? The answer is not obvious, but three concluding observations might help clarify the issue.

First, under the usual interpretation of the 1946 Employment Act and subsequent legislation, the Federal Reserve System has had a dual mandate in the postwar era: high employment and price stability, not a triadic mandate with the third element being the preservation of fixed exchange rates. In contrast with the early years of the Federal Reserve discussed by Barry Eichengreen in Chapter 2, the primary policy goals were macroeconomic.

The global record on employment and economic growth during the Bretton Woods era vastly exceeded the founders' wildest dreams. It can scarcely be faulted. The record on price stability is a little more mixed and more difficult to assess, but it was much better than our collective memory might suggest.

In the United States, consumer price inflation exceeded 5 percent per annum only twice in the Bretton Woods period: 1951 and 1969. In 1972, the last year before the final end of the par-value system, US consumer prices rose by just 3.5 percent. Inflation became a seriously destabilizing force only after the dissolution of the 1971 Smithsonian Agreements and the advent of generalized floating, peaking in 1980 at 13.6 percent. Judged by the primary objectives of macroeconomic policy, Federal Reserve actions throughout the Bretton Woods era appear to be rather more successful than if they are judged by the distinctly secondary standard of whether they contributed to the preservation of fixed exchange rates.

Second, the US dollar is still the underpinning of the international financial system, and the United States still dominates the world economy. The proportions have been and continue to be diminished by the emergence of successful economies elsewhere, but whatever the failures of economic policy may have been in the Bretton Woods era, they did not result in lasting damage to the US role in international finance and economics.

Third, the post–Bretton Woods era has been less successful globally than it should have been. Not only has global economic growth been slower, financial stability has also been compromised even more than in the Bretton Woods era. On the bright side, inflation has essentially been conquered, after the disastrous flare-up of the 1970s. Also on the bright side, the geographic spread of prosperity has continued, and more people in more countries are rising above poverty. The number of creditor countries in the IMF has risen from 17 in 1972 to nearly 50 today. But those successes are tempered by the recurrence and spread of international financial crises and the consequent setbacks to economic growth.

To a large extent, the pervasive financial crises of the 1980s through today can be traced to the relegation of the goals of high employment and growth to secondary status, subservient to fiscal and monetary discipline, a development that I call the New Anglo-Saxon Consensus (Boughton, 2014). Weak or inconsistent growth and rising unemployment create adverse incentives for policymakers and give rise to vicious cycles of instability punctuated by banking and exchange crises. A return to the Bretton Woods system, or to any system of fixed exchange rates, is neither desirable nor feasible. Perhaps if the US Treasury and the Federal Reserve had been more successful in managing the centrifugal forces that ultimately destabilized the Bretton Woods system, the more dynamic and diversified system that emerged from the ashes might have been more stable. In any event, the general lesson for the future is that without full attention to the primary goals, neither they nor the secondary goals will be achievable over the longer run.

References

Ala'i, Padideh, Tomer Broude, and Colin Picker, eds., 2006. *Trade as Guarantor of Peace, Liberty and Security?* Studies in Transnational Legal Policy, No. 37. Washington, DC: The American Society of International Law.

Bordo, Michael D. and Owen Humpage, "Federal Reserve Policy and Bretton Woods," this volume.

Boughton, James M. 2014. "Stabilizing International Finance: Can the System Be Saved?" *CIGI Essays in International Finance*, No. 2, September 2014. Available at www.cigionline.org/publications/cigi-essays-international-finance-volume-2-international-finance-can-system-be-saved?utm_source=homepage-feature&utm_medium=web&utm_campaign=UX

Carlson, Mark and David Wheelock, "Navigating Constraints: The Evolution of Federal Reserve Monetary Policy, 1935–1959," this volume.

Eichengreen, Barry, "Doctrinal Determinants, Domestic and International, of Federal Reserve Policy 1914–1933," this volume.

Henning, C. Randall, 1999. *The Exchange Stabilization Fund: Slush Money or War Chest?* Policy Analyses in International Economics 57. Washington, DC: Peterson Institute for International Economics.

5

The Federal Reserve Engages the World
(1970–2000)

An Insider's Narrative of the Transition to
Managed Floating and Financial Turbulence

Edwin M. Truman

The Federal Reserve enters its second century as the closest the world has to a global central bank. The US central bank is more influential and engaged globally than at any previous time in its history and more than any other central bank.

In formulating US monetary policy, the Federal Reserve increasingly has to take account of the developments outside of the US economy and the impacts of its policy decisions on other economies and global financial markets. These trends intensified in the twenty-first century, but they emerged in the last three decades of the twentieth century, the focus in this chapter.[1] I review four areas of the Federal Reserve's role in the global economy: (1) the emergence and taming of the Great Inflation; (2) developments in US external accounts; (3) the foreign exchange value of the US dollar, US exchange rate policy, and international financial markets; and (4) external financial crises. These interrelated areas absorbed the majority of Federal Reserve activity on international economic and financial policy issues in this period.

[1] Other chapters in this volume address earlier and more recent periods.

I thank Kent Troutman for his dedicated assistance in preparing the charts for this chapter. I am also indebted, without implicating them in any of the content of this chapter, to Carol Bertaut, Ralph Bryant, Terrence Checki, Thomas Connors, Sam Cross, Hali Edison, Joe Gagnon, Dale Henderson, C. Randall Henning, George Henry, Peter Hooper, Nancy Jacklin, Karen Johnson, Dino Kos, Catherine Mann, Jaime Marquez, Maurice Obstfeld, Adam Posen, Larry Promisel, Jeffrey Shafer, Charles Siegman, David Stockton, Charles Thomas, Tracy P. Truman, and participants in the Federal Reserve Bank of Dallas conference, "The Federal Reserve System's Role in the Global Economy," for their advice, comments, and support.

On the Great Inflation, the intellectual and policy challenge facing the Federal Reserve in the 1970s was not only to recognize the inflation problem but also to diagnose the phenomenon not as something imported from abroad via increases in energy prices and exogenous dollar depreciation, but primarily as homegrown, nurtured if not propagated primarily by Federal Reserve policy.

Prospects for the US trade and current account balances and the asymmetrical global adjustment process were a principal policy preoccupation in the wake of the disintegration of the Bretton Woods system of fixed exchange rates. That policy focus persisted into the 1980s. By 2000, trends in the US external accounts and the sustainability of the US international investment position had largely receded as a pressing policy concern of the Federal Reserve, but were about to reemerge.

The foreign exchange value of the US dollar is central to the analysis of prospects for the US external accounts, but has many other dimensions. For the Federal Reserve, the most controversial dimension was the involvement of the Federal Reserve System (System) in US foreign currency operations. By the mid-1990s, this issue had become less salient because the tool of foreign exchange market intervention fell into disuse.

Throughout the last third of the twentieth century, the Federal Reserve was deeply engaged in the management and prevention of external financial crises of a growing list of countries of importance. This conditioned its emerging global role.

5.1 The Setting

Contrary to the common narrative, the collapse of the Bretton Woods exchange rate system in the early 1970s did not free the Federal Reserve to focus exclusively on the domestic economy largely because the US economy was becoming increasingly globally integrated. The United States and its central bank became enmeshed in global economic and financial developments to a much greater degree than under the Bretton Woods system.

In 1970 US exports of goods and services – one measure of the influence of economic activity in the rest of the world on the US economy – were 5 percent of US GDP. By 2000, they were almost 10 percent. Imports – a measure of the economic influence of the United States on the rest of the world – rose from 5 percent of GDP in 1970 to 14 percent, by 2000; see Figure 5.1.

The increasing integration of the United States with the global financial system was even more dramatic. US foreign assets at the end of 2000

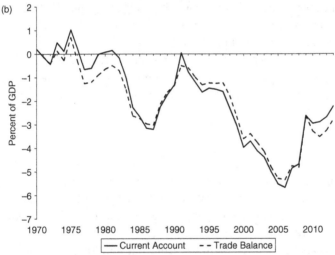

Figure 5.1. US exports and imports of goods and services and external balances, 1970–2013.
Sources: Bureau of Economic Analysis, US Commerce Department.

were $6.2 trillion (60 percent of US nominal GDP), compared with a mere 20 percent in 1970. On the other side of the ledger, foreign assets in the United States in 2000 were $7.6 trillion (72 percent of nominal GDP), up from a mere $120 billion in 1970 (only 11 percent of nominal GDP); see Figure 5.2.

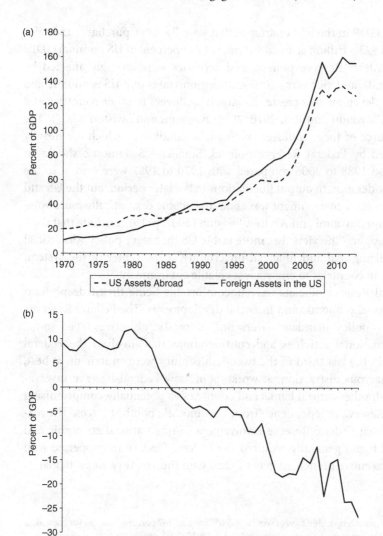

Figure 5.2. US assets abroad and foreign assets in the United States, 1970–2013.
Sources: Bureau of Economic Analysis, US Commerce Department; updated and extended dataset by Lane and Milesi-Ferretti, 2007; author's calculations.

An examination of transactions data reinforces this picture of growing US global financial involvement. In the first five months of 1977, the earliest available data, foreign purchases and sales of long-term domestic and foreign securities averaged $105 billion at an annual rate of 5 percent of US nominal GDP in the first quarter of that year. By 2000, purchases and sales averaged \$23.3 trillion at an annual rate of 232 percent of US nominal GDP.[2]

The Federal Reserve policies and activities were strongly affected by these trends, and vice versa. Research demonstrates that US economic and financial developments create the largest spillovers to other countries and regions (Bayoumi and Bui, 2010, 2012; Bayoumi and Swiston, 2007). The main source of these spillovers is financial conditions, which are heavily influenced by Federal Reserve policies. Smaller US domestic shocks in the period 1988 to 2006 compared with 1970 to 1987 were central to the global moderation in output fluctuations in the later period, but the US and global financial environment was about to become dramatically more volatile. Tamim Bayoumi and Andrew Swiston (2007, p. 15) conclude that their results support "the view that more stable US monetary policy was crucial for stabilizing real and financial uncertainty at the center of the system, allowing all countries to enjoy a less volatile environment."

Federal Reserve officials were uncomfortable being thrust deeply into international economic and financial developments. The Federal Reserve's monetary policy mandate covers only domestic objectives.[3] For some, the international activities and considerations that involved the Federal Reserve in the last third of the twentieth century were an irritant, at best, or a dangerous distraction, at worst. Some saw Federal Reserve involvement with other central banks and countries as potentially compromising Federal Reserve independence from US domestic political forces. The reason was that Federal Reserve involvement in international economic and financial issues generally required the Federal Reserve to cooperate with the US executive branch, in general, and with the Treasury, in particular.

---

[2] By 2014, the comparable figures were \$74.3 trillion and 467 percent. Sources for these data are the US Treasury, www.treasury.gov/ticdata/Publish/s1_99996.txt (accessed on August 8, 2014), and the US Department of Commerce, http://bea.gov/national/index.htm#gdp (accessed on August 8, 2014).

[3] The Federal Reserve's monetary policy objectives to "maintain long run growth of the monetary and credit aggregates commensurate with the economy's long run potential to increase production, so as to promote effectively the goals of maximum employment, stable prices, and moderate long-term interest rates, " which are specified in section 2A of the Federal Reserve Act, do not recognize the openness of the US economy. However, section 2B (b) of the act, prescribing the content of semiannual reports to the Congress on monetary policy, explicitly requires "a discussion of the conduct of monetary policy and economic developments and prospects for the future, taking into account past and prospective developments in employment, unemployment, production, investment, real income, productivity, *exchange rates, international trade and payments,* and prices [emphasis added by author]."

My purpose in this chapter is not to resolve questions of motivation of monetary policy decisions during this period (e.g., Bordo and Eichengreen, 2013a; Cooper and Little, 2000; Eichengreen, 2013; and Meltzer, 2013). Federal Reserve chairs, governors, and reserve bank presidents often use multiple arguments to support their policy preferences in meetings of the Federal Open Market Committee (FOMC, or Committee) and other discussions of policy. Thus, it is quixotic to try to establish the evolution of the relative weight of international considerations in Federal Reserve policies, including policies other than monetary policy narrowly defined. My aim is to demonstrate that between 1970 and 2000, despite the reluctance of many in the Federal Reserve, monetary policy and other activities unavoidably became embedded in an increasingly globalized economic and financial system.

I review the evolution of Federal Reserve analyses of, as well as involvement in, the four areas listed earlier. I treat each decade in turn. Because the areas are intertwined, I vary the order in which I treat them in each decade.[4] In the process, I do identify eighteen instances in which either developments in the global economy or policies of other countries substantially affected Federal Reserve decision making or activities (type A); Federal Reserve decisions were undertaken primarily to support other countries but with commensurate benefits for the United States (type B); or occasions of decisions in win-win cooperation (type C).

As background, I reviewed the titles and, where available, the abstracts, summaries, and content of 695 International Finance Discussion Papers (IFDPs) released between August 1971 and December 2000 (Table 5.1). These papers illustrate the depth and range of issues on which the staff worked during the thirty years covered by this chapter, not only at the Board but by logical extension throughout the System.[5] In many cases, the papers were based on work that had been previously or was subsequently presented to the Board or FOMC. Interestingly, the number of IFDPs was 75 percent more in the 1990s than in the 1970s, even though the staffing level in the

---

[4]   The three decades cover most of the period in which I was at the Board of Governors as an economist starting in 1972, as director of the Division of International Finance starting in 1977, and as a collaborator while I was at the Treasury from late 1998 until early 2001. (Hence, I often write *we*.) For a more personal view of the same period, see Truman (2016).

[5]   Although many papers touch on more than one area, I classify them under only one of the four areas that I cover in this paper plus three additional headings: large-scale econometric modeling, foreign economies other than economies in crisis, and a diverse "other" group of papers.

Table 5.1. *Classification of International Finance Discussion Papers: Number of Papers (in Parentheses) and Percent of Total Papers, 1971–2000*

Decade(s)	Inflation	External accounts	US dollar and policy	Financial crises	Modeling	Countries	Other	Total papers
1970s	(7) 4	(28) 16	(26) 15	(5) 3	(18) 11	(11) 6	(76) 44	171
1980s	(3) 1	(29) 13	(39) 18	(17) 8	(10) 4	(30) 14	(94) 42	222
1990s	(10) 3	(28) 9	(40) 13	(43) 14	(4) 1	(41) 14	(136) 45	302
1971 to 2000	(20) 3	(85) 12	(105) 15	(65) 9	(32) 5	(82) 12	(306) 44	695

Note: Percentages may not add to 100 because of rounding.
Sources: Board of Governors of the Federal Reserve System, www.federalreserve.gov/pubs/ifdp/2014/default.htm, and author's classification.

Division of International Finance (IF) was essentially unchanged over this thirty-year period at between 100 and 110 people.

5.2 The 1970s: Monetary Freedom and the Battle against Inflation

Allan Meltzer (2009, p. 843) writes, "The years 1973 to 1979 were the least successful period for postwar Federal Reserve policy." Few observers disagree with his bottom line even if many, as I, reject his view that the principal cause of the Federal Reserve's failure was that, starting in the mid-1960s, it cooperated too extensively with the executive branch.

The 1970s was a turbulent decade. The Bretton Woods exchange rate system collapsed amid associated concerns about the US external accounts. Gyrations in exchange rates and exchange rate arrangements were poorly understood and analyzed. Increases in energy prices along with mistakes in macroeconomic policies contributed to global recession, rising inflation, and external financial crises. The Federal Reserve finally addressed the US inflation crisis in October 1979.

5.2.1 The International Monetary System and US External Accounts

In August 1971, the link between the dollar and the official price of gold was suspended, which turned out to be permanent. The Bretton Woods system began its final unraveling. Contrary to some expectations at the time, it did not liberate Federal Reserve monetary policy or the Federal Reserve from concerns about the US external accounts; see Bryant (2016) and Solomon (1977, 2016).[6]

From 1960 to 1970, the United States had a current account surplus, but the surplus was not large enough to cover net private capital outflows. The result was official settlements deficits in the form of reductions in reserves

---

[6] Chairman Arthur Burns chose Ralph Bryant in 1972 to succeed Robert Solomon as the IF division director to address new and continuing policy challenges. Bryant and his colleagues hired additional staff, expanding the total size of the division by about a third. Bryant also initiated a project to construct a multicountry model (MCM) to analyze global economic and financial developments. The project, unique at the time, resulted in a large number of papers and ultimately a book (Stevens et al., 1984). Many of the papers were released in 1976. See Berner et al. (1975, 1977) for initial results. See Brayton et al. (1997) for an account of the evolution of macro models at the Federal Reserve Board and how the MCM fit into that history.

of gold and other assets and increases in foreign official claims on the United States. The Nixon administration sought a negotiated devaluation of the US dollar against other currencies to achieve a US current account surplus of sufficient size that the combination of the current account surplus and net private capital outflows, which were taken as a given, would not lead to a significant further buildup of foreign official claims on the United States.

In the 1970s, US external adjustment continued to preoccupy the staff and, to a lesser extent, the FOMC. In 1970 US exports and imports of goods and services were only 5 percent of GDP. Fluctuations in net exports in the 1960s and early 1970s hardly mattered for the projected path of economic activity and employment (Cooper and Little, 2000, Figure 5.2). By 1980, this was no longer true.

Robert Solomon (1977, p. 209) reports that the Board staff calculated that the Smithsonian Agreement had resulted in a nominal devaluation of the dollar of between 6.5 and 7.75 percent, depending on the weights chosen. Under the methodology now used by the Board staff, the depreciation was 5.5 percent in real, or price-adjusted, terms between July 1971 and January 1972; see Figure 5.3. The question was whether the devaluation was large enough to achieve a sufficient adjustment in the US current account balance. The initial objective had been an improvement of $13 billion, about 0.3 percent of GDP. After the Smithsonian Agreement, the staff calculated that the total improvement would be only $8 billion (Solomon, 1977, p. 210). But it was slow in coming. The staff forecast in January 1972, immediately after the Smithsonian Agreement, was for an improvement of $1 billion in that year.

As the year progressed, the forecast turned into a projected deterioration of $5 billion. This forced the staff to analyze the effects of the dollar's devaluation that resulted from the Smithsonian Agreement and how much adjustment was left in the pipeline. In early 1973, the staff made a major presentation to the Board of its results, concluding that the adjustment would fall short of what was needed (e.g., Junz, 1973; Clark, 1974).

Shortly thereafter, Treasury Secretary George Shultz sent Undersecretary Paul Volcker around the world to negotiate a second devaluation of the dollar on February 12, 1973. But by early March, the new fixed exchange rates had become unstuck, and – something that would be inconceivable today – foreign exchange markets in Europe and Japan were closed for two days. In mid-March, the exchange rate system lurched into generalized managed floating to the delight of many economists and dismay of many other observers.

The dollar continued to decline. It was enough to bring the cumulative real effective depreciation of the dollar from January 1970 to July 1973, to

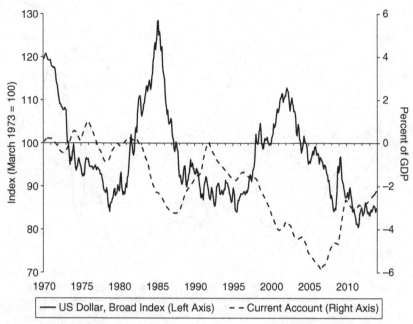

Figure 5.3. US current account balance and price-adjusted foreign exchange value of the US dollar, 1970–2013.
Sources: Bureau of Economic Analysis, US Commerce Department; Board of Governors of the Federal Reserve System; author's calculations.

20 percent.[7] Consequently, in the December 1973 *Greenbook* report on current economic and financial conditions (FRB, 1973), nominal net exports were projected to improve by $9.4 billion in 1973 and to increase a further $6.4 billion in 1974. In part due to the oil embargo imposed during the Arab–Israeli war in October 1973 and the subsequent quadrupling of the oil price, the 1974 forecast did not materialize.

The FOMC initially reacted to the oil price shock by continuing to ease monetary policy, indexed by the federal funds rate, starting at the September 1973 meeting (type A impact). The aim was to counter the effects of higher oil prices on US real economic activity. The easing continued until March 1974. The Committee then began to take into consideration that increases in oil prices also contributed to inflation and that it was unwise to ratify those increases via lower short-term real interest rates; see Figure 5.4.

---

[7] Here and below, except where otherwise noted, I cite the change in the foreign exchange value of the dollar in nominal or real (price-adjusted) terms using the methodology that the staff of the Federal Reserve Board uses today; see footnote 8.

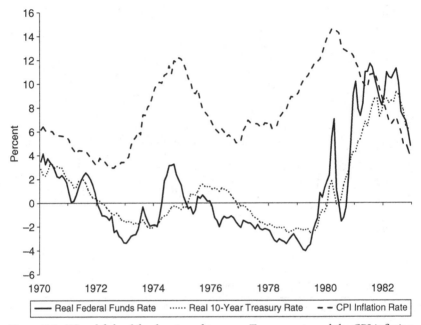

Figure 5.4. US real federal funds rate and ten-year Treasury rate and the CPI inflation rate, 1970–82.
Note: CPI = consumer price index.
Sources: Board of Governors of the Federal Reserve System; US Bureau of Labor Statistics; author's calculations.

The dollar's depreciation and the increase in global oil and other commodity prices spawned a cottage industry in estimating rules of thumb of the effects of such shocks on inflation in which IF staff participated (Katz, 1973; Kwack, 1973; Berner et al., 1974; Hooper and Lowery, 1979). In IF, we were uncomfortable that our rules of thumb, which we used in forecasting, contributed to the opinion that inflation was merely caused by rising prices with little the central bank could do about it.

5.2.2 Exchange Rates: Analysis and Operations

Policy and analysis of exchange rates involved more than just measuring effects on the price level and inflation. It involved five interrelated dimensions: measurement, exchange rate determination, US intervention operations, effectiveness of such operations, and the Federal Reserve's role in them.

On measurement, one issue was the relevant exchange rate for the US dollar. Financial market participants, and our colleagues at the Federal

Reserve Bank of New York, tended to think of the exchange rate for the US dollar vis-à-vis at most four other currencies: the German mark, the Swiss franc, the Japanese yen, and the British pound (and most frequently just the German mark). At the Board, we tended to think about exchange rates as macroeconomic variables rather than financial variables and – recognizing that no single country or currency dominated US economic or financial transactions – preferred not to focus on one bilateral exchange rate. Following the move to generalized floating in 1973, we adopted a measure of the dollar's foreign exchange value in terms of the currencies of the other Group of Ten (G-10) countries.[8]

A second measurement issue was the definition of exchange market intervention (Adams and Henderson, 1983). Here analysis and reporting was constrained by the availability of data shared by other countries with the Open Market Desk at the Federal Reserve Bank of New York (Desk), and the conventions associated with the foreign currency operations of other monetary authorities. The principal distinction was between intervention in the open market and off-market transactions with customers, which some people did not regard as intervention. Another related to intervention in the forward rather than the spot market.

Once nominal exchange rates became detached from parities, the challenge was how to think about exchange rate determination. Richard Meese and Kenneth Rogoff (1981, 1982, 1983) produced the seminal contribution, concluding that, except in the long run, existing models of exchange rate determination were of limited use out of sample. This work was inspired by the need to provide forecasts for the Federal Reserve Board and FOMC and by questions from members.[9]

---

[8] In addition to Germany, Japan, Switzerland, and the United Kingdom, these were Belgium, Canada, France, Italy, the Netherlands, and Sweden, making a total of eleven, including the United States. A considerable amount of research went into the question of whether we should use different weights for different purposes, but in the end it was decided that little was gained from differentiation. See Mico Loretan (2005) for a report on the index used in this paper, which is now more sophisticated and covers the currencies of twenty-six countries or currency areas, and historically ten of the fifteen countries now included within the euro area. Earlier reports and analyses include Leahy (1998), Pauls (1987), and Hooper and Morton (1978a, 1978b).

[9] The Meese-Rogoff analysis builds on earlier investigations of exchange rates and exchange rate determination. Michael P. Dooley and Jeffrey R. Shafer (1976) find that foreign exchange markets do not satisfy weak tests of efficiency. Peter Isard (1977) presents an early survey of the literature on exchange rate determination. (This paper later appeared in 1978 in *Princeton Studies in International Finance* 42 with the title "Exchange-Rate Determination: A Survey of Popular Views and Recent Models.") Peter Hooper and John Morton (1980) produce their own model of exchange rate determination. It combines the monetary approach explaining movements in equilibrium relative price levels with

Turning to US foreign exchange operations, they are conducted by the Desk on behalf of the FOMC and/or the Exchange Stabilization Fund (ESF) of the US Treasury. Under Bretton Woods, and until August 1971, US operations were almost entirely conducted for the System's account but were limited in size and scope. Many of those operations consisted of drawing foreign currencies on reciprocal currency (swap) arrangements to buy dollars purchased by other central banks to provide cover and/or to protect the US gold stock with the hope of buying the foreign currency in the market before the swap matured and the foreign currency had to be repaid.[10] Foreign exchange operations were conducted for multiple purposes under an authorization and directive of the FOMC that were revised or reaffirmed at least once a year.[11]

After the closing of the gold window, the United States refrained from operating in the foreign exchange market until July 19, 1972. Once resumed, operations continued until the dollar was devalued for a second time on March 12, 1973. Once again, US authorities withdrew from the market. That withdrawal lasted only until July 10 when, under heavy pressure from partner countries with concerns about a de facto third devaluation of the dollar, the Federal Reserve resumed operations.

5.2.3 Global Recession and Financial Turmoil

With inflation increasingly becoming a pressing issue, the FOMC pushed up the federal funds rate from March to July 1974. The Committee then responded to the recession that had started in November 1973 by reducing the rate. Fueled by the change in the global monetary regime, increases in petroleum prices, and inconsistent if not incoherent policy responses to both in the early 1970s, the recession was not confined to the United States.

---

the portfolio balance approach involving supplies and demands for assets that are imperfect substitutes; they use as a proxy for the latter the US cumulative current account balance. Hali Edison's evaluation and briefing (1988a, 1988b, respectively) examine the staff's exchange rate forecasting record from 1979 to 1987 and find that it slightly outperformed the random walk model as well as the Hooper-Morton model.

[10] A foreign currency swap involves the simultaneous purchase (sale) of a currency for another accompanied by a commitment to reverse the transaction in the future, which is normally ninety days.

[11] See, for example, FRB (1971, pp. 9–15) for the authorization and directive in effect when President Nixon closed the US gold window in 1971. It states that the purposes of System operations in foreign currency are to safeguard the value of the dollar, make international payments more effective, further monetary cooperation, insure that exchange rate movements (within IMF limits) reflected underlying economic forces, and promote growth in international liquidity in accordance with the needs of the world economy.

Global growth averaged about 5.5 percent in 1972 and 1973, and slumped to 2.2 percent in 1974 and 1.2 percent in 1975.[12]

The increases in oil prices and global economic and financial turmoil were associated with external financial crises in both advanced and developing countries. The Federal Reserve was drawn into several of them, increasing the size of swap lines with the central banks of Italy, Mexico, and the United Kingdom and allowing them to be drawn upon (type B impact).[13]

In all three of these financial crises, drawings on swap lines with the Federal Reserve were explicitly or implicitly linked to the establishment of IMF-supported economic stabilization and reform programs. In the case of the United Kingdom, Arthur Burns wrote to the British authorities explicitly linking its swap drawing in 1976 to a commitment to go to the IMF if the Bank of England could not repay the drawing within six months.

Burns took an intense interest in the external financial crises of the mid-1970s and their impact on the international financial system. One of his last major speeches as chairman (Burns, 1985) was titled "Need for Order in International Finance." He advocated a stronger role for the IMF in surveillance, better information about international lending from both borrowers and lenders, avoidance of persistent payments deficits and surpluses, and energy conservation.

In this period, IF staff members started to produce semiannual papers for the Board on economic and financial trouble spots around the world. They contained assessments of countries likely to have external financing problems or were already experiencing such problems. These "strictly confidential" reports were sent to the Board but not to the full FOMC. They did inform other presentations to the Committee.

In 1979, the Federal Reserve, Office of the Comptroller of the Currency (OCC), Federal Deposit Insurance Corporation (FDIC), and several state banking agencies established the Interagency Country Exposure Review Committee (ICERC) to evaluate US banks' foreign exposures and transfer risks in a consistent manner across agencies (FRB, 1999b). This was not a high-profile activity except at times of international financial stress, but it meant the staff was constantly involved in such issues.

---

[12] These data are GDP volume measures from the International Monetary Fund's *International Financial Statistics Yearbook* for 1999.

[13] The United Kingdom had the additional challenge of managing the continued unwinding of the reserve role of sterling, and the Federal Reserve agreed to help backstop that process (Schenk, 2010). Raymond Lubitz (1978) wrote about the Italian economic crises of the 1970s long before they were over.

5.2.4 International Monetary System Reform and
Federal Reserve Foreign Exchange Policy

Following the Smithsonian Agreement, reform of the international monetary system was completed in stages. The Committee of Twenty (C-20), established in 1972 to reform the Bretton Woods system, released its Outline of Reform in June 1974. It sketched out a possible course of evolutionary reform, but was not a full blueprint for replacing the Bretton Woods system, except it preserved the central role for the IMF. In August 1975, the matter of the treatment of gold was resolved, principally between the United States and France. Historically, France had an interest in the topic, and the United States wanted to banish gold from the international monetary system. In November 1975, the issue of exchange rate arrangements was settled. This topic also principally involved the differing philosophic positions of the US Treasury, by then firmly in the camp of supporters of floating exchange rates, and the French authorities. The agreement, which was later transformed into the revised Article IV of the IMF Articles of Agreement, was embraced at the first Group of Six (G-6) Economic Summit in Rambouillet, France.[14]

Once the revised Article IV had been agreed to, but before it technically became effective in April 1978, the Federal Reserve, with Henry Wallich taking the lead, undertook to reflect the agreement in revisions of the FOMC's Foreign Currency Authorization and Directive (FRB, 1976a). Wallich and Treasury Undersecretary Edwin H. Yeo painstakingly negotiated this language in six meetings lasting more than ten hours (FRB, 1976b, p. 12). The new directive used only one sentence to state the purpose of Federal Reserve foreign currency operations: "System operations in foreign currencies shall generally be directed at countering disorderly market conditions, provided that market exchange rates for the U.S. dollar reflect actions and behavior consistent with the proposed IMF Article IV, Section 1."

Wallich was sent back to discuss with Yeo the FOMC's discomfort with initial language stating that the Desk should conduct its operations in "collaboration" with the US Treasury, on grounds that "collaboration" implied

---

[14] The G-6 countries were the G-5 countries (France, Germany, Japan, the United Kingdom, and the United States) plus Italy; membership did not include Canada (added at the 1976 summit in San Juan, Puerto Rico, to create the G-7). The G-5 first met in Washington in March 1973 at the White House and included only finance ministers. When Burns learned this, he demanded that in the future central bank governors be included as well (which they were, along with finance ministry deputies, but normally not central bank deputies). In the late 1990s, the G-7 central bank deputies began to meet separately.

a sacrifice of Federal Reserve independence. The word "collaboration" was replaced by six words: "close and continuous consultation and cooperation."

The FOMC in 1976 added a new foreign currency instrument: a set of procedural instructions governing decision making on Federal Reserve foreign exchange operations. Burns intended the procedural instructions, in part, to limit the discretion of the Desk in conducting foreign exchange operations for the System. They required the Manager of the System's Open Market Account to clear with the foreign currency subcommittee of the FOMC, and for the subcommittee to clear with the full FOMC, swap drawings of any or a certain size and to approve changes in the System's "overall open position" in foreign currencies beyond certain limits for intermeeting periods as well as in any day.[15]

5.2.5 The US Inflation Crisis

Through much of the second half of the 1970s, US authorities struggled with slow growth, rising inflation, a weak foreign exchange value of the dollar, and the reemergence of the US current account deficit. All this was in the context of a global economic and financial system that was at best untested and some would say lacked any structure (Truman, 2012).

Starting again in July 1973, the Federal Reserve had been periodically active in both buying and selling dollars (Greene, 1984a). However, with the deteriorating US current account position, and the prevailing view in the market that the US authorities were practicing benign neglect of the dollar (wanting a lower dollar and actively talking down the dollar), the dollar was under downward pressure.

The pressure on the dollar intensified in 1978 (Greene, 1984c). Partly as a consequence, and demonstrating their own fear of floating, Europeans created a mutual protection scheme in the form of the European Monetary System (EMS) and a mechanism of fixed rates within pre-established limits. The Federal Reserve was increasingly behind the curve. The funds rate and interest rate on ten-year Treasury securities were negative in real terms,

---

[15] The foreign currency subcommittee consisted of the chairman and vice chairman of the committee, the vice chairman of the Board of Governors, and one other member of the Board. A limit on the size of the System's "overall open position" was introduced into the foreign currency authorization. It was defined as the "sum (disregarding signs) of open positions in each currency." The open position in each currency (later changed to the net position) was defined as the spot position plus forward position with due regard for sign. In addition to the formal limit on the overall open position, there were informal understandings about foreign currency holdings in total and currency-by-currency.

had been for some time, and continued to decline (Figure 5.4).[16] The overall message from foreign policymakers and the markets was that US inflation had gotten out of hand, US monetary policy was too easy, and the US dollar was fast losing its remaining luster (Truman, 2006, pp. 174–81).

At the Bonn Economic Summit in June 1978, as part of a bargain aimed at stimulating the world economy and reducing the US current account deficit, the US administration pledged to reduce inflation via a voluntary program to decelerate wages and prices, promote a tighter fiscal policy, and deregulate domestic petroleum prices. The program of budget restraint and voluntary wage and price guidelines released in mid-October was a disappointment to the market, as Chairman G. William Miller had anticipated and had warned his Federal Reserve Board colleagues.

To deal with this situation, Miller helped craft the November 1, 1978, dollar rescue package in cooperation with the US Treasury. He convinced the Treasury that it could issue foreign currency–denominated US government debt in the market (Carter Bonds), putting the US Treasury's money where its mouth was. The Federal Reserve agreed to a supplemental reserve requirement on large time deposits and to a 1 percentage point boost in the discount rate to a historic high of 9.5 percent, with the federal funds rate quickly following.[17] The last element was to meet a condition imposed by the Bundesbank for its participation in the package. On the whole, this was a dramatic demonstration of external discipline from market and official sources that affected Federal Reserve policies on a scale not witnessed during the Bretton Woods era (type A impact); see Greene (1984b) and Truman (2004, 2006) for more details.

However, it was not enough to arrest US inflation, and real interest rates continued to be deeply negative (Figure 5.4). After a brief recovery, the dollar resumed its decline and US inflation continued to rise. The stage was set for the FOMC on October 6, 1979, to adopt the new operating procedures. They aimed to better control the monetary aggregates by focusing on the

---

[16] From the end of 1974 through September 1979, the real federal funds rate had been positive in only eight of fifty-seven months. Figures 5.4, 5.5, and 5.7 use the headline consumer price index (CPI) over the previous twelve months. The real federal funds rate uses the twelve-month leading CPI inflation rate, and the real ten-year Treasury rate uses the thirty-six-month centered average of twelve-month CPI inflation rates. These were the conventions we used in IF during most of this period.

[17] Chairman Miller convinced the Treasury that it could absorb any exchange risk in the general account as a cost of issuing debt rather than potentially draining the account of the ESF. Other elements of the package included a doubling of FOMC swap lines with the Bundesbank, Bank of Japan, and Swiss National Bank; drawing intervention resources from the IMF; and stepping up US gold sales that had been underway.

supply of nonborrowed reserves to the market and by tolerating a higher level of and greater movements in the federal funds rate.

At the IMF annual meeting in Belgrade, Yugoslavia, former Chairman Burns delivered the Per Jacobsson lecture. His title was "The Anguish of Central Banking." His theme was that the Federal Reserve could not conquer inflation alone: it needed changes in fiscal, regulatory, and tax policies in addition to explicit endorsement of restrictive policies by the central bank.

Paul Volcker arrived at the lecture late, sat on the floor, skimmed the text, and tossed it onto the floor saying, "I have it all wrong." I understood his remark because I knew about the proposed new operating procedures, which were the basis for his reaction. More important, Volcker en route to Belgrade had obtained a commitment from the Treasury and Council of Economic Advisors not to object to the proposed approach. Both the administration and the FOMC had become convinced that everything else had been tried and had failed to reduce US inflation. In retrospect, it was necessary to have tried and failed many other approaches before policymakers, including within the Federal Reserve, agreed that the US inflation problem was principally homegrown and could be addressed only through monetary policy (type A impact) (Truman, 2005).

Experience with the new operating procedures was not smooth, in part, because of the imposition of credit controls in March 1980. The procedures also generated technical and policy controversy inside and outside the Federal Reserve. In response to those criticisms, in late 1980 and early 1981 the staff of the System, under the direction of Stephen Axilrod, undertook a comprehensive review of the experience to date (FRB, 1981). The study consisted of twelve papers. Two dealt with international aspects. One by Margaret Greene offered views of the new approach from the foreign exchange trading desk. A second paper that my colleagues and I in IF drafted considered, in part, exchange market developments, foreign experience, and effects on US international capital flows (Truman, 1981).

Two aspects of the study are noteworthy. First, it was a cooperative effort: exemplifying the Federal Reserve System at its best. Second, it helped to convince Volcker that the academic-quality economic research conducted at the Board was useful to him and his leadership of the Federal Reserve.

In 1980, the Federal Reserve devoted substantial attention to the implementation of the new operating procedures, but not to the exclusion of global concerns. At the February 1980 FOMC, Jeff Shafer, George

Henry, and I made a special presentation on international financial trends (FRB, 1980).

Shafer reviewed trends in the dollar under floating and explanations for those trends. He presented data on reserve diversification and patterns of intervention by the G-10 countries. Henry reviewed developments in oil markets and their implications for global imbalances. He flagged the growing deficits of the non-oil developing countries, their increasing reliance of foreign banks to finance those deficits, and the availability of other resources in the event that they experienced external financing difficulties. In my concluding remarks, I said:

> Thus, there are risks, and they have increased significantly in recent months with the further rise in oil prices on top of an expected slowdown in global economic activity ... Disruptions in the international financial system would almost certainly spill over into exchange markets, although the implications for the foreign exchange value of the dollar might be either positive or negative. Perhaps more importantly, many such disruptions would have serious, adverse implications for inflation, for the health of the U.S. banking system, and for prospects for economic growth in the near and long term.

With respect to the health of the US banking system and the potential external financial problems of non-oil developing countries, Volcker (1980) delivered a speech on March 1, 1980, at New York University on recycling the oil exporters' surpluses. The speech drew on a Board briefing by Henry Terrell. Volcker was so preoccupied with the credit control program that he spent less time on that speech than any other speech or testimony in my experience with him at the Board. However, the next to last paragraph was pure Volcker:

> Though we have been concerned with the financial integrity of U.S. banks in urging them to be prudent in their foreign lending, we also believe such a posture is consistent with the long-run best interests of the borrowers. I believe we could live with the recycling situation as it is today for a period of time, though it would be foolish not to expect some hard cases to emerge. But I also believe that our capacity to deal with this problem as time passes could increasingly be stretched close to the limit. In that light, borrowing countries should lose no time in developing policies to maintain their credit worthiness. And it seems to me lenders and borrowers alike – that is the great bulk of the world – have the strongest kind of self-interest in actions to avoid appreciable further increases in oil prices at a time when adjustment and financing capabilities already will be increasingly stretched.

In light of subsequent developments, it is too facile to say that Volcker had warned the world of the coming global debt crisis. However, it equally would be too facile to say that the Federal Reserve was not aware of the potential risks.

5.3 The 1980s: Sovereign Debt, External Deficits, and Exchange Rates

The Federal Reserve's successful attack on inflation had dramatic, negative repercussions on the global economy. One manifestation was the Third World debt crises that dominated the 1980s. In addition, the US dollar soared and the US current account balance tanked. The abrupt U-turns in US foreign exchange policy prompted deep concerns about the Federal Reserve's role in such operations.

5.3.1 International Concerns Contribute to Federal Reserve Easing

The imposition of credit controls in the United States in March 1980 exacerbated the recession already under way. The lifting of those controls produced a twelve-month expansion through July 1981, but the recession resumed and continued until November 1982. The federal funds rate began to decline in May 1982 for these and other reasons: The new operating procedures permitted the decline; the FOMC, Congress, and the country were becoming restless about the continuing recession; and the Committee began to pay more attention to the level of the federal funds rate. At the FOMC meeting on October 5, Axilrod (FRB, 1982) told the Committee that the behavior of the monetary aggregates, which were above the targets for the year, and the behavior of the real economy were out of sync.

The day before the November 16, 1982, FOMC meeting, Volcker asked me to make a special presentation to the FOMC. He wanted me to address the risks to the US economy from the global economy, which was in its third year of recession.[18] He told me that I did not have to hold back. I concluded:

In the best of circumstances, significant real and financial adjustments will be required by all. On the real side, we have roughly calculated that the external component of the expected adjustment by developing countries next year will reduce U.S. exports by at least five percent and lower U.S. real GNP by about 1/3 of a percentage point. These impacts could easily be larger. The financial implications are more difficult to quantify. But the real and financial risks could be significant especially if we have underestimated the negative real interactions among countries

---

[18] The convention at the time was that global growth of less than 2.5 percent – on a purchasing power parity (PPP) basis used in the IMF's *World Economic Outlook* – was a recession. Growth in 1980 was 1.9 percent; in 1981, 2.3 percent; and in 1982, 0.7 percent, climbing only to 2.9 percent in 1983.

or miscalculated the capacity of the international financial system to bridge over recent and potential disturbances (Truman, 1982, p. 5).

Our estimate was that net exports would subtract 0.7 percent from US real GDP from the second quarter of 1982 to the second quarter of 1983, with all the negative action from lower real exports. The decline in exports turned out to be about 50 percent larger, as the current account balance moved further into deficit.[19]

The Federal Reserve monetary policy responded to international influences during this period as they were impacting the US economy but also to how Federal Reserve policy was impacting the global economy (type B impact). The FOMC allowed the funds rate to decline until February 1983. By the end of 1982, the twelve-month rate of inflation was 4.0 percent, down from 8.6 percent in 1981 and 11.9 percent in 1980 (Figure 5.5).

5.3.2 The End of the Battle against Inflation?

Was the battle against inflation over? That is for others to judge. With the economy picking up and a projected rise in inflation, the FOMC raised the funds rate starting in May 1983 through August 1984.[20] Some say that was the decisive action to establish the Federal Reserve's inflation credibility. In 1986, there was a whiff of deflation; headline inflation slowed to 1.7 percent by the end of the year on the back of falling energy and other commodity prices. Inflation averaged about 3 percent in 1991–93, and the funds rate was in the same range for about eighteen months after the brief 1990–91 recession.[21]

---

[19] Using the Federal Reserve Board staff's weights for the broad index for the foreign exchange value of the dollar and GDP data from national sources, foreign growth averaged 0.42 percent from the first quarter of 1982 to the first quarter of 1983.

[20] At the May 25, 1983, meeting there were five dissents, which was unusual. "These members also referred to the potentially disruptive international impact of rising U.S. interest rates. Anthony Solomon, Roger Guffey, and Frank Morris in particular believed that the already strong dollar in foreign exchange markets, the tenuous situation of some of the developing countries, the still fragile economic recovery in other industrial countries, and the continuing weak outlook for U.S. exports counseled against an increase in reserve restraint" (FRB, 1983b). The other two dissenters were Nancy Teeters and Emmet Rice.

[21] That recession was largely caused by the run up in energy prices in the wake of Iraq's invasion of Kuwait and in the lead up to the first Gulf War. By this time, staff and the FOMC had a more coherent framework for calibrating policy: Look at the previous projection of growth in nominal GDP and adjust policy to keep it steady. As a result, part of the projected increase in nominal GDP would be taken in the form of an increase in inflation and part in the form of a decrease in the growth rate. This framework can be found in the material prepared for the August 21, 1990, FOMC (FRB, 1990a).

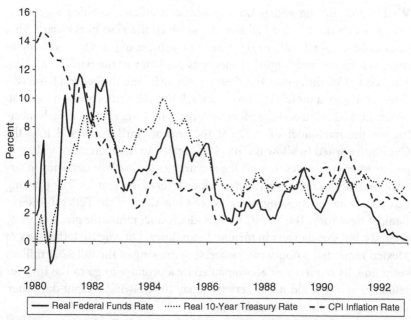

Figure 5.5. US real federal funds rate and ten-year Treasury rate versus CPI inflation rate, 1980–92.
Note: CPI = consumer price index.
Sources: Board of Governors of the Federal Reserve System; US Bureau of Labor Statistics; author's calculations.

By 1982, the US inflation threat was reduced to a considerable extent. But the experience of the 1970s had been costly for the United States and for the world economy. The Federal Reserve was not the only central bank that pursued a monetary policy that was too easy in the 1970s, but it demonstrated a lack of leadership. Technical changes in financial markets, such as the growth of syndicated lending by banks to sovereign governments of developing countries, played a role in the crisis. Parallels between the global economic and financial crisis in 2007–09 and the economic and financial crisis of the early 1980s are stronger than is often appreciated today, in particular with respect to the role and responsibility of the United States in contributing to the crisis.

5.3.3 The Third World Debt Crises

The onset of the 1980s Third World debt crises is conventionally dated to when the government of Mexico closed its foreign exchange market on Thursday, August 12, 1982, and the subsequent Mexican Weekend in

Washington, during which US and Mexican officials cobbled together a rescue operation. Mexico had already devalued the peso in February. That devaluation was accompanied by the appointment of Jesus Silva Herzog as finance minister and Miguel Mancera as governor of the Bank of Mexico. They visited Washington – the Treasury, the IMF, and the Federal Reserve – essentially once a month starting in March until the crisis broke in August.

The FOMC discussed the Mexican situation in March and at each meeting for the remainder of 1982. At the end of April, June, and July, the Committee voted to allow the Bank of Mexico to draw on its swap line to pad its foreign reserves to meet the requirement to back its currency in circulation without revealing the precarious level of its reserves. The drawing was pure window dressing; the proceeds remained at the Federal Reserve Bank of New York. The FOMC was decidedly uncomfortable granting these requests, but saw dangers in turning them down. On August 4, the Bank of Mexico requested a non-window dressing drawing of the full $700 million swap line. Its request was accompanied by a promise to go to the IMF for refinancing if it could not otherwise repay the drawing.[22] Eight days later, the acute crisis phase was underway.

Back in early May, I had accompanied Volcker to the Bank of International Settlements (BIS) for the monthly meeting of G-10 governors. Volcker warned his central bank colleagues that Mexico was likely facing an external financial crisis and that other developing countries would likely experience external financial problems as well.

Despite these warnings, when we contacted G-10 central bankers during the Mexican Weekend to say that the crisis had erupted, many officials were surprised. A senior official at the Bank of Japan asked why Mexico's crisis mattered to Japan. At that time, the BIS banking data were based on balance-of-payments accounting concepts and the location of the institution advancing credit; they were not based on the consolidated exposures across all the offices of a bank regardless of where they were located. I told my interlocutor that even the deficient location data revealed large Japanese bank exposures to Mexico.[23]

---

[22] The basic framework for this drawing had been agreed at the end of July; I had received an oral commitment of Treasury support at that time. On August 4, Volcker received a written commitment from Secretary Regan to facilitate the Bank of Mexico's repayment to the Federal Reserve by January 31, 1983, by permitting Mexico to draw on its swap line with the ESF.

[23] In the wake of the financial crises of the 1970s, the US banking agencies began to collect "country exposure" data on the consolidated operations of US banks. As a consequence of the 1980s debt crises, we were able to convince other countries to do the same.

The Federal Reserve Engages the World (1970–2000)   151

The basic framework used for the Mexican rescue was employed in several other cases. Governments and central banks, often acting through the BIS, provided countries with bridge financing while programs with the IMF were negotiated. In some cases, the drawings on the bridge loans did not occur until the economic reform program had been agreed with the Fund. Commercial banks were asked to agree to a standstill on principal payments while still receiving interest payments. As part of the financing of the IMF program, banks were asked to reschedule principal payments due, initially for the next year, and to make new loans to the country.[24] A critical mass of the bank exposures to the country had to agree to these conditions before the IMF would disburse.[25]

This was the Volcker Plan; it had a global approach. The template was used, with variations, for Brazil, Argentina, Yugoslavia, and the Philippines in 1982–83, and for several other countries.

The plan was developed at the Federal Reserve in November 1982, in large part by Charles J. Siegman working with Volcker (type B impact). Volcker sold the plan to the Treasury and to James Baker at the White House.[26] In later years, bank loans coming due over several years were rescheduled, and the interest rate on the rescheduled and new loans was lowered to LIBOR (London Interbank Offered Rate) plus 13/16, in principle barely covering the banks' cost of funds (Boughton, 2001, chapter 9).

The Volcker Plan was successful in arresting the crisis, but economic and financial recovery proved to be more difficult. Consequently, in 1985 the United States put forward the Baker Plan. The Baker Plan sought to restore growth through structural reforms linked to greater use of World Bank assistance. Countries also were expected to have IMF programs. Banks were expected to contribute through rescheduling old loans and making new loans.[27] Although Mexico and a number of other countries eventually participated in the plan, it too failed to achieve its economic objectives.[28]

---

[24] The rationale for adding to countries' external debts was that they were thought to be facing liquidity crises not insolvency crises (Cline, 1983).

[25] This approach was later changed because of delays in bank approvals. The IMF adopted a policy that allowed it to lend to members with arrears to the banks.

[26] Deputy Secretary Tim McNamar took the lead at Treasury on these debt issues. He worked with Volcker on the plan and, in turn, relied on Deputy Assistant Secretary Tom Leddy, a civil servant in the great tradition of Treasury career officials, with whom I worked closely (see Volcker and Gyohten, 1992, chapter 7, for their account of those days).

[27] The Baker Plan focused on seventeen countries, raised from an initial fifteen, of which five were not in Latin America (Cline, 1995, chapter 5).

[28] Mexico had another crisis episode in 1988, again during an election year, and drew on the Federal Reserve and US Treasury swap lines on August 1 and repaid them on September

The Baker Plan was followed in 1989 by the Brady Plan. The Brady Plan involved writing down and securitizing bank debt backed by a collateralization of near-term interest payments (via deposits in escrow accounts) and of full payment of principal, normally in thirty years (via zero-coupon bonds).

The Federal Reserve played three roles with respect to the Brady Plan. First, we convinced the Treasury to drop the all-or-nothing approach to debt reduction in favor of a menu approach, which included not only debt reduction but also debt service reduction and new loans at concessional interest rates. Second, we worked with the IMF, bankers, and countries to help implement the approach; Terry Checki at the Federal Reserve Bank of New York played a crucial role.[29] Third, the Board of Governors approved the Federal Reserve Bank of New York's role in holding the escrow and collateral accounts for the Brady exchanges. This was an unusual role for the Federal Reserve to play, and the Board placed conditions on doing so, such as requiring the country to have an IMF program.[30]

The management of the Third World debt crises of the 1980s has been criticized for imposing on the countries involved a decade of lost growth. Most countries suffered, though Chile after its crisis in 1982–83 was an exception. Could or should there have been better alternatives? Did the Federal Reserve and other central banks and governments around the world protect banks too much from the consequences of their mistakes? My answer is no, at least in the first few years. No government facing an external financial crisis at that time even considered an open default or write-down of its debt to foreign banks. Policymakers were eager to get back to borrowing as soon as possible.

The Federal Reserve, the US bank supervisors collectively, and their counterparts in every advanced country exercised forbearance with respect to forcing banks to recognize actual or potential losses. That strategy was dictated by the scale of crisis affecting the banks and the condition of economies in the United States and elsewhere. The creditor banks ultimately took some losses. One might argue that the banks too would have been better off acting more quickly, but there was not much appetite for that.[31]

---

15 to pad its international reserves in connection with the announcements of their levels on August 4 and September 1.

[29] Meltzer (2009, p. 1182) incorrectly credits Checki with the design of the Brady Plan.

[30] One consequence of these conditions was that when Brazil and its bankers got around to completing a Brady package in 1994 without the support of an IMF program, the BIS was used to hold the collateral (Boughton, 2012, pp. 421–427).

[31] The debates in the 1980s and 1990s about so-called private sector involvement and the role of debt rescheduling, reprofiling, and write-downs were similar to those still swirling today (IMF, 2014).

Crisis prevention efforts were stepped up during and after the outbreak of the Third World debt crises. The United States and other countries agreed to increase IMF quota resources by almost half and to almost triple the size of the IMF's General Arrangements to Borrow (GAB), through which the IMF could borrow additional resources from certain members to finance its lending programs. The terms of the GAB were changed so that the extra resources were no longer reserved for IMF lending to the G-10 participating countries, but could be used to help finance any IMF program. The Federal Reserve presented to the US Treasury the case for embracing this change.

Passage of the resulting legislation by Congress was not an easy task. It passed the House of Representatives by five votes. The Reagan administration had to "buy" approval from Democrats by agreeing to housing legislation that it did not support. The IMF legislation was incorporated into that legislation. Also included was the International Lending Supervision Act (ILSA), which tightened up some rules and regulations involving international lending, such as the ICERC process and accounting for origination fees (forcing them to be taken into earnings over the life of a loan rather than upfront). The legislation also called for the Federal Reserve and Treasury to undertake discussions with supervisors in other major countries to establish a common and higher level of capital for internationally active banks. Those discussions led to the 1988 Basel Capital Accord, in which the Federal Reserve played a major role.

IF staff at the Board, and by extension other parts of the Federal Reserve System, examined the evolving issues of sovereign debt. As shown in Table 5.1, during the decade of the 1980s, seventeen IFDPs were written on various aspects of financial crises, constituting 8 percent of the total. One of the most influential was an early paper by Michael P. Dooley et al. (1983), which examines the origins of debt problems of eight key countries and uses a simulation model to project their prospects for the rest of the decade. Dooley and his colleagues were among the first to point to the issue of capital flight, which could undermine any progress in reducing countries' current account deficits.

5.3.4 The US Dollar and Current Account Deficits

In addition to the Third World debt crises, international economic policy discussions at the Federal Reserve in the 1980s were dominated by the emergence of a large US current account deficit, which peaked at more than 3 percent of GDP, and wide swings in the foreign exchange value of the dollar (Figure 5.3).

During the first two months of 1981, the Desk bought substantial amounts of foreign currency as the dollar strengthened, having already covered the Carter Bonds. However, in late February, Undersecretary Beryl Sprinkel signaled that the Reagan administration and the Regan Treasury favored a minimalist approach to foreign exchange market intervention, and the Desk's purchases stopped (Greene, 1984b). In early April Sprinkel delivered congressional testimony outlining the Treasury's approach. Volcker had reviewed and toned down that testimony to emphasize that the minimalist approach to US intervention could still encompass operations to "counter disorderly market conditions."

Volcker's view was that the Secretary of the Treasury was the chief financial officer of the United States and should set the framework for US intervention policy even if the Federal Reserve and Treasury had independent legal authority to operate in the foreign exchange market.[32] In his oral remarks, Sprinkel expanded on his text and cast doubt on the need for the Federal Reserve's swap lines and for US foreign currency balances, part of which were subsequently used to subscribe to an increase in the US quota in the IMF (Pardee, 1981).[33]

By June 1982, the dollar had appreciated by 25 percent in price-adjusted terms over the previous two years, and officials in other countries were complaining that the US unwillingness to cap the dollar's rise was undermining their own efforts to lower inflation. Consequently, at the G-7 Summit in June 1982, the United States agreed to a study of experience under floating exchange rates, including the effectiveness of exchange market intervention.

Philippe Jurgensen of the French finance ministry chaired the working group of officials. The Federal Reserve produced a number of background papers for the study (type C impact).[34] Much of the effort was directed at trying to determine if sterilized intervention had been effective during the floating rate period, based on a portfolio balance model that assumes that securities denominated in different currencies are not perfect substitutes.[35]

---

[32] Indeed, on March 30, following the assassination attempt on President Reagan, I obtained Volcker's permission to authorize the Desk to buy dollars when we were unable to reach the Treasury. The Desk subsequently split the sales between System and ESF accounts.

[33] US intervention subsequently was minimal but not nonexistent. From April 1981 to January 1985, the Desk operated on twenty days.

[34] Ten US studies, including three by Margaret Greene of the Federal Reserve Bank of New York and one by a team from the Treasury, were later published as Staff Studies (Henderson and Sampson, 1983).

[35] As was stressed by Michael Dooley in his comments, the effectiveness of the recent large-scale asset purchases by the Federal Reserve and other central banks relies on the same basic assumption. Researchers, in some cases using more modern techniques, have found substantial effectiveness in such purchases. However, recent central bank operations

The research results supply weak support for the effectiveness of intervention via the portfolio balance channel but also acknowledge the possibility of a signaling channel for effectiveness.

The working group's report contributed to a better understanding in official circles of the distinction between sterilized and unsterilized intervention and examined the issues associated with foreign exchange market intervention from a number of perspectives. On the effectiveness of intervention, the working group concludes: "[S]terilized intervention did not generally have a lasting effect, but ... intervention in conjunction with domestic policy changes did have more durable impact" (Jurgensen, 1983, p. 17).

The report of the working group went first to the Summit finance ministers, central bank governors, and representatives of the European Community, who issued a statement (1983) on April 29, 1983, in which they agreed "on the need for closer consultations on policies and market conditions; and, while retaining our freedom to operate independently, are willing to undertake coordinated intervention in instances where it is agreed that such intervention would be helpful."[36]

The release of the working group's report and the associated statement on April 29 did not attract much attention either in the markets or at the FOMC table. Sam Cross (FRB, 1983a), manager of the Desk at the time, commented that perhaps the nonreaction was because Secretary Regan immediately after the April 29 meeting said that US policy had not changed. It did not for another twenty-one months.

By May 1984, the dollar's real effective value had risen more than 30 percent from its level in July 1980, and the US current account deficit had ballooned to more than 2 percent of GDP. Although staff consistently projected that the dollar would soon start to depreciate, we continued to be wrong. Larry Promisel chaired a special FOMC presentation involving Peter Hooper, Peter Isard, and Dale Henderson on the deteriorating prospects for the US external position (FRB, 1984). The presentation reviewed how the deficit had evolved to that point; presented some projections of the deficit if the dollar's value were to remain unchanged; and considered the implications of various alternative scenarios of (monetary and fiscal) policy

---

in domestic securities have been on a wholly different scale than operations in foreign currencies in the 1970s and early 1980s.

[36] My hope in participating in the intervention study was that we would be able to preserve a role for sterilized intervention as a supportive tool of economic, including monetary, policy. In that, we were successful, though I was disappointed by the weakness of the empirical results. Writing twenty years later (Truman, 2003b), I conclude that the research still had not established a more robust role for intervention, at least on the scale that it was then practiced.

induced or exogenous adjustment in the dollar. The presentation looked at the issue of sustainability in terms of the US international investment position, which was about to turn negative. The US current account deficit continued to expand through the end of 1987.[37]

US exchange rate policy began to change in January 1985. On January 17, at a dinner meeting of the G-5 finance ministers and central bank governors at the Federal Reserve Board, in which both Secretary Regan and Secretary-designate Baker participated, it was decided to issue a statement inter alia to help ease the intense selling pressure on the British pound sterling. The statement referenced the 1983 Williamsburg G-7 Summit's commitment "to undertake coordinated intervention in the markets as necessary." It was followed up by a small amount of coordinated intervention in which the United States (Federal Reserve and Treasury) participated.

The FOMC had a conference call on January 18, 1985, in which Volcker briefed the Committee on the G-5 meeting and the extent to which it was about sterling or the dollar. He observed: "I think everybody would be relatively content, or more than relatively content, if the net result with intervention or without intervention was that the dollar ended up somewhat lower than it has been."

Governor Charles Partee commented, "I'm no great supporter of intervention as you know, but I do think the situation has become extreme enough that it is called for. I think it is a good move" (FRB, 1985c).

For the February 1985 FOMC meeting, the staff again projected that the price-adjusted foreign exchange value of the dollar against the major currencies would depreciate under the weight of the rising current account deficit by about 15 percent over the next two years. The dollar finally peaked in March 1985 and then fell by 30 percent on the real broad index through early 1988 (Figure 5.3).[38]

Market forces alone might have continued the dollar's decline beyond the summer of 1985, but they were reinforced by the Baker-inspired

---

[37] The continued deterioration of the US external position and its sustainability received extensive staff analysis for the rest of the decade (e.g., Danker and Hooper, 1990; Helkie and Hooper, 1987, 1989; Hooper and Mann, 1987; Howard, 1989; and Stekler and Helkie, 1989). Staff of the Federal Reserve Board also participated during the 1980s in projects investigating policy rules that might promote better international economic policy coordination and results (e.g., Bryant et al., 1988; Bryant, Holtham, and Hooper, 1988; Bryant, Hooper, and Mann, 1993; Hooper et al., 1990).

[38] Against major currencies, the decline was 40 percent. In assessing this period in Truman (2006), I conclude that the message from the markets was that the US monetary/fiscal mix was flawed, the dollar had experienced a bubble, and concerns about protectionism were real.

announcement by the G-5 finance ministers and central bank governors following their September 22 meeting at the Plaza Hotel in New York that "some further orderly appreciation of the main non-dollar currencies against the dollar is desirable."

Baker's initiative was in response to growing protectionist sentiments in the United States. Following the meeting in New York, an FOMC conference call was held on September 23 to explain that there could well be substantial intervention in subsequent days. Sam Cross's report to the FOMC on October 1 provided a full account of the effects of the announcement along with other events that produced a substantial decline in the dollar without a great deal of intervention (FRB, 1985a).

At the October 1985 FOMC meeting, concerns were raised about the implications of a "precipitous decline of the dollar" and a request was made for a special briefing. On the way to the IMF meetings in Seoul later in the week, Volcker – in what should have been treated as an off-the-record comment to *Washington Post* columnist Hobart Rowen – commented that "one could have too much of a good thing."[39] At the subsequent November FOMC meeting, Axilrod chaired a presentation by Peter Hooper, David Stockton, Larry Slifman, and himself that outlined the possible path of external adjustment, the implications for the real economy, the dynamics of possible interest rate and price changes, and associated monetary policy issues in terms of the risks to inflation and/or growth. Axilrod favored engineering a gradual adjustment of the dollar (FRB, 1985b). Gradual adjustment was not in the cards, but neither was recession or inflation. Aided by the collapse of energy prices in 1986, inflation did not rise appreciably until late in the decade. Real interest rates, in particular long-term rates, did not increase much either (Figure 5.5).

The dollar's depreciation went further and faster than anyone had anticipated. By early February 1986, it had declined by about 12 percent in real terms against the major currencies from its value in September 1985, and 20 percent from its peak the previous March. This triggered another instance in which international considerations impacted Federal Reserve monetary policy decisions in the form of the Board's aborted decision on February 24 to lower the discount rate. Volcker was concerned about the impact of a unilateral cut in the discount rate on the already weakening US dollar and voted against a change (type A impact). He was outvoted by Preston Martin, Martha Seger, Wayne Angell, and Manuel Johnson; the latter two had just joined the Board. Fortunately, changes in the discount rate

[39] The quotation appeared in a column by Hobart Rowen a number of weeks later.

were announced after the US markets closed rather than immediately, as is now the case. This allowed time not only for Volcker to draft his resignation letter and convey his intentions to Baker but also for cooler heads to prevail. The Board met again in the late afternoon and agreed that Volcker could have two weeks to negotiate downward adjustments in the German and Japanese discount rates prior to a reduction in the US rate, which occurred on March 7.[40]

The depreciation of the US dollar continued. By the February 1987 FOMC meeting, the dollar was down 30 percent from its early 1985 peak in real terms against the major foreign currencies, and the staff projected that the depreciation would continue at a reduced pace at least through the end of 1988 (FRB, 1987).

Starting in the fall of 1986, authorities in foreign countries became increasingly concerned about the pace and extent of the dollar's depreciation, in particular against the Japanese yen. On February 22, Baker and Volcker met with their counterparts from the other G-6 countries in Paris and announced in the Louvre Accord that "they agreed to cooperate closely to foster stability of exchange rates around current levels."[41]

In IF, we thought that it was a mistake to try to cut short the dollar's depreciation, in part, because the depreciation to date would not be sufficient to eliminate the US current account deficit and, in part, because we anticipated that downward pressures on the dollar would continue to be intense. We sent a memorandum to Chairman Volcker outlining our arguments. He did not buy them. In Volcker and Gyohten (1992, p. 243), Volcker explained that he was concerned about the impact of further depreciation on the US inflation rate and subsequently on interest rates. In a discussion many years later, Volcker told me that he also was concerned about the broader impact of further dollar depreciation on growth in other countries (type B impact).

This announcement inaugurated a brief international experiment with target zones or reference ranges for exchange rates.[42] The experiment quickly unwound: The reference rates were recalibrated several times, and

---

[40] I know of no definitive account of who initially agreed to delay the Board's action and why. William Silber (2012, pp. 254–58) provides a plausible version of the events.

[41] The Italian officials were invited, but boycotted when they learned that the G-5 had met the day before.

[42] The Louvre communiqué (G-6, 1987) also states: "It is important that the newly industrialized developing economies should assume greater responsibility for preserving an open world trading system by reducing trade barriers and pursuing policies that allow their currencies to reflect more fully underlying economic fundamentals." Similar concerns led to the enactment of the Omnibus Trade and Competitiveness Act of 1988, which mandated that the Treasury twice a year report on developments in international economic and exchange rate policies in consultation with the Board and the International Monetary Fund.

by September 1987 they were ancient history as far as we at the Federal Reserve were concerned.[43]

The dollar continued to depreciate through the spring of 1987 and staged a brief recovery in the summer before tailing off again. At the September FOMC meeting, Chairman Greenspan's second, the federal funds rate was snugged up to support the dollar (type A impact).

The upward creep in US interest rates contributed to international financial tensions and led to public criticism by Baker of German economic and – in particular – Bundesbank monetary policy. Whether by coincidence or not, the US and global stock market crash followed on Monday, October 19. The Federal Reserve promptly eased its policy. However, other countries that were also affected by the global rush from equities did not immediately follow suit. International cooperation was not entirely absent. The relevant US authorities did consult with their counterparts almost daily.

The equity markets calmed down, but the dollar's slide accelerated. The G-7 ministers and governors issued a statement (for the first time negotiated without a meeting, hence a "telephone communiqué") on December 22 and followed up with substantial amounts of intervention to support the dollar to little avail. The delay in issuing the statement was because the other countries, Germany in particular, were waiting for the US administration to agree with Congress on measures to cut the US budget deficit, which turned out to be quite modest after protracted negotiations in which Greenspan was an active participant (type A impact).

However, after the turn of the year, in the words of Cross (FRB, 1988): "Central banks intervened in concert aggressively, visibly and noisily. The market had been looking for a signal, especially from the U.S., and these operations convinced many market participants that the G-7 countries were indeed now committed to halting the dollar's decline." The decline on a weighted-average price-adjusted basis did not bottom out until April, but the worst was over (see Truman, 2006, pp. 186–91, for a longer account of this episode).

5.3.5 The Federal Reserve's Role in US Intervention

The Federal Reserve was a full participant in US intervention operations associated with the decline of the dollar and attempts to halt that decline. But by the end of the 1980s change was in the air.

---

[43] Randall Henning (1994) argues – incorrectly in my view (Truman, 2006, p. 194) – that the reference ranges continued through Baker's departure from the Treasury in August 1988 and gradually unraveled in 1989–90. It is possible that the framework persisted in the thinking of some Treasury officials, but their thoughts were never communicated to me in this manner.

After the intervention operations in January 1988, the dollar's recovery persisted, perhaps aided by increases in the federal funds rate, which started in the spring of 1988 and continued through the middle of 1989. Largely following the desires of the Treasury, the Desk initially used the dollar's rise to rebuild US reserves of foreign currencies and later actively to resist the dollar's appreciation.[44] The scale of these activities became controversial within the Federal Reserve, in part, because of the potential for losses on the Federal Reserve's share of US foreign currency reserves. In addition, the intervention appeared to be stepping on the gas at the same time the FOMC was stepping on the brakes with respect to consumer price inflation, which was creeping up to above 5 percent.

In response, Cross and I recommended to Greenspan that the staff conduct a study of Federal Reserve System foreign currency operations to review those operations from an institutional and historical perspective. Greenspan agreed, as did the August 1989 FOMC (type A impact).[45]

We presented the *Report of the Task Force on System Foreign Currency Operations* to the March 1990 FOMC meeting. It contains an overview by Cross and me and eleven papers covering the legal, historical, and procedural aspects of Federal Reserve foreign currency operations; policy, strategy, and tactics; institutional frameworks for decision making here and abroad; resources for financing intervention, including the history of the "swap network"; and analytical issues.[46] The papers were reviewed by a conference of System Research Directors.[47]

---

[44] From January 1989 through April 1990, the US monetary authorities bought $24.4 billion in foreign currencies operating on 114 of 346 business days (Truman, 2006, p. 193).

[45] At that meeting, Johnson abstained from an increase in the size of the warehousing agreement for the Treasury or ESF from $5 billion to $10 billion, and he and Angell voted against an increase in the limit on the System's overall open position in all foreign currencies from $18 billion to $20 billion. Federal Reserve "warehousing" of foreign currencies for the Treasury or the ESF involves a spot purchase of foreign currency from the Treasury or ESF with a simultaneous forward sale of that currency at the same exchange rate. It involves no exchange rate risk to the System on the principal amount; such arrangements date back to 1962. See Henning (1999, pp. 49–52) for some additional history.

[46] The papers are available in redacted form from the FOMC Secretariat. One paper (Edison, 1990) was released as an IFDP; it reviews the literature on foreign exchange market intervention including its effectiveness. A second paper (Pauls, 1990) appears in modified form as a Federal Reserve *Bulletin* article.

[47] In 1979, the System had an earlier related project on the implications of the exchange rate regime; see summary of forty-one papers in Gray and Shafer (1981).

In the overview, Cross and I (Cross and Truman, 1990) offer a number of summary observations:

- US exchange rate policy is set by the Secretary of the Treasury and has evolved since 1962 with the active participation of the Federal Reserve.
- The rubric under which US foreign currency operations are conducted, "countering disorderly market conditions," has been interpreted in an elastic manner.
- Federal Reserve foreign currency operations are routinely sterilized, but exchange market considerations have at times influenced the day-to-day implementation of monetary policy.[48]
- There is no evidence that Federal Reserve monetary policy had been subverted by inappropriate exchange rate considerations or by international exchange rate understandings.
- The consensus on the limited effectiveness of sterilized intervention was as outlined earlier in this chapter.
- On the issue of warehousing foreign currency for the Treasury or its ESF, we advised against denying to the Treasury the US dollar resources it might need to purchase foreign currency.

In late February and early March 1990, pending the FOMC's discussion of the task force's report, Greenspan declined to participate in US purchases of Japanese yen and German marks (Cross, 1990). At the FOMC meeting, the report and related issues were extensively discussed (FRB, 1990d, pp. 46–84). The immediate questions for the Committee were whether it would approve a further increase in the limit on the System's overall open position in foreign currency from $21 billion to $25 billion and whether it would approve a further increase in warehousing eligible foreign currencies for the Treasury or ESF from $10 billion to $15 billion.

The task force and its report may have cleared the air with respect to some of the issues surrounding Federal Reserve foreign currency operations, but a substantial degree of skepticism remained, as was noted in the *Record of Policy Actions* for the March meeting, released on May 18 (FRB, 1990c). Wayne Angell, Lee Hoskins, and John LaWare voted against both actions largely on policy grounds. Angell and Hoskins also questioned the lack of congressional and constitutional authority to warehouse foreign currencies for the Treasury and ESF. Not by accident, the *Record of Policy Actions* introduced the questioning dissents by noting, "Under a

---

[48] The Treasury's operations via the ESF do not raise the question of sterilization because they do not impact the Federal Reserve's balance sheet.

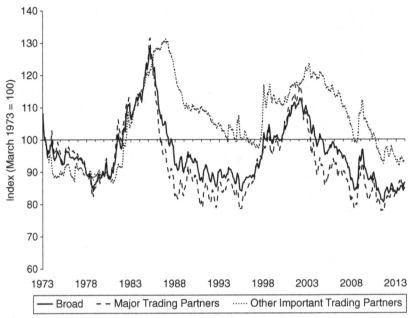

Figure 5.6. Indices of the price-adjusted foreign exchange value of the US dollar, 1973–2013.
Source: Board of Governors of the Federal Reserve System.

longstanding interpretation by the Committee and its General Counsel, warehousing transactions are open market operations in foreign currency that are authorized under the Federal Reserve Act."

Subsequently, on April 9, 1990, the Federal Reserve joined the Treasury in a symbolic purchase of yen at the request of the Japanese at a G-7 meeting in Paris. The US dollar peaked that month on a price-adjusted weighted-average basis against the major currencies and continued to decline in terms of the currencies of other important trading partners. See Figure 5.6 for the three indices of the dollar price-adjusted foreign exchange value using the current staff methodology.

5.4 The 1990s: The Federal Reserve Goes Global

During the 1990s, developments in the rest of the world attracted increasing Federal Reserve intellectual resources and attention, not to the exclusion of, but in addition to, domestic economic and financial developments. The US economy was not nearly as closed in real or financial terms as it had been in the 1960s. Global political developments accompanied the economic and financial trends and also could not be ignored.

In some respects, these economic, financial, and political trends exacerbated disagreements within the Federal Reserve about the System's involvement in US foreign currency operations and about the Federal Reserve's role in international financial cooperation more generally. But the Federal Reserve's role was evolving.

5.4.1 From Managed Floating to Limited Intervention

Responding to concerns expressed by some members of the FOMC about Federal Reserve involvement in US foreign exchange operations, in particular about the Federal Reserve's warehousing facility for the Treasury and ESF, Greenspan persuaded the Treasury to liquidate some of its foreign currency holdings via sales to other central banks and to use some of its dollar proceeds to unwind some of the warehousing with the Federal Reserve. At the February 1992 FOMC meeting, the facility was unanimously reduced back to the traditional level of $5 billion. This decision was accompanied by an exchange of letters between Brady and Greenspan that noted the reduction in the size of the facility, committed the Treasury to reduce its use of the facility by an additional $2 billion, noted some other modest changes in terms, and expressed Brady's hope that the Committee would consider positively any future request to increase the size of the facility (see FRB, 1992b).

Although the dollar declined a bit from May 1990 to early 1991, it appreciated again through June 1991. It again reached a low in September 1992 in the context of the turmoil in the exchange rate mechanism (ERM) of the EMS.

Domestic financial markets were cheered after July 1992, when the FOMC cut the federal funds rate by fifty basis points. Foreign exchange market participants were less enthusiastic and were dismayed by remarks by Brady – after the Munich Economic Summit – that were interpreted as welcoming dollar depreciation. These two events led US authorities to cooperate with several other countries to buy dollars on July 20. Those purchases only temporarily arrested the dollar's decline, but operations continued through August 24. Bill McDonough, who was then manager of the Desk, and others in the Federal Reserve ultimately persuaded the Treasury to cease. This was another occasion in which the Federal Reserve was able to restrain the Treasury, in part, because the Federal Reserve could have declined to participate, which would subsequently have become public. Where we were less than prescient was in our lack of appreciation that the

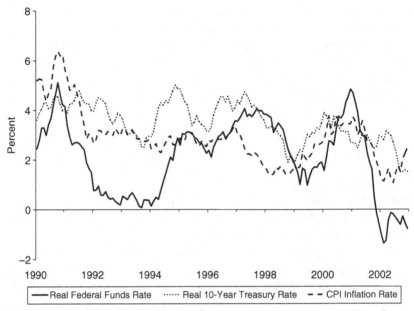

Figure 5.7. US real federal funds rate and ten-year Treasury rate versus CPI inflation rate, 1990–2002.
Note: CPI = consumer price index.
Sources: Board of Governors of the Federal Reserve System; US Bureau of Labor Statistics; author's calculations.

pressures on the dollar were primarily a reflection of tensions within the ERM that exploded in September.

The dollar fluctuated in a narrow range from September 1992 until early 1994, with only five days of US dollar purchases during 1993. Dollar purchases occurred on another five days during 1994, as the dollar weakened. Substantial purchases on June 24 triggered an extensive subsequent FOMC discussion on July 5. In the end, Lawrence Lindsey and Jerry Jordan declined to approve the June transactions. Lindsey and Jordan (FRB, 1992a) "agreed that the foreign exchange transactions conducted during the inter-meeting period were authorized under the Committee's rules. Their dissents were based on their strong reservations about the efficacy of sterilized intervention in most circumstances, including those prevailing during the intermeeting period. In their view, to the extent that repeated intervention failed to achieve stated or perceived objectives, questions would tend to arise about the credibility of monetary policy more generally."

The real federal funds rate increased by almost 300 basis points (Figure 5.7) and the price-adjusted dollar depreciated about 4 percent against all currencies and more than twice that much against the major currencies from January 1994 to March 1995. That was a bit of a puzzle. The FOMC and staff also were surprised that the interest rate on ten-year US government securities rose by about 200 basis points over the period of tightening. Our explanation at the time was that markets had overreacted to information that the global economy, not just the US economy, was growing more rapidly than had been expected.

The US dollar continued to weaken into July 1994, reaching lows against the Japanese yen and German mark on July 19. In his testimony on July 20, Greenspan said in a blunt response to a question worthy of his predecessor, Paul Volcker, "Any evidences of weakness in [the dollar] are neither good for the international financial system, nor good for the American economy" because of what they say about what is going on in the American system.[49]

The next day, by prior design, Treasury Undersecretary Lawrence Summers stated in his testimony before the same Committee:

The Administration believes that a strengthening of the dollar against the yen and the mark would have important economic benefits for the United States. It would restore confidence in financial markets that is important to sustaining recovery. It would boost the attractiveness of U.S. assets and the incentive for longer-term investment in the economy, and it would help to keep inflation low. In addition, we believe – and this view is shared by other G-7 countries – a renewed decline in the dollar would be counterproductive to global recovery. (Fisher, 1994, p. 2)

These words were not followed by action in the foreign exchange market. There was no US intervention to support the dollar until early November. The support of the other G-7 countries was implicit. In January 1995, Secretary Rubin, who replaced Secretary Bentsen, morphed the policy from a "stronger dollar" to a "strong dollar" during his confirmation hearings – an important distinction that apparently is too subtle for most commentators.

The strong dollar policy has now been maintained by three US administrations for twenty years, and the Federal Reserve played a pivotal role in its articulation (type C impact). Of course, some observers want the United States to have – and for the Federal Reserve to support – policies for the dollar that are keyed to the state of the US economy and the US external accounts and that point in different directions in different circumstances. For the US and the Federal Reserve's role in the global financial system, that is an impossible luxury.

The issue of US exchange rate and intervention policy, its relation to monetary policy, and the involvement of the Federal Reserve in the former again was discussed extensively by the FOMC following November 2–3, 1994,

---

[49] Greenspan's formal testimony made the same point but less directly.

purchases of dollars. This discussion helped establish a stronger consensus in the Committee. The point was repeatedly made, and generally accepted, that the Federal Reserve exercised considerable influence over US intervention operations. The Treasury had the capacity to ignore Federal Reserve advice. But because the Federal Reserve could and had declined to participate in the past, its views acted as a brake on the Treasury. If the Federal Reserve were to take its skin permanently out of the game, the influence of its voice would be substantially weakened. Following this discussion, the November operations were unanimously approved.[50]

The Treasury and Federal Reserve operated jointly to support the dollar on eight occasions in the first eight months of 1995. The dollar bottomed out on a real effective basis in June or July 1995, depending on your choice of index.

The era of active US and Federal Reserve foreign currency operations ended in 1995. During the first two and a half years of the Clinton administration, US authorities operated eighteen times in the foreign exchange markets, two fewer occasions than from April 1981 to December 1984 under the first Reagan administration.[51] The Clinton administration, under the influence of the Federal Reserve and other factors, refrained from operating again until June 1998, with a substantial purchase of yen, and September 2000, with a substantial purchase of the new and weakening euro (type B impact).

US thinking about such operations had changed, and the Federal Reserve played a major role in effecting that change. First, concerted (multilateral) operations have the greatest chance of success, which means that many countries have to turn on their off switches, and this raises the hurdles to such operations. This was the case in June 1998 and September 2000. Second, if one does operate, one should be prepared to operate in scale. Third, operations are more likely to have an impact if they are linked to other policy or economic and financial developments.

Contrary to the view in Bordo, Humpage, and Schwartz (2015, chapter 7), the evolution to a minimalist approach to Federal Reserve foreign currency

---

[50] At the same meeting Al Broaddus, as was his custom, dissented from approving the renewal of the Federal Reserve's swap lines for 1995.

[51] The answer to the puzzle posed by Cooper and Little (2000) about why in 1994–5 with the dollar weakening there was not more Federal Reserve concern about the effects on US inflation is that (1) the depreciation was not all that significant (the dollar's real effective depreciation was only 8 percent over the 18-month period from its prior peak in January 1994 to its low in August 1995), and (2) the inflation effects were viewed as modest – staff forecasts of the CPI excluding food and energy fluctuated narrowly around 3 percent.

operations in the mid-1990s was motivated primarily by pragmatic considerations of objectives, tactics, and effects rather than concerns about Federal Reserve independence and credibility. Some within the System and members of the FOMC strongly expressed the latter perspective, but their views were not decisive. As evidence, the Federal Reserve has operated in foreign exchange markets with the US Treasury three times since 1995, in 1998 and 2000, as well as in March 2011, following the Japanese earthquake and tsunami. And there have been no changes in the FOMC's foreign currency authorization, directive, or procedural instructions.[52]

5.4.2 Dismantling the Swap Network

In 1996, the FOMC returned to the issue of foreign exchange market intervention in the guise of discussing the future of the Federal Reserve swap network. The swap network, at least historically, was associated with the Federal Reserve's involvement in foreign currency operations. Moreover, aside from the Bank of Mexico, no central bank had drawn on the swap network since the Swedish Riksbank did in 1981. The swap network was seen by many as an anachronism. Finally, with the European Central Bank (ECB) scheduled to start operations on January 1, 1999, at a minimum swap arrangements with the central banks that would be subsumed into the euro area would have to be renegotiated. Against this background, Fisher, Kohn, and Truman (1996) sent a memorandum to the FOMC discussing issues and alternatives. The topic was discussed on July 2, 1996 (FRB, 1996b, pp. 95–113).

FOMC sentiment generally favored dismantling the swap network. But three countervailing arguments were advanced. First, the swap network was seen by some as symbolic of Federal Reserve engagement with other central banks, and most FOMC members were reluctant to send the wrong signal about the Federal Reserve's continued interest in international monetary cooperation. Second, a few members spoke with considerable foresight about the potential dollar liquidity needs of foreign central banks in the future. In light of potential liquidity problems of Japanese banks with large presences in the United States, the Federal Reserve had recently entered into an agreement with the Bank of Japan to use Japan's US Treasury securities as a backstop for borrowings by Japanese banks from the discount

---

[52] The FOMC had an extensive discussion of the September 2000 operation in euro, and some members advocated changing the framework governing those operations. That view was not widely supported (FRB, 2000), and the operation was unanimously approved.

window. The staff paper discusses the possibility of establishing a reverse repurchase facility for foreign central banks.[53] Third, in this connection a few members mentioned not only international payment system issues but also the implications of closing down the swap network in whole or in part for the international role of the US dollar.

The conclusion was that Greenspan and McDonough, who had become president of the Federal Reserve Bank of New York, should consult with the president of the Bundesbank and the governor of the Bank of Japan at the next BIS meeting, which they did. They reported to the August FOMC meeting (FRB, 1996b, pp. 4–8) that the Bundesbank was receptive to dismantling the swap network, but it was reluctant to do so until the membership in the ECB had been established, and the Bank of Japan was not. The Committee agreed to return to the issue at a later date.

At the September 1998 FOMC meeting, Fisher and I (1998) presented a memorandum to the FOMC in which we reported that the Bank of Japan was less reluctant and other central banks were willing to dismantle the swap network. Consequently, with the exception of the swap arrangements with Mexico and Canada, the Federal Reserve's swap network, first established in 1962, was terminated as of the end of 1998. A coordinated announcement was made on December 23, 1998, in connection with the release of the minutes of the November 17 meeting (FRB, 1998b).

The FOMC's decision did not address the swap arrangements with Mexico and Canada. In recent years, the use of the swap line with the Bank of Mexico had sparked most of the controversy within the FOMC on this topic. Some FOMC members and my successor as director of the Division of International Finance, Karen Johnson, subsequently endeavored to dismantle those arrangements, but without success.

The irony is that the swap network was resurrected for use to provide liquidity in connection with the millennium (Y2K) changeover, but was not needed. It was again revived and used in the wake of the attack on the World Trade Center on September 11, 2001. And it was used extensively and with an expanded set of participating countries during the global financial crisis starting in 2008. Portions of the network are again permanent and are available now without limits on the size of possible drawings, though activation still requires mutual consent.

Cooper and Little (2000, p. 102) are correct in their comment on the 1998 FOMC decision and the role of the swap network in facilitating the Federal Reserve's role as international lender of last resort: "World politics

---

[53] Some interest was shown in this proposal, but it was not acted upon.

are not yet as global as world financial crises." In 1998, the FOMC may have been in denial.

5.4.3 The US External Accounts

After a brief surplus in 1991, the US current account moved back into the red. By late 1996, the staff was projecting a deficit of more than 2 percent of GDP. A deficit of that size did not immediately materialize, but the trend was sufficiently disturbing that the staff under Johnson began a fresh, exhaustive look at prospects for the US external position. The primary focus was the sustainability of the US current account position in a projected environment in which US growth was expected (incorrectly) to be stronger than growth in the rest of the world. In addition, trends in US exports and imports appeared still to be affected by the finding of Houthakker and Magee (1969) that the income elasticity of foreign demand for US exports was less than the income elasticity of US demand for imports. The bottom line was that whatever the definition of a sustainable US international investment position in terms of the appetite of the rest of the world for claims on the United States, substantial continuous real dollar depreciation would likely be necessary to maintain that position. The secondary questions were whether markets would bring about the adjustment and whether policy – in particular US fiscal policy – would be a necessary complement to facilitate the adjustment.

The results of this study and related research were presented to the Board of Governors and to the Treasury. The substance made its way into Board and FOMC briefings. But the study was not formally presented and at the moment is not available to the general public.[54]

Johnson recently shared with me two observations about this topic: first, there was the lack of clear thinking from those who demanded that the United States narrow its current account deficit but did not want to see a drop in the dollar. They claimed a change in US fiscal policy magically would pass through to the current account deficit. But we know better. A tighter US fiscal policy works through the dollar via its impact on interest rates and through income just as any shock would. So either the United States goes into recession, the dollar adjusts, or both. If you define successful

---

[54] One paper that was an input to this project was released as an IFDP (Hooper, Johnson, and Marquez, 1998) and later appeared with the same title in *Princeton Study in International Economics* 87 (2000), Princeton, NJ: International Finance Section, Department of Economics, Princeton University. Mann (1999) also drew on her work on this project before she left the staff of the Federal Reserve Board.

adjustment to mean that the United States gets back to full employment, then the dollar is the principal channel.

Second, at most of the discussions at BIS and IMF meetings on the topic of US external adjustment, the representatives of each country wanted the United States to adjust, but they did not want to be the counterpart to that adjustment. The Federal Reserve is the central bank of the nth, or residual, currency in the international monetary system, with even less capacity to influence the adjustment process than it had under the Bretton Woods system; see Johnson (2016) for elaboration.

The project directed by Johnson was not the last such effort at the Federal Reserve Board. William Helkie coordinated a later project in this period. As part of both the Johnson and Helkie projects, the staff devoted greater attention and analysis to the US financial account and associated issues than in earlier work (e.g., Ahearne, Griever, and Warnock, 2000; Warnock and Mason, 2000). In addition, Freund (2000) produced her well-known paper on the experiences of industrial countries with current account adjustments: the point at which reversal often begins (5 percent of GDP), the typical negative impact on growth, and associated real depreciation (10–20 percent).

5.5 External Financial Crises and International Relations

The 1990s saw its share of external financial crises. The Federal Reserve played a role in addressing many of them and in their aftermaths. Moreover, during this decade the Federal Reserve became increasingly involved with countries, their central banks, and institutions outside its traditional G-10 (plus Mexico) circle.

5.5.1 The Mexican Crisis

The North American Free Trade Agreement (NAFTA) with Mexico and Canada was the first order of Mexican business for the Clinton administration. A $6 billion contingency swap facility, equally shared between the Treasury and the Federal Reserve, for the Bank of Mexico was available to activate if the legislation did not pass. It narrowly passed the House of Representatives by 234–200.

Subsequently, the North American Financial Group (NAFG) was established as a consultative body alongside NAFTA, with an associated North American Framework Arrangement (NAFA) involving increased Treasury and Federal Reserve swap lines with Mexico of $3 billion each; a

Canada–Mexico swap line of C$1 billion; and the existing Federal Reserve swap line with the Bank of Canada of $2 billion. Before the NAFA was formally signed on April 26, 1994, Mexican presidential candidate Luis Donaldo Colosio was assassinated on March 23. The Federal Reserve and Treasury immediately agreed to provide a special swap facility, as had been arranged the previous November, for the Mexicans to draw upon to support their markets when they reopened on March 25. The facility was announced but not drawn upon.

Mexico was again running a current account deficit in part because its exchange-rate-based stabilization policy did not allow the peso's crawl to keep up with the widening inflation differential between Mexico and the United States. As in 1976, 1982, and 1988, the issue was whether Mexico's policy regime would hold until after the Mexican presidential election and the expected handover from Carlos Salinas to Ernesto Zedillo on December 1. In connection with the election on August 21, the Federal Reserve coordinated a contingent multilateral support package of $12 billion, half of which was to come from the existing Treasury and Federal Reserve swap arrangements and half was to be provided by other central banks through the BIS. It was understood that if Mexico drew it would be obligated to reexamine its exchange rate policy (FRB, 1994) with the understanding, at least on the US side, that it would lead to an accelerated depreciation of the peso and preferably more aggressive actions to address Mexico's macroeconomic problems.

Mexico got through the election without the need to activate the facility. But pressure mounted again after the FOMC, on November 15, raised the target for the federal funds rate by seventy-five basis points. This was a surprise to the market and to the Bank of Mexico, which chose not to match the increase. Increased pressure on the peso resulted, and a weekend of telephone consultations between Mexican and US authorities, including those at the Federal Reserve, followed. On Sunday night, November 20, Secretary Bentsen delivered the US consensus advice to his Mexican counterpart Pedro Aspe: adjust your exchange rate policy sooner rather than later. The advice was rejected. Three weeks later Summers called me and said, "We were wrong: nothing has happened."

I replied, "Wait and see."

Sure enough, on Tuesday, December 20, as the FOMC was meeting, the Mexican authorities announced that they had moved their intervention band 15 percent but were retaining the rate of crawl of four centavos a day.

The new exchange rate regime did not hold, in part, because it was not supported by any other policy measures or an announcement that Mexico would turn to the IMF for help. The Federal Reserve, in early January, allowed the Bank of Mexico to draw on its swap line after Mexico had agreed to go to the IMF and promised henceforth to announce its reserve holdings at least once a month. However, the run on the peso continued. The Zedillo administration's second finance minister during its first month in office, Guillermo Ortiz, visited the Treasury and Federal Reserve and asked for help.

After considering several alternatives, the Treasury proposed a $20 billion package of loan guarantees for Mexico. Accompanying the proposal, which was reviewed by an interagency group before going to President Clinton on the evening of January 11, was a Federal Reserve staff analysis, at the Treasury's request. It concluded that in a worst-case scenario of knock-on effects to other countries, the Mexican crisis *could* lead to a 2 percent decline in US GDP from the current trajectory.[55]

Clinton accepted the Treasury proposal. For much of the remainder of January, Rubin, Summers, and Greenspan were on Capitol Hill trying to sell the package, which had grown in size to $40 billion. Although congressional leadership had initially endorsed the proposal, the selling job became increasingly tough.

I suggested to Summers that the Treasury might use the ESF as an alternative. He said the Treasury had explored that option, but there were not enough dollars in the ESF. I noted that some of the ESF's holdings of German marks mark and Japanese yen could be warehoused with the Federal Reserve to provide the ESF with more dollars if necessary, as long as the FOMC was willing to expand the warehousing facility (which I certainly could not guarantee). Summers subsequently discussed this approach with Rubin and Greenspan, and this second plan was adopted. It involved a $20 billion swap line for Mexico from the Treasury's ESF, an augmentation of Mexico's $7.5 billion IMF program by $10 billion, and an increased commitment from the BIS for a window-dressing swap arrangement of $10 billion in place of the previously agreed $5 billion.

The second plan was announced on the morning of January 31. In the afternoon, I briefed the FOMC on the plan, its rationale, and the proposed facilitating role for the Federal Reserve (FRB, 1995). In the end, only Larry Lindsey and Tom Melzer dissented from the decision to increase the size

---

[55] Woodward (2000) incorrectly wrote that the analysis used the word *would* instead of *could*. Despite the fact that I had told him that the analysis had used the word *could* (in good central bank speak), Woodward insisted in writing *would* unless I produced the document; I could not do this, because I was then at the Treasury.

of the warehousing facility to $20 billion, but a number of other governors and presidents were unhappy (type B impact). No one could be confident that the plan would work, much less what the consequences for the Federal Reserve would be either way. The plan worked better than anyone expected; by the middle of 1995, Mexico had turned the corner under Zedillo. Indeed, in 2000, Mexico did not experience a financial crisis in its presidential election year for the first time since 1970. Staff in the Division of International Finance also wrote a number of ex post assessments of the Mexican crisis and its experience with a type of exchange-rate-based stabilization policy. Several were written by Steve Kamin, a future Division Director who did yeoman service during the Mexican crisis (Kamin, 1996; Kamin and Rogers, 1996, 1997).

In the wake of the Mexican financial crisis, Federal Reserve representatives participated in two efforts to improve what later became known as the "international financial architecture" (type C impact). A central bank group and, later, the G-10 deputies of finance ministers and central bank governors endeavored to learn the lessons from Mexico's sovereign liquidity crisis. This initiative resulted in a report (G-10, 1996) that laid the initial groundwork for what are now known as collective action clauses; they were not embraced broadly until the early part of this century.

Second, the Federal Reserve worked with the Treasury to design and gain international, and ultimately congressional, approval of the IMF's New Arrangements to Borrow (NAB). This mechanism for permanently adding to the capacity of the IMF to borrow from certain members in addition to their quota subscriptions was endorsed in principal at the Halifax G-7 summit in 1995 but did not become effective until the end of 1998. The NAB was built on the model of the GAB except the group of participating countries was expanded to include many more members, including emerging market and developing countries.

5.5.2 Asian Financial Crises

During the Asian financial crises of 1997–98, Federal Reserve staff, including reserve bank staff, worked with the Treasury on programs for various affected countries, but the Federal Reserve in general had a secondary role. The FOMC discussed the Asian crises at their meetings in the summer and fall of 1997. The principal issue was the implications for the US outlook. In the Greenbook forecast of November 11, 1997, we had real GDP growth in developing countries at 2.4 percent for 1998, down from 5.4 percent in 1997 and bouncing back to 4.3 percent in 1999 (FRB, 1997). A year later, the three figures were 5.1, –1.8, and 1.1 percent, respectively (FRB, 1998a).[56] We got that forecast wrong too. By November 1999, the data and staff forecast were 5.1, –0.3, and 4.4 percent, respectively (FRB, 1999a). The downturn was not quite as deep as we once thought it might be, and the bounce back was substantial.[57]

The Federal Reserve role changed at the end of the year, when the initial program for Korea failed to arrest its crisis. Korea had run down its foreign exchange reserves through investments in Korean banks that had lost access to dollar financing and through defending its exchange rate before the crisis broke in November and Korea called in the IMF in December. But financing from the IMF was coming in the front door and was being paid out to foreign banks through the back door via Korean banks. This situation was not sustainable.

Treasury Assistant Secretary Tim Geithner and I proposed to Rubin and Greenspan that we seek international cooperation on a standstill and roll-over of payments due from Korean banks to United States and other foreign banks and to a subsequent reprofiling of those claims. Rubin and Greenspan agreed it was worth a try (type B impact). The G-7 ministers and governors launched the plan on December 24, 1997 (G-7, 1997). The announcement concludes: "A successful program will require a continued sustained commitment to reform by the Korean authorities, appropriate financial support from the official sector as outlined above conditioned on the strong policies necessary to restore confidence, and a successful effort by the Korean authorities to secure longer term financing from private creditors and the international capital markets." For about six weeks, I chaired a daily international conference call among central banks and the IMF to monitor progress in getting banks to agree to the standstill and, later, compliance with their commitments.

The official international financial community, with the participation of the Federal Reserve, responded to the Asian financial crises with an

---

[56] One explanation for our error was that the crisis countries refused to accept in the background material for the IMF programs forecasts of negative growth. This was true for Thailand and Korea in particular. Another explanation is that we forgot the devaluations can be contractionary, in particular when they are associated with crises in the country's financial system. Even if exports expand and imports contract, domestic investment tends to collapse.

[57] Steve Kamin, who by then had principal staff responsibility for the forecasts for emerging market and developing countries, though ultimate responsibility was with the Division Director, wrote a nice paper (Kamin and Marc Klau, 1998) examining the issue of contractionary devaluations that concluded that they were not generally contractionary, at least in the long run.

additional set of reports on reforming the international financial architecture (BIS, 1998). The reports covered enhancing transparency and accountability, strengthening financial systems, and managing international financial crises. The Federal Reserve also was a driving force behind the establishment in 1999 of the Data Template on International Reserves and Foreign Currency Liquidity. It was designed to ensure that countries accurately and regularly report their international reserves to the market and their own citizens, as Mexico and later Thailand and Korea had not done.

5.5.3 Engagement with Other Countries and Regions

In October 1989 Greenspan, at the request of the White House, went to Moscow to meet with Leonid Abalkin (charged by Mikhail Gorbachev to try to reform the Soviet economy) and his colleagues.[58] Our advice was to develop a capital market to support increased domestic investment. But it was too late for reform to save the Soviet economy and system. A month later the Berlin Wall came down. Two years later the Soviet Union was dissolved.

The collapse of the Soviet Union led to an extensive involvement of the Federal Reserve Bank of New York with the reform government of Boris Yeltsin that focused on the Russian banking system. It also led to an international cooperative effort involving many people in the Federal Reserve System to help Russia and the post-Soviet states establish credible and effective central banks in the wake of the hyperinflation that accompanied the collapse of the ruble area. Nathan Sheets, a future director of the Division of International Finance, started his career at the Federal Reserve covering Russia and the transition economies formerly in the orbit of the Soviet Union. Among his many papers was one that examined the experience of countries in transition with capital flight (Sheets, 1995). A second examined the export performance of the transition economies (Sheets and Boata, 1996).

The fall of the Berlin Wall and the subsequent unification of Germany led to several important and penetrating IFDPs by Alexander and Gagnon (1990); Adams, Alexander, and Gagnon (1992); and Gagnon, Masson, and McKibbin (1996). These papers demonstrate that German monetary and

---

[58] I accompanied Greenspan along with Robert Zoellick, who was then at the State Department as economic counselor and undersecretary for economic and agricultural affairs. See Greenspan (2007, chapter 6) for an account of this visit.

political unification was an asymmetrical demand shock that put strains on fixed exchange rates within the ERM of the EMS.

Federal Reserve Board economists also were among the few US-based economists who took seriously the prospect of a European Economic and Monetary Union (EMU) and wrote a number of papers on its implications and prospects. Bryson (1993) questions the limits on the flexibility of fiscal policies suggested in the Delors Report. Johnson (1994) looks at the implications of EMU for the dollar and concludes that its effect on the international role of the dollar would be benign as long as the US economic policy in general and the Federal Reserve policy in particular appropriately discharged their mandates. Edison and Kole (1994) look at the lessons from the 1992 to 1993 ERM crises for the path toward the establishment of the euro.

The Federal Reserve's extensive relations with China started in the spring of 1980, when a 25-person delegation from China representing the People's Bank, Bank of China, and Agricultural Bank of China visited the Federal Reserve Board as well as Federal Reserve banks and offices in New York, Chicago, Houston, and San Francisco. A few months later, Volcker led a six-person group, on a return visit. Soon every member of the Board and most presidents of reserve banks had visited China and hosted delegations from the People's Bank of China. In 1994 Greenspan led an interagency visit to the People's Bank of China, then headed by Zhu Rongji, who was later premier. The Summers Treasury and Clinton White House enlisted Greenspan's support for granting China permanent normal trade relations in the context of China's joining the World Trade Organization.

On August 17, 1998, a year after the outbreak of the Asian financial crises, Russia announced that it would float the ruble and suspend payments on certain debts. Financial markets reacted adversely; many market participants had thought Russia was too nuclear to fail. Financial conditions tightened further over the next couple of weeks. The resultant deteriorating global economic and financial outlook led Greenspan, after consultation with colleagues at the Federal Reserve Bank of Kansas City symposium in Jackson Hole on August 27–29, to declare in a subsequent speech at Berkeley on September 4:

[I]t is just not credible that the United States can remain an oasis of prosperity unaffected by a world that is experiencing greatly increased stress. Developments overseas have contributed to holding down prices and aggregate demand in the United States in the face of strong domestic spending. As dislocations abroad mount, feeding back on our financial markets, restraint is likely to intensify. In the spring and early summer, the Federal Open Market Committee was concerned that a rise in inflation was the primary threat to the continued expansion of the economy. By the time of the Committee's August meeting, the risks had become balanced, and the Committee will need to consider carefully the potential ramifications of ongoing developments since that meeting. (Greenspan, 1998)

The market got the signal, but it was not enough to relieve market tensions, which were intensified by the problems of Long-Term Capital Management. The FOMC subsequently reduced the federal funds rate by seventy-five basis points. The United States and world economies were being strongly affected by the slowdown in global growth (type C impact).[59]

Symbolic of the Federal Reserve's expanding engagement with the rest of the world was the decision to take up the Federal Reserve's seats on the Board of the Bank for International Settlements in 1994.[60] Once on the BIS Board, the Federal Reserve, represented by Greenspan and McDonough, successfully pressed to expand BIS membership beyond European and a few other central banks.

The Federal Reserve also was a key participant in the creation of the Financial Stability Forum (FSF) in 1999, which became the expanded Financial Stability Board in 2009, to monitor international financial developments, coordinate regulatory activities, and broaden existing oversight to include finance ministries. Roger Ferguson was the second FSF chair, from 2003 to 2006. Federal Reserve officials from both the Federal Reserve Bank of New York and Board of Governors had participated in the BIS Euro-currency Standing Committee since its establishment in 1971. It was the principal international forum for discussing what are now known as "macro-prudential" issues. In 1999 the committee was renamed the Committee on the Global Financial System. Donald L. Kohn served as its chair from 2006 until his retirement in 2010, at which point William C. Dudley, president of the Federal Reserve Bank of New York, succeeded him.[61]

By the turn of the twentieth century, the Federal Reserve had become fully engaged with the world. International concerns were too numerous to be managed primarily by the president and staff at the Federal Reserve

---

[59] In the fourth quarter of 1998, the US export-weighted index of global growth over the previous four quarters had reached its lowest level since the first quarter of 1983.

[60] See Siegman (1994) for a history of the Federal Reserve's involvement with the BIS up until September 1994.

[61] The Federal Reserve was a charter member of the Basel Committee on Banking Supervision and supplied two of its chairs Jerry Corrigan (1991–93) and Bill McDonough (1998–2002). The Federal Reserve was also a driving force behind what is now the BIS Committee on Payment and Settlement Systems, supplying an early chair, Wayne Angell (1988–90), and more recently Tim Geithner (2005–09) and Bill Dudley (2009–12).

Bank of New York, one governor (Dewey Daane in the late 1960s and early 1970s and after him Henry Wallich) of the Federal Reserve Board, and occasionally the chairman. All governors had acquired important international responsibilities, and reserve bank presidents were much more engaged internationally as well.

5.6 Concluding Observations

By 2000, the principal changes in the four areas addressed in this chapter were that the issues were now spread on a global canvas and the Federal Reserve had become the principal artist. The Federal Reserve was deeply enmeshed in an economically and in particular financially globalized world.

I have identified in this chapter eighteen instances in which either (A) developments in the global economy or policies of other countries substantially affected Federal Reserve decision making or activities; (B) Federal Reserve decisions were undertaken primarily to support other countries but with commensurate benefits for the United States; or (C) occasions of decisions in win-win cooperation.

The first category comprises

- 1973 oil shocks;
- 1978 dollar rescue package;
- 1979 adoption of the new operating procedures;
- February 1986 discount rate decision;
- September 1987 tightening to support the dollar;
- December 1987 fiscal package and related G-7 announcement; and
- 1989–90 tensions over intervention and Federal Reserve monetary policy.

In the second category are

- Swap drawings by Italy, Mexico, and the United Kingdom in 1974–76;
- Monetary policy easing in 1982;
- The Third World debt crises of the 1980s;
- Support for the Louvre Accord;
- The 1994–95 Mexican crisis;
- Organization of the Korean standstill in 1997–98; and
- The 1998 and 2000 intervention purchases of yen and euro.

The final category includes

- 1983 Jurgensen report on exchange market intervention;
- July 1994 Greenspan statement on the dollar;

- Post-Mexico 1994–95 cooperation on international financial architecture issues; and
- September-October 1998 FOMC easing.

Some may disagree with my identifications, classifications, and interpretations. Others may add to this list, which is not exhaustive. My view is that these examples are sufficient to support my thesis that the Federal Reserve by 2000 had emerged as the closest the world has to a global central bank. No other central bank was as engaged with the global economy and financial system.

Long before 2000, the Federal Reserve had implicitly embraced the view that inflation should be the central bank's primary objective and is essentially a homegrown product. As I advocated in Truman (2003a), the Federal Reserve in 2012 formally adopted a long-term inflation goal. Today the only question is whether one could have too little as well as too much inflation.

By the mid-1990s, the issue of Federal Reserve involvement in US foreign exchange operations had been resolved through a combination of Federal Reserve influence on US intervention policy, the emerging consensus among most advanced countries on the limited role that such operations should have in macroeconomic policy management, and an end for most advanced countries of their fear of floating.

By 2000 the associated issues of the US current account position and the sustainability of the US international debt position had largely receded from receiving high-level policy attention within the Federal Reserve. However, those concerns reemerged after 2000.

With the growing globalization of financial markets, the international role of the US dollar in 2000 was more significant than it had been within the narrow confines of official currency arrangements that characterized the Bretton Woods period. Other currencies, including the nascent euro, the waning yen, and the yet to be internationalized Chinese renminbi, were acquiring roles in the international financial system alongside a large number currencies of smaller economies. But the international financial system had become so large and integrated that even as the US dollar's share of international financial flows and stocks declined somewhat, the dollar's absolute importance, and with it the responsibilities of the Federal Reserve, expanded.

The dollar's increased international role meant that the United States and the Federal Reserve had even less scope to employ exchange rate policy directly or indirectly to address actual or potential concerns about the sustainability of the US external accounts. The US dollar's role may be privileged but, as illustrated by US preference for a passive strong dollar policy, the privilege is constrained.

By the end of the 1990s, the Federal Reserve could run from global economic and financial developments but it could not hide from them. The Federal Reserve had become heavily involved in financial crises of a growing number of countries around the world. This expansion mirrored the emergence in the twenty-first century of the Federal Reserve as the closest the world has to a global central bank.

My view of Federal Reserve involvement in the external financial crises during the last third of the twentieth century, as well as now, is that central banks should do what they think is right in terms of the overall common good and deal with the consequences in ex post assessments. You do not keep the fire trucks in the firehouse when the city is burning even if the risk is that you will save the undeserving and lose firefighters, trucks, and firehouses as an indirect consequence of cooperation internally or externally.

The Federal Reserve should interpret the global common good broadly. Because of the increase in international economic and financial integration, its existing mandate can accommodate such an interpretation. At the conclusion of the sixth meeting of the Strategic and Economic Dialogue on July 11, 2014, Chair Yellen agreed to include in the US–China Joint Fact Sheet (US Treasury, 2014): "The Federal Reserve is sensitive to the effects of its policies on the international financial system. A key goal of the Federal Reserve is to maintain financial stability both domestically and internationally." This statement of the Federal Reserve's posture does not mean it will put the interests of one or more other countries before the interests of US economic and financial stability. One practical reason is that the interests of countries will not always coincide; what is best for India may not be best for Canada or Turkey. But the Federal Reserve takes a broad view of its responsibilities because it has a shared goal and responsibility for economic and financial stability domestically and internationally. Nevertheless, the Federal Reserve cannot solve all US domestic economic and financial problems. Likewise, it cannot do so for the rest of the world.

In my oral presentation of the Foreign Exchange Task Force report to the FOMC in March 1990 (FRB, 1990b), I said, "I believe that the Federal Reserve's cooperation with the Treasury in exchange rate matters, on the whole, has served the System's and the nation's interest." That was my view with respect to US intervention activity at the time, and it is my view today on the broad range of Federal Reserve international activities that involve its working with the US Treasury and other institutions around the world.

The nation is served, and the interest of the Federal Reserve is served, by economic and financial policies of high quality. The Federal Reserve is right to employ its intellectual and other resources to contribute to better US and global economic and financial policies even when those policies do not lie narrowly within the Federal Reserve's mandate. The Federal Reserve is independent within the government. It enjoys a degree of insulation from short-run political pressures, and it benefits from a stable institutional structure. Along with these protections, the Federal Reserve has commensurate responsibility for the full range of economic and financial outcomes produced by governmental processes, domestically and internationally.

References

Adams, Donald B. and Dale W. Henderson, 1983. "Definition and Measurement of Exchange Market Intervention." Staff Studies 126. Washington, DC: Board of Governors of the Federal Reserve System.

Adams, Gwyn, Lewis S. Alexander, and Joseph E. Gagnon, 1992. "German Unification and the European Monetary System: A Quantitative Analysis." International Finance Discussion Papers 421 (January). Washington, DC: Board of Governors of the Federal Reserve System.

Ahearne, Alan G., William L. Griever, and Francis E. Warnock, 2000. "Information Costs and Home Bias: An Analysis of US Holdings of Foreign Equities." International Finance Discussion Papers 691 (December, latest version May 2002). Washington, DC: Board of Governors of the Federal Reserve System.

Alexander, Lewis S. and Joseph E. Gagnon, 1990. "The Global Economic Consequences of German Unification." International Finance Discussion Papers 379 (April). Washington, DC: Board of Governors of the Federal Reserve System.

Bayoumi, Tamim and Trung Bui, 2010. "Deconstructing the International Business Cycle: Why Does A US Sneeze Give the Rest of the World A Cold?" IMF Discussion Paper WP/10/239 (July). Washington, DC: International Monetary Fund.

2012. "Global Bonding: Do U.S. Bond and Equity Spillovers Dominate Global Financial Markets?" IMF Discussion Paper WP/12/298 (December). Washington, DC: International Monetary Fund.

Bayoumi, Tamim and Andrew Swiston, 2007. "Foreign Entanglements: Estimating the Source and Size of Spillovers Across Industrial Countries." IMF Discussion Paper WP/07/182 (July). Washington, DC: International Monetary Fund.

Berner, Richard, Peter B. Clark, Jared Enzler, and Barbara Lowrey, 1974. "International Sources of Domestic Inflation." International Finance Discussion Papers 55 (November). Washington, DC: Board of Governors of the Federal Reserve System.

Berner, Richard, Peter B. Clark, Howard Howe, Sung Kwack, and Guy Stevens, 1975. "Simultaneous Determination of the US Balance of Payments and Exchange Rates: An Exploratory Report." International Finance Discussion Papers 59 (February). Washington, DC: Board of Governors of the Federal Reserve System.

1977. "A Multi-Country Model of the International Influences on the US Economy: Preliminary Results." International Finance Discussion Papers 115 (December). Washington, DC: Board of Governors of the Federal Reserve System.

BIS (Bank for International Settlements), 1998. *Reports on the International Financial Architecture: Reports of Working Groups*. Basel. Available at www.bis.org/publ/othp01.htm (accessed on June 30, 2014).

Bordo, Michael D. and Barry Eichengreen, 2013. "Bretton Woods and the Great Inflation" in Michael D. Bordo and Athanasios Orphanides (eds.), *The Great Inflation: The Rebirth of Modern Central Banking*. Chicago, IL: University of Chicago Press.

Bordo, Michael D., Owen F. Humpage, and Anna J. Schwartz, 2015. *Strained Relations: US Monetary Policy and Foreign-Exchange Operations in the Twentieth Century*. Chicago, IL: University of Chicago Press.

Boughton, James M., 2001. *Silent Revolution: The International Monetary Fund 1979–1989*. Washington, DC: International Monetary Fund.

———— 2012. *Tearing Down Walls: The International Monetary Fund 1990–1999*. Washington, DC: International Monetary Fund.

Brayton, Flint, Andrew Levin, Ralph Tryon, and John C. Williams, 1997. *The Evolution of Macro Models at the Federal Reserve Board*. Washington, DC: Board of Governors of the Federal Reserve System. Available at www.federalreserve.gov/PUBS/FEDS/1997/199729/199729pap.pdf (accessed on June 6, 2014).

Bryant, Ralph C., 2016. Oral history. Washington: Board of Governors of the Federal Reserve System. Available when released at www.federalreserve.gov

Bryant, Ralph C., Dale W. Henderson, Gerald Holtham, Peter Hooper, and Steven A. Symansky, eds., 1988. *Empirical Macroeconomics for Interdependent Economies* (two volumes). Washington, DC: Brookings Institution.

Bryant, Ralph C., Gerald Holtham, and Peter Hooper, eds., 1988. *External Deficits and the Dollar: The Pit and the Pendulum*. Washington, DC: Brookings Institution.

Bryant, Ralph C., Peter Hooper, and Catherine L. Mann, 1993. *Evaluating Policy Regimes: New Research in Empirical Macroeconomics*. Washington, DC: Brookings Institution.

Bryson, Jay H., 1993. "Macroeconomic Stabilization through Monetary and Fiscal Policy Coordination: Implications for European Monetary Union." International Finance Discussion Papers 453 (September). Washington, DC: Board of Governors of the Federal Reserve System.

Burns, Arthur F., 1978. *The Anguish of Central Banking*. Washington, DC: Per Jacobsson Foundation.

———— 1985. "Need for Order in International Finance" in Arthur F. Burns (ed.), *Reflections of an Economic Policy Maker: Speeches and Congressional Statements: 1969–1978*. Washington, DC: American Enterprise Institute for Public Policy Research.

Clark, Peter B., 1974. "The Effects of Recent Exchange Rates Changes on the US Trade Balance." International Finance Discussion Papers 52 (September). Washington, DC: Board of Governors of the Federal Reserve System.

Cline, William C., 1983. "International Debt and the Stability of the World Economy." Policy Analyses in International Economics 4 (September). Washington, DC: Peterson Institute for International Economics.

Cline, William R., 1995. *International Debt Reexamined*. Washington, DC: Peterson Institute for International Economics.

Cooper, Richard N. and Jane Sneddon Little, 2000. "US Monetary Policy in an Integrating World: 1960–2000" in Richard W. Kopcke and Lynn Elaine Browne (eds.), *The Evolution of Monetary Policy and the Federal Reserve System Over the Past Thirty Years: A Conference in Honor of Frank E. Morris*, Conference Series 45. Boston, MA: Federal Reserve Bank of Boston.

Cross, Sam Y., 1990. "Treasury and Federal Reserve Foreign Exchange Operations: February–April 1990." *Federal Reserve Bank of New York Quarterly Review* 15: 66–72.

Cross, Sam Y. and Edwin M. Truman, 1990. *Task Force on System Foreign Currency Operations*. Memorandum to the Federal Open Market Committee (March 9). Available from the FOMC Secretariat, Board of Governors of the Federal Reserve System. Washington, DC.

Danker, Deborah and Peter Hooper, 1990. "International Financial Markets and the US External Imbalance." International Finance Discussion Papers 372 (January). Washington, DC: Board of Governors of the Federal Reserve System.

Dooley, Michael P., William Helkie, Ralph Tryon, and John Underwood, 1983. "An Analysis of External Debt Positions of Eight Developing Countries Through 1990." International Finance Discussion Papers 227 (August). Washington, DC: Board of Governors of the Federal Reserve System.

Dooley, Michael P. and Jeffrey R. Shafer, 1976. "Analysis of Short-Run Exchange Rate Behavior March 1973 to September 1975." International Finance Discussion Papers 76 (February). Washington, DC: Board of Governors of the Federal Reserve System.

Edison, Hali J., 1988a. Evaluation of IF's Exchange Rate Forecasts 1979–1987. Memorandum to the Exchange Rate Forecasting Group (April 19). Photocopy.

  1988b. Special Board Briefing on Exchange Rate Forecasting (May 23). Photocopy.

  1990. "Foreign Currency Operations: An Annotated Bibliography." International Finance Discussion Papers 380 (May). Washington, DC: Board of Governors of the Federal Reserve System.

Edison, Hali J. and Linda S. Kole, 1994. "European Monetary Arrangements: Implications for the Dollar, Exchange Rate Variability, and Credibility." International Finance Discussion Papers 468 (May). Washington, DC: Board of Governors of the Federal Reserve System.

Eichengreen, Barry, 2013. "Does the Federal Reserve Care about the Rest of the World?" *Journal of Economic Perspectives* 27: 87–104.

Fisher, Peter R., 1994. "Treasury and Federal Reserve Foreign Exchange Operations: July to September 1994." *FRBNY Quarterly Review* 19: 1–10.

Fisher, Peter, Donald Kohn, and Edwin Truman, 1996. *Issues Related to Review of System's Swap Arrangements* (March 14). Washington, DC: Board of Governors, FOMC Service Center. Photocopy.

Fisher, Peter and Edwin Truman, 1998. *Update on the Federal Reserve Swap Network* (September 28). Washington, DC: Board of Governors, FOMC Service Center. Photocopy.

FRB (Board of Governors of the Federal Reserve System), 1971. *Meeting of the Federal Open Market Committee: Minutes of Actions* (March 9). Washington, DC. Available at www.federalreserve.gov/monetarypolicy/files/fomcmoa19710309.pdf (accessed on June 9, 2014).

1973. *Greenbook* (December). Washington, DC. Available at www.federalreserve
.gov/monetarypolicy/files/FOMC19731218 19731212.pdf (accessed on June 9,
2014).

1976a. *Record of Policy Actions of the Federal Open Market Committee: December
20–21, 1996.* Washington, DC. Available at www.federalreserve.gov/monetarypolicy/
files/fomcropa19761221.pdf (accessed on June 11, 2014).

1976b. *Transcript: December 20–21, 1996.* Washington, DC. Available at www
.federalreserve.gov/monetarypolicy/files/FOMC19761221meeting.pdf (accessed
on June 11, 2014).

1980. *FOMC Presentation: International Financial Trends.* Washington, DC. Available
at   www.federalreserve.gov/monetarypolicy/files/FOMC19800205material.pdf
(accessed on June 13, 2014).

1981. *New Monetary Control Procedures.* Federal Reserve Staff Study Volumes I and
II. Washington, DC.

1982. *Presentation Materials, October 5, 1982.* Washington, DC. Available at www
.federalreserve.gov/monetarypolicy/files/FOMC19821005material.pdf (accessed
on July 4, 2014).

1983a. *Presentation Materials, May 24, 1983.* Washington, DC. Available at www
.federalreserve.gov/monetarypolicy/files/FOMC19830524material.pdf (accessed
on August 12, 2014).

1983b. *Record of Policy Actions, May 24, 1983.* Washington, DC. Available at www
.federalreserve.gov/monetarypolicy/files/fomcropa19830524.pdf (accessed on June
28, 2014).

1984. *The US External Position, May 21, 1984.* Washington, DC. Available at www
.federalreserve.gov/monetarypolicy/files/FOMC19840522material.pdf (accessed
on June 24, 2014).

1985a. *Notes for FOMC Meeting, October 1, 1985.* Washington, DC. Available at www
.federalreserve.gov/monetarypolicy/files/FOMC19851001material.pdf (accessed
on June 24, 2014).

1985b. *Presentation Materials, November 4–5, 1985.* Washington, DC. Available at
www.federalreserve.gov/monetarypolicy/files/FOMC19851217material.pdf
(accessed on July 27, 2014).

1985c. *Transcript of Conference Call, January 18, 1985.* Washington, DC. Available at
www.federalreserve.gov/monetarypolicy/files/FOMC19850118confcall.pdf
(accessed on June 24, 2014).

1987. *Presentation Materials: February 10–11, 1987.* Washington, DC. Available at
www.federalreserve.gov/monetarypolicy/files/FOMC19870211material.pdf
(accessed on June 25, 2014).

1988. *Presentation Materials: February 9–10, 1988.* Washington, DC. Available at
www.federalreserve.gov/monetarypolicy/files/FOMC19880210material.pdf
(accessed on June 25, 2014).

1990a. *Presentation Materials: August 21, 1990.* Washington, DC. Available at www
.federalreserve.gov/monetarypolicy/files/FOMC19900821material.pdf (accessed
on June 24, 2014).

1990b. *Presentation Materials: March 27, 1990.* Washington, DC. Available at www
.federalreserve.gov/monetarypolicy/files/FOMC19900327material.pdf (accessed
on June 26, 2014).

1990c. *Record of Policy Actions: March 27, 1990.* Washington, DC. Available at www .federalreserve.gov/monetarypolicy/files/fomcropa19900327.pdf (accessed on June 25, 2014).

1990d. *Transcript: March 27, 1990.* Washington, DC. Available at www.federal reserve.gov/monetarypolicy/files/FOMC19900327meeting.pdf (accessed on June 25, 2014).

1992a. *Minutes, July 5–6, 1992.* Washington, DC. Available at www.federalreserve .gov/fomc/MINUTES/1994/19940706min.htm (accessed on June 29, 2014).

1992b. *Presentation Materials, March 31, 1992.* Washington, DC. Available at www.federalreserve.gov/monetarypolicy/files/FOMC19920331material.pdf (accessed on June 29, 2014).

1994. *Transcript: Conference Call July 20, 1994.* Washington, DC. Available at www .federalreserve.gov/monetarypolicy/files/FOMC19940720confcall.pdf (accessed on June 30, 2014).

1996a. *Transcript: August 20, 1996.* Washington, DC. Available at www.federal reserve.gov/monetarypolicy/files/FOMC19960820meeting.pdf (accessed on June 30, 2014).

1996b. *Transcript: July 2–3, 1996.* Washington, DC. Available at www.federal reserve.gov/monetarypolicy/files/FOMC19960703meeting.pdf (accessed on June 30, 2014).

1997. *Greenbook* (November). Available at www.federalreserve.gov/monetary policy/files/fomc19971216gbpt119971211.pdf (accessed on August 5, 2014).

1998a. *Greenbook* (November). Available at www.federalreserve.gov/monetary policy/files/fomc19981117gbpt119981112.pdf (accessed on August 5, 2014).

1998b. *Minutes: November 17, 1998.* Washington, DC. Available at www.federal reserve.gov/fomc/minutes/19981117.htm (accessed on June 30, 2014).

1999a. *Greenbook* (November). Available at www.federalreserve.gov/monetary policy/files/fomc19991116gbpt119991110.pdf (accessed on August 5, 2014).

1999b. *Guide to the Interagency Country Exposure Review Committee Process.* Washington, DC. Available at www.federalreserve.gov/boarddocs/SRLETTERS/ 1999/sr9935a1.pdf (accessed on June 13, 2014).

2000. *Transcript: October 3.* Washington, DC. Available at www.federalreserve.gov/ monetarypolicy/files/FOMC20001003meeting.pdf (accessed on October 28, 2014).

Freund, Caroline L., 2000. "Current Account Adjustment in Industrial Countries." International Finance Discussion Papers 692 (December). Washington, DC: Board of Governors of the Federal Reserve System.

G-6 (Group of Six), 1987. *Statement of the G6 Finance Ministers and Central Bank Governors* (Louvre Accord). Paris. Available at www.g8.utoronto.ca/finance/ fm870222.htm (accessed on July 17, 2014).

G-7 (Group of Seven), 1997. *G-7 Statement on the Korean Situation* (December 24). Available at www.g8.utoronto.ca/finance/fin_dec2497.htm (accessed on July 24, 2014).

G-10 (Group of Ten), 1996. *The Resolution of Sovereign Liquidity Crises: A Report to the Ministers and Governors Prepared under the Auspices of the Deputies.* Basel: Bank for International Settlements.

Gagnon, Joseph E., Paul Masson, and Warwick J. McKibbin, 1996. "German Unification: What Have We Learned from Multi-Country Models?" International Finance

Discussion Papers 547 (April). Washington, DC: Board of Governors of the Federal Reserve System.

Gray, Jo Anna and Jeffrey R. Shafer, 1981. "The Implications of a Floating Exchange Rate Regime: A Survey of Federal Reserve System Papers." International Finance Discussion Papers 173 (January). Washington, DC: Board of Governors of the Federal Reserve System.

Greene, Margaret L., 1984a. "US Experience with Exchange Market Intervention: January–March 1975." Staff Studies 127. Washington, DC: Board of Governors of the Federal Reserve System.

1984b. "US Experience with Exchange Market Intervention: October 1980–September 1981." Staff Studies 129. Washington, DC: Board of Governors of the Federal Reserve System.

1984c. "US Experience with Exchange Market Intervention: September 1977–December 1979." Staff Studies 128. Washington, DC: Board of Governors of the Federal Reserve System.

Greenspan, Alan, 1998. *Is There a New Economy?* Remarks at the Haas Annual Business Faculty Research Dialogue (September 4). Berkeley, CA. Available at http://fraser.stlouisfed.org/docs/historical/greenspan/Greenspan_19980904.pdf (accessed on June 26, 2014).

2007. *The Age of Turbulence: Adventures in a New World.* New York, NY: Penguin Press.

Helkie, William L. and Peter Hooper, 1987. "The US External Deficit in the 1980's: An Empirical Analysis." International Finance Discussion Papers 304 (February). Washington, DC: Board of Governors of the Federal Reserve System.

1989. "US External Adjustment: Progress and Prospects." International Finance Discussion Papers 345 (March). Washington, DC: Board of Governors of the Federal Reserve System.

Henderson, Dale W. and Stephanie Sampson, 1983. "Intervention in Foreign Exchange Markets: A Summary of Ten Staff Studies." *Federal Reserve Bulletin* 69: 830–36.

Henning, C. Randall, 1994. *Currencies and Politics in the United States, Germany, and Japan.* Washington, DC: Peterson Institute for International Economics.

Henning, C. Randall, 1999. "The Exchange Stabilization Fund: Slush Money or War Chest?" Policy Analyses in International Economics No. 57. Washington, DC: Peterson Institute for International Economics.

Hooper, Peter, Karen Johnson, Donald L. Kohn, David E. Lindsey, Richard D. Porter, and Ralph W. Tyron, eds., 1990. *Monetary Aggregates and Financial Sector Behavior in Interdependent Economies.* Washington, DC: Board of Governors of the Federal Reserve System.

Hooper, Peter, Karen Johnson, and Jaime Marquez, 1998. "Trade Elasticities for G-7 Countries." International Finance Discussion Papers 609 (April). Washington, DC: Board of Governors of the Federal Reserve System.

Hooper, Peter and Catherine L. Mann, 1987. "The US External Deficit: Its Causes and Persistence." International Finance Discussion Papers 316 (November). Washington, DC: Board of Governors of the Federal Reserve System.

Hooper, Peter, Karen Johnson, and Jaime Marquez, 1998. "Trade Elasticities for G-7 Countries." International Finance Discussion Papers 609 (April). Washington, DC: Board of Governors of the Federal Reserve System.

Hooper, Peter and John Morton, 1978a. "Index of the Weighted-Average Exchange Value of the US Dollar: Revision." *Federal Reserve Bulletin* 64: 700.

1978b. "Summary Measures of the Dollar's Foreign Exchange Value." *Federal Reserve Bulletin* 64: 783–89.

1980. "Fluctuations in the Dollar: A Model of Nominal and Real Exchange Rate Determination." International Finance Discussion Papers 169 (October). Washington, DC: Board of Governors of the Federal Reserve System.

Houthakker, Hendrik S. and Stephen P. Magee, 1969. "Income and Price Elasticities in World Trade." *Review of Economics and Statistics* 51: 111–25.

Howard, David H., 1989. "The United States as a Heavily Indebted Country." International Finance Discussion Papers 353 (May). Washington, DC: Board of Governors of the Federal Reserve System.

IMF (International Monetary Fund), 2014. *The Fund's Lending Framework and Sovereign Debt – Preliminary Considerations* (May). Washington, DC.

Isard, Peter, 1977. "The Process of Exchange Rate Determination: A Survey of Popular Views and Recent Models." International Finance Discussion Papers 101 (September). Washington, DC: Board of Governors of the Federal Reserve System.

Johnson, Karen H., 1994. "International Dimension of European Monetary Union: Implications for the Dollar." International Finance Discussion Papers 469 (May). Washington, DC: Board of Governors of the Federal Reserve System.

2016. Oral history. Washington: Board of Governors of the Federal Reserve System. Available when released at www.federalreserve.gov

Junz, Helen B., 1973. "Balance of Payments Aims and Structures in the 1970s." International Finance Discussion Papers 38 (December). Washington, DC: Board of Governors of the Federal Reserve System.

Jurgensen, Philippe, 1983. *Report of the Working Group on Exchange Market Intervention*. Washington, DC: US Department of the Treasury (March). Photocopy.

Kamin, Steven B., 1996. "Real Exchange Rates and Inflation in Exchange-Rate Based Stabilizations: An Empirical Examination." International Finance Discussion Papers 554 (June). Washington, DC: Board of Governors of the Federal Reserve System.

Kamin, Steven B. and John H. Rogers, 1996. "Monetary Policy in the End-Game to Exchange-Rate Based Stabilizations: The Case of Mexico." International Finance Discussion Papers 540 (February). Washington, DC: Board of Governors of the Federal Reserve System.

1997. "Output and the Real Exchange Rates in Developing Countries: An Application to Mexico." International Finance Discussion Papers 580 (May). Washington, DC: Board of Governors of the Federal Reserve System.

Katz, Samuel I., 1973. "'Imported Inflation' and the Balance of Payments." International Finance Discussion Papers 115 (December). Washington, DC: Board of Governors of the Federal Reserve System.

Kwack, Sung Y., 1973. "The Effect of Foreign Inflation on Domestic Prices and the Relative Price Advantage of Exchange Rate Changes." International Finance Discussion Papers 35 (November). Washington, DC: Board of Governors of the Federal Reserve System.

Lane, Philip R. and Gian Maria Milesi-Ferretti, 2007. "The External Wealth of Nations Mark II: Revised and Extended Estimates of Foreign Assets and Liabilities, 1970–2004." *Journal of International Economics* 73: 223–50.

Leahy, Michael P., 1998. "New Summary Measures of the Foreign Exchange Value of the Dollar." *Federal Reserve Bulletin* 84: 811–18.

Loretan, Mico, 2005. "Indexes of the Foreign Exchange Value of the Dollar." *Federal Reserve Bulletin* 91: 1–8.

Lubitz, Raymond, 1978. "The Italian Economic Crises of the 1970s." International Finance Discussion Papers 120 (June). Washington, DC: Board of Governors of the Federal Reserve System.

Mann, Catherine L., 1999. *Is the US Trade Deficit Sustainable?* Washington, DC: Peterson Institute for International Economics.

Meltzer, Allan H., 2009. *A History of the Federal Reserve. Volume 2, Book 2, 1970–1986.* Chicago, IL: University of Chicago Press.

2013. "Comment on Bordo and Eichengreen" in Michael D. Bordo and Athanasios Orphanides (eds.), *The Great Inflation: The Rebirth of Modern Central Banking,* Chicago, IL: University of Chicago Press.

Meese, Richard and Kenneth Rogoff, 1981. "Empirical Exchange Rate Models of the Seventies: Are Any Fit to Survive?" International Finance Discussion Papers 184 (June). Washington, DC: Board of Governors of the Federal Reserve System.

1982. "The Out-of-Sample Failure of Exchange Rate Models: Sampling Error or Misspecification?" International Finance Discussion Papers 204 (March). Washington, DC: Board of Governors of the Federal Reserve System.

1983. "Empirical Exchange Rate Models of the Seventies: Do They Fit Out-of-Sample?" *Journal of International Economics* 14: 3–24.

Pardee, Scott E., 1981. *Notes for FOMC Meeting, May 18, 1981.* Washington, DC: Board of Governors of the Federal Reserve System. Available at www.federalreserve.gov/monetarypolicy/files/FOMC19810331material.pdf (accessed on June 24, 2014).

Pauls, B. Dianne, 1987. "Measuring the Foreign Exchange Value of the Dollar." *Federal Reserve Bulletin* 73: 411–22.

1990. "U.S. Exchange Rate Policy: Bretton Woods to Present." *Federal Reserve Bulletin* 76: 891–908.

Schenk, Catherine, 2010. *The Decline of Sterling: Managing the Retreat of an International Currency 1945–1992.* Cambridge, UK: Cambridge University Press.

Sheets, Nathan, 1995. "Capital Flight from the Countries in Transition: Some Theory and Empirical Evidence." International Finance Discussion Papers 514 (July). Washington, DC: Board of Governors of the Federal Reserve System.

Sheets, Nathan and Simona Boata, 1996. "Eastern European Export Performance during the Transition." International Finance Discussion Papers 562 (September). Washington, DC: Board of Governors of the Federal Reserve System.

Siegman, Charles J., 1994. "The Bank for International Settlements and the Federal Reserve." *Federal Reserve Bulletin* 80: 900–06.

Silber, William L., 2012. *Volcker: The Triumph of Persistence.* New York, NY: Bloomsbury Press.

Solomon, Robert, 1977. *The International Monetary System 1945–1981: An Insider's View*. New York, NY: Harper and Row.

———. 2016. Oral history. Washington: Board of Governors of the Federal Reserve System. Available when released at www.federalreserve.gov

Stekler, Lois E. and William L. Helkie, 1989. "Implications for Future US Net International Investment Position of Growing US Net International Indebtedness." *International Finance Discussion Papers* 358 (July). Washington, DC: Board of Governors of the Federal Reserve System.

Stevens, Guy, Richard Berner, Peter B. Clark, Ernesto Hernandez-Cata, Howard Howe, and Sung Kwack, 1984. *The U.S. Economy in an Interdependent World: A Multicountry Model*. Washington, DC: Board of Governors of the Federal Reserve System.

Summit Finance Ministers, Central Bank Governors, and Representatives of the European Community, 1983. Statement on the Intervention Study, April 29.

Truman, Edwin M., 1982. *International Economic and Financial Conditions*. Available at www.federalreserve.gov/monetarypolicy/files/FOMC19821116material.pdf (accessed on June 15, 2014).

———. 2003a. *Inflation Targeting in the World Economy*. Washington, DC: Peterson Institute for International Economics.

———. 2003b. "The Limits of Exchange Market Intervention" in C. Fred Bergsten and John Williamson (eds.), *Dollar Overvaluation and the World Economy*. Washington, DC: Peterson Institute for International Economics.

———. 2004. "A Critical Review of Coordination Efforts in the Past" in Horst Siebert (ed.), *Macroeconomic Policies in the World Economy*. Berlin: Springer Verlag.

———. 2005. Reflections [Monetary Policy 25 Years after October 1979]. *Federal Reserve Bank of St. Louis Review* 87: 353–57.

———. 2006. "What Can Exchange Rates Tell Us?" in Michael Mussa (ed.), *C. Fred Bergsten and the World Economy*. Washington, DC: Peterson Institute for International Economics.

———. 2012. "John Williamson and the Evolution of the International Monetary System." PIIE Working Paper 12–13 (August). Washington, DC: Peterson Institute for International Economics.

———. 2016. *Oral History*. Washington, DC: Board of Governors of the Federal Reserve System. Available when released at www.federalreserve.gov

Truman, Edwin M., et al., 1981. "The New Federal Reserve Operating Procedures: An External Perspective" in *New Monetary Control Procedures*. Federal Reserve Staff Study Volumes I and II. Washington, DC: Board of Governors of the Federal Reserve System.

US Treasury, 2014. *U.S.–China Joint Fact Sheet: Sixth Meeting of the Strategic and Economic Dialogue*. Washington, DC. Available at www.treasury.gov/press-center/press-releases/Pages/jl2561.aspx (accessed on July 24, 2014).

Volcker, Paul A., 1980. *The Recycling Problem Revisited*. Remarks before the Graduate School of Business Administration, New York University (March 1). New York, NY. Available at http://fraser.stlouisfed.org/docs/historical/volcker/Volcker_19800301.pdf (accessed on June 13, 2014).

Volcker, Paul A. and Toyoo Gyohten, 1992. *Changing Fortunes: The World's Money and the Threat to American Leadership.* New York, NY: Times Books.

Warnock, Francis E. and Molly Mason, 2000. "The Geography of Capital Flows: What We Can Learn from Benchmark Surveys of Foreign Equity Holdings." International Finance Discussion Papers 688 (December, latest version April 2001). Washington, DC: Board of Governors of the Federal Reserve System.

Woodward, Bob, 2000. *Maestro: Greenspan's Fed and the American Boom.* New York, NY: Simon and Schuster.

Comments on Edwin M. Truman, "The Federal Reserve Engages the World (1970–2000): An Insider's Narrative of the Transition to Managed Floating and Financial Turbulence"

Michael P. Dooley

The narrative Ted has provided for the conference provides a personal and engaging review of the ways in which the international economy shaped and was shaped by the Federal Reserve System from 1970 through 2000. I enjoyed most his treatment of the early years, the '70s, perhaps because I was at the Fed at the time and worked with Ted and most of the characters that appear in these pages.

The challenge of those years was that we knew almost nothing about the floating exchange rate system that arrived unexpected and uninvited. We certainly knew nothing useful about the Federal Reserve's role in this new system. The International Finance Division at the Board of Governors brought together young economists from the Ivy League to Chicago to Stanford (and one Penn Stater) in an environment where interesting and important questions arose almost daily. We were not competing with one another for tenure and this encouraged collaboration. In my view the defining feature of this moment in history was that good ideas (and probably some bad ones) were formulated, presented to the Board of Governors and, as Ted documents, were influential with policymakers (some more than others).

What is missing from the narrative is the ferocity of the debate before the staff's view was presented to the policymakers. Our audience included very well informed governors and chairmen and believe me there was considerable conflict in deciding what version of the staff's view should be presented.

I will focus on one of the debates from the 1970s and 1980s that in my view was never resolved and which remains relevant today. Ted documents the gradual decline of sterilized intervention as a policy alternative for the United States and other industrial countries. This historical fact is not in dispute. But I believe the reasons behind this outcome are not well understood. It could be that sterilized intervention proved to be ineffective in influencing exchange rates among major currencies. Or policymakers may have decided that the risk of losses associated with accumulating net positions in other currencies was too high a price to pay for influencing the exchange rate. Finally, policymakers may have concluded that they do not know enough about exchange rate determination to have a coherent objective for the exchange rate.

Revisiting these issues is timely because, as Ted points out, sterilized intervention has striking similarities with quantitative easing.[1] My view is that sterilized intervention in foreign exchange markets is a relatively powerful form of quantitative easing. I will approach the problem in the context of a portfolio balance framework. This is itself a controversial point of view, but the portfolio balance approach remains the dominant framework today for thinking about quantitative easing.

In the context of a portfolio balance framework, the effectiveness of sterilized intervention and QE depends on the assumption that the financial assets the government is buying and selling are imperfect substitutes in private portfolios.[2] In crude terms QE consists of the government buying its own long duration bonds and selling its own short duration bonds. SI consists of the government buying its own domestic-currency-denominated bonds and selling its own foreign-currency-denominated bonds.[3]

Consider Japan's current efforts to weaken the yen. To date they have intervened in yen-denominated bond markets in the hope that private investors will consider the resulting new mix of yen bonds as less attractive and so bid for dollar bonds and thus weaken the yen. SI would be a more direct alternative policy since it would force the private sector to hold more yen and fewer dollar bonds. Moreover the two policies could be combined. So why has QE been widely assumed to be effective and pursued in massive amounts while SI has not?

It could be that government bonds of different durations are imperfect substitutes while government bonds denominated in different currencies are perfect substitutes. This, however, seems unlikely and I know of no evidence or logic that might support such an assumption.

---

[1]   See Truman this volume, notes 35 and 36.
[2]   A number of arguments have been offered for why a set of assets bought and sold in the Federal Reserve's QE are imperfect substitutes. For simplicity I will lump these together in duration. See Krishnamurthy and Vissing-Jorgensen (2011).
[3]   I focus on net changes to the private sector's portfolio and assume the central bank's balance sheet and the Treasury's balance sheet are consolidated. It follows that the size of the central bank's balance sheet does not matter because it is simply intermediating between the government and the private sector.

To the contrary it seems very likely that currency denomination is a much more potent source of imperfect substitution as compared to duration. Why is it that the conventional wisdom that SI is not an effective policy tool? I think there are two reasons.

First, the portfolio balance model was never widely accepted by the economics profession.[4] I learned this the hard way by presenting a portfolio balance model at the University of Chicago in 1974. Monetarists didn't care about financial markets then, and since then it is no exaggeration to say that all financial markets have been banished from macro models. Getting rid of the messy details of financial markets was a major intellectual achievement. Financial transactions trade current for future consumption. It seems to follow that intertemporal maximization models drive intertemporal prices. Intertemporal prices are determined in markets for current and future goods and can then be applied to any assortment of financial assets that might exist at the time. In such models there are no meaningful demand or supply relationships for financial assets.

I would like to think that the subprime crisis itself discredited the view in the economics profession that financial markets are just a set of arbitrage conditions that play no role in the performance of the economy. But especially when traveling to emerging markets, I often hear the assertion that sterilized intervention is ineffective. It is as if the gradual rejection of this policy tool in the industrial countries that Ted documents was based on a theoretical fundamental truth.

An alternative reason for the disuse of intervention with very different implications is that empirical work testing the effectiveness of SI was at best inconclusive. My view on this literature has been that it missed the most important empirical regularity in the data. Intervention did not have lasting effects because for industrial countries it was very, very small and for the United States was systematically reversed.[5]

Why small? In my memory Federal Reserve officials were very sensitive to potential criticism if they had to report losses on foreign currency positions. In popular terms "speculating on foreign exchange rates with the taxpayers' money" was frowned upon. Moreover, potential losses were large and unpredictable because officials had very little confidence that they knew what the right exchange rate was. It is curious that the inability to find empirical evidence that sterilized intervention affected exchange rates was

---

[4] See Backus and Kehoe (1989).
[5] See Dooley (1982).

not eclipsed by the inability to find any variable systematically related to exchange rates.

Today we have the curious mix of conventional wisdoms. QE is effective but SI is not. If the portfolio balance framework is correct, this makes no sense. But our faith in QE makes sense if sterilized intervention can be effective but has not been used, at least by industrial countries. I remain convinced that in emerging markets where sterilized intervention has been used on a meaningful scale that it has been an effective policy tool. China's $6 trillion in reserves is in my view meaningful and has influenced the real exchange rate over an extended time period.

Why is QE a policy tool that is actually used in industrial countries? For some reason most of us do not frown on the Federal Reserve's speculating on interest rates with the taxpayers' money. Moreover, it is clear the Federal Reserve policymakers are not greatly concerned about potential losses on their multitrillion-dollar long duration position. When US interest rates rise, there are likely to be noticeable losses on the Federal Reserve's mark-to-market balance sheet. Some judicious accounting however could result in a smaller flow of profits to the Treasury.[6]

Finally, I think industrial countries have used QE because there has been no doubt that central banks knew what they wanted to do with long-term interest rates. Moreover every central bank wanted to do the same thing and everyone cannot do sterilized intervention in the same direction at the same time. It remains to be seen whether or not industrial countries will use sterilized intervention as a logical extension of quantitative easing. A careful reading of the history of the debate is certainly warranted to inform that decision.

References

Backus, David and Patrick Kehoe, 1989. On the Denomination of Government Debt: A Critique of the Portfolio Balance Approach. *Journal of Monetary Economics* 25(3): 359–79.

Dooley, Michael, 1982. An Analysis of Exchange Market Intervention of Industrial and Developing Countries. *IMF Staff Papers* 29: 233–69.

Krishnamurthy, Arvind and Annette Vissing-Jorgensen, 2011. "The Effects of Quantitative Easing on Interest Rates: Channels and Implications for Policy," *Brookings Papers on Economic Activity*, 215–65.

Rudebusch, Glenn D., 2011. "The Fed's Interest Rate Risk," *Economic Letter*, Federal Reserve Bank of San Francisco, April 11.

---

[6] See Rudebusch (2011).

6

The Federal Reserve in a Globalized World Economy

John B. Taylor

Economic research as far back as the early 1980s showed that simple rules-based monetary policy would result in good economic performance in a globalized world economy.[1] According to this research, if each central bank in the world followed a steady monetary policy rule that was optimal for its own country's price and output stability, it would also contribute to a framework of stability for the other countries. In fact, quantitative research showed that there would be little additional gain from the central banks' jointly optimizing their policies. This finding was, and still is, the implication of empirically estimated multicountry monetary models with highly integrated international capital markets, no-arbitrage conditions in the term structure of interest rates, forward-looking expectations, and price and wage rigidities.

The historical experience of the Great Moderation period of the 1980s, 1990s, and until recently largely validated this result. As central banks moved toward more transparent rules-based monetary policies – including through inflation targeting – economic performance improved. The improvement was especially dramatic compared with the instability of the 1970s, when, following the demise of the Bretton Woods system, monetary

[1] See, for example, the studies by Carlozzi and Taylor (1985), Taylor (1985, 1993), Clarida, Galí, and Gertler (2002), and Obstfeld and Rogoff (2002).

This chapter was prepared for the conference "The Federal Reserve's Role in the Global Economy: A Historical Perspective," hosted by the Federal Reserve Bank of Dallas. The chapter focuses on monetary policy rather than on the regulatory parts of Federal Reserve policy. Some of the results are based on research prepared for the Bank for International Settlements (BIS) (Taylor, 2013c). I thank Michael Bordo, Claudio Borio, Steve Cecchetti, Richard Clarida, Richard Fisher, Arminio Fraga, Lawrence Goodman, Simon Hilpert, David Mauler, Ronald McKinnon, David Papell, Kenneth Rogoff, George Shultz, Volker Wieland, and the staff of the Globalization and Monetary Policy Institute at the Federal Reserve Bank of Dallas for helpful comments and assistance.

policy was highly discretionary and unfocused. King (2003) called it a NICE period for it was noninflationary and consistently expansionary. Toward the later part of this NICE Great Moderation, central banks in many emerging market countries also moved toward more rule-like policies with long-run price stability goals. Their performance and their contribution to global stability also improved, especially compared with the earlier periods of frequent emerging market financial crises.

The situation had similarities to a game-theory equilibrium in which each country chose its own good monetary policy taking as given that other countries would do much the same under a basic understanding that the outcome would be nearly as good as if they coordinated their policy choices in a cooperative fashion. Attempts to coordinate policy choices across countries would likely have added little to the large improvement in macroeconomic stability during the Great Moderation, much as the monetary theory implied. For this reason, I doubled down on King's (2003) acronym and called the period a *near internationally cooperative equilibrium* (NICE). So we had Twice-NICE or NICE-squared.[2]

But during the past decade, the situation has changed for the worse. We have seen the end of NICE in both senses of the word. The Great Recession and the Not-So-Great-Recovery in much of the developed world put an end for the time being to the Great Moderation. The large negative spillover effects and apparent lack of international monetary coordination have again become a major international policy issue. Policymakers in large emerging market countries, including Brazil, China, and India, have complained about adverse spillover of monetary policy in the developed countries on their economies. Policymakers in developed countries including Japan and Europe have pointed to the adverse exchange rate effects of monetary policies in other developed countries, and some have raised concerns about currency wars and competitive devaluations. Many central banks in small open economies, such as Singapore, Hong Kong, and Switzerland, have had to take unusual actions to prevent excesses in their countries.

As Volcker (2014) recently put it, "new questions have been raised about the sensitivity of markets in small and emerging economies to the prospect of even small policy adjustments by the Federal Reserve. While the concerns and complaints of some officials in those countries may seem exaggerated, the volatility of short-term capital flows responsive to even a small shift in policy perception does raise important issues. And, there can be no

---

[2]   Taylor (2013c)

doubt that major changes in circumstances and policies in industrialized countries do inevitably have world-wide repercussions."

For these reasons there have been calls for a new approach to the international monetary system. The Globalization and Monetary Policy Institute at the Dallas Fed was set up with the explicit purpose of researching the issue, and Fisher (2014) has pinpointed some of the most serious concerns about the current situation in monetary policy. The Bank for International Settlements (BIS) has been researching the causes of the increased spillovers and looking for reforms of the process of international monetary policy cooperation (Caruana, 2012a, 2012b). The Center for Financial Stability held a seventieth anniversary conference in Bretton Woods in 2014 to consider such issues. Harking back to the 1944 Bretton Woods conference and "memories of a more orderly, rule-based world of financial stability, and close cooperation among nations," Volcker (2014) asks the fundamental question:

What is the approach (or presumably combination of approaches) that can better reconcile reasonably free and open markets with independent national policies, maintaining in the process the stability in markets and economies that is in the common interest?

Deciding on what is the correct approach requires a good diagnosis of the problem. In my view, the recent change in the international monetary situation is mainly due to monetary actions deviating from steady-as-you-go rule-like policies. The same monetary research from the 1980s that predicted that NICE-squared would be the result of rule-like policy would also predict the demise of NICE-squared in the event of a prolonged deviation from rule-like policy. And in fact, recent empirical research shows that such a deviation occurred in the United States and some other countries, starting about a decade ago – well before the financial crisis – when interest rates were held very low.[3]

Indeed, there has been a "Global Great Deviation" to use the terminology of Hofmann and Bogdanova (2012), who show that the deviation is continuing to the present when unconventional central bank interventions and large-scale balance sheet operations are included. The response of central banks to the deviations of policy of other central banks causes them to deviate together from the optimal policy that would otherwise be appropriate based on their own domestic considerations. The quantitative easing actions undertaken by the Bank of Japan in the spring of 2013 were in part

---

[3] See Ahrend (2010), Kahn (2010), and Taylor (2007).

a response to the adverse spillover on the exchange rate of the easier policy in other G-7 countries.[4]

This chapter starts from these theoretical and historical observations and tries to answer the question posed by Paul Volcker. It starts by explaining the basic theoretical framework, its policy implications, and its historical relevance. It then reviews the empirical evidence on the size of the international spillovers caused by deviations from rules-based monetary policy, and explores the many ways in which these spillovers affect and interfere with policy decisions globally. Finally, it considers ways in which individual monetary authorities and the world monetary system as a whole could adhere better to rules-based policies in the future and whether this would be enough to achieve the goal of stability in the globalized world economy.

6.1 Policy Tradeoffs in a Globalized World Economy

The idea that monetary policy rules deliver good economic performance in a globalized world economy comes out of a multicountry monetary modeling framework that I have been using in research and graduate teaching for many years (Carlozzi and Taylor, 1985; Taylor, 1993, 2013a).[5] It assumes perfect capital mobility (as in the original Dornbusch-Mundell-Fleming model), which is of course quite appropriate for a "globalized world economy." It also assumes staggered wage and price setting as in the Taylor (1980) model, so that inflation today depends in part on inflation in the future. Domestic prices in each country are affected by both domestic wages and the price of foreign imports, so the law of one price does not hold in the short run. Output in each country is influenced by the real interest rate, the real exchange rate, and expectations of future output due to forward-looking

---

[4] The Bank of Japan also announced an inflation target of 2 percent, which has an element of international cooperation because that is close to the numerical target of the Fed and the ECB.

[5] The field of multieconomy monetary economics is, of course, vast and has evolved significantly over the years inside and outside central banks. The calibrated two-country model of Carlozzi and Taylor (1985) was a project at the Federal Reserve Bank of Philadelphia and evolved into the fully estimated model described in Taylor (1993). Clarida, Galí, and Gertler (2002) built a two-country model with explicit microfoundations in order to evaluate monetary policy rules in a global context. Carabenciov et al. (2013) have built on such work in empirical research that can be traced back to the empirical models compared by Bryant, Hooper, and Mann (1993). Clarida (2014) provides a modern and practical perspective and Obstfeld (2014) adds a useful discussion. Since the financial crisis, many other policy issues have required consideration, including forward guidance, quantitative easing, the incorporation of credit spreads into policy rules, and the comparison of rules actually used by the Fed as found in recently released transcripts.

consumers who take account of their future income prospects when deciding how much to consume. Shocks can hit anywhere in the economy and may be due to shifts in preferences or technology. Shocks to the wage and price setting process are central to the modeling framework and preclude from the start any miraculous divine coincidence, as defined by Blanchard and Galí (2007). Indeed, the essence of the monetary policy problem is characterized by a policy tradeoff between price stability and output stability. The task of monetary policy in each country is to find a policy in which the policy instrument is adjusted so as to reach an efficient point on that tradeoff.

In such a model, the problem for the central bank is to decide how to respond to shocks and fluctuations in the economy while not creating its own shocks and disturbances either domestically or internationally. By choosing the size of its response coefficients, it can affect the relative amount of price stability and output stability. For example, when the interest rate reaction coefficient on inflation increases, then price stability increases and output stability falls. Conversely, if the central bank chooses to react less to inflation changes, then there will be less price stability but more output stability. And by minimizing deviations from its optimal policy responses – that is, by not adding shocks to its policy rule – it will minimize monetary policy-induced fluctuations.

The sense in which the gains from international policy coordination are small in such a modeling framework is that the central bank's choice of a policy rule – in this case the decisions to be more or less responsive – has relatively little impact on output and price stability in the other countries. Figure 6.1 illustrates the idea in the case of two countries. It shows the tradeoff between output and price stability in Country 1, on the left, and Country 2, on the right. Measures of the size of output and price fluctuations are on the vertical and horizontal axes, respectively. The tradeoff curve is like a frontier. Points on the curve represent optimal policy. Monetary policy cannot take the economy to infeasible positions to the left of or below the curve. But suboptimal monetary policy – due to policy errors, reacting to the wrong variables, etc. – can take the economy to inefficient higher variability points above and to the right of the curve. Along the curve, lower price variability can only be achieved with greater output variability corresponding to different values of the reaction coefficient. The existence of such a tradeoff curve is quite general, and the curve has been used in many different monetary policy studies going back to the 1970s and continuing today.[6]

---

[6] See Taylor (1979), Bernanke (2004), and King (2012).

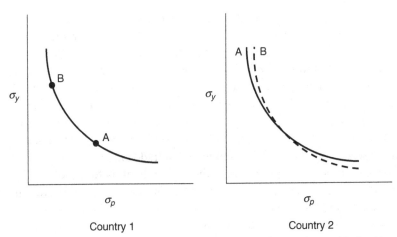

Country 1   Country 2

Figure 6.1. Illustration of the NICE idea. If Country 1 chooses Optimal Policy B rather than Optimal Policy A, then the policy frontier in Country 2 shifts from Curve A to Curve B, or by a very small amount. This result also holds in reverse if Country 2 changes its policy.

The shape and the position of the tradeoff curve depend on the parameters of the model and the size of the shocks. An increase in the variance of the shock to wage setting in one country, for example, will move that country's curve up and to the right. A reduction in the size of the response of wages to the state of the economy – effectively more price-wage stickiness – will also result in a shift in the tradeoff curve in the northeast direction.

Points A and B, which are on the tradeoff curve for Country 1, represent two alternative choices for optimal policy, reflecting different weights on the macroeconomic objective function for Country 1. The policy at point A results in a relatively small variance of output and a relatively large variance of prices compared with point B. The two different tradeoff curves for Country 2 show the effect on Country 2 of a change in policy in Country 1 from A to B. The important point is that the tradeoff curve for Country 2 is virtually the same regardless of which of the optimal policies are chosen by Country 1. Curve B is drawn with a slight twist relative to Curve A, but that is not a general result. Note that the same type of diagram would show that a change in policy in Country 2 would have little change in Country 1.

This is the sense in which monetary policy research, as in Taylor (1985, 1993), implies that there is little to be gained by Country 2 coordinating its own policy rule with Country 1 if both Country 1 and Country 2 are following policy rules that are optimal domestically. In game-theory terminology, macroeconomic performance under a Nash non-cooperative monetary policy is nearly as good as under the optimal cooperative monetary policy, and far superior to a policy which is suboptimal on purely domestic grounds. If the modeling approach implied that the Country 2 curve shifted by a lot with a change from one optimal policy to another optimal policy in Country 1, and vice versa, then the cooperative monetary policy might be worth pursuing even if the policies were optimal from a domestic point of view.[7]

The converse situation where monetary policy in one or both countries does not follow an optimal rule is less clear cut theoretically because it requires defining the nature of the deviation. Nevertheless, the tradeoff curves can be used to illustrate how such deviations from an optimal policy rule can lead to a breakdown in the international policy equilibrium. This is shown in Figure 6.2. Suppose Country 1 deviates from its optimal monetary policy rule and moves in the direction of an inefficient policy as shown by point C in Figure 6.2. The impact in Country 2 will most likely be large for two separate, but not mutually exclusive, reasons.

First, the tradeoff curve in Country 2 would likely shift out. The instability caused by the change in policy in Country 1 could spillover to Country 2, for example, in the form of more volatile export demand, as was demonstrated vividly in the financial panic in late 2008, or simply in more volatile exchange rates or commodity prices. Bordo and Lane (2013) have shown that policy deviations can have a variety of adverse effects on economic performance which can be transmitted globally. These shocks would be very hard for even the best monetary policy to fully counteract. Figure 6.2 shows this shift in the tradeoff curve in Country 2; the original curve – either A or B – moves out to the curve with the long dashed lines. Hence Country 2 is forced to the point C, or perhaps to another point on the new less-favorable tradeoff.

Second, the change to a less efficient monetary policy in Country 1 might bring about a change to a less efficient monetary policy in Country 2. For example, if the policy change in Country 1 is to bring about an excessively easy policy with very low interest rates, then the policymakers in Country 2 may be concerned about exchange rate appreciation and thus keep their interest rate too low too – deviating from their policy rule – which could cause an increase in price volatility and output instability. The central bank might do this even if there was an offsetting effect from

---

[7]   Recall that I am only considering monetary policy here. Eichengreen (2013) argues that countries can use fiscal policy if they are constrained in the use of monetary policy due to international considerations.

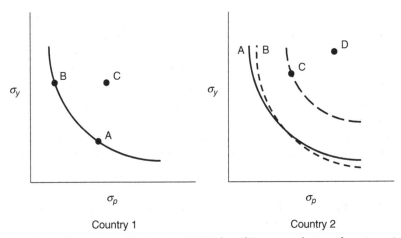

Country 1   Country 2

Figure 6.2. Illustration of the Not-So-NICE idea. If Country 1 deviates from its optimal policy rule, moving to point C, then the impact on Country 2 can be quite large: It either causes Country 2 to choose a poor policy rule C with no change in the tradeoff, or it causes the tradeoff curve to shift out, or both as in point D.

higher export demand from higher output in Country 1. They might perceive that offsetting effect to be too low or too delayed or they may be concerned about the hit to certain export sectors. Of course it is possible that both international effects of the change in policy in Country 1 occur at the same time, in which case the outcome could be point D in the right-hand panel of Figure 6.2.

6.2 Historical Interpretation

The historical interpretation of the past half century put forth in this chapter is that the world economy moved from the situation like Figure 6.2 to Figure 6.1 and then back to Figure 6.2 as policy became more rules-based and then less rules-based. Evidence for the first shift in policy was provided early on by Clarida, Galí, and Gertler (1998) and later confirmed by many others including recently by Nikolsko-Rzhevskyy, Papell, and Prodan (2014) who use modern time series techniques and also provide evidence for the second shift. Clarida (2014) cites considerable research that shows that the connection between the policy and the economic performance "was no coincidence," adding that many research papers "show that, in dynamic stochastic general equilibrium models with nominal rigidities, flexible exchange rates and inflation targeting produce desirable macroeconomic outcomes in open economies."

While there is general agreement about the first shift in policy, there are different views about the second. The main alternative view is based on the idea that the monetary policies undertaken by the central banks have been appropriate in recent years, even if they are not consistent with the rule-like behavior followed during the NICE-squared period. Yellen (2012) argues, for example, that "the simple rules that perform well under ordinary circumstances just won't perform well with persistently strong headwinds restraining recovery."

According to this alternative view, the shift in economic performance in Figure 6.2 was not due to monetary policy deviating from a rules-based approach. Any shift in the tradeoff curve was due to other factors. Rather than being due to monetary policy in Country 1 moving off the tradeoff curve to the inefficient point C, the curve in Country 2 shifted for other reasons.

Mervyn King (2012), for example, has made this argument using the same tradeoff curve diagram. He argues that the tradeoff curve shifted out because financial stability during the Great Moderation eventually bred instability, largely through the complacency of investors who, thinking that stability conditions would continue, took on too much risk and thereby increased instability. The idea is due to Hyman Minsky, so King argues that the Taylor curve shifted to a new Minsky–Taylor curve. As he puts it, "A failure to take financial instability into account creates an unduly optimistic view of where the Taylor frontier lies, especially when it is based on data drawn from a period of stability. Relative to a Taylor frontier that reflects only aggregate demand and cost shocks, the addition of financial instability shocks generates what I call the Minsky–Taylor frontier."

Bernanke (2013) seems to go further than King (2012) in this line of argument. In terms of Figure 6.2, he argues that the effect of what I call a policy deviation in Country 1 on policy in Country 2 is actually entirely appropriate. He compares recent monetary policy shifts to what happened during the Great Depression when countries moved off the gold standard and started what were called competitive devaluations, but in essence were a move toward more monetary ease.

6.3 Global Impacts of Deviations from Monetary Policy Rules

Now consider the quantitative size and nature of the spillover effects of deviations from policy rules as evidenced by empirical multieconomy modeling frameworks. I consider two multicountry monetary models: the Taylor Multicountry Model (TMCM) that includes the United States and other developed countries, described in Taylor (1993)[8] and GPM6, the IMF global model, which includes the United States, other developed countries, and emerging market countries in Latin American and Asia. GPM6 is described in Carabenciov et al. (2013).[9] Calculations by Taylor and Wieland (2012) show that the TMCM has effects in the United States of monetary shocks that are very similar to the new Keynesian models of Christiano, Eichenbaum, and Evans (2005) and Smets and Wouters (2007).

Figure 6.3 and Figure 6.4 show the impact of deviations from monetary policy rules in the two models for several key variables and a selection of countries or regions. In Figure 6.3, the impacts on the United States and Japan are compared while in Figure 6.4 the impact on the United States is compared with Japan as well as with the Latin American countries (LA6, which include Brazil, Chile, Colombia, Mexico, and Peru) and emerging Asia countries (EA6, which include China, India, South Korea, Indonesia, Taiwan, Thailand, Malaysia, Hong Kong, Philippines, and Singapore).

In each case, the monetary shock is a deviation from the monetary policy rule in the United States. Note that in interpreting the graphs, the deviations are of different sizes in the two models. In Figure 6.3, the deviation initially causes the interest rate to fall by about 0.8 percentage points and then slowly move up with the interest rate back to the starting point in about five quarters. In Figure 6.4, the deviation initially causes the interest rate to fall by about 0.2 percentage points and then the dynamics of the policy rule lead to a gradual rise in the interest rate back to its starting point in about five quarters. In both simulations, the interest rate overshoots before returning to normal due to the response of the policy rule to the economy after the shock.

First observe the large impact of the policy deviation on the exchange rate in both models. The simulations show that the dollar depreciates by 1.4 percent for each percentage point decrease in the US interest rate in the TMCM and by 1.0 percent in GPM6 (not shown in the figures).

Next consider the impact of the change in the short-term interest rate and the resulting change in the exchange rate on US output in both Figure 6.3 and Figure 6.4: the percentage increase in output for a percentage point reduction in the interest rate is about 0.5 in Figure 6.3 and 0.25 in Figure 6.4. Simulating other estimated multicountry models shows

---

[8] Simulations of the TMCM model reported here were run via the model database constructed and maintained by Volker Wieland; see Wieland et al. (2012).
[9] Simulations of the GPM6 model reported here were run at the IMF by Roberto Garcia-Saltos.

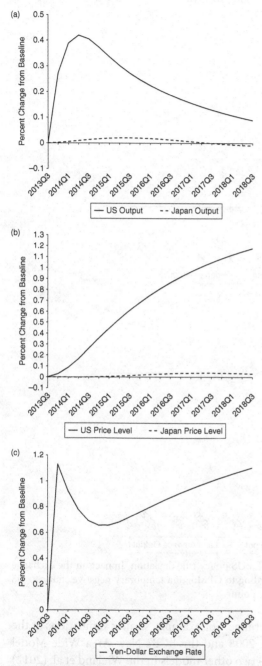

Figure 6.3. Exchange rate and output-price effect of a US policy rule deviation. The figure shows the impact, according to the TMCM, on the exchange rate and on output and prices in the United States and Japan of a 1 percent negative deviation (reduction) from the policy rule phased out at rate 0.9.

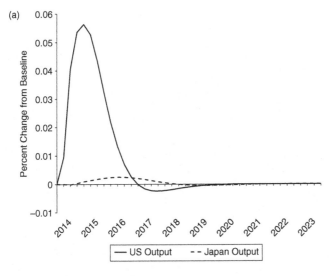

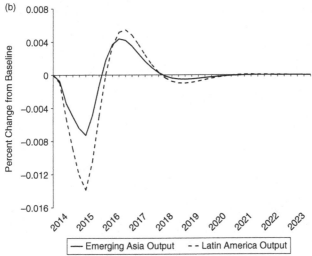

Figure 6.4. Output-price effect of a US policy rule deviation. Impact on the exchange rate and output and prices, according to GPM6, of a temporary negative shock to US interest rate rule of 0.2 percentage points.

impacts in this same general range. For example, similar simulations of the Fed's SIGMA model vintage 2008 and the ECB's New Area Wide Model (NAWM) also vintage 2008 – two other models in the Wieland et al. (2012) model database – show, respectively, impact effects on output of 0.19 and 0.28 percent for each percentage point deviation in the policy rule for the short-term interest rate.

Finally, consider the impact on output in other countries. According to the GPM6 model, this exchange rate change translates into a *negative* effect on output in the Latin American and the Asian emerging market economies. For each percentage point monetary policy-induced increase in output in the United States, output falls by 0.25 percentage points in the Latin American countries and by 0.13 percentage points in the emerging Asian countries. As described by the authors of the IMF's GPM6 model, this occurs in these countries because "the exchange rate channel is stronger than the direct output gap effect." The impact on other developed economies' output is not negative, but it is quite small. For example, Japan's output increases by only about 1/20th of the US output increase in both models.

These estimates contradict the view sometimes put forth by central bankers in the United States and other developed countries when discussing policy spillovers. Bernanke (2013), for example, argued that "The benefits of monetary accommodation in the advanced economies are not created in any significant way by changes in exchange rates; they come instead from the support for domestic aggregate demand in each country or region. Moreover, because stronger growth in each economy confers beneficial spillovers to trading partners, these policies are not 'beggar-thy-neighbor' but rather are positive-sum, 'enrich-thy-neighbor' actions." The policy simulations in these empirical multicountry models do not, however, support an enrich-thy-neighbor view.

When one moves beyond these multieconomy models and considers unconventional monetary policy, there are more reasons to doubt the enrich-thy-neighbor characterization. If the monetary policy action is mainly in the form of quantitative easing, the standard term structure models are not applicable, and there is a great deal of debate about whether there is a positive effect on aggregate demand. Stroebel and Taylor (2012) found very little effect of large-scale purchases on mortgage rates when controlling for other risks, and the announcement effects detected by Gagnon et al. (2011) likely phase out over time.

6.4 Monetary Policy Contagion

These simulations illustrate why in practice a large policy deviation at one central bank puts pressures on central banks in other countries to deviate from their otherwise optimal policy. As the empirical models show, a reduction in policy interest rates abroad causes the exchange rate to appreciate. Even though there may be countervailing effects of the low foreign interest rates because economic output abroad is stimulated (the trade effect in the model simulations), this effect may occur with a lag in practice and is less visible than the exchange rate appreciation. Moreover, for the emerging market countries in Latin America and Asia, the exchange rate effect dominates according to the empirical model simulations. More generally, there is not enough empirical evidence to support the view that a pickup in output abroad will offset the appreciation. Moreover, in recent years the pickup abroad has not materialized. Hence, many central banks will tend to resist large appreciations of their currency, and one way to do so is to reduce their own policy rate relative to what it would be otherwise. This will reduce the difference between the foreign interest rate and the domestic interest rate and will thus mitigate the appreciation of their exchange rate.

Another concern of some central banks is that very low interest rates at the major central banks can increase risky capital flows in their countries, as shown by Bruno and Shin (2012), and one way to combat this is to lower the policy interest rate. Firms abroad are able to borrow in dollars to finance investment projects even though the returns on these projects are denominated in local currency. The loans made to the firms by banks to fund these projects are subject to default in the event that the project earns less than the loan, including interest payments. In such a circumstance, a central bank can mitigate the increase in foreign lending by keeping its own interest rate lower than it otherwise would for domestic stability purposes. This reduces the incentive to borrow abroad and the associated risk. In the end, an extra low interest rate policy in one country leads to a similar deviation in other countries.[10]

There is considerable empirical evidence of the impact of foreign interest rates on central bank decisions. The best evidence comes from central bankers themselves, many who readily admit to these reactions in conversations. Some issue public reports. Consider the Norges Bank which provides a great deal of detail about its decisions and the rationale for them.[11] In 2010, for example, the Norges Bank explicitly reported that it lowered its policy interest rate because interest rates were lower abroad. The Norges Bank provides reports on the details of its own policy rules, and there was a

---

[10] In discussions with many central bankers, I hear more concerns about exchange rates than about capital inflows, but the actual reasons for deviating from conventional policy rules are inherently complex. A preference for discretion rather than rules-based policies has become more common among central bankers, especially in the aftermath of a financial crisis when the "rulebook" is often thrown away. Moreover, governments have become more aggressive in asking central banks to take unconventional actions if other central banks are doing so.

[11] See Røisland (2010), the OECD Survey (2010), and Taylor (2013b).

large deviation in 2010. The actual policy rate, at about 2 percent, was much lower than the rate implied by its domestic monetary policy rule, which called for a policy rate of about 4 percent. This deviation was almost entirely due to the very low interest rate abroad, according to the Norges Bank. It reported that a policy rule with external interest rates included came much closer to describing the actual decisions than the policy rules without external interest rates.

The case of the Bank of Japan's move in the spring of 2013 toward quantitative easing and large-scale asset purchases provides another example. Following the financial crisis and into recovery, the yen significantly appreciated against the dollar as the Fed repeatedly extended its zero interest rate policy and its large-scale asset purchases. Concerned about the adverse economic effects of the currency appreciation, the new government of Japan urged the Bank of Japan to ease up on policy and implement its own massive quantitative easing, and, with a new Governor at the Bank of Japan, this is exactly what happened. As a result of this change in policy, the yen fully reversed its course and has returned to the exchange rate just before the panic of 2008. In this way, the policy of one central bank appeared to affect the policy of another central bank.

The moves of the ECB in 2014 toward quantitative easing of some kind may have similar motivations. An appreciating euro was in the view of the ECB a cause of both the low inflation and the weak economy. With the prolonged zero interest rates in the United States, an understandable response was to shift to even lower rates in the euro area and the initiation of quantitative easing. Indeed, the shift and initiation was followed by a dollar strengthening and a weaker euro.

There is considerable econometric evidence of the spread of central bank policies based on the statistical correlations between policy interest rates in different countries. Gray (2013) estimated policy rate reaction functions in which the US federal funds rate or other measures of foreign interest rates entered on the right-hand side as deviations from their respective policy rules. He used panel data from twelve central banks (Australia, Canada, South Korea, the United Kingdom, Norway, New Zealand, Denmark, Israel, Brazil, the euro area, China, and Indonesia), and found that the average reaction coefficient on the foreign rate was large and significant.

There is also evidence that shifts in monetary policy in the form of quantitative easing have an impact on monetary policy decisions abroad. Chen et al. (2012) examine the impact of various types of quantitative easing in the United States, the United Kingdom, the ECB, and Japan on monetary conditions in emerging market countries and in other advanced economies.

They find that "the announcement of QE measures in one economy contributed to easier global liquidity conditions."

6.5 A Policy Deviations Multiplier

Deviations from rules-based monetary policy aimed at avoiding the competitive devaluation effects of exchange rate changes can have large multiplier effects. Consider the case of an interest rate rule and two countries. In this case, the multiplier can be illustrated with a simple diagram.[12]

Suppose i is the policy interest rate at one central bank and i_f is the policy interest rate at the other central bank. Assume that each central bank tends to deviate from its own policy rule in order to prevent competitive devaluations effects originating from abroad from actually having a competitive effect. Thus, the amount of the deviation would depend on interest rate settings at the central bank in the other country (Taylor, 2009, 2013c).

Figure 6.5 shows an example of two reaction functions in which the first central bank has a response coefficient of 0.5 on the second central bank's policy interest rate and the second central bank has a response coefficient of 1 on the first central bank's interest rate. Suppose the first central bank cuts its interest rate i by 1 percentage point below its normal policy rule setting. Then, the second central bank will also reduce its policy rate i_f by 1 percentage point, which causes the first central bank to cut its interest rate by another 0.5 percentage point leading to another cut at the second central bank, and so on. In this example, the end result is a 2 percentage point rate cut once the iterative process settles down. The initial deviation from the policy rule of 1 percentage point by the first central bank is multiplied by 2 in this example, ending up reducing the policy rates in both countries by 2 percentage points.

The end effect of these iterations is to thwart the competitive devaluation. But what may have appeared as a currency war ends up as an interest rate war, or even an unconventional monetary policy war.

6.6 Capital Controls

Concerned about the ramifications of deviating from their normal monetary policy, many central banks have looked for other ways to deal with the impacts of policy deviations abroad, which during recent years have been characterized mainly by unusually low interest rates at foreign central

---

[12] A similar case can be made if the policy instrument is quantitative easing.

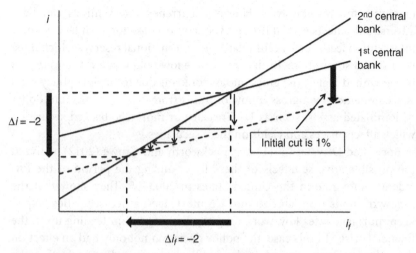

Figure 6.5. The policy deviations multiplier. Each central bank matches, at least in part, the interest rate change at the other central bank. This creates a multiplier effect in which the final interest rate change is much larger than the initial change.

banks. The imposition of capital controls is one approach. Capital controls limit the flow of capital and are usually aimed at containing the demand for local currency and its appreciation, but also at mitigating risky borrowing and volatile capital flows.

However, capital controls create market distortions and may lead to instability as borrowers and lenders try to circumvent them and policymakers seek even more controls to prevent the circumventions. Indeed, capital controls are one reason why the output and price stability frontier will shift adversely. Capital controls also conflict with the goal of a more integrated global economy and higher long-term economic growth.

Nevertheless, the unusual spillovers of recent years have led even the IMF to suggest that capital controls might be used as a defense despite these harmful side effects. And the Federal Reserve has endorsed the approach, with, for example, Bernanke (2013) saying that "... the International Monetary Fund has suggested that, in carefully circumscribed circumstances, capital controls may be a useful tool."

6.7 Currency Intervention

Currency intervention is another way to prevent unwanted appreciation of a currency either as an alternative or as a supplement to lower interest rates. In fact, currency intervention has been used widely in recent years by many emerging market countries. However, currency interventions can have adverse side effects even if they prevent appreciation for a while. Currency intervention leads to an accumulation of international reserves which must be invested somewhere. In the case where low policy interest rates are set in the United States, the gross outflow of loans due to the low policy rates is accompanied by a gross inflow of funds from central banks into dollar denominated assets, such as US Treasury or mortgage-backed securities, which affects prices and yields on these securities.

Borio and Disyatat (2011) and Beckworth and Crowe (2012) analyzed the possible adverse effects of these flows during the period of the low federal funds rate in the United States in 2003–05. They show that the inflow of funds from abroad into US mortgage-backed securities helped keep mortgage rates low, worsening the housing boom leading up to the financial crisis. In this case, the policy deviation not only had an effect on the policy tradeoffs abroad, it also fed back on the policy tradeoff in the United States.

6.8 Macro-Prudential Policies as an Imperfect Substitute for Good Monetary Policy

Another policy reaction has been the increased use of substitutes for monetary policy when the conventional policy is impacted by policies from abroad. This is most obvious in small open economies closely tied to the major currencies. Both Singapore and Hong Kong have had near-zero short-term interest rates in recent years because the Fed has had zero rates. Their pegged exchange rate regimes and open capital markets have left no alternative. So in order to contain inflationary pressures, they have had no choice but to resort to discretionary interventions in housing or durable goods markets, lowering required loan-to-value ratios in housing or requiring larger down payments for automobile purchases. Similarly, Switzerland has introduced explicit restrictions on housing in order to contain a housing boom in the face of near-zero interest rates.

These policies are also becoming more popular in inflation-targeting countries with flexible exchange rates. Discouraged from leaving interest rates at appropriate levels because of exchange rate concerns, they turn to such market specific measures. These so-called macro-prudential actions are inherently discretionary, expand the mission of central banks, and bring them closer to politically sensitive areas. They also run the risk of becoming permanent even after unconventional policies abroad are removed. A regulatory regime aimed at containing risk taking is entirely appropriate, but that entails getting the levels right, not manipulating them as a substitute for overall monetary policy.

6.9 What to Do

For all these reasons, deviations from rules-based monetary policy are likely to be a key driver of instabilities in the international monetary system. There are many reasons for the spread of these deviations and other potentially distortionary policies – which I have documented here – but the understandable desire to prevent excessive exchange rate fluctuations and large risky capital flows are the main ones.

The obvious implication is that going forward the goal should be to return to more rules-based monetary policies similar to what existed during the 1980s, 1990s, and until recently, and now certainly including the emerging market countries. Such a system would likely operate near an international cooperative equilibrium as described above.

Can anything be done to help this along? I have argued that, for the United States, legislation may be needed, and recently some legislative action is underway. The first main section, "Requirements for Policy Rules for the Fed," of a bill recently passed out of Committee in the United States House of Representatives would require that the Federal Reserve report publicly a rule or strategy for how the policy instruments, such as the federal funds rate, would change in a systematic way in response to changes in inflation, real GDP, or other inputs. The rule would have to be consistent with the setting of the actual federal funds rate at the time of its report.

The Fed would choose the rule and how to describe it. But if it decided to deviate from its rule or modify its rule – say because the Fed's estimates of the long-run equilibrium real interest rate change – then the Chair of the Fed would have to testify in Congress and explain why.

Such legislation preserves the independence of the Fed to choose its monetary policy strategy. It does not require that the central bank hold any instrument of policy fixed, but rather that it make adjustments in a systematic and predictable way. The central bank can serve as lender of last resort or take appropriate actions to provide liquidity in a crisis, and even change its rule or deviate from it if policymakers decide that is necessary, but if it did it would submit an explanation.

Some say that such legislation would reduce central bank independence, but since the central bank chooses its own rule, its independence is effectively maintained. The purpose of the act is to prevent the damaging departures from rules-based policy, which central bank independence has not prevented.

Such legislation would limit discretion and excessive intervention in an accountable way. It meets Milton Friedman's goal of "legislating rules for the conduct of monetary policy that will have the effect of enabling the public to exercise control over monetary policy through its political authorities, while at the same time … prevent[ing] monetary policy from being subject to the day-by-day whim of political authorities" Friedman (1962, p. 51).

But what about other central banks in the globalized world economy? A clear commitment by the Federal Reserve to move in this direction – whether aided by legislation or not – would help by influencing other central banks and the international financial institutions. An international understanding and agreement would help further. The major central banks now have a common inflation target and converging views about how the policy instruments should respond. This makes agreement about a policy strategy for the instruments more feasible. Such an agreement could instruct the IMF or the BIS, or even ask nonprofit groups, to monitor the extent to which central bank policies are steady and rule-like. They could use the same procedures as in the current US legislation, or something which recognizes the widely different institutional frameworks within each country.

Would such an approach be enough? Empirical evidence points in that direction. The large destabilizing capital flows motivated by search for yields would diminish. Rey (2013) has shown that a good portion of these flows has been induced by erratic swings in monetary policy which would be reduced greatly. And the large capital movements associated with "fear of free falling" exchange rates, which Vegh and Vuletin (2012) have documented, would likely be calmed as reliable central bank actions come to be expected. Research by Vegh and Vuletin (2012) indicates that the adoption of rules-based inflation targeting had that effect in a number of emerging market countries. This is consistent with the empirical finding of Eichengreen and Taylor (2003) that "countries that target inflation have significantly less volatile exchange rates."

Historical experience, informed by economic theory and research, indicates that with this approach each country could choose its own independent monetary policy strategy while contributing to the common interest of global financial and economic stability and without interfering with the principles of free and open markets.

References

Ahrend, Rudiger, 2010. "Monetary Ease: A Factor Behind Financial Crises? Some Evidence from OECD Countries." *Economics: The Open Access, Open Assessment E-Journal* 4: 1–30.

Beckworth, David and Christopher Crowe, 2012. "The Great Liquidity Boom and the Monetary Superpower Hypotheses" in David Beckworth (ed.), *Boom and Bust in Banking: Causes and Cures of the Great Recession*. Oakland, CA: The Independent Institute, 17–54.

Bernanke, Ben, 2004. "The Great Moderation." Eastern Economic Association, Washington, DC, February 20.

2013. "Monetary Policy and the Global Economy." London School of Economics, March 25.

Blanchard, Olivier and Jordi Galí, 2007. "Real Wage Rigidities and the New Keynesian Model." *Journal of Money, Credit, and Banking* 39: 35–65.

Bordo, Michael and John Landon Lane, 2013. "Does Expansionary Monetary Policy Cause Asset Price Booms: Some Historical and Empirical Evidence." NBER Working Paper no. 19585, October.

Borio, Claudio and Piti Disyatat, 2011. "Global Imbalances and the Financial Crisis: Link or No Link?" Bank for International Settlements, Working Paper, 346, May.

Bruno, Valentina and Hyun Song Shin, 2012. "Capital Flows and the Risk-Taking Channel of Monetary Policy." Paper presented at the 11th BIS Annual Conference, June.

Bryant, Ralph, Catherine L. Mann, and Peter Hooper (eds.), 1993. *Evaluating Policy Regimes: New Research in Empirical Macroeconomics*. Washington, DC: The Brookings Institution.

Carabenciov, Ioan, Charles Freedman, Roberto Garcia-Saltos, Douglas Laxton, Ondra Kamenik, and Petar Manchev, 2013. "GPM6: The Global Projection Model with 6 Regions." IMF Working Paper, WP/13/87.

Carlozzi, Nicholas and John B. Taylor, 1985. "International Capital Mobility and the Coordination of Monetary Rules" in J. Bhandhari (ed.) *Exchange Rate Management Under Uncertainty*. Cambridge, MA: MIT Press, Also available at http://web.stanford .edu/~johntayl/Onlinepaperscombinedbyyear/1985/International_Capital_ Mobility_and_the_Coordination_of_Monetary_Rules.pdf

Caruana, Jamie, 2012a. "Policymaking in an Interconnected World." Presented at Federal Reserve Bank of Kansas City Policy Symposium on *The Changing Policy Landscape*, Jackson Hole, Wyoming, August 31.

2012b. "International Monetary Policy Interactions: Challenges and Prospects." Bank for International Settlements, Speech in Punta del Este, Uruguay, November 16.

Chen, Qianying, Andrew Filardo, Dong He, and Feng Zhu, 2012. "International Spillovers of Central Bank Balance Sheet Policies." BIS Papers, Number 66.

Christiano, Lawrence, Martin Eichenbaum, and Charles Evans, 2005. "Nominal Rigidities and the Dynamic Effects of a Shock to Monetary Policy." *Journal of Political Economy* 113: 1–45.

Clarida, Richard, 2014. "Monetary Policy in Open Economies: Practical Perspectives for Pragmatic Central Bankers." *Journal of Economic Dynamics and Control* 49: 21–30.

Clarida, Richard, Jordi Galí, and Mark Gertler, 1998. "Monetary Policy Rules in Practice: Some International Evidence." *European Economic Review* 42: 1033–67.

2002. "A Simple Framework for International Monetary Policy Analysis." *Journal of Monetary Economics* 49: 879–904.

Eichengreen, Barry, 2013. "Currency War or International Policy Coordination?" University of California, Berkeley, January, http://eml.berkeley.edu/~eichengr/curr_war_JPM_2013.pdf

Eichengreen, Barry and Alan M. Taylor, 2003. "The Monetary Consequences of a Free Trade Area of the Americas." NBER Working Paper no. 9666, April.

Fisher, Richard W. 2014. "Monetary Policy and the Maginot Line." Remarks at the University of Southern California, July 16.

Friedman, Milton, 1962. *Capitalism and Freedom.* Chicago, IL: University of Chicago Press.

Gagnon, Joseph, Matthew Raskin, Julie Remanche, and Brian Sack, 2011. "The Financial Market Effects of the Federal Reserve's Large-Scale Asset Purchases." *International Journal of Central Banking* 7: 3–44.

Gray, Colin, 2013. "Responding to a Monetary Superpower: Investigating the Behavioral Spillovers of U.S. Monetary Policy." *Atlantic Economic Journal* 41: 173–84.

Hofmann, Boris and Bilyana Bogdanova, 2012. "Taylor Rules and Monetary Policy: A Global Great Deviation?" *BIS Quarterly Review* September.

Kahn, George A., 2010. "Taylor Rule Deviations and Financial Imbalances." Federal Reserve Bank of Kansas City *Economic Review,* Second Quarter, 63–99.

King, Mervyn, 2003. "Speech at the East Midlands Development Agency/Bank of England Dinner." Leicester, October 14.

2012. "Twenty Years of Inflation Targeting." Stamp Memorial Lecture, London School of Economics, London, October 9.

Nikolsko-Rzhevskyy, Alex, David H. Papell, and Ruxandra Prodan, 2014. "Deviations from Rules-Based Policy and Their Effects." *Journal of Economic Dynamics and Control* 49: 4–17.

Obstfeld, Maurice, 2014. "On the Use of Open Economy New Keynesian Models to Evaluate Policy Rules." *Journal of Economic Dynamics and Control* 49: 31–34.

Obstfeld, Maurice and Kenneth Rogoff, 2002. "Global Implications of Self-Oriented National Monetary Rules." *Quarterly Journal of Economics* 117: 503–36.

OECD, 2010. *Economic Survey: Norway,* 32.

Rey, Hélène, 2013. "Dilemma not Trilemma: The Global Financial Cycle and Monetary Policy Independence." *Global Dimensions of Unconventional Monetary Policy,* Federal Reserve Bank of Kansas City, August.

Røisland, Øistein, 2010. "Monetary Policy in Norway." Slide presentation, Norges Bank, http://www.uio.no/studier/emner/sv/oekonomi/ECON4325/v10/undervisnings-materiale/MonetaryPolicyNorway.pdf

Smets, Frank and Raf Wouters, 2007." Shocks and Frictions in U.S. Business Cycles: A Bayesian DSGE Approach." *American Economic Review* 97: 506–606.

Stroebel, Johannes and John B. Taylor, 2012. "Estimated Impact of the Fed's Mortgage-Backed Securities Purchase Program." *International Journal of Central Banking* 8: 1–42.

Taylor, John B., 1979. "Estimation and Control of a Macroeconomic Model with Rational Expectations." *Econometrica* 47: 1267–86.

1980. "Aggregate Dynamics and Staggered Contracts." *Journal of Political Economy* 88: 1–23.

1985. "International Coordination in the Design of Macroeconomic Policy Rules." *European Economic Review* 28: 53–81.

1993. *Macroeconomic Policy in a World Economy: From Econometric Design to Practical Operation.* New York, NY: W.W. Norton.

2007. "Housing and Monetary Policy." *Housing, Housing Finance, and Monetary Policy*, Federal Reserve Bank of Kansas City, September, 463–76.

2009. "Globalization and Monetary Policy: Missions Impossible" in Mark Gertler and Jordi Galí (eds.) *The International Dimensions of Monetary Policy*, Chicago, IL: The University of Chicago Press, 609–24.

2013a. "Lectures on Monetary Theory and Policy." Stanford University. Also available at http://web.stanford.edu/~johntayl/Spring2013PhDclass/IndexSpring2013.html

2013b. "International Monetary Coordination and the Great Deviation." *Journal of Policy Modeling* 35: 463–72.

2013c. "International Monetary Policy Coordination: Past, Present and Future." BIS Working Papers, no. 437, Monetary and Economic Department, December.

Taylor, John B. and Volker Wieland, 2012. "Surprising Comparative Properties of Monetary Models: Results from a New Model Data Base." *Review of Economics and Statistics* 94: 800–16.

Vegh, Carlos and Guillermo Vuletin, 2012. "Overcoming the Fear of Free Falling: Monetary Policy Graduation in Emerging Markets." NBER Working Paper no. 18175, June.

Volcker, Paul, 2014. "Remarks." Bretton Woods Committee Annual Meeting, June 17, www.brettonwoods.org/sites/default/files/publications/Paul%20Volcker%20 final%20Remarks%20June%2017.pdf.

Wieland, Volker, Tobias Cwik, Gernot Mueller, Sebastian Schmidt, and Maik Wolters, 2012. "A New Comparative Approach to Macroeconomic Modeling and Policy Analysis." *Journal of Economic Behavior and Organization* 83: 523–41.

Yellen, Janet, 2012. "Revolution and Evolution in Central Bank Communications." Haas School of Business, University of California, Berkeley, November 13.

Comments on John B. Taylor, "The Federal Reserve in a Globalized World Economy"

Richard H. Clarida

The potential for gains to international monetary policy cooperation is an important subject of long-standing interest in international finance. In this chapter, John Taylor provides a concise overview of some of the findings of previous research, but also introduces an original insight on this topic that I at least had not seen before. In fact, I think John's result may be more robust and applicable than his chapter might suggest.

In the chapter John discussed recent historical periods for many countries that feature noninflationary, consistently expanding (NICE) levels of economic activity. These periods do not appear to result or benefit from any evident efforts by countries to cooperate globally on monetary policy. As John reminds us, from thirty-five years of research – much of it inspired by John's own work – we know that typically, one finds only modest potential gains from international monetary policy cooperation in calibrated models. But in these simulations, the non-cooperative policies that are analyzed are usually pretty sensible. In other words, there are not a lot of studies that focus on the gain to policy cooperation when one country is running terrible policies. Invoking a version of the envelope theorem, John makes the conceptual case that gains to cooperation are locally small if a country takes as given a sensible (perhaps even Nash non-cooperative optimal) monetary policy of another country, but they may be very large if, instead, the other country runs a terrible policy (which is not Nash optimal).

I think John's hypothesis could be stated more crisply as follows: the potential gains from monetary policy cooperation are large if one of the countries is running a terrible policy, but if so this cooperation can take a simple form: just cooperate and agree to run sensible (non-cooperative optimal) if 'selfish' policy. In the language of reaction functions, the home country runs a policy rule that feeds back only on home macrovariables (inflation, unemployment) in a sensible way, and the foreign country runs a policy rule that feeds back only on foreign macrovariables (inflation, unemployment) in a sensible way. I think that this is an insight that has a practical implication that is potentially relevant in real-world policy formulation. This is because optimal cooperative rules implied by models can be very complicated rules that would be hard to monitor and hard to implement in practice.

Let's now talk about a real-world example of the phenomenon John is describing. Let's talk about Switzerland which confronted a crisis in the euro area that to some extent was exacerbated by a policy mistake. You're Switzerland; you are a rich economy, but you're small. You're being inundated with vast waves - Tsunamis - of flight capital. It's moving your currency, 30 to 40 percent beyond what PPP would indicate. So you do what the textbook says. You cut rates to zero and then eventually go negative on rates paid (received!) on excess reserve balances. You are an inflation targeter, but your inflation rate is falling toward zero. So what do you do? You've got to do something you never would have considered had there been no euro area crisis.

So you announce in 2011 and stand ready to defend with unlimited monetization a floor on the EURCHF exchange rate (a floor that prevents it from appreciating). The point of this approach is that there are limits to how much a central bank can intervene to defend a currency from weakening, but there is no limit to prevent your currency from appreciating.

Now, I think this is a good example of John's point. I think the SNB made the right policy call given the euro area crisis, but clearly, this was a response that they likely never would have considered had there not been the crisis next door.

7

Unprecedented Actions

The Federal Reserve's Response to the Global
Financial Crisis in Historical Perspective

Frederic S. Mishkin and Eugene N. White

In response to the Great Inflation, governments were more willing to cede greater independence to central banks, giving them better specified mandates, and central banks were more willing to pledge adherence to rules and transparency, with both, apparently, limiting discretionary intervention.[1] The resulting Great Moderation was thus, in large part, seen as a triumph of rules over discretion, and a recognition by policymakers of the time consistency problem. The success of reducing and stabilizing the inflation rate produced a consensus on the appropriate role and mandate for central banks (Mishkin, 2011). The global financial crisis that started in August 2007 and the disruptions of the subsequent seven years upset this consensus, and seemingly novel and unprecedented interventions were employed to address the panic and then revive markets and economies.

These "unprecedented" interventions included monetary policy easing at a time of robust growth and rising inflation, bailouts, new lending facilities, nonconventional monetary policy, such as quantitative easing, and large-scale international swap arrangements. By April 2008, these developments provoked former Fed Chairman Paul Volcker to comment that the

---

[1] See for example, Bernanke et al. (1999), Mishkin and Schmidt-Hebbel (2002).

Prepared for the conference, "The Federal Reserve's Role in the Global Economy: A Historical Perspective" at the Federal Reserve Bank of Dallas, September 18–19, 2014. We particularly want to thank Michael Bordo and Steven Kamin for their helpful comments. We are also grateful for suggestions made by participants at the Federal Reserve Bank of Dallas' September 18–19, 2014, conference, the Columbia University Macroeconomics workshop, and the Banque de France. The views expressed here are our own and are not necessarily those of Columbia University, Rutgers University, or the National Bureau of Economic Research. Disclosure of outside compensated activities for Mishkin can be found at www0.gsb.columbia.edu/faculty/fmishkin/

Federal Reserve had "taken actions that extend to the very edge of its lawful and implied powers, transcending certain long-embedded central banking principles and practices."[2] Solemn warnings have been issued about the perils of deviating from the mandates and rules that emerged out of the Great Moderation. Meltzer (2009) and Taylor (2009), for example, criticized the Fed for veering away from a clear and simple lender of last resort (LOLR) policy rule, as prescribed by Bagehot (1873) and other nineteenth century authorities, where it is clearly announced that financial institutions will not be bailed out. On the other hand, others like Madigan (2009) have asserted that the Fed's actions were in line with Bagehot's prescriptions.

In this chapter, we provide a historical framework to evaluate the "unprecedented" actions of the Fed, comparing its actions to central bank responses to crises in the nineteenth and twentieth centuries. This exercise reveals that there is less novelty in the Federal Reserve's recent actions and that central banks over the last hundred and fifty years have often not followed the simple LOLR policy rule. Historical exploration of actual LOLR practices provides a context for deciding whether the Federal Reserve's deviation from a Bagehot rule was appropriate.

Our review of leading financial crises in Britain, France, and the United States, from the Overend-Gurney panic of 1866 to the collapse of Long-Term Capital Management (LTCM) in 1998, documents that "unprecedented" actions by central banks are the norm rather than the exception. The reason for this observation lies in the necessity of reconciling central banks' mandates for price stability and financial stability. Under fixed and flexible exchanges rate regimes, there are important benefits from a price-stability rule that can be easily monitored so that central banks, and the political authorities who delegate policy responsibility to them, will be induced to follow credible policies that avoid time-consistency problems. The nature of financial crises, however, is such that addressing them almost invariably requires a temporary violation of rules, or the adoption of more flexible, less easily monitored, rules. Attempts to set a policy rule for financial stability by following Bagehot's recommendations accepts that policy will not seek to forestall a crisis but only respond when a financial crisis has hit, taking remedial action to assist solvent institutions but allowing the shock from the crisis to percolate through the whole economy. However, in most episodes, central banks have acted preemptively to manage failures of large financial institutions and buffer the economy from the shocks emanating from the crisis. While the reactive approach risks a recession or a deeper recession, the pre-emptive approach

---

[2] As quoted in Coy (2008).

creates incentives for moral hazard. For the latter approach to be successful, two elements are essential. First, the conditions when a rule may be temporarily violated must be well understood so that it becomes a contingent rule and there will be no market penalty. Alternatively, a more flexible, less easily monitored, rule must make the central bank sufficiently accountable so that it constrains discretion and avoids the time-consistency problem. Second, in order to ensure that the pre-emptive approach does not set the stage for the next crisis, actions must be taken to mitigate moral hazard.

7.1 Instrument, Contingent, and Target Rules for Central Banks

The problem of setting a proper mandate for a central bank dates to their very origin. Central banks became a common feature of sovereign nations in the nineteenth century, although there were precursors, notably the Bank of England and the Riksbank. They evolved as governments grappled with the problem of how to provide price stability and financial stability for their economies.[3]

To understand how governments provided mandates to their central banks, we need to be very clear about three different types of rules that central banks have followed: instrument rules, contingent rules, and target rules. For an *instrument rule,* a central bank agrees to set a policy instrument either to a particular value or to values that depend on states of the economy that are easily verified. The classic instrument rule is a metallic standard, where monitoring is managed by ascertaining the gold or silver content of coins. Nations employed metallic standards that converged toward the gold standard, which provided a monetary anchor, ensuring long- but not short-term price stability. However, for transactions, a coin-only regime proved very costly, and banks became the issuers of currency and deposits. Governments also directly issued currency, and this often led to abandonment of metallic-standard, instrument rules, resulting in high- and hyper-inflations, a manifestation of the time-inconsistency problem of Kydland and Prescott (1977) and Calvo (1978) arising from the temptation to exploit seigniorage. This problem illustrated the need to delegate the responsibility for money creation to independent agencies. The standard origin of a nineteenth century central bank was as a privileged government-chartered joint stock firm, privately owned, with clearly specified instrument rules for money creation that were easy to monitor by transparency rules and/or the appointment of some of its officials by the government (Grossman, 2010). Control of these

---

[3] For a recent survey of the evolution of banking and central banking, see Grossman (2010).

banks was also exercised by the limited duration of their charter. For the pre-
miere central banks, the Bank of England and the Banque de France, their
charters were for fixed periods, well over a decade – to minimize short-term
political interference. Upon expiration, their charters were subject to modification prior to renewal by Parliament.[4]

The key, simple point here is that central banks were agents delegated by
the legislature to conduct policy. To ensure that central banks avoided the
time-consistency problem, they were expected to follow instrument rules
that limited excessive money creation. Although instrument rules have the
advantage that they are easily verified, they have the disadvantage that they
can be too rigid, either because the evolution of the financial markets alters
the structure of the economy or because of unforeseen events.[5] In either
case, instrument rules can then result in very poor and sometimes even
disastrous economic performance. This problem with instrument rules
points to the difficulty that the principal has in writing a contract for the
agent that will cover all contingencies. The legislative process is often slow
and unable to respond quickly to a financial crisis. Consequently, in certain
circumstances escape clauses or practices permitting the violation of the
rules for price stability have been engineered, yielding the second type of
rule, *contingent rules*. Contingent rules allow departures from the instrument rule in which discretionary policy is allowed in extraordinary circumstances. Bordo and Kydland (1995) have argued that the gold standard
functioned as a contingent rule in the nineteenth century.[6] Permitting its

---

[4] Although Canada did not have a central bank, its decennial bank act of the nineteenth
century served a similar purpose; American national banks had finite charters until the
McFadden Act of 1927.

[5] A striking, modern example of the failure of an instrument rule as a result of a change
in the structure of the economy is the failure of the Swiss monetary targeting rule in the
1980s. In 1975, the Swiss National Bank (SNB) announced a growth target for the monetary aggregate M1. Beginning in 1980, the SNB switched the money growth target to an
even narrower monetary aggregate, the monetary base. Although monetary targeting was
quite successful in controlling inflation in Switzerland for many years, it ran into serious
problems with the introduction of a new interbank payment system, the Swiss Interbank
Clearing (SIC), and a wide-ranging revision of the commercial banks' liquidity requirements in 1988. These structural changes caused a severe drop in banks' desired holdings
of deposits, which were the major component of the monetary base, at the SNB. A smaller
amount of the monetary base was now needed relative to aggregate spending, altering the
relationship between the two, and so the 2 percent target growth rate for the monetary
base was far too expansionary. Inflation subsequently rose to over 5 percent, well above
that of other European countries. These problems with monetary targeting led the Swiss
to abandon it in the 1990s and adopt a much more flexible framework for the conduct of
monetary policy. For a detailed discussion of this episode, see Bernanke et al. (1999).

[6] In the literature on sovereign debt, "excusable defaults" represent a similar phenomenon
(Grossman and van Huyck, 1988).

suspension in times of war or financial crisis gave the monetary authorities (provided they were not responsible for the crisis) flexibility to cushion the shock to the economy.[7] This use of discretion did not necessarily result in the market imposing a penalty on the violating country, such as a higher risk premium for its sovereign bonds, as long as discretion was constrained by a transparent commitment to return to the instrument rule when conditions returned to normal.

Another alternative to instrument rules is *target rules*, which in the history of central banking represent an evolution, requiring increased trust as they cannot be monitored over the short run as instrument rules can. A target rule makes the policymaker accountable to achieve a certain objective, say an inflation target. Target rules have the advantage over instrument rules that they can respond to unforeseen shocks or changes in the structure of the economy. However, target rules have the disadvantage over instrument rules in that they are less easy to verify because there are lags from the policy instruments to the objective. For example, monetary policy affects inflation with long lags, so inflation-targeting central banks typically commit to achieving their targets over the medium term, say two years. This medium-term horizon for the target means that verification of the success of policies today will not come until two or so years in the future. Target rules may also have elements of contingent rules and be quite flexible. Inflation targeting as practiced is often described as "flexible inflation targeting" (Bernanke et al., 1999), and allows for short-run deviations from the target depending on the state of the economy. The flexibility and greater difficulty for verification of target rules has led critics of target rules to argue that they allow policymakers too much discretion. However, Bernanke and Mishkin (1997) argue that this criticism of target rules is misplaced. Rather, they see target rules, if they are sufficiently transparent (as is inflation targeting), as "constrained discretion." In other words, a transparent target rule can constrain central banks from systematically engaging in policies with undesirable long-run consequences, thereby avoiding the time-consistency problem. However, target rules allow central banks some discretion for dealing with unforeseen or unusual circumstances.

For the Bank of England, the Act of 1844 or Peel's Act set the instrument rules under which it would operate. The law set the total fiduciary issue

---

[7]   Adherence to the gold standard was rarely a mechanical process and central banks often responded to domestic economic objectives (such as interest rate smoothing) in addition to movements in gold reserves (See Bordo, 1986; Eschweiler and Bordo, 1994; Dutton, 1984; Pippenger, 1984; Giovannini, 1986). However, these actions were subordinated to the dominant commitment to keep the exchange rate within the gold points.

of banknotes that could be backed by securities at £14 million; any issue above this required 100 percent backing with specie. A rush for liquidity by financial institutions, discounting notes at the Bank of England, sometimes threatened a violation of the law. The Treasury could offer the Bank a "chancellor's letter" that would guarantee to indemnify the Bank and secure any needed legislation to protect the Bank (Wood, 2005; Giannini, 2011). During the panics in 1847, 1857, and 1866, the Banking Act of 1844 was effectively suspended, relieving the specie constraint on the Bank of England's discretionary issue of currency. Understood to be only for the duration of the crisis, these exceptions "did no damage to the convertibility commitment."[8]

As was recognized at the time, the problem is, of course, defining what constitutes an emergency. Perhaps the most notable example of a suspension of an instrument rule during the gold standard was the United Kingdom's suspension of convertibility from 1797 to 1821. In response to the threat of a French invasion, the United Kingdom shifted to a nonconvertible paper pound that permitted inflationary finance. This long, temporary suspension lasted for the remainder of the Napoleonic wars, until a postwar deflation returned the pound to its prewar gold parity. Believed to be following a contingent rule, the government was allowed by the market to borrow at very low nominal rates in the inflationary environment that were consistent with a credible government promise to eventually return the pound to its prewar parity (Bordo and White, 1994).

Too rigidly adhering to an instrument rule may impose huge costs. For example, it might be argued that during the Great Depression of the 1930s, the Federal Reserve interpreted its mandate too narrowly by failing to respond adequately to the financial crisis and thereby contributing to the depression. To ensure that the Fed had greater flexibility, in the aftermath of the economic collapse, Congress put Section 13(3) into the Federal Reserve Act that permitted the Fed to use discretion to provide credit beyond its usually constrained limits in "unusual and exigent circumstances."

A vital question facing central banks today is how to combine the mandates for price stability and financial stability. In times of crisis, a target rule with "constrained discretion" may be superior to an instrument rule by permitting temporary deviations to accommodate certain

---

[8] Bordo and Kydland (1995, p. 431). These authors provide a table for twenty-one countries covering the period of the classical and interwar gold standards that documents clearly defined circumstances when suspension of the gold standard was credibly consistent with the exchange rate regime.

types of shocks that both policymakers and the market understand to be exceptional. The historical evidence suggests that it is possible to design target and contingent rules that overcome the potential for moral hazard that is inherent in permitting some discretionary authority. In this chapter, we detail several important crises that illustrate the benefits of following a target or contingent rule, provided that discretionary policy interventions are followed by actions that substantially reduce the moral hazard that follows from such interventions. To frame our discussion, we begin by identifying the generally accepted "unprecedented" actions that the Fed took in response to the Crisis of 2008 that violate the policy rule advocated by Thornton, Bagehot, and their modern adherents. Then, we compare them to actions taken by the monetary authorities in previous crises. The monetary authorities are considered very broadly to include not only the central bank but also the Treasury and any central bank substitutes, including clearing houses.

7.2 The Fed's Unprecedented Actions in the Recent Financial Crisis

There were seven actions that were considered extraordinary or unprecedented in the recent crisis:

1. *Unusually Easy Monetary Policy.* The first glimmers of the global financial crisis appeared on August 9, 2007, when BNP Paribas announced that it had suspended redemptions on three of their funds, indicating that they were unable to value the collateralized debt obligations (CDOs) held by these funds because of an evaporation of liquidity for the underlying subprime mortgage assets. As a result, lending in the interbank markets seized up, with the spread between the Libor rate and the overnight index swap (OIS) rate shooting up from less than 10 basis points to over 100 basis points in the next several weeks. In response, the Fed lowered the spread between discount rate and the federal funds rate target by 50 basis points on August 17. Then, at its September 18 meeting, the FOMC cut the federal funds rate target by 50 basis points. What was unusual was that monetary policy eased while the momentum in the economy was quite strong, with real GDP growing at nearly 3 percent and inflation rising. By the time that the recession began in December 2007, the Fed had lowered the federal funds rate target by 100 basis points, reducing it further by May 2008 for a total decline of 325 basis points, even though the CPI did not peak at nearly 6 percent until July 2008. These actions well in advance of the panic arising

from the collapse of Lehman Brothers in September 2008 emphasize the preemptive character of monetary policy.

2. *New Non-Bagehot Liquidity Facilities.* During the global financial crisis, the Federal Reserve created a number of new credit facilities that provided liquidity, but not at high interest rates as proposed by Bagehot. Although the discount rate was further reduced so that it was only 25 basis points above the federal funds target in March 2008, borrowing from the discount window did not appear to provide sufficient liquidity. Discount window borrowing had a "stigma" because it suggested that a borrowing bank might be desperate for funds and thus be in trouble. To encourage additional borrowing, the Fed set up a temporary Term Auction Facility (TAF) in December 2007 to auction federal funds. The TAF facility became more widely used than the discount window because it avoided the stigma problem and enabled banks to borrow at a competitive rate lower than the discount rate. The TAF auctions started at $20 billion and rose as the crisis worsened to over $400 billion. The Fed further broadened its provision of liquidity to the financial system, well beyond its traditional lending to banking institutions, by creating lending facilities for investment banks in March 2008 (the Term Securities Lending Facility – TSLF, Primary Dealer Credit Facility – PDCF), as well as lending facilities to promote purchases of commercial paper, mortgage-backed securities, other asset-backed securities, and money-market-mutual fund assets after the collapse of Lehman Brothers in September 2008 (Asset-Backed Commercial Paper Money Market Mutual Fund Liquidity Facility – AMLF, Commercial Paper Funding Facility – CPFF, Money Market Investor Funding Facility – MMIFF, Term Asset-Backed Securities Loan Facility – TALF). The enlargement of the Fed's lending programs during the 2007–09 financial crisis was remarkable, reaching a peak of over $1.5 trillion dollars by the end of 2008.

3. *International Central Bank Cooperation.* The Fed also became an international lender of last resort to central banks during the crisis. In December 2007, the Fed set up swap lines for the European Central Bank and the Swiss National Bank to allow them to borrow dollars from the Fed so that they could make dollar loans to their domestic banks. After the Lehman Brothers collapse, the Fed arranged swap lines with the central banks of Japan, the United Kingdom, Canada, Australia, Sweden, Norway, Denmark, New Zealand, Mexico, Brazil, Korea, and Singapore. At its peak in December 2008, the Fed had extended almost $600 billion of these swaps to foreign central banks.

4. *Nonconventional Monetary Policy.* In the last few decades, the Fed's open market operations normally involved only the purchase of short-term government securities. However, during this crisis, the Fed saw a need to adopt a nonconventional monetary policy of large-scale asset purchases (LSAPs) to lower interest rates for particular types of credit. To support the mortgage-backed securities market (MBS) and lower interest rates on residential mortgages, the Fed set up a government sponsored entities purchase program in November 2008, through which the Fed eventually purchased $1.25 trillion of MBS guaranteed by Fannie Mae and Freddie Mac. This program was dubbed *quantitative easing* (later known as QE1) because it resulted in a large increase in the Fed's balance sheet and the monetary base. However, as argued by former Chairman Bernanke, this program was directed not at expanding the Fed's balance sheet, but at improving the function of particular credit markets, hence he referred to the program as *credit easing*, rather than *quantitative easing*. By the time that financial markets recovered, the federal funds rate was effectively at zero. To further pursue an expansionary policy and revive the economy, the Fed announced in November 2010 that it would purchase $600 billion of long-term Treasury securities at a rate of about $75 billion per month. This large-scale purchase program, which became known as QE2, was intended to lower long-term interest rates. In September 2012, the Federal Reserve announced a third large-scale asset-purchase program, QE3 which combined elements of QE1 and QE2 by conducting purchases of $40 billion of mortgage-backed securities and $45 billion of long-term Treasuries. However, QE3 differed from the previous QE programs in that it was not for a fixed dollar amount, but was instead open-ended, with the purchases continuing "if the outlook for the labor market does not improve substantially." Starting in December 2013, the Fed announced that this program would be phased out gradually over time.

5. *Central Bank Rescues of Financial Institutions/Provision for Orderly Liquidations.* In early March 2008, short-term financing for the investment bank, Bear Stearns, dried up because of a run on the shadow banking system (Gorton and Metrick, 2009). Uncertain of the value of the collateral backing Bear Stearns repurchase agreements, the market would not roll over these loans. Because the value of Bear Stearns' long-term assets would plummet if quickly sold, the firm faced imminent failure. The Fed worried that the failure of Bear Stearns might trigger a full-fledged financial crisis, so it brokered a deal for JPMorgan/Chase to purchase Bear Stearns, with the Fed taking $30 billion of Bear Stearns'

toxic assets on to its books.[9] The Fed arranged a bailout because JPMorgan was unwilling to take these hard-to-value assets on to its books. Then, on Monday, September 15, 2008, after suffering losses in the subprime market, Lehman Brothers filed for bankruptcy – the largest bankruptcy filing in US history – as the Fed stood aside. Officials at the Federal Reserve and the US Treasury have argued that they did not have the legal resolution authority to intervene to prevent a Lehman bankruptcy. On the other hand, given the extraordinary efforts the Federal Reserve made to bail out Bear Stearns, it seems plausible that the Fed and the Treasury made a conscious decision not to bail out Lehman Brothers.[10] The Fed's safety net was soon extended to insurance companies. The Financial Products Unit of American International Group (AIG) had written over $400 billion of credit default swaps, which after Lehman Brothers' collapse, left it facing enormous payments. Observing these potential losses, the market refused to continue short-term funding to AIG. In response, on September 16, 2008, the Fed stepped in with an $85 billion loan to keep AIG afloat.[11]

6. *Treasury Collaboration/Intervention/Aid.* When the financial crisis entered a particularly virulent phase after the collapse of Lehman Brothers (Mishkin, 2010), further assistance to failing financial institutions was viewed as urgent. After a messy fight in Congress, the Bush administration's Economic Recovery Act of 2008 was passed on October 3, 2008, creating the Troubled Asset Relief Plan (TARP). This program initially intended to purchase subprime mortgage assets to prop up financial institutions' balance sheets. However, it soon became clear that agreeing on prices for assets was impossible. The Treasury then switched to using the TARP funds to inject capital into financial institutions, thereby shoring up their balance sheets directly. In addition, on September 29, the US Treasury had announced a Temporary Guarantee Program for Money Market Funds, which insured that MMMFs would not "break the buck" and investors would receive at least the $1 par value per share. Subsequently, on October 14, 2008, the Federal Deposit Insurance Corporation (FDIC) announced the Temporary Liquidity Guarantee Program (TLGP) that guaranteed newly issued senior

---

[9] Legally, the Fed could not purchase these assets directly. Instead, it in effect acquired them by making a non-recourse loan to JPMorgan, where the Fed could not require the bank to pay back the loan and so took ownership of the toxic collateral, which ended being worth less than what the Fed paid.

[10] Many commentators have argued that allowing Lehman to go bankrupt was a colossal mistake that turned a mild financial disruption into a global financial crisis, but there was a plausible case for letting Lehman go into bankruptcy, as argued in Mishkin (2011).

[11] Total loans to AIG from the Fed and the United State government rose to over $170 billion.

unsecured bank debt, such as federal funds and commercial paper, as well as noninterest-bearing transaction accounts. Its stated purpose was to "strengthen confidence and encourage liquidity in the banking system" (FDIC, 2008). Although the Federal Reserve was not directly involved in administering these programs, they were part of a package of bailouts of financial institutions, and the Federal Reserve lobbied Congress to implement these programs.

7. *Supervisory Actions.* Concerned about public confidence in the solvency and viability of the leading financial institutions, the Treasury announced in February 2009 that the nineteen largest banking institutions would be placed in the Supervisory Capital Assessment Program (SCAP) that would administer *stress tests* led by the Federal Reserve in cooperation with the Office of the Comptroller of the Currency (OCC) and the FDIC. The initial stress test was designed as a forward-looking exercise to estimate the possible erosion of bank capital under two scenarios: the February 2009 baseline consensus forecast by private-sector economists of a continuing decline in economic activity and a worst-case scenario of a much more severe recession (Board of Governors of the Federal Reserve System, 2009). The Treasury announced the results in early May 2009, which were well received by market participants. The stress test improved market confidence and encouraged the recapitalization of these banks and the stabilization of the financial system (Acharya and Seru, 2013).[12] To put these "unprecedented" actions during the Crisis of 2008 into a historical perspective, Table 7.1 divides them into seven categories, with an "X" in the top row indicating that they were undertaken. In the following rows, we present selected crises from the previous 150 years for comparison, which are accompanied by brief narratives explaining how and why exceptional or "rule-violating" actions were undertaken by the monetary authorities to quell the crisis.

7.3 Bagehot's Rule and the Crises of 1866, 1889, and 1890

Contemporary policy debates about how a LOLR should respond to a financial crisis are framed as much by history as by theory. This history is largely informed by a "classical" view of how the Bank of England checked financial crises in the late nineteenth century. The progenitors of this view, Thornton

---

[12] Hoshi and Kashyap (2010) found that similar stress tests in Japan in 2003 were a key element of the recovery of the Japanese banking system after the "lost decade" from 1992 to 2002.

Table 7.1. *Unprecedented Actions by Monetary Authorities in Financial Crises*

	Unusual Monetary Easing	Non-Bagehot Liquidity Facilities	International Central Bank Cooperation	Nonconventional Monetary Policy	Rescue/ Orderly Liquidation of Financial Institution	Direct Treasury Collaboration/ Intervention/Aid	Supervision
	1	2	3	4	5	6	7
United States 2008	X	X	X	X	X	X	
United Kingdom 1866						X	X
France 1889					X	X	
United Kingdom 1890			X		X	X	
United States 1907		X	X			X	
United States 1929	X	X					
United States 1930–33				X	X	X	X
Penn Central 1970		X					
Continental Illinois 1984					X		
Crash of 1987	X	X					
LTCM 1998	X				X		

(1802) and Bagehot (1873), argued that the Bank of England should react to a banking panic by lending freely through the discount window at a high rate of interest on all collateral that would be considered good in normal, noncrisis times, preventing illiquid but not insolvent banks from failing.[13] This advice was predicated on the fact that the United Kingdom was on the gold standard and a high rate would protect the Bank of England's reserves and prevent a currency crisis from following a banking crisis (Grossman and Rockoff, 2014). It should also be remembered how the discount rate was supposed to be managed in ordinary, noncrisis times. Changes in the discount rate were supposed to follow the gold standard's "rules of the game," rising in response to a balance of payments deficit and reduced when there was a surplus. The objective was to speed up the operation of the gold standard's adjustment process and reduce the associated and costly gold flows. The discount rate then reacted to the balance of payments movements. The recommendation given by Bagehot to the Bank of England for crisis times complements the "rules" for ordinary times.

Humphrey (1975) and Bordo (1990) point out that according to the Thornton-Bagehot approach, it is not the duty of the LOLR to prevent financial shocks but to neutralize them once they have occurred by halting the spread of a panic. The Thornton-Bagehot approach is a reactive policy, unlike the "unprecedented" actions that may be considered to be preemptive policies; but it has attractive characteristics, as the refusal to save insolvent institutions keeps moral hazard at bay and the high rate provides an automatic exit strategy, as banks quickly pay off loans from the bank.

The Thornton-Bagehot approach does have elements of an instrument rule because it makes recommendations for how a policy instrument, the discount rate, should be set and how the discount facility should be administered. However, it is important to note that the Thornton-Bagehot approach is not nearly as precise and easily monitored as the gold standard or more modern instrument rules such as the Taylor rule or the monetarist constant-money-growth rate rule. For want of a better name, we refer to the Thornton-Bagehot approach as Bagehot's rule throughout the rest of this chapter, keeping in mind that it is not quite as rigid as many instrument rules.

Reviewing the history of the Bank of England, Bagehot emphasized that the Bank, having the greatest reserves, could quell a panic by providing

---

[13] Bagehot's explanation of how the Bank should act was partly a response to criticism that his proposed LOLR operations would bring upon moral hazard (Wood, 2005; Grossman, 2010, p. 91).

cash for good collateral at a rate sufficiently high to deter excessive use of the Bank's facility. Although Bagehot's book was written after the Overend, Gurney, and Co. Panic of 1866, it has been recently documented (Bignon, Flandreau, and Ugolini, 2012) that his prescription was put into effect after a crisis in 1847. In this panic, the Bank kept its discount rate below the market rate and rationed credit, exacerbating the crisis. The Bank of England's full adherence to Bagehot's rule was made plain in 1866 when the large Overend-Gurney bank was recognized to be insolvent and the Bank of England signaled that it had no intention of aiding the bank, precipitating a panic (Flandreau and Ugolini, 2014). When it was announced that Overend-Gurney had suspended, the bank rate was raised from 7 to 9 percent and then to 10 percent, well above the market rate for bills. Banks and bills brokers crowded the discount window at the Bank, but there was no decline in the quality accepted as collateral. Eventually, the panic abated. While the Bank's response to the 1866 panic is considered by many to be the correct response that can be announced ahead of time, thereby providing commitment, it should be noted that the Bank was only able to act as a LOLR because it had secured a "chancellor's letter" from the Treasury. The chancellor's letter promised indemnification, if needed, via a bill in Parliament. The letter from the Chancellor of the Exchequer permitted the Bank of England to violate the instrument, price-stability rule governing reserves for banknotes, set by the Bank Act of 1844. Overend-Gurney was thus understood to be an emergency when the Bank could credibly violate the price-stability rule in order to ensure financial stability, with the backing of the Treasury. Hence this application of Bagehot's rule was not a pure application of an instrument rule, but had elements of a contingent rule. As this action violated the price-stability, instrument rule, we classify the issuance of a chancellor's letter as an unconventional policy action, in terms of a gold standard regime, in Table 7.1.

While most economists and policymakers treat Bagehot and the Bank of England's behavior from the 1866 crisis to 1914 as the "gold standard" for a LOLR, both the Bank of England and the Banque de France – the two most important central banks of the era – deviated from this policy advice and engaged in what would be termed today as unprecedented policy actions that deviated from the gold standard instrument rule.[14] First, in 1889, the Banque de France engineered a lifeboat operation to rescue one the largest Paris banks, and then in 1890, the Bank of England followed suit with a

---

[14] Grossman (2010) discusses some early examples of bailout in Australia (1826), Belgium (1839), and Germany (1848).

lifeboat for Baring Brothers *à la française*. These actions get little attention in the debate over the appropriate rules for a LOLR, but they were important steps in the evolution of central banking policy in response to the evolution of the financial system in the 1880s.

In 1882, a crash on the Paris stock market led to the collapse of Union Générale, one of France's largest banks, as well as several smaller banks. Defaulting counterparties in the forward market for stocks caused a crucial number of brokers to fail, threatening the solvency of the whole Paris Bourse. The brokers lacked the statutory collateral the Banque de France required for loans, but a consortium of banks, with the right collateral, stepped in as an intermediary, ensuring that the brokers had sufficient liquidity. Although the Banque de France also lent freely to the rest of the market, it refused to provide any assistance to the insolvent Union Générale, the Bourse in Lyon, and other banks (White, 2007). A long deep recession ensued that caused some in the Banque to question whether they had acted correctly. Thus, when a run on one of the largest banks, the Comptoir d'Escompte, began in 1889, the Banque lent freely at a rate higher than the market rate to all borrowers with good collateral; but it also saved the insolvent Comptoir (Hautcoeur, Riva, and White, 2014). This bank had supported an attempt to corner the copper market with large loans and massive guarantees of copper forward contracts. When the price of copper collapsed, the bank was insolvent. Pressed by the Minister of Finance who offered an early renewal of the Banque's charter as an inducement, the Banque provided loans of 140 million francs against all the Comptoir's assets, good and bad – a violation of the strict, statutory, instrument rules governing collateral for lending. A guarantee syndicate of banks, whose membership was determined partly on ability to pay and partly on involvement in the copper speculation, was induced to cover any losses up to 40 million francs (Hautcoeur, Riva, and White, 2014). Some on the Banque de France's Council of Regents were opposed to this unprecedented action, but credit to the Comptoir halted a run that appeared to presage a general panic. The Banque then held the Comptoir's bad assets, permitting the copper market to recover and an orderly resolution to proceed through the courts. The buildings and accounts of the failed bank were transferred to its recapitalized successor. Severe financial penalties were meted out to the Comptoir's board of directors and others involved in the disaster, actions that appear to have been designed to mitigate moral hazard from this intervention. No other major financial crisis occurred in France until the outbreak of World War I. In Table 7.1, this 1889 crisis is tagged as having two unprecedented interventions – a bailout/resolution and Treasury intervention.

A year after the French crisis, in November 1890, one of the leading British banks, Baring Brothers, was found to be on the brink of failure. Before a panic could take hold, the Bank of England took unprecedented preemptive actions (Clapham, 1945). Barings had originated and under-written vast issues of Argentine securities. Having borrowed heavily and unable to sell off its portfolio of these bonds, as their value dropped, the bank approached the Bank of England. Alarmed that this leading house might be insolvent, the Bank informed the Treasury of the situation. In contrast to France in 1889, the initiative for action came from the central bank, and the British Treasury refused to countenance any direct support, even though the Chancellor of the Exchequer believed that if Barings went under, the crisis would be far more severe than the Overend-Gurney Crisis of 1866. Following the example of 1866, he offered a "chancellor's letter," which have would permitted the Bank to increase its circulation beyond its legal limits. This offer was refused by the Governor of the Bank of England who apparently was afraid that news of this action might set off a panic.

However, the gold reserves of the Bank were threatened as institutions discounted with the Bank, presenting the possibility of a currency crisis in the globalized capital market of the period. To shore up its gold reserves, the Bank of England borrowed £3 million from the Banque de France, pro-viding Treasury bills as collateral, which were obtained by selling consols to the Commissioners of the National Debt. The Governor explained to his French counterpart that although the Bank could induce gold to flow to England by raising the bank rate, such a measure "would have been too severe," alarming the City, and he "preferred not to adopt the course usually taken" (Clapham, 1945, Vol. 1, p. 330). In addition, £1.5 million was pur-chased from Russia by the sale of Exchequer bonds. Thus, the Bank recog-nized that following Bagehot's rule might signal a weakness that could bring about further bank runs or a run on the pound. Borrowing from foreign central banks and governments was preferable.

Meanwhile, it was quietly ascertained that Barings was probably insol-vent. Sensing these problems, the market flooded Bank of England with requests to discount Barings paper (Clapham, 1945). Faced with accept-ing bad collateral, the Governor demanded that the Treasury provisionally guarantee loans to Barings to maintain its liquidity so that the Bank would have time to form a guarantee syndicate to absorb any potential losses. The Governor quickly assembled a syndicate of banks and other financial houses whose pledges totaled £17,105,000. This sum was more than sufficient to protect the Bank from losses, as its maximum advance was £7,526,600. The guarantee syndicate was set to last for three years, while the Bank "nursed" Barings' assets. However, this task was not completed and, over the protests of some syndicate members, it was renewed for another two years, with a reduction in the pledge to a quarter of the initial sum. Liquidation was finally completed in 1895; and although the funds of the syndicate were not drawn upon, the Baring family was compelled to cover losses with their private fortunes – a step to mitigate the moral hazard consequences of intervention. Although the Bank of England was generally praised for this action that preempted a panic, *The Economist* warned its readers that this was a dangerous precedent, describing the potential risk of moral hazard. In Table 7.1, the Barings episode includes three unusual actions: central bank cooperation, managing an insolvent institution, and Treasury cooperation with a promise of intervention if needed.

The unprecedented actions of 1889 and 1890 raise the obvious question: why didn't the Banque de France and the Bank of England strictly follow Bagehot's rule, or perhaps why didn't Thornton or Bagehot discuss the possibility of a lifeboat? The answer would seem to be that certainly in 1802 and even as late as 1873, the British financial system was not yet dominated by large leveraged institutions that were highly interconnected with other large institutions, and the globalized financial markets of the late nineteenth century were just emerging. To use an anachronistic term, no "systemically important financial institutions" or "SIFIs" had emerged. The merger waves that ultimately produced a nationally concentrated industry were still in the future (Capie and Rodrik-Bali, 1982). While a panic could render many banks illiquid, Thornton and Bagehot saw individual banks' solvency questions as relatively unconnected. Two decades after *Lombard Street* was written, the financial industry presented a problem that the Banque de France and the Bank of England addressed by taking unprecedented actions beyond following Bagehot's rule.

7.4 The Crisis of 1907

Analyzing the Crisis of 1907 from the point of view of a LOLR is an awkward exercise as the United States did not, of course, have a central bank yet. The New York Clearing House (NYCH) might be categorized as a quasi-central bank because of its ability to add to interbank liquidity via the issue of clearinghouse loan certificates, but it was not a government-sponsored central bank and had no mandate for price stability. Nevertheless, it is useful to detail the interventions that were deployed in the United States by the NYCH and the Treasury and in Europe by the central banks.

Like the 1889 crisis in France, the panic of 1907 in the United States was set off by the failure of an attempted copper corner at the time when liquidity was particularly tight. In response to gold outflows from British insurance companies' payments for the San Francisco earthquake of 1906 (Odell and Weidenmier, 2004), the Bank of England raised its discount rate and the Banque de France created a special facility to draw gold from the United States by paying interest on gold in transit to France. During the week of October 14, 1907, five members and three nonmembers sought assistance from the NYCH and were accommodated. But, when a run on the nonmember Knickerbocker Trust began on October 21, it was denied assistance from the NYCH; and runs broke out against other trust companies. Secretary of the Treasury George Cortelyou tried to provide some liquidity by depositing $25 million in the major central reserve city banks on October 24 but with little effect (Friedman and Schwartz, 1963).

As credit dried up, interest rates shot up and stock prices fell. On the same day as the Treasury acted, J. P. Morgan persuaded the member banks of the NYCH to lend to a "money pool" to enable brokers on the New York Stock Exchange to complete a settlement. The rush for liquidity did not abate and on October 25, the NYCH announced the issuance of clearing house loan certificates – an action that eased the demand for liquidity by increasing liquidity for interbank transactions – and the suspension of deposit convertibility (Moen and Tallman, 2000). As a consequence a premium on currency and coin arose, creating an incentive to import gold from abroad.

The international dimension of 1907 is particularly important. Although the Bank of England has been referred to as the "conductor of the orchestra" of the globalized financial markets because London was the world's largest financial center and changes in the Bank's discount rate usually led other central banks to follow suit, it was the Banque de France, with Paris as the second largest financial center, that had far greater gold reserves that provided assistance to other central banks. Thus, in the immediate aftermath of the American crisis in October, when the Bank of England's high discount rate did not end gold exports that were causing its reserves to shrink, the Banque de France announced on November 7 that it would purchase 80 million francs of sterling bills and forwarded 80 million francs of US gold eagles to London to allay the drain. When gold outflows in France became acute, Banque de France announced on November 22 that it would create a special facility that eased liquidity both in France and the United States (Rodgers and Payne, 2014). The high premium on gold in New York led to an outflow of circulating gold in France. To allay this temporary, extraordinary demand, the Banque created a special loan facility where

French bankers could discount commercial paper on very favorable terms to obtain US gold eagles from the vaults of the Banque. Estimated to be 80 million francs or $16 million, the eagles were then shipped to the United States in lieu of French coin that remained in circulation (Rodgers and Payne, 2014). In Table 7.1, the 1907 crisis had three unusual actions: new liquidity facilities, central bank cooperation, and Treasury assistance.

In the United States, the failure of the NYCH to provide liquidity to Knickerbocker Trust to enable it to ride out the crisis or liquidate it in a more orderly fashion is central to the story of the panic's generation, although intervention would have required further actions to mitigate moral hazard. The severe panic and recession were, of course, what led to the creation of the Federal Reserve. Although established in 1913, the Fed did not become an independent central bank until it had finished assisting the Treasury with the financing of World War I. In the 1920s, the Fed fine-tuned its policy techniques, managing a period of low inflation and low unemployment, not unlike the Great Moderation. This period abruptly closed with multiple crises that yielded the Great Depression. Here we divide the crises of the Great Depression into the Stock Market Crash of 1929, where the Federal Reserve acted appropriately as a LOLR, and the banking crises of 1930–33, where the Fed failed as a central bank.

7.5 The Stock Market Crash of 1929

The stock market boom and bust of 1928–29 provided the first big test for the Federal Reserve. The October 1929 crash hit the largest market for short-term funds – brokers' loans. Banks, individuals, and companies with extra cash lent to brokers, who in turn lent on margin to investors. Panicked that investors might default on their margin loans from brokers, lenders to brokers withdrew their call loans and refused to renew their time loans, creating the possibility of broker bankruptcies and fire sales of collateral, with the effects spilling over to other markets. When the New York City banks stepped in to replace loans to brokers, supplying approximately $1 billion, the Federal Reserve Bank of New York let it be known that "the discount window was wide open" for member banks. The discount rate remained low in violation of Bagehot's rule. The New York Fed also gave these banks additional reserves through open market purchases of $160 million, ensuring that the crash was confined to the stock market and did not fuel a banking panic (Friedman and Schwartz, 1963, p. 339).

In the aftermath of the New York Fed's action, credit spreads declined to levels below those before the stock market crash (Mishkin, 1991). The low level of credit spreads up until October 1930 is remarkable given the sharp economic contraction up to that point and the over 40 percent decline in the value of common stocks. This phenomenon suggests that the unprecedented actions of the New York Fed were successful in containing the initial financial disruption.

However, the purchases of securities that the New York Fed made were in excess of those approved by the Open Market Investment Committee, an unprecedented action that departed from established, instrument-rule, operating procedures, angering the Board. In Table 7.1, this unusual monetary easing is indicated in Column 1 for 1929. New York's policy came to an end when the Board indicated its displeasure with the New York Fed for bailing out speculators and policy tightened. This stance was maintained by the Fed, even as the economy slowed through 1930–32 and three major banking panics swept through the financial system. The Fed reduced the discount rate, but deflation kept real rates high and open market operations remained feeble. The Federal Reserve's inaction in these years is well known and has been held largely responsible for the economic collapse. For this essay, what is striking is the absence of unprecedented actions by the Fed when banking panics began to occur, starting in the fall of 1930; indeed, innovative policy responses did not come from the Fed but from Republican and Democratic administrations working with Congress.

7.6 The Banking Panics of 1930–1933

The Federal Reserve's policy mistakes that contributed to the onset and duration of the Great Depression have been well documented.[15] In accounts of the economic collapse, the failure of the Fed to act promptly and forcefully as a LOLR to halt and offset the four banking panics has played a central role (Friedman and Schwartz, 1963; Romer, 1990). A variety of reasons for these mistakes have been offered: poor institutional design of the Fed, poor theory and interpretation of the effects of monetary actions, and the fear that the nation's ability to remain on the gold standard was imperiled (Bordo and Wheelock, 2013). From our vantage point, these factors all contributed to induce the Fed – especially, the Board and some Federal Reserve banks – to adhere too strictly to the instrument rules laid down by the Federal Reserve Act presumably to ensure price stability and financial stability. Unlike its pre-1914 European counterparts and the New York Fed in

---

[15] A short list of seminal works would include Friedman and Schwartz (1963), Wicker (1966), Meltzer (2003), Wheelock (1991), and Bordo and Wheelock (2013).

1929, the Fed undertook no unprecedented actions. Faced with crisis after crisis, the Fed maintained its very circumscribed mandate, while presidents and the Congress sought innovative interventions. However, trusting to the Fed, they did not act promptly, and given the slow nature of the legislative process, which allowed special interests to exercise influence, the effectiveness of their actions varied considerably.

The limits on the central bank were engineered by the Federal Reserve Act of 1913 that created a decentralized central bank of twelve regional banks supervised by the Federal Reserve Board in Washington, DC. Each of the Federal Reserve banks was empowered to discount eligible paper for its member banks – national banks and state-chartered banks that opted to join. The reserve banks set their own discount rates subject to Board approval.[16] The Fed focused on ensuring that only "real bills" were discounted, narrowly defining the type of collateral – eligible paper – that would be acceptable.[17] Discounting member banks would receive Federal Reserve notes or deposits at the Fed, with the total notes and deposits created by each reserve bank constrained by gold cover – instrument rule – requirements of 40 percent for notes and 35 percent for deposits, with eligible paper equal to 100 percent of outstanding notes. Although the 1913 Act's precursor, the Aldrich Bill, had broader discounting provisions, where any direct bank obligation, if approved by the Secretary of the Treasury, was allowable, this was omitted from the Federal Reserve Act. Furthermore, the Fed could only lend to member banks, not the more numerous nonmember banks, except in extraordinary circumstances approved by the Board.[18] Thus, by design, the Fed was constrained and had potentially less flexibility in responding to a crisis than European banks. While events would prove differently, the founders of the Fed, strong believers in the real bills doctrine, may have thought that by enshrining the real bills doctrine in the Federal Reserve Act "they had created a foolproof mechanism that would prevent panics from occurring in the first place" (Bordo and Wheelock, 2013).

There was another crucial difference between Fed discount rate policy and those of the Bank of England and the Banque de France. Instead of

---

[16] The discount rate declined somewhat as a policy tool and open market operations gained importance, being used to hit a borrowed reserves target.

[17] The Act permitted discounting of "notes, drafts, and bills of exchange arising out of actual commercial transactions." Discounting of loans for "the purpose of carrying or trading in stocks, bonds or other investment securities" was forbidden, with the exception of US government securities. Discounting was only permitted for loans with a maximum term of ninety days (180 days for agricultural loans).

[18] A rare exercise of this power was during a local banking panic in Florida in 1929 (Carlson, Mitchener, and Richardson, 2011).

maintaining a discount rate above the market rate, discount rates tended to be below. The adverse selection problem quickly arose. The Fed found that it was not simply accommodating borrowers with temporary liquidity problems: it had a substantial number of habitually weak borrowing banks. Good borrowers were discouraged by the stigma they incurred. Nevertheless, the Fed's accommodation of seasonal money market demands is believed to have eliminated banking distress and panics in the 1920s (Miron, 1986; White, 2013).

The first banking crisis, and in particular, the demise of the Bank of United States, offers an interesting contrast to the rescues of the Comptoir d'Escompte, Baring Brothers, and LTCM in 1998. Although it was relatively smaller, runs on the bank caused both the New York Fed and the New York Superintendent of Banks to fear that its failure might spawn more runs. Pumping liquidity into this bank, the Fed provided over $20 million (Lucia, 1985). Federal and New York authorities then sponsored a plan to merge the Bank of United States with Manufacturers Trust, Public National Bank, and International Trust, with the Clearing House banks subscribing $30 million of new capital (Friedman and Schwartz, 1963, p. 309). Unlike the LTCM episode where the New York Federal Reserve Bank managed the crucial meetings, the New York Superintendent was kept out of the discussions of the Clearing House banks who scuttled the plan because they disapproved of the real estate loans of the Bank of United States and because they believed that its failure would have no repercussions. The Superintendent then closed the bank and began liquidation. Friedman and Schwartz (1963, p. 311) viewed this action as a serious failure:

The withdrawal of support by the Clearing House banks from the concerted measures sponsored by the Federal Reserve Bank of New York to save the bank – measures of a kind the banking community had often taken in similar circumstances in the past – was a serious blow to the System's prestige. (1963, p. 311)

Other banks responded to news of the Bank of United States failure by borrowing $200 million from the New York Fed, part of the rising demand for liquidity of the first banking panic.

By 1932, the president and the Congress, horrified by the steady economic decline, reacted to what they considered to be the insufficient actions of the Fed. Following President Herbert Hoover's recommendation, Congress created the Reconstruction Finance Corporation (RFC) in January 1932. The RFC was empowered to make loans to banks, other financial institutions and railroads up to $1.5 billion to halt the rise in failures. In July 1932, the Emergency Relief and Construction Act increased the RFC's lending capacity to $3.3 billion. In the Glass-Steagall Act of 1932, Congress gave the Fed permission to lend on any satisfactory collateral in an emergency – including government bonds, previously excluded by real bills concerns. The act went further to provide a means to lend to banks that had insufficient eligible assets for collateral, trying to broaden the Fed's ability to provide liquidity (Friedman and Schwartz, 1963, pp. 320–321). For a longer-term market, the mortgage market, the Federal Home Loan Bank Act was passed in 1932 to provide a means for savings and loans, savings banks, and insurance companies to borrow on collateral of first mortgages (Friedman and Schwartz, 1963). Although this legislation was influenced by the building and loan associations lobby (Snowden, 1995), its passage reflected the limitations on the Fed's ability to create additional lending facilities. In addition, Congress put heavy pressure on the Fed, which in April 1932 embarked on large-scale open market purchases of $1 billion but backed off when Congress' session was over.

Facing a huge fourth banking panic, President Franklin D. Roosevelt declared a bank holiday on March 6, 1933, and moved the United States off the gold standard. On March 9, Congress passed the Emergency Banking Act confirming the powers of the president to declare a bank holiday and authorizing emergency issues of Federal Reserve banknotes. It also permitted the RFC to buy preferred stock from national and state banks (Friedman and Schwartz, 1963). The banking holiday included a "stress test." In December 1932, there were 17,796 commercial banks, with 447 failing between the end of the year and the declaration of the holiday. To restore public confidence, examiners and auditors assessed the solvency and viability of the remaining banks, and only 11,878 were quickly opened. This activity resembles the 2009 stress test that was administered to the largest American banks, with similar positive effects on confidence. Although some national banks would be liquidated, the Comptroller of the Currency was empowered to manage national banks with impaired assets, appointing conservators who would monitor deposit inflows and outflows and oversee the reorganization of these institutions. The RFC played a major role in strengthening the weak banks by providing $1 billion in bank capital, buying stock from 6,139 banks.

Lastly, the Emergency Banking Act sought to give the Fed more flexibility to aid banks by permitting the Fed to make advances in "exceptional and exigent circumstances" to member banks on any acceptable assets. This last provision was permanently adopted by the Banking Act of 1935 as Section 13(3) of the Federal Reserve Act, permitting Federal Reserve banks in "unusual and exigent circumstances" to discount, for any participant in a program or facility, notes approved by the Federal Reserve bank provided they are "unable to secure adequate credit accommodations from other banking institutions." Thus, the Fed was granted the authority to take unprecedented actions, recognizing that it had been too constrained by law and outlook. In Table 7.1, we identify four unprecedented actions for 1930–33, but they were not initiated by the Fed. Congress broadened the Fed's means to conduct monetary policy (4), the bank holiday provided a means to have an orderly reopening and closure of banks (5), the RFC and Federal Home Loan banks provided more aid via Treasury contributions (6), and the bank holiday led to a novel auditing ("stress test") of the banks (7).

In earlier crises, the monetary authorities sought to limit future risk-taking; did Congress seek to do this as well in the 1930s? It has been argued that the package of New Deal reforms did much to undermine the incentives to limit risk-taking in banking, notably the elimination of double liability for bank stock and the introduction of deposit insurance (White, 2013). Nevertheless, Congress was aware of the moral hazard implications of deposit insurance (Calomiris and White, 1994). It refused to bail out depositors in banks that failed before the creation of the FDIC, and it created a fairly limited insurance program aimed at protecting smaller depositors. The expansion of deposit insurance in later years was the product of a regulatory dynamic, largely driven by lobbying of interest groups in the banking industry (White, 1998).

7.7 The Penn Central Bankruptcy

Prior to 1970, commercial paper was considered one of the safest money market instruments because only corporations with very high credit ratings issued it. It was common practice for corporations to continually roll over their commercial paper, that is, issue new commercial paper to pay off the old. Penn Central Railroad was a major issuer of commercial paper, with more than $200 million outstanding; but by May 1970 it was on the verge of bankruptcy and it requested federal assistance from the Nixon administration.[19] Despite administration support for a bailout of Penn Central, Congress decided after six weeks of debate not to pass bailout legislation. Meanwhile, the Nixon administration asked the Board of Governors of the Federal Reserve to authorize a direct loan from the Federal Reserve Bank of

[19] See Maisel (1973) and Brimmer (1989) for further discussion of the Penn Central bankruptcy episode.

New York to Penn Central. However, on Thursday, June 18, the New York Fed informed the Board of Governors that its staff studies indicated that Penn Central would not be able to repay the loan, and as a result the Board decided not to authorize the loan. Without this loan, Penn Central was forced to declare bankruptcy on Sunday, June 21, 1970.

Once the Federal Reserve made the decision to let Penn Central go into bankruptcy, it was concerned that Penn Central's default on its commercial paper would, as Brimmer (1989) puts it, have had a "chilling effect on the commercial paper market" (p. 6), making it impossible for other corporations to roll over their commercial paper. The Penn Central bankruptcy, then, had the potential for sending other companies into bankruptcy which, in turn, might have triggered a full-scale financial panic. To avoid this scenario, the New York Fed contacted several large money center banks on Saturday and Sunday, June 20 and 21, alerted them to the impending bankruptcy, and encouraged them to lend to their customers who were unable to roll over their commercial paper, indicating that the discount window would be open to them to facilitate their loans. With the interest rate on discount loans below market interest rates, banks borrowed $575 million. In addition, on June 22 the Fed decided to suspend Regulation Q ceilings on deposits of $100,000 and over in order to keep short-term interest rates from rising, and the formal vote was taken the next day to allow the FDIC and the Federal Home Loan Bank Board to take parallel action. The net result was that the Federal Reserve provided liquidity to ensure the continued smooth functioning of the commercial paper market.

The rationale for the Fed's actions was that an unprecedented bankruptcy in the commercial paper market would lead lenders to pull out because they would no longer be confident that they could accurately screen borrowers, which was reflected in credit markets by a widening of credit spreads. After these actions, credit spreads came back down and commercial paper rates fell sharply, indicating a rapid recovery in the commercial paper market. The financial disruption from the Penn Central bankruptcy therefore turned out to be small and the recession which started shortly before the Penn Central bankruptcy occurred was mild.

This policy action clearly was unprecedented and a violation of the Bagehot rule because lending was done at below-market interest rates. However, these below-market rates and the Fed's commitment to provide funds to keep that market functioning had the advantage that it made it profitable for banks to lend directly to a market where credit had dried up. This approach enabled the Fed to direct credit to nonfinancial firms that it was not monitoring, having the banks lend to them instead. These banks then had the incentive to monitor these firms to prevent them from taking on excessive risk because the banks would be on the hook if the loans went sour. The Fed thus used the banks as delegated monitors to ameliorate potential moral hazard that could lead to excessive risk taking. This action avoided the necessity for the Fed to lend to firms that it did not supervise and had little expertise in monitoring. It is treated in Table 7.1 as a non-Bagehot liquidity facility even though the action was indirect. The Federal Reserve's actions did have elements of discretion, but because the Fed used delegated monitors to constrain moral hazard risk, these actions can be characterized as constrained discretion.

7.8 Continental Illinois 1984

In 1984, Continental Illinois, the seventh largest bank in the United States, experienced a bank run when uninsured depositors became convinced that it was insolvent. In its drive to become the nation's largest commercial and industrial lender, Continental Illinois became imperiled by large oil and gas loans that it had purchased. Rumors of Continental Illinois' problems started runs by large uninsured depositors in early May 1984, leading the bank to borrow heavily from the Federal Reserve Bank of Chicago. Its borrowings from the Fed reached $3.5 billion by May 11. Continental Illinois then sought an additional $4.5 billion from a group of banks, collateralized by $17 billion of assets on deposit at the Fed (Wall and Peterson, 1990).

The size of the institution and its ties to other banks led the Federal Reserve and the FDIC to conclude that intervention was necessary to prevent a general banking panic. A bailout plan was put forward on May 17, where the FDIC gave the bank $1.5 billion in new capital and a group of banks injected $500 million. A group of 28 banks provided a $5.5 billion line of credit, with the Fed supplying additional liquidity. Crucially, the FDIC promised 100 percent protection to *all* creditors of the bank, thus halting the run (FDIC, 1997).

In the next two months, regulators sought a merger partner for Continental but failed. For the final resolution, in July 1984, the FDIC agreed to buy $4.5 billion of bad loans from the bank, with a $1 billion charge-off by the bank and a capital infusion of $1 billion from the FDIC. The FDIC assumed Continental's $3.5 billion debt to the Federal Reserve Bank of Chicago in exchange for a transfer to the FDIC of assets from Continental Illinois, which had a book value of $4.5 billion and an adjusted book value of $3.5 billion. The FDIC also received a package of nonperforming, classified, or poor quality loans with a book value of $3 billion. These were valued at $2 billion, with the $1 billion taken by the bank as a charge against its capital. Furthermore, Continental Illinois gave the FDIC a note for $1.5 billion to be repaid within three years by transferring loans with a book value of $1.5 billion to the agency. To offset the $1 billion charge to capital, the FDIC purchased preferred stock issues in the bank holding company that were delivered to the bank as equity. The top management and board of directors were removed (FDIC, 1998). In Table 7.1, intervention for Continental Illinois is treated as part of an orderly rescue or liquidation, in Column 5.

The Continental Illinois episode provides an interesting contrast to pre-Great Depression interventions by central banks. In the earlier period, bank failures would have been handled either by the courts, as in the United Kingdom or France, or by a specialized agency like the Comptroller of the Currency in the United States. The courts and the OCC had no option but to liquidate banks, and they had no funds to assist with a failed bank's continued operation; but a central bank might intervene, having the resources to provide for a more orderly resolution, as in the case of the Comptoir d'Escompte and Barings. The creation of the FDIC reduced the need for the Fed to take this action, but the size of the FDIC's fund limited the agency, and a bank might still need liquidity from the Fed, as in the case of Continental Illinois.

However, there was a marked difference between the actions of the monetary authorities in 1984 and the Banque de France in 1889 and the Bank of England in 1890. Unlike earlier European bank failures or even the failures during the Great Depression, the FDIC preemptively stepped forward to insure all creditors, instead of cooperating with the Fed to ensure that only insured depositors were made whole. This action was clearly discretionary and was contrary to the need to mitigate the effect of moral hazard arising from its intervention. Indeed, the FDIC's actions established that large banks were "too big to fail," which was confirmed by the Comptroller of the Currency at a Congressional hearing shortly after the Continental Illinois bailout. This too-big-to-fail policy encouraged large banks to take on excessive risks because their creditors knew that they would be protected from any losses and so no longer needed to monitor the bank's risky activities as closely. The too-big-to-fail policy then played a role in excessive risk taking that led to the banking crisis of the late 1980s and early 1990s, as well as the banking crisis that accompanied the global financial crisis from 2007 to 2009 (Stern and Feldman, 2004).

7.9 Stock Market Crash of 1987

The biggest danger to the economy from the stock market crash of 1987 did not come from the decline in wealth resulting from the crash itself, but rather from the threat to the clearing and settlement system in the stock and futures markets.[20] From the peak on August 25, 1987, until October 16, just prior to the crash, the Dow Jones Industrial Average had declined 17.5 percent. On Monday, October 19, the market fell by 22.6 percent on a record volume of 604 million shares. Although October 19, 1987, dubbed "Black Monday," was the largest one-day percentage decline in stock prices to date, it was the next day,. Tuesday, October 20, 1987, that imperiled financial markets. To keep the stock market and the related index futures market functioning in an orderly fashion, brokers needed to extend massive credits to their customers as margin calls were made. The magnitude of the problem is illustrated by the fact that just two brokerage firms, Kidder, Peabody and Goldman Sachs, had advanced $1.5 billion in response to margin calls on their customers by noon of October 20. Brokerage firms and specialists were in dire need of additional funds to finance their activities. However, understandably enough, banks had grown nervous about the financial health of securities firms and were reluctant to lend.

Upon learning of the plight of the securities industry, Alan Greenspan and E. Gerald Corrigan, the president of the New York Federal Reserve Bank and the Fed official most closely in touch with Wall Street, began to fear a breakdown in the clearing and settlement systems and the collapse of securities firms. To prevent this from occurring, Greenspan announced, before the market opened on Tuesday, October 20, the Federal Reserve System's "readiness to serve as a source of liquidity to support the economic and financial system." In addition to this extraordinary announcement, the Fed encouraged key money center banks to lend freely to their brokerage firm customers, and, as in the Penn Central bankruptcy episode, made it clear that it would provide discount loans to banks so that they could make these loans. However, as in the Penn Central episode, the banks making the loans would face losses if the firms they lent to run into difficulties after the crisis was over, so the Federal Reserve was again using the banks as delegated monitors to reduce moral hazard risk taking. The Federal Reserve's actions can thus be thought of as being discretionary, but nonetheless representing constrained discretion because they addressed

---

[20] See the *Wall Street Journal* (1987) and Brimmer (1989) for a description of the events surrounding the stock market crash.

moral hazard risk. Given this backstop, banks increased their loans to brokers and to individuals to purchase or hold securities by $7.7 billion. As a result, the markets were not disrupted and a market rally ensued, raising the DJIA by over 100 points (over 5 percent) on October 22. This action by the Fed was reminiscent of the actions taken by the Federal Reserve Bank of New York during the October 1929 panic period in which it provided liquidity to enable money center banks to take over call loans which had been called by others.

Credit spreads did rise in the immediate aftermath of the crash; the junk bond-Treasury spread jumped by 130 basis points the week of the crash and by another 60 basis points over the next two weeks. However, within two months, this credit spread returned to precrash levels (Mishkin, 1991). The failure to enter a recession after the stock market crash, despite many forecasters' predictions along these lines, is consistent with the view that the Fed's actions were effective in calming the credit markets. In Table 7.1, we treat 1987 as we did 1929, as having unusual monetary easing.

7.10 LTCM 1998

The rise and collapse of Long-Term Capital Management in 1998 demonstrated for the first time the potential of individual nonbanking intermediaries – particularly hedge funds – to spawn a general financial crisis that required the Federal Reserve to intervene, though not to make use of its broad Federal Reserve Act 13(3) powers.

Organized as a limited liability partnership for high wealth and institutional investors, like most hedge funds, LTCM's purpose was to engage in speculative strategies virtually free of regulation and oversight. Starting with a capital of $1.3 billion in 1994, LTCM grew quickly to $7 billion in 1997 when the management concluded that there were limits to its strategy and returned $2.7 billion of equity to investors, leaving the firm with $4.8 billion in early 1998. LTCM sought to reap extraordinary returns by "market-neutral arbitrage" (Edwards, 1999; Lowenstein, 2000). Using derivative contracts it took long positions in bonds that it believed to be overvalued, and short positions in bonds it considered to be undervalued. In early post-Asian crisis in 1998, this strategy focused on the large spread between high-risk bonds and low-risk bonds that they believed to be a temporary and soon-to-be reversed phenomenon. Certain of their forecast, LTCM borrowed at least $125 billion from banks and entered into derivative contracts with a notional value in excess of $1 trillion – creating the potential for very large gains or losses if spreads narrowed or widened. This risk was amplified by the fact that LTCM held large quantities of illiquid securities in its portfolio.

Lenders and counterparties were willing to accept LTCM's huge exposure because of the outsize reputation of its partners and because they were largely unaware of the magnitude of the risks it had incurred thanks to LTCM's unchallenged secretiveness. Disaster hit when Russia defaulted on its bonds and spreads surged. Combined with a rush to liquidity and quality, LTCM sustained huge losses that nearly wiped out its equity by September. If LTCM had dumped its portfolio, asset values might have collapsed, threatening many financial institutions, owing to their position as counterparties to LTCM's swaps. Desperate for capital, LTCM sought to find one or more white knights to provide new equity but failed. The Federal Reserve Board showed no signs of providing liquidity; and on September 16, Greenspan ruled out a reduction in interest rates and stated that "Hedge funds are strongly regulated by those who lend the money" (Quoted in Lowenstein, 2000, p. 178). However, with the risk of a general market meltdown, the president of the Federal Reserve Bank of New York, William McDonough, convened a meeting on September 22, 1998, of all major financial institutions involved with LTCM. After considerable wrangling, on September 28, a sixteen-member consortium provided $3.6 billion in capital in exchange for 90 percent of LTCM's equity – a lifeboat for LTCM. Although the Fed did not provide any equity or loans, supplying only "office space" and "some guidance" (Edwards, 1999), its intervention with a "creditor rescue" helped LTCM to avoid a formal default, a contrast to the failure of the New York Superintendent of Banks intervention on behalf of the Bank of United States in 1930.

A key problem in the crisis was LTCM's vast derivative contracts, which had no automatic stay if LTCM defaulted and became bankrupt, leaving counterparties to liquidate any of LTCM's assets in their control. Thus, there was a potential for a fire sale that would have reduced the value of LTCM and potentially other institutions with similar assets. In effect, the Fed indirectly ensured that there was an orderly resolution of LTCM.

Immediately after the formation of the lifeboat for LTCM, the Fed cut the fed funds target rate on September 29 from 5.5 to 5.3 percent. This cut was in direct response to the crisis' eruption in the United States; and, as during the recent financial crisis, it was done while the economy was still in the midst of a boom that had begun in March 1991 and would not peak until March 2001 (NBER Business Cycles, www.nber.org). Yet this cut was insufficient, and with swap spreads continuing to widen and LTCM continuing to weaken, other financial institutions with similar exposure, took large hits against their capital. Only when the Fed cut rates for a second time and third time on October 15 and November 17 when the fed funds rate reached 4.75 percent did spreads narrow and calm return to the markets (Lowenstein, 2000). In Table 7.1, the exceptional actions of the Fed include the unusual easing of monetary policy and assisting with an orderly resolution of a firm on the brink of insolvency.

Once the shock dissipated, pursuing a contingent rule would have indicated that the Federal Reserve would take away the federal funds rate cuts. This was not done, and we consider this to be one of the serious mistakes made by the Federal Reserve under Greenspan. Not only did inflation subsequently rise, going above 2 percent, a level that is considered to be an appropriate objective currently by the Federal Reserve and other central banks, but these monetary actions indicated that the Federal Reserve would react asymmetrically to shocks, lowering interest rates in the event of a financial disruption, but not raising them upon reversal of the adverse shock. Federal Reserve monetary policy actions during this period were therefore purely discretionary because they helped contribute to the belief in the "Greenspan put," a form of moral hazard in which financial institutions expect monetary policy to help them recover from bad investments (e.g., see Tirole and Farhi, 2009; Keister, 2010). The failure of the Greenspan put to constrain moral hazard is one factor that has been cited as playing a role in the excessive risk taking that helped lead to the global financial crisis from 2007 to 2009.

7.11 Overview of the Historical Experience

It is common for economists to recommend that central banks adopt an instrument rule, like Bagehot's rule, for managing financial crises. By signaling a commitment to this instrument rule, central banks can limit moral hazard and discourage risk-taking that can pave the way for the next financial crisis. While central banks have had over two centuries to consider this advice, put forward by Thornton in 1802 and then forcefully argued by Bagehot in 1873, they typically don't follow it.

The central banks in our historical survey – the Bank of England, the Banque de France, and the Federal Reserve – initially attempted to follow versions of Bagehot's rule. In 1866, to confront the panic begun by the collapse of Overend-Gurney, the Bank of England lent freely at a high rate of interest on only good collateral, after securing permission from the Treasury to violate the currency-issue/gold reserve instrument rule. Solvent institutions were given the liquidity to ride out the crisis, and the economy absorbed the heavy shock of the failing banks. Yet, when Baring Brothers collapsed in 1890, neither the Bank of England nor the leading bankers were willing to strictly apply Bagehot's rule, the discount rate was not jacked up, and swaps were arranged with other central banks to obtain liquidity. For Baring Brothers, a lifeboat was formed to ensure an orderly liquidation of the bank, with the Bank of England providing liquidity as needed for the rest of the financial system, according to Bagehot's precepts. Losses from this failure were not born by the taxpayer or the Bank of England but primarily by the partners of the failing bank, especially the Baring family. The recognition of the Bank's success gave credibility to its contingent rule for combining price and financial stability.

This same shift is observed for the Banque de France. In 1882, when a large bank, Union Générale, failed, its demise bankrupted the stock exchange in Lyon and threatened to do the same for the Paris Bourse. The Banque de France could not assist the Paris exchange directly because it lacked the exact collateral prescribed by the Banque's statutes. However, a lifeboat for the Bourse was provided via a group of banks that had the correct collateral and intermediated the loan. The exchange survived, though hobbled under its debt for the next several years, and the crisis set off a severe recession that had a slow recovery. This experience seems to have altered the Banque de France's response to the imminent failure of one of the top banks in 1889, the Comptoir d'Escompte. This time the Banque did not hesitate to lend to the Comptoir on questionable assets and formed a lifeboat operation before a panic took hold, providing additional credit with no higher interest rates to other financial institutions seeking liquidity but imposing harsh penalties for those involved in precipitating the crisis. This prompt preemptive strike may well have informed the Bank of England's response the next year and influenced the Banque's decision to set up special lending facilities to cope with the crisis 1907.

The trajectory of the Fed was similar, but it was Congress that initiated the shift to contingent rules for addressing financial crises, not the Fed. The panic of 1907, where a number of extraordinary measures were taken by the Treasury and the New York Clearing House, set the stage for the creation of the Federal Reserve System. As a new institution, the Fed took its mandate – with its limitations – very seriously. However, when the first major crisis, the Stock Market Crash of 1929, hit, the Federal Reserve Bank of New York, anxious to contain the crisis, exceeded its authority, temporarily breeching the instrument-rule procedures designed to ensure price stability by expanding open market operations. Encouraging banks to borrow at the discount window without stigma so that they could lend to troubled brokers kept the crisis contained. The correctness of this action is reflected by the fact that a very similar action was taken by the Federal Reserve Board in 1987 in response to the stock market crash of that year. The difference between 1987 and 1929 was that in 1929, the Board did not initiate or approve of this bold action and censured the New York Fed. The Fed then returned to a very strict interpretation of its mandate, effectively dismissing the need to address the mounting bank failures and panics of 1930–33. If banks needed liquidity, the discount window was open; but since there was no line at the window, expansionary measures were assumed to be unnecessary. As the Fed was unwilling to initiate flexibility, Congress responded with new legislation to expand the Fed's ability to lend and intervene, most notably giving the Fed discretionary authority to provide credit via Section 13(3). Significantly, no morally hazardous bailout was seriously considered for the depositors or shareholders of banks that failed during 1930–33.

The bankruptcy of Penn Central in 1970 seems to have followed this playbook. Although subject to significant political pressure to help the railroad, the Fed refused to provide assistance. But concerned that Penn Central's bankruptcy would hammer the commercial paper market, the Fed signaled to banks that they could readily borrow from the discount window with no stigma if their customers could not roll over their commercial paper and needed short-term credits. Penn Central received no favors, and the rest of the market was assured access to short-term lending.

The drastic measures needed to constrain moral hazard when there is a preemptive central bank intervention are evident in these late nineteenth and early to mid-twentieth century cases. Beginning in the late twentieth century, preemptive discretionary interventions increased but the safety net for bank stakeholders was expanded, creating growing incentives for risk-taking. The rising tide of bank and savings and loan failures in the late 1970s and early 1980s appears to have altered the earlier strict policy.

The failure and bailout of Continental Illinois in 1984 represented a key shift in policy, effectively inaugurating the Too-Big-To-Fail (TBTF) doctrine. Runs by uninsured depositors of Continental Illinois persuaded regulators that its failure could produce a full-scale banking panic. With the Fed supplying liquidity and the FDIC supplying capital, Continental Illinois was bailed out, providing 100 percent insurance for creditors and bond holders. The contrast in the penalties assessed against stakeholders in the earlier crises surveyed here is striking, especially since the authorities' actions in 1984 were recognized as creating substantial moral hazard. Even when the Fed has appeared to avoid intervention, as in the case of LTCM, by holding meetings to induce banks to form a lifeboat to rescue the hedge fund, managers of LTCM and other involved financial institutions continued in the business, though they sustained huge losses. In addition, the widening of interest rate and swap spreads was met by the Fed's lowering of interest rates. While this was effective in narrowing spreads, interest rates were not raised afterwards and Greenspan's promise to prevent crises became the "Greenspan put." The discretionary violation of the target rule thus did not appear to be temporary, and the resolve to contain moral hazard was sharply diminished.

This overview of the historical episodes suggests that they can be classified into three categories. The first category includes episodes in which the central bank adhered too strictly to instrument rules and thus took no preemptive actions to deal with financial crises: the 1930–33 period in the United States is the classic example. It is commonly agreed that the Federal Reserve's inactivity during this period was a disaster, not only for the United States, but for the world economy. The second category includes episodes in which central banks deviated from the currency-issue/gold reserve rules, but were clearly committed to take actions to reduce moral hazard: these include the United Kingdom in 1890, France in 1889, and the United States in 1929, 1970, and 1987. We would argue that these central bank deviations from instrument rules were highly successful in limiting the damage from the financial disruption to the economy, and yet were conducted so that moral hazard was limited and therefore did not make the financial system more vulnerable. The third category includes episodes where the central bank and the government engaged in discretionary actions where efforts to limit moral hazard were weak: these include the Continental Illinois episode in 1984 and monetary policy easing taken in 1998 in the aftermath of the LTCM crisis. Although these discretionary actions limited the damage from the financial disruption, they should not be viewed as successful interventions because they created moral hazard incentives for financial institutions to take on excessive risk that set the stage for later financial crises.

7.12 Conclusions

The historical experience provides several lessons.

- First, the "unprecedented" actions of the Federal Reserve during the global financial crisis were in line with what central banks, including the Federal Reserve, did in previous episodes of financial disturbances.

Unprecedented actions have been a part of a central bank's arsenal since the nineteenth century.

- Second, unprecedented actions in which instrument rules were temporarily abandoned, but discretion was constrained, were frequently successful in stabilizing the financial system and the aggregate economy. Indeed, unwillingness to deviate from instrument rules, as occurred during the 1930–33 episode, led to a disastrous outcome. This episode provides an important rationale for the Federal Reserve's adoption of unprecedented actions during the recent global financial crisis.
- Third, the historical experience indicates that discretionary deviations from Bagehot's rule can promote financial instability if steps are not taken to mitigate the moral hazard that these actions encourage. The unprecedented actions associated with Continental Illinois in 1984 and LTCM in 1998 increased morally hazardous risk-taking by financial institutions and were an important factor that led to the banking crisis of the late 1980s and early 1990s and the global financial crisis of 2007–09.

The historical experience therefore suggests that the concerns for designing a central bank's mandate should not focus on whether a central bank should strictly follow instrument rules. Rather, the concerns for designing a central bank's mandate should focus on how an appropriate target rule or contingent rule can be developed to constrain discretion and mitigate moral hazard. The Federal Reserve's unprecedented actions during the global financial crisis should thus be judged not on whether they should have been pursued but rather on whether they were accompanied by adequate measures to maintain a target rule and constrain moral hazard.

References

Acharya, Viral and Amit Seru, 2013. "What Do Macro-Prudential Stress Tests Resolve: Asymmetric Information, Debt Overhang or Regulatory Uncertainty?" New York University, Manuscript.

Bagehot, Walter, 1873. *Lombard Street: A Description of the Money Market*. London: H.S. King.

Bernanke, Ben S., Thomas Laubach, Frederic S. Mishkin, and Adam Posen, 1999. *Inflation Targeting: Lessons from the International Experience*. Princeton, NY: Princeton University Press.

Bernanke, Ben S. and Frederic S. Mishkin, 1997. "Inflation Targeting: A New Framework for Monetary Policy?" *Journal of Economic Perspectives* 11: 97–116.

Bignon, Vincent, Marc Flandreau, and Stefano Ugolini, 2012. "Bagehot for beginners: the making of lender-of-last resort operations in the mid-nineteenth century." *Economic History Review* 65: 580–608.

Board of Governors of the Federal Reserve System, 2009. "The Supervisory Capital Assessment Program: Design and Implementation." April 24, www.federalreserve.gov/bankinforeg/bcreg20090424a1.pdf

Bordo, Michael D., 1986. "Financial Crises, Banking Crises, Stock Market Crashes and the Money Supply: Some International Evidence" in Forrest Capie and Geffrey Wood (eds.), *Financial Crises and the World Banking System*. London: Macmillan.
    1990. "The Lender of Last Resort: Alternative Views and Historical Experience." *Federal Reserve Bank of Richmond Economic Review*, (January/February), 18–29.

Bordo, Michael D., and Finn E. Kydland, 1995. "The Gold Standard As a Rule: An Essay in Exploration." *Exporations in Economic History* 32: 423–464.

Bordo, Michael D., and Eugene N. White, 1994. "British and French Finance during the Napoleonic Wars," in Michael D. Bordo and Forrest Capie (eds.), *Monetary Regimes in Transition*. Cambridge: Cambridge University Press, 241–73.

Bordo, Michael D., and David C. Wheelock, 2013. "The Promise and Performance of the Federal Reserve as Lender of Last Resort, 1914–1933" in Michael D. Bordo and Will Roberds (eds.), *The Origins, History and Future of the Federal Reserve: A Return to Jekyll Island*. Cambridge: Cambridge University Press, 59–98.

Brimmer, Andrew F. 1989. "Distinguished Lecture on Economics in Government: Central Banking and Systemic Risks in Capital Markets." *Journal of Economic Perspectives* 3: 3–16.

Calvo, Guillermo A., 1978. "On the Time Consistency of Optimal Policy in a Monetary Economy." *Econometrica* 46: 1411–28.

Capie, Forrest and Ghila Rodrik-Bali, 1982. "Concentration in British Banking, 1870–1920." *Business History* 24: 280–92.

Calomiris, Charles W. and Eugene N. White, 1994. "The Origins of Federal Deposit Insurance" in Claudia Goldin and Gary D. Libecap (eds.), *The Regulated Economy: A Historical Approach to Political Economy*. Cambridge: Cambridge University Press, 145–88.

Carlson, Mark, Kris J. Mitchener, and Gary Richardson, 2011. "Arresting Banking Panics: Federal Reserve Liquidity Provision and the Forgotten Panic of 1929." *Journal of Political Economy* 119: 889–924.

Clapham, John 1945. *The Bank of England: A History*. Vol. II, New York, NY: The Macmillan Company.

Coy, Peter, 2008. "Volcker Shuns the Blame Game." *Business Week*, April 10.

Dutton, John, 1984. "The Bank of England the Rules of the Game under the International Gold Standard: New Evidence" in Michael D. Bordo and Anna J. Schwartz (eds.), *A Retrospective on the Classical Gold Standard, 1821–1931*. Chicago, IL: University of Chicago Press, 173–202.

Edwards, Franklin R., 1999. "Hedge Funds and the Collapse of Long-Term Capital Management." *Journal of Economic Perspectives* 13: 189–210.

Eschweiler, Bernhard and Michael D. Bordo, 1994. "Rules, Discretion, and Central Bank Independence: the German Experience, 1880–1989" in Pierre L. Siklos (ed.), *Varieties of Monetary Reforms*. New York, NY: Springer.

Federal Deposit Insurance Corporation, 1997. *History of the Eighties – Lessons for the Future*. Washington, DC: FDIC.

1998. *Managing the Crisis: The FDIC and RTC Experience, 1980–1994*. Washington, DC: FDIC.

2008. "FDIC Announces Plan to Free Up Bank Liquidity." Press Release, October 14, www.fdic.gov/news/news/press/2008/pr08100.html

Flandreau, Marc and Stefano Ugolini, 2014. "The Crisis of 1866." Geneva: Graduate Institute of International and Development Studies, Working Paper, No. 10.

Friedman, Milton and Anna J. Schwartz, 1963. *A Monetary History of the United States, 1867–1960*. Princeton, NJ: Princeton University Press.

Giannini, Curzio, 2011. *The Age of Central Banks*. Cheltenham: Edward Elgar.

Giovannini, Alberto, 1986. "Rules of the Game' During the International Gold Standard, England and Germany." *Journal of International Money and Finance* 5: 467–83.

Grossman, Herschel I. and John B. van Huyck, 1988. "Sovereign Debt as a Contingent Claim: Excusable Default, Repudiation and Reputation." *American Economic Review* 78: 1088–97.

Grossman, Richard S., 2010. *Unsettled Account: The Evolution of Banking in the Industrialized World Since 1800*. Princeton, NJ: Princeton University Press.

Grossman, Richard S. and Hugh Rockoff, 2014. "Fight the Last War: Economists on the Lender of Last Resort." Of the Uses of Central Banks: Lessons of History, Norges Bank Conference, June 5–6.

Hautcoeur, Pierre-Cyrille, Angelo Riva, and Eugene N. White, 2014. "Floating a Lifeboat: the Banque de France and the Crisis of 1889." *Journal of Monetary Economics* 65: 104–19.

Hoshi, Takeo and Anil Kashyap, 2010. "Will the U.S. Bank Recapitalization Succeed? Eight Lessons from Japan." *Journal of Financial Economics* 97: 398–417.

Humphrey, Thomas, 1975. "Lender of Last Resort: The Concept in History. *Federal Reserve Bank of Richmond Economic Review.*" 75: 8–16.

Keister, Todd, 2010. "Bailouts and Financial Fragility." Federal Reserve Bank of New York, Unpublished manuscript.

Kydland, Finn E. and Edward C. Prescott, 1977. "Rules Rather Than Discretion: The Inconsistency of Optimal Plans." *Journal of Political Economy* 85: 473–92.

Lowenstein, Roger, 2000. *When Genius Failed: The Rise and Fall of Long-Term Capital Management*. New York, NY: Random House.

Lucia, Joseph L., 1985. "The Failure of the Bank of United States: A Reappraisal." *Explorations in Economic History* 22: 402–16.

Madigan, Brian F., 2009. "Bagehot's Dictum in Practice: Formulating and Implementing Policies to Combat the Financial Crisis." Jackson Hole, Wyoming Symposium, Federal Reserve Bank of Kansas City, August 21.

Maisel, Sherman J., 1973. *Managing the Dollar*. New York, NY: Norton.

Meltzer, Allan H., 2003. *A History of the Federal Reserve Volume 1, 1913–1951*. Chicago, IL: University of Chicago Press.

2009. "Reflections on the Financial Crisis." *Cato Journal* 29: 45–51.

Miron, Jeffrey, 1986. "Financial Panics, the Seasonality of the Interest Rate and the Founding of the Fed." *American Economic Review* 76: 125–40.

Mishkin, Frederic S., 1991. "Asymmetric Information and Financial Crises: A Historical Perspective" in R. Glenn Hubbard (ed.), *Financial Markets and Financial Crises*. Chicago, IL: University of Chicago Press, 69–108.

2011a. "Over the Cliff: From the Subprime to the Global Financial Crisis." *Journal of Economic Perspectives* 25: 49–70.

2011b. "Monetary Policy Strategy: Lessons From the Crisis" in Marek Jarocinski, Frank Smets, and Christian Thimann (eds.), *Monetary Policy Revisited: Lessons from the Crisis, Sixth ECB Central Banking Conference.* Frankfurt: European Central Bank, 67–118.

Mishkin, Frederic S. and Klaus Schmidt-Hebbel, 2002. "One Decade of Inflation Targeting in the World: What Do We Know and What Do We Need to Know?" in N. Loayza and R. Soto (eds.), *Inflation Targeting: Design, Performance, Challenges.* Santiago: Central Bank of Chile, 171–219.

Moen, Jon R. and Ellis W. Tallman, 2000. "Clearinghouse Membership and Deposit Contraction During the Panic of 1907." *Journal of Economic History* 60: 145–63.

NBER, Business Cycles, www.nber.org.

Odell, Kerry and Marc Weidenmier, 2004. "Real Shock, Monetary Aftershock: the 1906 San Francisco Earthquake and the Panic of 1907." *Journal of Economic History* 64: 1002–27.

Pippenger, John, 1984. "Bank of England Operations 1893-1913" in Michael D. Bordo and Anna J. Schwartz (eds.), *A Retrospective on the Classical Gold Standard 1821-1931.* Chicago, IL: Chicago University Press, 233–76.

Rodgers, Mary Tone and James E. Payne, 2014. "How the Bank of France Changed U.S. Equity Expectations and Ended the Panic of 1907." *Journal of Economic History* 74: 420–48.

Romer, Christina D., 1993. "The Nation in Depression." *Journal of Economic Perspectives* 7: 19–39.

Snowden, Kenneth A., 1995."Mortgage Securitization in the United States: Twentieth Century Developments in Historical Perspective" in Michael D. Bordo and Richard Sylla (eds.), *Anglo-American Financial Systems: Institutions and Markets in the Twentieth Century.* New York, NY: Irwin, 261–98.

Stern, Gary H. and Ron J. Feldman, 2004. *Too Big to Fail: The Hazards of Bank Bailouts.* Washington, DC: The Brookings Institution.

Taylor, John, B., 2009. *Getting Off Track: How Government Actions and Interventions, Caused, Prolonged and Worsened the Financial Crisis.* Stanford, CA: Hoover Institution Press.

Taylor, John, B. and John Williams, 2009. "A Black Swan in the Money Market." *American Economic Journal: Macroeconomics* 1: 58–83.

Thornton, Henry, 1802. *An Enquiry into the Nature and Effects of the Paper Credit of Great Britain.* F. Hayek (ed.), Fairfield: August M. Kelley.

Tirole, Jean and Emmanuel Farhi, 2009. "Collective Moral Hazard, Maturity Mismatch and Systemic Bailouts." NBER Working Paper No. 15138.

Wall, Larry D. and David R. Petersen, 1990. "The Effect of Continental Illinois' Failure on the Financial Performance of Other Banks." *Journal of Monetary Economics* 26: 77–99.

Wall Street Journal, 1987. "Terrible Tuesday: How the Stock Market Almost Disintegrated a Day After the Crash." November 20.

White, Eugene N., 1998. "The Legacy of Deposit Insurance: The Growth, Spread, and Cost of Insuring Financial Intermediaries" in Michael D. Bordo, Claudia Goldin, and Eugene N. White (eds.), *The Defining Moment: The Great Depression and the*

American Economy in the Twentieth Century. Cambridge: Cambridge University Press, 87–124.

2007. "The Crash of 1882 and the Bailout of the Paris Bourse." *Cliometrica* 1: 115–44.

2013. "To Establish More Effective Supervision: How the Birth of the Fed Altered Bank Supervision" in Michael D. Bordo and Will Roberds (eds.), *A Return to Jekyll Island: The Origins, History and Future of the Federal Reserve.* Cambridge: Cambridge University Press, 7–55.

Wheelock, David C., 1991. *The Strategy and Consistency of Federal Reserve Monetary Policy, 1924–1933.* Cambridge: Cambridge University Press.

Wicker, Elmus R., 1966. *Federal Reserve Monetary Policy, 1917–1933.* New York, NY: Random House.

Wood, John H., 2005. *A History of Central Banking in Great Britain and the United States.* Cambridge: Cambridge University Press.

Comments on Frederic S. Mishkin and Eugene N. White, "Unprecedented Actions: The Federal Reserve's Response to the Global Financial Crisis in Historical Perspective"

Steven B. Kamin

Introduction

Rick Mishkin and Eugene White's paper, "Unprecedented Actions: The Federal Reserve's Response to the Global Financial Crisis in Historical Perspective," addresses a critical issue for central banks today: the interplay between the use of monetary policy for macroeconomic stabilization and financial stability. This issue has received a great deal of attention since the global financial crisis (GFC), but Mishkin and White bring useful new perspectives to the analysis. First, they discuss potential tensions between the central bank's rules or strategies for achieving their macro objectives and those for addressing bouts of financial instability. Second, and in that vein, they assess the actions taken by the Federal Reserve since the GFC against the benchmark of the most elemental framework for central bank lender-of-last-resort (LOLR) policy, Bagehot's rule. Finally, and this is in some ways the most interesting contribution of the paper, Mishkin and White compare the Federal Reserve's recent actions to those undertaken by several major central banks over a long period of history, from the mid-nineteenth century.

I found both the analytic issues raised by the paper, as well as the narratives of the historical episodes in which central banks in the United States and Europe addressed financial crises, to be very provocative and informative. I also agree with the central conclusions of the paper: discretionary deviations from monetary policy rules may be necessary to address financial crises, but measures should be taken to rein in any resulting moral hazard. That said, Mishkin and White do not resolve all of the issues raised by their analysis, and I will highlight some of those in my remarks.

I would like to thank Mark Carey, Ricardo Correa, and Chris Erceg for their assistance and insightful comments in writing this discussion.

Summary of Paper

By my reading, Mishkin and White's paper starts with several key premises. First, central bank strategies for achieving price stability have evolved over time. Central banks started out being constrained by clear, transparent rules that minimized discretion (so-called instrument rules) but evolved over time to more discretionary strategies focused on achieving their ultimate macroeconomic objectives ("contingent rules" and, ultimately, "target rules"). Second, there is a potential tension between financial stability and instrument-rule driven strategies to achieve price stability, because tamping down financial crises may require monetary creation in excess of the limits provided by the price-stability rule. However, there may be less tension between contingent or target rules and actions to promote financial stability. Finally, although the paper isn't entirely clear on this, Bagehot's rule – which limits LOLR lending to solvent institutions with good collateral, and at a penalty rate – is a way to ensure that financial stability actions are consistent with either less or more discretionary approaches to price stability, since it limits money creation to the amount of available good collateral, and since it limits the moral hazard problem related to provision of a safety net.

Starting from these premises, Mishkin and White examine the Fed's recent actions against the backdrop of the historical record. They note that the Fed undertook a wide range of unprecedented actions during the GFC, ranging from unconventional monetary easing to the creation of new liquidity facilities to international swap lines to rescues or orderly liquidations of certain financial institutions. In many cases, they argue, these actions went beyond the limits prescribed by monetary policy instrument rules, especially Bagehot's rule. However, the authors go on to show, these actions generally were not as unprecedented as they might seem at first blush. The paper documents how, starting in the late nineteenth century, central banks in the United Kingdom, France, and the United States consistently violated Bagehot's rule by rescuing financial institutions or providing for their orderly liquidation.

Mishkin and White argue that these actions were necessary to calm the financial system and avert disorderly spillovers and crisis. As long as policies reverted to more conventional standards soon afterwards, and as long as care was taken to limit moral hazard by ensuring stakeholders took losses, these policies did not pose problems. For the most part, the rescues undertaken by the authorities in the nineteenth century and first part of the twentieth century met these criteria. The paper argues, however, that more recently, the authorities have taken actions that promote moral hazard, citing the bailout of creditors of Continental Illinois and the overly-persistent loosening of monetary policy after LTCM, which gave rise to talk of the "Greenspan put." These actions purportedly set the stage for subsequent financial crises, including the GFC.

Discussion

I would like to start by highlighting several important contributions of Mishkin and White's paper. To begin with, at a time when the central bank's responsibilities as guardian of financial stability, alongside its responsibility for ensuring macroeconomic equilibrium, are receiving renewed attention, it makes sense to take a closer look at potential tensions between these two objectives. I interpret the paper's "takeaway" message on this score to be that in the past, conflicts may have arisen between simple instrument rules for monetary policy and the response to financial crisis. However, with target rules such as flexible inflation targeting, which impose no short-term constraints on monetary emission, no such conflicts present themselves as long as responses to financial instability are well designed, transitory, and do not promote moral hazard.

Second, I applaud the paper's efforts in putting the Fed's and other authorities' responses to the GFC in the context of the broader sweep of the history of policy responses to financial crises. The authors' finding that the historical response to financial crisis often involved actions that went beyond Bagehot's rule, especially as financial institutions became more interconnected and subject to spillovers, strikes me as quite useful and informative. Similarly, their argument that more recently, authorities have become less diligent in punishing stakeholders and thus more condoning of moral hazard, is interesting and provocative. I would be interested in seeing more comprehensive (perhaps statistical) evidence for this shift in behavior, however. Additionally, if such a shift in behavior actually occurred, it would be useful to know why – perhaps because as financial systems became increasingly interconnected, nothing short of full bailout was considered sufficient to quell a crisis?

There are several other issues in the paper that merit further consideration.

Bagehot's Rule and Monetary Policy

The relationship between Bagehot's rule for LOLR action and monetary policy rules more generally is an interesting issue highlighted by the authors, and I think the paper could have made the evolution of this relationship a bit clearer. Certainly, when the Bank of England faced legal limits on the expansion of its balance sheet, as in 1867, or when gold standards impeded the flexibility of monetary policy, the rules in effect may have limited the provision of liquidity. Under those circumstances, Bagehot's rule – which limits lending to the supply of good collateral – would have been a useful adjunct to the more general instrument rule constraining monetary emission, and the paper notes that accordingly.

But under more flexible monetary policy strategies such as prevail in modern central banking, there is generally no conflict between macroeconomic objectives such as price stability and lending for financial stability, as long as central banks and the currency they create are credible. In fact, under those circumstances, financial crises tend to boost the demand for narrow money, thereby further reducing the risk that liquidity creation will cause inflation. Accordingly, just as credible monetary policy no longer requires strict adherence to nondiscretionary rules on interest rates or money creation, so long as policymakers focus on achieving their ultimate macro objectives, neither does credible monetary policy require strict adherence to Bagehot's rule, so long as policymakers focus on controlling moral hazard. The authors clearly recognize this, but it would be worth underscoring more explicitly in their paper.

Fed Actions During the GFC

A second issue I'd like to raise concerns the actions taken by the Fed during the GFC, which Mishkin and White refer to as "unprecedented," "exceptional," and, at least in one passage, "rule-violating." To begin with, of the seven action categories cited in the paper as "unprecedented," five of them had little to do with possible violations of Bagehot's rule: unusual monetary easing, international central bank cooperation, nonconventional monetary policy, direct Treasury collaboration/intervention/aid, and supervision. These policies might have violated old-fashioned instrument rules for monetary policy like the gold standard, but by focusing on averting a damaging recession and deflation, they were entirely consistent with a modern focus on achieving macroeconomic mandates.

Turning to a sixth type of Fed action identified by the paper, "non-Bagehot liquidity facilities," it is not clear how many of the new facilities were indeed non-Bagehot. They generally involved lending freely, for good collateral, to solvent institutions and markets in order to avert collapse of intermediation and the financial system. To be sure, this lending was not always at penalty rate, but that was to offset the stigma of borrowing from the Fed. And while much of the lending was highly untraditional in that it was extended to nonbanks, by some interpretations, Bagehot's rule was not intended to apply exclusively to banks. Particularly in the modern age, banks are but one channel of intermediation, and stabilizing financial conditions may of necessity involve other types of institutions.[1]

Finally, the seventh type of Federal Reserve action cited by Mishkin and White is the "rescue/orderly liquidation of financial institutions." These actions are certainly among the most controversial undertaken by the Fed during the GFC, but a few points are worth recalling. All funding for troubled institutions was collateralized by marked-to-market assets, with haircuts. The Fed didn't lose a dime on its actions in connection with either Bear Stearns or AIG. And, finally, as indicated in Figure 7.1, the total lending in support of specific institutions accounted for only $120.5 billion at its peak on May 5, 2010, compared to total assets of the Fed of $2.3 trillion at that time.

Sources of Moral Hazard

A third issue worth considering is Mishkin and White's argument that a number of actions in recent decades – the bailout of Continental Illinois, the coordinated rescue of LTCM, and the easing of monetary policy after LTCM – all ratcheted up moral hazard and thus contributed, to some extent, to the eruption of the GFC. To begin with, the paper provides only scant support for its contention that monetary policy remained too loose after LTCM – this is hardly a consensus view, and a reliable evaluation of that policy would require a much more detailed analysis of developments during that period. I would note that the rate cut being discussed – from 5½ to 4¾ percent – was relatively modest and left the fed funds rate at a still-high level. Furthermore, while Mishkin and White draw attention to inflation subsequently rising above 2 percent, this was true only for headline CPI inflation, which was boosted by a bounceback in energy prices; the core PCE inflation rate stayed below 2 percent.

More generally, the paper's contention that all of these actions (Continental Illinois, LTCM, and the Greenspan put) led to moral hazard and contributed to the excessive risk-taking underlying the GFC is provocative, but no

---

[1] On these points, see Brian Madigan, "Bagehot's Dictum in Practice: Formulating and Implementing Policies to Combat the Financial Crisis," speech presented at the Federal Reserve Bank of Kansas City conference at Jackson Hole, Wyoming, August 21, 2009.

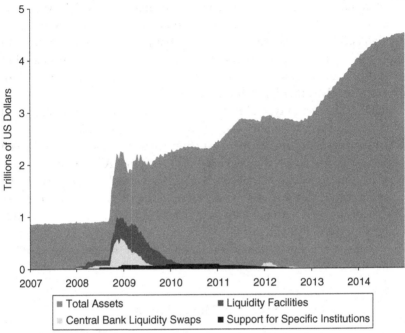

Figure 7.1. Selected assets of the Federal Reserve.
Note: Liquidity Facilities = term auction credit, loans, net portfolio holdings of commercial paper funding facility, net portfolio holdings of TALF LLC. Support for Specific Institutions = net portfolio holdings of Maiden Lane LLC, Maiden Lane II LLC, Maiden Lane III LLC, preferred interests in AIA Aurora LLC & Alico Holdings LLC.
Source: Haver Analytics.

more than speculation – I would have liked to see some evidence linking measures of risk-taking to the actions taken by the authorities, although I'm not sure what kind of evidence might exist for this. Finally, it is worth noting that Mishkin and White's paper focuses exclusively on the actions taken by US authorities from the 1980s onward that promoted moral hazard – yet financial institutions in Europe engaged in equally risky behavior in the lead-up to the GFC.

Other Tensions between Monetary Policy and Financial Stability

Mishkin and White's paper focuses on the challenge of responding appropriately to financial crisis while limiting moral hazard and pursuing monetary policy goals. This is an entirely appropriate focus of study, and in many respects, the authors are preaching to the choir: since the GFC, authorities around the world have taken actions to rein in moral hazard, including the Dodd-Frank Act and Orderly Liquidation Authority in the United States, new requirements for "bail in" in Europe, and the Basel III rules on bank capital and liquidity throughout the world. It is worth noting, however, that since the GFC, another potential tension between monetary policy and financial stability has garnered renewed attention: how to calibrate monetary and macroprudential policies to support economic recovery and move inflation back up to target rates without encouraging future financial imbalances? This question involves a very different set of issues than those addressed by Mishkin and White, but is one that certainly merits further research.

Conclusion

All told, I found Mishkin and White's paper to be interesting, informative, and provocative. As I have discussed, there are aspects of their research that could use further attention. However, I certainly agree with their conclusion that financial crises require extraordinary responses, but measures must be taken to control any resulting moral hazard.

8

Panel Discussion on the Federal Reserve's Role in International Financial Crises

The Fed's Role in International Crises

Donald Kohn

For my contribution to this panel, I will reflect on the role of the Federal Reserve in the last crisis – focusing on the 2007–09 period when the crisis was most intense in the United States and tending to spread to the rest of the world, and I was inside the institution helping to formulate policy. The Fed played a central role in dealing with the international aspects of the crisis through this period. We provided liquidity to many foreign banks – to their US subsidiaries and affiliates at our discount window here at home, but importantly and innovatively also to their home offices through a network of liquidity swap arrangements with other central banks, which I will discuss at length. But we also were central to the monetary policy response around the world, and I will touch on this aspect of our involvement briefly at the end of my remarks.

The centrality of the Fed's role reflects a number of factors. US financial markets and institutions are themselves at the center of an increasingly integrated global financial system. Deep, liquid markets for dollar assets are a natural investment outlet for investors in the rest of the world, including many official entities. The dollar remains the most important reserve currency, many international transactions are denominated in dollars, and dollar foreign exchange and swap markets are critical venues for managing risk. The largest US financial institutions are global in reach and any impairment of their normal functioning – their provision of intermediary, risk management, liquidity, and payment services – affects economies around the world.

Moreover, the buildup of risks in the period leading up to the crisis and the transmission of their realization around the globe had a lot to do with domestic US markets. The United States was "ground zero" in the 2007–09 crisis years – especially the subprime mortgage market. US subprime assets were widely held around the globe, so problems with those assets were quickly transmitted overseas, and the United States was exposed to the decisions of foreign financial institutions and governments about how to respond. Those global interconnections were key to understanding the Fed's response in the international sphere.

Barry Eichengreen and others have noted a "modern Triffin dilemma." The original Triffin dilemma in the Bretton Woods exchange rate system pointed out the tension for the United States and the global financial system between providing for the world's growing needs for dollar liquidity, which required that the United States run a current account deficit, and assuring that the growing amount of foreign dollar holdings was exchangeable into gold from what was a relatively stable stock. The modern Triffin dilemma highlights the tension between the growing demands for dollar assets – primarily the debt of US entities – and financial stability. Stability could be threatened when the increasing demand for dollar assets induces a buildup in US debt to levels that might be difficult to service, especially when it is based on inflated collateral values. In the run up to the crisis, foreign demands for US debt were rising rapidly for several reasons.

One was the US current account deficit, which reached 6 percent of GDP. The United States was spending far more than it was producing, importing the difference, and financing those net imports by borrowing from abroad, resulting in a faster increase in net indebtedness than in income. This deficit was shaped to some extent by exogenous spending/saving decisions in the United States – that is, the federal fiscal deficit stoked by tax cuts. But it also was the consequence of the choices of foreign governments – in particular the decisions of the Chinese and other governments to pursue export-led growth. This entailed artificially holding down the value of their currencies on foreign exchange markets and in the process accumulating huge dollar reserves. These were invested mostly in safe, liquid assets, and the demand for these assets depressed longer-term interest rates in the United States and globally.

The buildup of vulnerabilities was exacerbated by the investment choices made by foreign private parties – and here I will emphasize gross as well as net flows from overseas into dollar markets. Foreign banks looking for low-risk higher-yield investments latched onto various types of US securities, most especially super senior tranches of pools of subprime mortgages. Their demand, along with demand from US sources, fed the inventiveness of the US financial sector in constructing a supply of increasingly opaque, but nominally very safe, instruments and contributed to the loosening of credit standards for subprime mortgages. Foreign financial institutions financed their holdings of these fundamentally long-term assets in large part with wholesale short-term liabilities. These included asset-backed commercial paper (ABCP) issued by SIVs (conduits sponsored by the banks) and deposits from money funds. They were also funded by domestic deposits converted into dollars in short-term swap markets. European banks were prominent in these trades.

On the eve of the crisis, then, foreign institutions were looking at a currency mismatch and a maturity mismatch, and they were relying on the illusion of liquidity, especially in the MBS market, to manage risks. I'm not blaming the crisis on these foreign governments or institutions. Obviously many of the same weaknesses (not the currency mismatch) and more were shared by US domestic lenders and it was US regulators that had responsibility for overseeing US markets. But the actions of foreign banks and governments contributed, and the role of the Fed in the international aspects of the crisis very much reflected the character of the risks that had built up across borders.

After house prices started to decline and the adequacy of the collateral backing for many of those subprime loans was called into question, uncertainty about where the losses would fall disrupted interbank lending markets – both here and abroad. The functioning of these markets was impaired, and funding tenors became even shorter. The runoff of ABCP increased the direct exposure to subprime and other mortgage loans of foreign and domestic banks that had provided liquidity backstops to these conduits and SIVs, further increasing uncertainty about solvency. The pullback by global banks as funding became more expensive and its availability uncertain, along with the onset of recessions in some industrial economies, transmitted problems to economies where banks hadn't taken risks – including many emerging markets.

Swaps with foreign central banks for the purposes of allowing those central banks to provide dollar liquidity to their commercial banks was a major aspect of the Fed's response and one that was new to this crisis. We saw it as a logical extension in interconnected global financial markets of a basic central bank function – supplying liquidity when uncertainty causes the usual funders of banks and other financial institutions to back away. In these circumstances, central bank liquidity becomes necessary to break or at least to damp the adverse feedback loop between funding difficulties and credit supplies to the economy.

From the onset of the crisis in August 2007, the financial markets were characterized by disruptions to bank and later nonbank funding as uncertainty about the solvency and viability of counterparties mounted. The lack of transparency in structured investments and in the balance sheets of some complex institutions and the sense that events were moving fast with unknown outcomes meant that market participants could not and did not discriminate well between good and bad counterparties. Their actions came to be dominated by fear and a run to safety and liquidity, resulting in a sharp cutback in lending to businesses and households as well as rapid sales of assets at declining market prices. Reduced lending and lower asset prices contributed in turn to a weakening economy, greater disruption of funding markets, and adverse effects on market liquidity. We were in a doom loop, whose intensity varied from late 2007 on, but didn't fully abate in the United States until after the banks were recapitalized and the stress tests of 2009 brought transparency to their condition. This type of market response could not be countered by open market operations because the reserves and liquidity would not be distributed through the financial system to where they were needed.

As a consequence, from the beginning central banks utilized their lending facilities to respond to the emerging crisis. This was seen as classic Bagehot central banking: when funding is generally disrupted, lend freely at a penalty rate against good collateral (valued as in normal times) to solvent institutions. This is the way to stem the panic, avoid fire sales, limit the reduction in credit availability, shore up confidence, and enhance market functioning.

The first liquidity swaps to deal with the cross-border aspects of disruptions to funding markets were announced in December 2007 with the European Central Bank and the Swiss National Bank. Increasingly intense foreign bank bidding for short-term dollar funding was putting upward pressure on the federal funds and other short-term dollar interest rates. Sales by foreign banks were adding to downward pressure on the prices of mortgage assets and having adverse effects on the liquidity in US financial markets.

By doing swaps with other central banks in addition to domestic discount window lending, the Federal Reserve was able to help relieve pressure in US funding markets without itself needing to make judgments about the solvency of foreign institutions and without taking risks of lending to these institutions. And they allowed the foreign central bank to make the moral hazard judgment that necessarily accompanies any provision of liquidity insurance. This seemed appropriate since home country authorities were overseeing these large globally active banks, and it would be home country taxpayers that could bear the consequences if liquidity failure turned into capital failure and if the failure of an institution impaired the functioning of home country financial markets. Moreover, global banks are often managed on a consolidated basis; the swaps enabled the banks to borrow dollars where collateral was located and then to redistribute that liquidity around their systems. The initial press release emphasized that the swaps were intended to help the functioning of United States and global markets.

The December 2007 announcement was coordinated across several foreign central banks in addition to the ECB and SNB in the context of a broad array of measures to relieve pressures and enhance the functioning of funding markets. For example, in the United States, the same press release announced the Term Auction Facility (TAF) for auctioning discount window credit here. The swaps were one element in a broad effort to make liquidity available so as to bolster confidence and reduce the adverse effects of market disruptions.

As the crisis deepened after the failure of Bear Stearns and then Lehman Brothers, the dollar swaps network grew in scope and size. It came to include fourteen countries; the ECB, Bank of Japan, SNB, and Bank of England were running TAF-like auctions of dollar loans, with no upper bound on what they swapped with us and lent to their banks. At the end of 2008, $554 billion was outstanding to nine different authorities; Mexico borrowed later, so at least ten central bank counterparties took advantage of these facilities. At the same time, of course, the scope and size of discount window lending in the United States was greatly expanding. The volume of lending through swaps came down rapidly as panic abated; this indicates that they were priced right in accordance with Bagehot principals – at a penalty to rates that would prevail if markets were functioning normally.

Did they work? Here's the bottom line of an extensive study published in 2010 by William Allen and Richhild Moessner in a BIS working paper: "We conclude that the swap lines provided by the Federal Reserve were very effective in relieving U.S. dollar liquidity stresses and stresses in foreign exchange markets, so that the Fed's objectives were substantially met. It seems plausible that had the Fed not acted as it did, global financial instability would have been much more serious and that the recession consequently would have been deeper. The effectiveness of the Fed's actions was most likely due to the fact that funds were provided quickly, limits were raised flexibly as the financial crisis intensified, especially after the failure of Lehman Brothers, and that large amounts were provided via the swap lines."[1]

Still, the swap lines raised some difficult issues as the FOMC debated their expansion in the fall of 2008. The first issue was the boundary problem: who to include and exclude. This came to the fore in particular when the swaps were extended to emerging market economies. We included Brazil, Korea, Mexico, and Singapore, which were characterized as "four large and systemically important economies" in the press release that announced the expansion, but undoubtedly other countries saw themselves as fitting into that category as well.

In the discussion at the October 2008 FOMC meeting, Nathan Sheets, the director of the Division of International Finance, put forth three criteria. First, that each country has significant economic and financial mass so problems there can spill over into the United States (Singapore was a systemically important financial center.) Second, that each had been well managed with prudent policies in place so that the stresses they were experiencing were a consequence of problems in the United States and other advanced economies. And third, that the swaps would help – that their banks had experienced or were subject to stresses related to dollar funding.[2]

The FOMC members generally agreed with these criteria and found that the four countries in question met them. Nonetheless, it was uncomfortable for the FOMC to be the arbiter of the soundness of other countries' policies, the liquidity requirements of their banks, and their systemic importance. The FOMC is always assessing the likely course of events in the rest of the world as they might affect the United States and progress toward the FOMC's objectives, but this issue raised the required knowledge and judgment to a very much higher and more detailed level, and the results of who might be in or out could have major effects on the countries involved. And how would the FOMC monitor whether the funds were being used for the intended purposes and not to avoid needed adjustment?

The second difficult issue related to the availability of alternative sources of liquidity for the authorities – to what extent should the Fed insist on other sources being utilized before it became the lender or swapper of last resort? Several of the fourteen had a large volume of dollar reserves that might be used to lend to their banks. In most cases, however, those reserves were being held for purposes of currency intervention, not liquidity provision

---

[1] Central Bank Cooperation and International Liquidity in the Financial Crisis of 2008–09, BIS Working Paper 310, May 2010, p. 75.
[2] www.federalreserve.gov/monetarypolicy/files/FOMC20081029meeting.pdf

to banks. Forcing them to run down their reserves before swaps were acti-
vated might send an adverse signal in exchange markets, where some were
already under pressure. Moreover, in most cases they didn't have enough
dollar reserves to meet the potential liquidity needs of their banks and those
limits would undermine confidence-enhancing effects of the dollar loans.
Being an effective lender of last resort requires the possibility of unlimited
resources, and the Fed was the only institution that met this criterion.

Another alternative might have been borrowing from the IMF. We
were in near-constant contact with the IMF as the swaps for Brazil, Korea,
Mexico, and Singapore were being put together. The IMF's resources are
quite limited, however, and loans from the IMF were perceived as carrying
a substantial stigma, as in the past those loans had signaled crisis conditions in the borrowing country and were accompanied by many conditions
for major reforms and often austerity. As such they carried considerable
political as well as economic risk for the leaders of the borrowing country.
The IMF initiated a new facility that relied on prequalification and was for
liquidity, not solvency, purposes and didn't have the conditionality of other
IMF facilities. But this facility was just getting started in the fall of 2008,
and it was unclear whether it would work with enough resources and with
largely unconditional access for sound economies and institutions.

How best to handle cross-border lender of last resort responsibilities for
a wide array of nations is still an open question – one that Steve Cecchetti
will address in his comments. It's important that the global policy community address this now. Uncertainty about whether a lender will be available in a crisis will only contribute to reserve accumulation as countries
self-insure, putting contractionary pressure on global growth and output.

As I noted at the beginning of these remarks, swaps and liquidity provision weren't the only areas in which the Fed was deeply involved in international aspects of the crisis. Another was monetary policy. On October 8,
2008, six major central banks, including the Federal Reserve, announced
simultaneous adjustments of their policy stances, with a view toward
"effecting some easing of global monetary conditions." This coordinated
action was unprecedented. I don't know who made the first phone call that
started the banks down this path, but the participation and leadership of
the Federal Reserve were essential. Importantly the coordinated cut provided a mechanism to help the ECB turn away from its focus on inflation,
which had precipitated an increase in rates in the euro area in August. It
was intended to boost confidence; the central banks were on the job coordinating actions on the thought that working together quite visibly would
be more effective than acting separately. Bank capital injections, borrowing

guarantees, and more expansionary fiscal policy would be required, but these would all take more time, and meanwhile central banks could act quickly and together.

More generally, the Federal Reserve, under the leadership of Ben Bernanke, led in innovating ways to ease financial conditions even after short-term rates had effectively hit zero – innovations that have been followed by other central banks. We cut rates aggressively at the early stages of the crisis and then after it deepened on the failure of Lehman Brothers. Once at the zero lower bound for nominal rates, the Fed used combinations of asset purchases and guidance about future interest rate targets to effect a further easing of financial conditions in order to stimulate growth and limit disinflation. Other central banks may have implemented parts of this program earlier, but the Fed put it together, innovated as more became needed, and explained why it was necessary for global economic recovery, even if some other countries were uncomfortable with the resulting capital flows. Over time other advanced economy central banks have adopted many of the elements of the Federal Reserve's program.

The Fed in International Crises

Charles Bean

I retired as the Bank of England's Deputy Governor for monetary policy in June 2014, having taken up the post just a couple of months before the collapse of Lehman Brothers. One of my roles was as the Bank's deputy at G7, G20, and IMF meetings and, given that, I thought that today I would reflect on some of the international aspects of the Fed's monetary policies during the Great Recession. In so doing, I aim to complement Don Kohn's discussion of the part played by the currency swap lines during the crisis.

As you are no doubt aware, there has been fairly vocal criticism in the G20 by some emerging economies of the highly stimulatory unconventional monetary policies pursued by the Federal Reserve – and by implication other central banks pursuing similar policies, including the Bank of England. The first bout occurred during 2010, when Guido Mantega, the Brazilian Finance Minister, famously accused the Fed of engaging in a "currency war" to depreciate the dollar. More recently, as the Fed moved to taper its asset purchases and began to prepare the ground for a normalization of policy rates, there was renewed criticism as emerging economies struggled to deal with the associated reversal in the flows of capital and a rise in the volatility of exchange rates and other asset prices.

The currency war argument rests on the view that the Fed's monetary policies were of the beggar-thy-neighbor variety. But, of course, there are several channels of international propagation, most of which generate positive, rather than negative, demand spillovers. Aside from the expenditure switching induced by dollar depreciation, expansionary monetary policies of either the conventional or unconventional variety generate an increase in US aggregate demand through intertemporal substitution and wealth effects, in turn generating positive demand spillovers to other countries through the import channel.

In addition, asset purchases reduce yields not only in the markets where the purchases take place, but also in the markets for substitute assets through portfolio balance effects. There are several papers that find the Fed's asset purchases also lowered yields in other countries' bond markets. For instance, Neely (2010) found that the impact on the yields on the sovereign bonds in other advanced economies was around half that of the impact on US yields, while Moore et al. (2013) found that the impact on emerging-economy government bond yields was around one-sixth of the impact on US yields. The falls in these bond yields will have further boosted foreign aggregate demand, through similar channels to which they raised US aggregate demand.

The net spillovers overseas associated with the Fed's aggressive monetary actions during the Great Recession were consequently theoretically ambiguous in sign. Moreover, simulations with global macroeconometric models invariably suggest that the net effect on activity in the rest of the world was likely to have been expansionary, not contractionary. Given that the world economy was – and still is – suffering from insufficient aggregate demand, I conclude that the Fed's monetary policies were helpful not only domestically but also for the rest of the world.

Rather than resulting from a deliberate attempt to shift the burden of the recession overseas through currency depreciation, the associated movements in exchange rates should obviously be seen instead as an incidental, and countervailing, by-product of a policy aimed at stimulating demand. Moreover, there is little sign that such a beggar-thy-neighbor depreciation actually took place, as both the dollar and the sterling effective exchange rates proved remarkably stable after the inception of quantitative easing.[1] That may have reflected the impact of enhanced growth prospects offsetting the impact of interest rate differentials.

As I see it, the problem lay less with the Fed's actions and more with the unwillingness of some other countries to adjust their policies enough to restore and rebalance the pattern of global aggregate demand, including permitting sufficient real exchange rate adjustment. Participants at successive G20 meetings from 2010 onwards agreed that a better outcome for the world economy could be achieved by combining three elements: steady fiscal consolidation in those advanced economies running large, and potentially unsustainable, fiscal deficits; structural reforms to product and labor markets in both advanced and emerging economies to boost supply

---

[1] Sterling did fall by almost a third in the early stages of the crisis, but the movement was complete by the time the Bank of England started buying assets in March 2009.

potential; and a rotation of the source of aggregate demand toward those countries running chronic current account surpluses before the crisis and away from those running chronic deficits.

This strategy was encapsulated in the G20 Framework for Strong, Sustainable, and Balanced Growth, but the recovery proved anything but strong, sustainable, and balanced. Why was it so difficult to achieve a superior coordinated outcome in practice? In part I believe that it reflects the inherent asymmetry, noted long ago by Keynes, that the pressure to adjust is typically greater on debtor than creditor nations; this asymmetry in the burden of adjustment can probably only be satisfactorily addressed if surplus countries attach a reasonably high probability to being on the other side of the fence in the not-too-distant future. Moreover, frequently layered on top is the moralistic view that saving and surpluses are somehow worthy while borrowing and deficits are shameful. In addition, because multiple actions by multiple actors are needed, there is real difficulty in ensuring that promises are kept and free riding is avoided. And that is more of a problem, the weaker are the political ties between countries.

I have more sympathy with the recent criticism of US policies prompted by 2013's "taper tantrum," if only because the economic rationale is more persuasive. In particular, the focus on this occasion has been the financial stability implications of large swings in capital flows, rather than the consequences for exchange rates or aggregate demand. Moreover, critics such as Raghu Rajan recognize that Fed policies need to normalize but are concerned that it should happen in a way that does not create financial instability overseas, for instance by leading to credit crunches or exposing currency mismatches on bank or corporate balance sheets.

I do not think, though, it is reasonable to ask the Fed to "aim off" achieving its domestic objectives of low and stable inflation and high and stable employment in order to take account of these financial stability concerns overseas. Not only would it run counter to the Fed's legal mandate, but it would also appear to constitute a suboptimal assignment of instruments to objectives.

The postcrisis conventional wisdom in the central bank fraternity is that monetary policy should remain focused on macroeconomic stability, while macroprudential policies should be assigned to the task of mitigating the risks to financial stability. Only once such macroprudential policies have proved ineffective or if the risks are building outside of the regulatory perimeter does it become appropriate to follow a second-best policy of mitigating those risks by following a "leaning against the wind" monetary policy.

By extension, the financial stability risks to emerging – and indeed other advanced – economies engendered by the monetary policies of the global financial system's hegemon are in the first instance best managed by the application of suitably targeted macroprudential policies in the affected countries. This includes not only conventional macroprudential policies designed to discourage excessive credit creation and risk concentration, but also those with an international dimension, such as avoiding currency mismatches or putting some "sand in the wheels" to discourage inflows and outflows of footloose foreign capital; see Pereira da Silva (2014) for a nice exposition of the use of such tools in the Brazilian case.

The use of such tools is not without risk, however. Recent experience provides a new legitimacy for so-called capital-management policies that moderate the international flow of capital. But some countries may deploy them to delay or prevent necessary macroeconomic adjustments. It is, therefore, important that bodies such as the IMF keep an eye out to ensure they are not abused.

In addition, macroprudential tools are most effective in attenuating the buildup of risk. They are arguably less likely to be effective in reducing the impact of risks that do crystallize. Here the conventional central bank armory of emergency liquidity support is more likely to be of value. Since the dollar is both a key funding currency for banks and often also functions as a safe haven for investors in times of stress, in the international context that requires countries either to have access to an emergency supply of dollars through the IMF or central bank swap lines, or else to self-insure by building up large reserve holdings and all that that entails.

Notwithstanding concerns about moral hazard, my sense from G20 discussions is that the emerging economies would feel considerably more comfortable about the Fed's exit from unconventional policies if they knew they could also rely on Fed support in the event of attendant financial instabilities. Indeed, that may represent a *quid pro quo* for the emerging economies' continued support for the current international monetary arrangements.

References

Moore, Jeffrey, Sunwoo Nam, Myeongguk Suh, and Alexander Tepper, 2013. "Estimating the Impacts of the U.S. LSAPs on Emerging Market Economies' Local Currency Bond Markets." Federal Reserve Bank of New York, Staff Report #595.

Neely, Christopher, 2010. "The Large Scale Asset Purchases Had Large International Effects." Federal Reserve Bank of St. Louis, Working Paper #2010-018D.

Pereira da Silva, Luiz A., 2014. "Global Dimensions of Unconventional Monetary Policy – an EME Perspective" in *Global Dimensions of Unconventional Monetary Policy*. Kansas, KS: Federal Reserve Bank of Kansas City.

The Global Dollar System

Stephen G. Cecchetti

The global financial crisis started in 2007 when European banks came under increasing strain. If forced to specify the crisis kickoff, I would pick Thursday, August 9, the day that BNP Paribas halted redemptions from three investment funds because it couldn't value their holdings of US mortgages.[1] Responding to the ensuing market scramble for liquidity, the ECB injected €95 billion that day into the European banking system and the Federal Reserve put $24 billion in theirs. Today, these numbers look quaint. Then, they seemed enormous.[2]

With time we learned that banks outside the United States, in Europe and elsewhere, had been borrowing a large volume of dollars in short-term money markets and investing it in US mortgage-backed securities. As the mortgages started to default and the securities lost value, the non-US banks had trouble rolling over their short-term debt. McGuire and von Peter (2009) eventually estimated the dollar shortfall to be well over $1 Trillion!

That there are significant parts of the global financial system that run on US dollars is no surprise. In 2013, the dollar accounted for 80 percent of trade finance[3] and 87 percent of foreign currency market transactions.[4]

---

[1] See *New York Times* (2007).
[2] For a contemporary account of the August 2007 event, see Cecchetti (2007).
[3] Data are from SWIFT, www.swift.com/about_swift/shownews?param_dcr=news.data/en/swift_com/2013/PR_RMB_nov.xml
[4] See the Bank for International Settlements (2013).

Professor of International Economics, Brandeis International Business School; research associate, National Bureau of Economic Research; and research fellow, Centre for Economic Policy Research. These remarks were prepared for the Federal Reserve Bank of Dallas conference on "The Federal Reserve's Role in the Global Economy: A Historical Perspective," September 18–19, 2014. These are largely based on Cecchetti (2014) and Cecchetti and Schoenholtz (2014b). I would like to thank Robert McCauley for guiding me through the data, and Kim Schoenholtz for his collaboration in preparing parts of these remarks. All errors are my own.

But the fact of the matter is that there is an enormous parallel dollar-based financial system – call it the Global Dollar system – that operates outside the United States.

Using data from the BIS, we can estimate the size of this Global Dollar system. Starting with US dollar liabilities of banks outside the United States, we quickly get to a sum around $13 trillion.[5] (If you have a dollar-denominated account in a bank in London, Zurich, or Hong Kong, it would be included in this total.) Now, not all countries report to the BIS, so this subtotal is incomplete.[6] China and Russia are missing, for example. In addition, Ecuador, El Salvador, and Panama are dollarized, so their banks are issuing dollar liabilities. Tallying these nonreporting sources may add another $1 trillion. Next come a few trillion dollars from dollar-denominated securities that are issued outside the United States (mostly in London).[7]

All of this leads to the conclusion that the Global Dollar system has issued dollar liabilities of more than $15 trillion; a volume that exceeds the total liabilities of banks operating within the United States.

Who should be concerned about this? In 1971, President Nixon's Treasury Secretary John Connally famously told an assembled group of European finance ministers: "The dollar is our currency, but your problem." He was speaking about exchange rates, expressing a view that was already questionable forty years ago.

Applied to the twenty-first century global system of dollar finance, Connally's view is patently false. The world's largest intermediaries are now so interdependent that if one gets into trouble, others are likely to follow. And the market for short-term dollar funding is unified globally. Consequently, if a systemically important bank in Europe finds itself unable to roll over dollar liabilities, it can be compelled to sell dollar assets at fire sale prices and, possibly, default, leading other banks to cut lending and hoard safe assets.

Such contagion puts the entire financial system at risk, making the US dollar everyone's problem. By lending to solvent but (temporarily) illiquid banks, a central bank can limit a liquidity crisis. Indeed, it was the frequent banking panics of the late nineteenth and early twentieth century that led to the creation of the Federal Reserve System as the US lender of last resort, the role already played by the European central banks of the day.[8]

---

[5]   This estimate comes from combining information from Tables 5A, 5D, 13A, and 14C from the BIS locational banking statistics available at www.bis.org/statistics/bankstats.htm

[6]   The list of reporting countries is available at www.bis.org/statistics/rep_countries.htm

[7]   Data are at www.bis.org/statistics/secstats.htm

[8]   According to Jalil (2015), from 1870 to 1910, there were four major and eight minor banking panics in the United States. This, even though banks appeared to have capital in

Yet, today's two dollar-based financial systems differ in one critical respect: banks operating or based in the United States have access to the Federal Reserve's discount window, so when they suddenly need dollars they can easily get them, provided that they are solvent. Other solvent banks, those in the parallel Global Dollar financial system, have no such access.

As Tucker (2014) so aptly puts it, we assign banks the task of providing liquidity insurance both by offering demand deposits and callable lines of credit. If we are going to have a liquidity insurer, Tucker goes on to say, then we need a liquidity reinsurer. This is a role that we normally assign to the central bank. So long as commercial banks offer liquidity insurance in domestic currency, we are fine. What about transactions in foreign currencies? What if an intermediary issues demandable deposits in a currency other than their domestic money? Who provides the reinsurance then?

Had the Federal Reserve merely accepted that dichotomy, the crisis of 2007–09 would have gotten much deeper much faster as leading European banks dumped assets or defaulted! Instead, in December 2007, the Fed introduced one of its most successful crisis mitigation tools, offering to lend US dollars to foreign central banks that they could in turn lend to their banks. Recognizing that fire sales and defaults of these foreign banks posed a systemic threat back home, the Fed eventually provided fourteen other central banks with large (in some cases, unlimited) dollar swap lines to meet the surge in funding dollar needs.[9] At the height of the crisis in December 2008, the amount lent peaked at nearly $600 billion.

Countries without access to the Federal Reserve swap lines had to find other alternatives. Some, like Argentina, Brazil, and the Philippines, offered banks access to the US dollar portion of their foreign exchange reserves. Others, including Colombia and Poland, obtained insurance from the IMF through its Flexible Credit Line (FCL).[10]

Policy innovation in the heat of a crisis is one thing. With the crisis over, we can now look forward a bit more calmly and ask: what mechanisms should we put in place to guard against future stresses? How should we manage the system's needs and risks of the Global Dollar system?

I see five possibilities:

1. Use prudential regulation to ban or restrict issuance of US dollar liabilities;

excess of 20 percent. (See the Tables C158 to C237 of the Historical Statistics of the United States.)

[9] The official announcements are on the Federal Reserve's website at www.federalreserve .gov/monetarypolicy/bst_liquidityswaps.htm

[10] See www.imf.org/external/np/exr/facts/fcl.htm for a description.

2. Make dollar supply the responsibility of the authorities where the activity is taking place;
3. Supply dollars through regional pooling of foreign exchange reserves;
4. Obtain dollars from a supranational institution such as the IMF; or,
5. Make the supply of dollars to the Global Dollar system the responsibility of the Fed.

Banning intermediaries from offering foreign currency accounts is not only naïve, it is foolish. It is naïve because people will find ways to transact in foreign currency regardless of the rules we might make; and it is foolish since it would dramatically reduce cross-border financial activity. Short of an outright ban, domestic prudential measures definitely have their place. But, in the end, restrictions of this sort will be limited to the degree that a country wishes to benefit from participation in the global system.

Moving to the second possibility, if the Banco Central do Brasil lets intermediaries in Rio de Janeiro create liabilities in US dollars, or the Bank of Korea allows banks in Seoul to do the same, isn't it their problem? Having sufficient foreign exchange reserves on hand to manage such a systemic event is surely one reason for the very dramatic accumulation over the past decade. As of mid-2014, aggregate foreign exchange reserves stood close to $14 trillion, or nearly 20 percent of global GDP. The cost of this is extraordinary. For each percentage point that the real return on these reserves is below the global marginal product of capital, someone is paying 0.2 percent of global GDP per year! And, those that are paying are primarily low-income countries.[11]

It is in an effort to reduce these costs that countries have worked to form regional reserve-pooling arrangements like the Chiang Mai Initiative.[12] But it is hard to see how the size of such a fund can be big enough without the ultimate support of the Fed.

The fourth approach is to have supranational institutions manage dollar shortages. The IMF's FCL, which provides qualified countries with guaranteed access to financing for a fee, is just such an arrangement.[13] But again, the question is one of size. Could the IMF have supplied the nearly $600

---

[11] Granted that countries hold foreign exchange reserves for a number of reasons, including defending their exchange rate. But in the end, these are held to manage capital outflows that will occur when their economies and financial systems are under stress.

[12] Initiated in 2000 and enhanced in 2007, the Chiang Mai Initiative is a multilateral swap agreement among ten countries in East Asia – the ASEAN + 3 – that draws on a reserves pool that is currently $240 billion.

[13] As noted earlier, during the crisis Colombia ($6.2 billion), Mexico ($73 billion), and Poland ($33.8 billion) have obtained committed lines of credit through the FCL. None of the credit lines were drawn.

billion that was drawn through the Federal Reserve swap facilities in late 2008? Unless there is a way to ensure resources that are nearly unlimited – as the swap lines are – it is hard to see how a supranational institution would be able to meet the demand for foreign currency in the case of a truly systemic event.

This brings me to the final option: the Federal Reserve itself provides the dollars through swap facilities. This is not only feasible, but given the enormous benefits accruing to the United States from the Global Dollar system, there is a sense in which it is just. To understand why I say this, we can do a rough accounting of the benefits and costs the US faces.

The benefits are a combination of reduced financing cost and the ability to run very large current account deficits to meet demand. On the first, the current consensus is that the United States receives a financing benefit in the range of 0.5 percent of GDP per year.[14] While, based on some rough calculations, it is possible to show that a current account deficit of between 2 and 2½ percent of US GDP is sustainable for years to come.[15] Adding these together, I conclude that the US gross benefit from being the issuer of the reserve currency is on something like 2½ to 3 percent of US GDP per year. Since the United States represents 23 percent of world GDP, this equals something in the range of 0.6 percent of global GDP.

Turning to the costs, the first and foremost is that this demand for reserve currency assets tends to push the value of the currency up and encourage borrowing from abroad. This flip side of the current account deficit has distortionary effects on the domestic economy. It creates sectoral imbalances, disadvantaging both export industries and domestic import competitors; and, in the process, it encourages borrowing from abroad. As we saw during the recent financial crisis, the latter can be particularly damaging if and when the leveraged asset prices turn from boom to bust. But it is difficult to see these as being even the same order of magnitude as the benefits.[16]

---

[14] This number is in substantial dispute. I have used the very conservative estimate of 50 basis points from Curcuru, Thomas, and Warnock (2013). Dividing foreign holdings of $14.6 trillion from the TIC data by 2014 GDP of $17.1 trillion and multiplying by 50 basis points yields 0.5 percent.

[15] See Cecchetti and Schoenholtz (2014a).

[16] A few years ago, a group of researchers at the McKinsey Global Institute put everything together and concluded that the net benefit to the United States is in the range of 0.5 percent of GDP. Their estimate seems quite small as a consequence of the fact that they treat the current account deficit as primarily a cost to exporters and import-competitors who supply less rather than a benefit to households that can consume more (for a very long time). See Dobbs et al. (2009).

In fairness, the rest of the world does gain from the existence of a reserve currency. The easiest benefit to see comes from the fact that the dollar is the de facto international numeraire. What this means is that, instead of having $n(n-1)/2$ currency markets, we only need $(n-1)$ with the US dollar as the other side of each. For a world with at least 150 currencies, that's the difference between 149 markets and 11,175. This is why the US dollar accounts for one side of nearly 90 percent of foreign exchange transactions. Even if there were no reserve currency, the market would create one simply as a way to reduce transactions costs. But it is hard to see these benefits as being anything close to the costs.

The natural conclusion is that, so long as the dollar remains in widespread use outside of the United States, the central bank liquidity swaps should be part of the Federal Reserve's permanent tool kit.[17] But, if that is to be the case, we will need to address a number of problems analogous to those faced by the domestic lender of last resort: moral hazard, adverse selection, and overstepping of one's mandate. On the first, if they have a backstop, countries will be tempted to allow their banks to provide too much foreign currency liquidity insurance to facilitate trade and capital flows. Controlling moral hazard will require a combination of international standards that restrict activity and a sufficiently high price charged by the Fed for the dollars – a penalty rate à la Bagehot. On adverse selection, there will have to be some mechanism for ensuring that the least creditworthy countries aren't the ones at the head of the line asking to swap their compromised currencies for dollars. Something similar to the IMF's prequalification mechanism may ultimately be required. And, since relying on an external organization is likely to be even more politically charged than doing it at home, one of the costs of being the supplier of the reserve currency may be that the Fed will have to employ a small staff of people who evaluate whether a country qualifies for a swap line. As for stepping on other people's toes, the US president may well view providing dollars to a foreign central bank, and hence to a foreign country, as foreign policy. Some people already view swap lines as beyond the bounds of the Fed's agreed activities. Political support for a broader extension of dollar liquidity provision is not in evidence.[18]

Among the many lessons that we learned from the events of the last decade is that a financial system requires a lender of last resort. Domestic financial stability requires having a central bank that can provide

---

[17] For a summary of the debate, see Truman (2013).
[18] There is also what I would consider to be a legal detail. The swap lines are the responsibility of the FOMC, and they require annual reauthorization as a matter of law, so permanence cannot be assumed.

domestic currency to ensure the system remains liquid. By the same token, if we are to continue to benefit from the movement of goods, services, and capital across borders, then we need a system that efficiently allocates the foreign exchange risk arising from the transactions that support these activities. And, the facilitation of cross-border transactions and the allocation of the associated risks inevitably requires that banks provide liquidity insurance in foreign currency. In the vast majority of cases, this means dollar liabilities. Ensuring financial stability in such circumstances requires that, when they face a liquidity crisis, banks outside the United States have access to dollars. So long as the global financial system runs on dollars, something that is likely for some time to come, it is to the benefit of the United States that the Federal Reserve finds a way to provide such access.

References

Bank for International Settlements, 2013. *Triennial Central Bank Survey of Foreign Exchange and Derivatives Market Activity in 2013*. December.

Cecchetti, Stephen G., 2007. "Federal Reserve Policy Actions in August 2007: Frequently Asked Questions (updated)." Available at www.voxeu.org, August 15.

2014. "Towards an International Lender of Last Resort." BIS Papers No. 79, September, 131–36.

Cecchetti, Stephen G. and Kermit L. Schoenholtz, 2014a. "How Big Can the U.S. Current Account Stay?" Available at www.moneyandbanking.com, July 24.

2014b. "The Dollar is Everyone's Problem." Available at www.moneyandbanking.com, September 29.

Curcuru, Stephanie E., Charles P. Thomas, and Frank E. Warnock, 2013. "On Returns Differentials." International Finance Discussion Papers, 1077, Board of Governors of the Federal Reserve System, April.

Dobbs, Richard, David Skilling, Wayne Hu, Susan Lund, James Manyika, and Charles Roxburgh. 2009. "An Exorbitant Privilege? Implications of Reserve Currencies for Competitiveness." Discussion Paper, McKinsey Global Institute, December.

Jalil, Andrew J., 2015. "A New History of Banking Panics in the United States, 1825–1929: Construction and Implications." *American Economic Journal: Macroeconomics* 7:295–330.

McGuire, Patrick M. and Goetz von Peter, 2009. "The US Dollar Shortage in Global Banking." *BIS Quarterly Review* March: 47–64.

New York Times, 2007. "BNP Paribas Suspends Funds Because of Subprime Problems." August 9.

Truman, Edwin M., 2013. "Enhancing the Global Financial Safety Net Through Central-Bank Cooperation." Available at www.voxeu.org, September 10.

Tucker, Paul M.W., 2014. "The Lender of Last Resort and Modern Central Banking: Principles and Reconstruction." BIS Papers No. 79, September, 10–42.

Perspectives of the Fed's Role in International Crises

Guillermo Ortiz

8.1 Introduction

I would like to thank the Dallas Fed, and particularly my friend Richard Fisher, for inviting me to participate in this roundtable.

These are challenging times for central banking all over the world and, especially, for the Fed, given the weight of the US economy and the international role of the dollar.

The Great Recession and the associated Global Financial Crisis have deeply eroded the broad consensus existing previously among economists and policymakers: flexible inflation targeting was considered to be the best operational rule for a central bank, and the short-term interest rate the basic, and almost unique instrument. That soothing and self-reassuring view has been seriously damaged.

In a world of near-zero interest rates, central banks have had to rely on unconventional policy tools – balance sheet expansion and forward guidance – to sustain aggregate demand. The Fed has played a pioneering and successful role in that respect.

It is now also clear that advanced economies are not immune to the financial instabilities that were of the essence of financial crises in emerging countries during the 1990s.

Financial stability has deep and complex connections with price stability and full employment. Whether financial stability is an objective on its own, implying complex trade-offs with inflation and output, is a controversial question. Certainly, macroprudential policies can address financial stability issues, but no doubt monetary policy could influence risk taking and contribute also to the fragility or strength of the financial system. In this context of intellectual reappraisal and policy experimentation, the question of the international role of the Fed has acquired a new dimension. Like that of any central bank, the mandate of the Fed is essentially domestic. In a strict sense, and notwithstanding the fact that international financial stability is a public good that any responsible national government may want to protect, any central bank should be concerned with international financial issues only to the extent that it affects domestic inflation and output.

However, it is difficult for a central bank to plug into its own decisions the consideration of their spillover effects on international financial markets and, even more so, the feedback on its own economy of such spillovers – the so-called spillback. This issue is paramount for the Fed notwithstanding its domestic legal mandate, given the international role of the dollar, as evidenced for example by the deep concerns existing today, especially among emerging countries, about the impact on international capital flows of a gradual reversal of the Fed's basic monetary policy.

8.2 The Fed's Role in International Crisis Management

To get some insights, it could be interesting to reassess the Fed's role in past international crisis management. I would like to make some remarks on this issue from the viewpoint of someone directly involved in the management of the 1994–95 Tequila Crisis and the impact on Mexico in 2008–09 of the Lehman Brothers collapse.

Due to the depth and breadth of the economic interaction between the two countries, Mexico has a special relationship with the United States and the Bank of Mexico also has a special relationship with the Fed ... and, even more so with the Dallas Fed as my friend Richard Fisher knows well. As observed over time, GDP growth, and particularly industrial production, in the United States directly impact output and employment in Mexico since our exports to the United States represent 23 percent of our GDP.

Interest rates and liquidity in US financial markets are key factors in determining the volume and composition of capital flows into Mexico: given the openness of the Mexican financial sector and the size of the US one, arbitrage is wide and fast, and it is almost impossible for Mexican monetary policy to significantly diverge from the Fed's. Over time market swings favored by financial integration with the United States have historically been a factor explaining the dynamics of Mexican financial crises, which have frequently been a sort of advanced indicator of financial trouble in other emerging economies. But, economic events in Mexico also impact the United States.

For example a downturn in Mexico has traditionally induced migration to the United States and a sizable negative impact on economic activity in southern Texas, given the real integration across the border economies. And the international contagion effect of financial crisis in Mexico has been a factor of concern for the Fed. For those reasons, Mexico has probably been in the Fed's agenda more than other emerging countries, as evidenced in its role during the 1994–95 and 2008–09 financial crises.

The causes of the Tequila Crisis are well known and out of the scope of this panel. I want just to say here that it was a paradigmatic banking crisis.

In a context of bullish expectations created by the upcoming NAFTA, capital inflows induced a bank lending boom to the private sector. Banks had just been privatized, financial regulation was weak, and macroprudential policies were badly institutionalized. Systemic risks were widespread, as evidenced in a mismatch of currencies and maturities.

However, the immediate cause of the crisis, in addition to the deteriorating political environment, was a deep change in the Fed's monetary policy from early 1994 on: the fed funds rate increase from 3 percent in January to 6 percent in December. In retrospect, given the impossibility to have in Mexico a monetary policy opposed to the US cycle, the optimal reaction should have been a change in the exchange rate regime (from managed to free float), supported by contractionary monetary and fiscal policies.

An underestimation of the length and depth of the Fed's turnaround, the political difficulty of a severe fiscal adjustment in an election year, and the concern of the Bank of Mexico about the impact of a sharp devaluation and high interest rates on an already fragile banking sector delayed the proper policy reaction and led to a full-fledged financial crisis.

Certainly, a better exchange of views between the Bank of Mexico and the Fed during 1994 would have been welcome. However, once the crisis exploded in December 1994, the role of the Fed was a key element for controlling and overcoming it. Three elements were of importance:

1. First, a sizable swap line between the Bank of Mexico and the Fed amounting to $4 billion, although the size and conditions for use were more like "window dressing" than a source of actual liquidity. However, the signaling effect of the Fed's support in the critical circumstances of early 1995 was very important to increase the credibility of Mexico's adjustment policies.
2. Second, the New York Fed's direct involvement in designing and implementing the trust fund that was to channel the revenues from Pemex oil exports as a guarantee for repayment of the loan granted from the US Stabilization Fund. That trust could probably have been put in place in another institution, for instance a large private US bank,

but the fact that the New York Fed was involved had also a strong signaling effect.

3. Third, goodwill. This may have been the least tangible but most important contribution of the Fed to the external financial package that was put in place to support Mexico's adjustment policies. As some of you may remember, the size and speed required for an efficient financial package was inconsistent with traditional IMF mechanisms and direct involvement of the US government was necessary. When the US Congress backed away, President Clinton and the Treasury decided to mobilize the executive Stabilization Fund. Since the number of $50 billion was floated around in the Congress deliberations and became the magical size of the required package in the minds of financial markets participants, that number had to be reached and $20 billion had to come from the Stabilization Fund ($17.5 billion came from the IMF, the largest contribution ever at that time).

Even though the Stabilization Fund is out of the scope of the Fed, it is clear that the Executive Branch would not have authorized it without the open support of the Fed. Undoubtedly, the constant institutional involvement of the Fed in the discussions between Mexican authorities and United States and IMF officials, the analytical contribution of its staff, and the personal good will of its Chairman made it possible to put together expeditiously a new kind of policy and support package to deal with a deep financial crisis in a big developing country.

It is well understood that this package became a reference when dealing with Asian crises and almost a "cookie cutter" for the IMF design of the corresponding international support and domestic adjustment policies. Perhaps things would have been bumpier if the first financial crisis of this kind (a banking crisis in a globalized economy) had taken place in Asia and not in Mexico, because the Fed's involvement in the design and implementation of the financial rescue package might have been less justified in a faraway country than in the case of its southern neighbor.

Another example, albeit much less dramatic, of the Fed's international role in Mexico refers to the 2008–09 financial crisis. Mexico, as most large emerging economies, did not suffer severe financial dislocations, at least not to the extent of developed economies. However, in the immediate post–Lehman Brothers collapse period, risk-averse capital flew out of the country, the exchange rate was left to float, and turmoil was apparent in derivative markets. In this occasion, coordination between the Bank of Mexico and the Fed was expeditious and efficient. The Fed was acting as a lender of last resort providing through central banks in developed countries (mostly in Europe) dollar liquidity in the face of an abrupt shrinking of money markets. The Bank of Mexico asked the Fed to put in place a large swap line between the two central banks to temper volatile expectations. The Fed was concerned about the possible spillover effects of the US crisis on Mexico (the first time things moved in that direction). We agreed on a $30 billion swap, but, as opposed to the line put in place in 1995, that swap was not window dressing but an effective credit line, the first of its kind in the case of emerging countries. We used it up to $3.5 billion, not because we needed it, but to show the markets that it could indeed be disposed of. The impact on expectations was immediate. In order not to single out Mexico (which neither we nor the Fed wanted to do), this facility was extended to some other emerging countries, especially in Asia.

8.3 Lessons from These Episodes

I think the two episodes I just briefly discussed provide some interesting perspective on the Fed's role in international financial crises. I would emphasize three lessons:

First, the Fed's monetary policy works as a very stringent restriction for the definition of Mexico's monetary policy, in the sense that any sustained deviation quickly tends to backfire through instabilities in the Mexican financial sector. Historically, the Fed has played a key role in supporting Mexico during various episodes of financial crisis, mostly through good will, signaling effects, and, occasionally, some more direct participation. To a large extent, the involvement of the Fed was justified because of the deep integration of the Mexican and the US economy. Looking forward, one can hope that the role of the Fed in Mexico will be less through a key support during crisis episodes and more through an ongoing cooperation to avoid them.

Second, as it has been widely acknowledged, the mandate of the Fed is domestic even though the spillover effects of its decisions are global. No matter how perverse or undesirable this situation may be, it is a fact of life derived from the evidence that the dollar is the reserve currency of the world. No matter how beneficial the international role of the dollar may be for the US economy, the reserve status of the dollar is not a decision of the US government but a decision of international financial markets, so one cannot realistically expect that the Fed can alter its policies only because of its international consequences: that is the basic foundation of the often quoted famous remark by John Connally, President Nixon's Treasury Secretary, to a European delegation worried about exchange rate fluctuations: "the dollar is our currency, but it's your problem."

Of course, the Fed does care about international financial stability, not only because of some sort of benevolent concern, but mostly because it affects the dynamics of the US economy in obvious ways. In the short run, as recent data show, slow global growth has reduced export demand for US products and to some extent foreign earnings of US corporations, acting as a strong headwind for the US economic recovery.

In the longer run, it is clear that financial stability in a large country is interlinked with financial stability globally and, thus, enhanced international cooperation among regulators is required in a post–Global Financial Crisis world. Impressive progress has been made in some areas but further progress is required in the most difficult and complex ones.

To the extent that a central bank shares responsibility for the regulatory oversight of the banking system, the financial stability objective has a significant effect on monetary policy discussions; from an a priori viewpoint, you may want monetary policy to internalize its effects on financial stability, mostly through its impact on risk-taking in some pockets of the financial sector, but one must acknowledge that these are new and difficult issues which are just being explored. Aiming to attain the dual goals of maximum employment and stable prices, while maintaining domestic and, even more so, international financial stability, requires dealing with new practical challenges that involve assessing extremely complex analytical issues. That is a daunting institutional and intellectual endeavor that may go beyond the scope of the Fed's mandate.

Third, one must acknowledge that the IMF is the only international institution that has a legal mandate to look after financial and economic stability globally. In the case of Mexico's financial crises, the effectiveness of the Fed's ad hoc role was increased because it was part of a wider effort formally and explicitly conducted by the IMF. In the future the Fed's role in financial crises, in avoiding them or confronting them, cannot be conceived without an enhanced cooperation with the IMF, but with a strengthened IMF. As the global economy becomes more interconnected, more balanced in terms of income shares, and more uncertain, the capacity to react efficiently and in a coordinated fashion to crises which are global in scope will be key in avoiding huge welfare losses. This implies making the IMF governance structures more "cooperation oriented" and fair; enhancing its analytical framework to incorporate new cross-border transmission channels and enhancing efficient "early warning indicators"; increasing and making more flexible crisis response facilities and resources; endowing it with the proper tools to achieve traction in risk mitigation though collective action; and, if warranted, extending its mandate to fully cover all potential sources of systemic global risk, including capital account dynamics.

9

The Robert V. Roosa Lecture

Excerpts from a Conversation between Richard W. Fisher and Paul A. Volcker

RICHARD FISHER: It's a great pleasure to introduce the "Moses of Central Banking," Paul Volcker. Paul and I are friends. He's been a mentor. There's a reason for it. We both were trained by a man named Robert V. Roosa, which is why this is called the Roosa Lecture. Well, actually, a Roosa conversation. Paul is Class of '49. I was Class of '75. Bob Roosa did this until he passed on and there were lots of good people that went through the program, but like the presidency of the United States, starting with the first, George Washington, with each generation, the quality has gone downhill. So you have here before you tonight the best and the worst! Before we get into the conversation, I want to just stand in front of this audience and thank this man for saving our country and for resisting enormous political pressure to get that done. So, please join me in applauding him and thanking him.

PAUL VOLCKER: I thought you were talking about George Washington.

RICHARD FISHER: The last thing I'll say is Paul Volcker has been on this earth for 87 percent of the time that the Federal Reserve System has been in existence. I asked him, "Are you 86 or 87?" He said, "My answer is, 'Oh, to be 80 again.'" Paul?

PAUL VOLCKER: Well, thank you! I'm delighted to be here. When I heard about this program and the subject, the first 100 years of the Federal Reserve, I thought it would be terrific to come down. I was listening as the lecture was being introduced and I thought I got to know Bob Roosa I think sixty-five years ago. We're here at the 100th year of the Federal Reserve. I cannot claim acquaintanceship with Woodrow Wilson who started the Federal Reserve, but I did know Robert Roosa at a critical time in the Federal Reserve Bank of New York. Let me just say a word about him. You don't hear much about him. He didn't win any Nobel Prizes, but he was a colleague or in the same group with

Paul Samuelson and some others. They were writers and scholars. He was a doer, and he spent his life in the Federal Reserve. He was the brains of the Federal Reserve Bank in New York. And in those days, we used to think the Federal Reserve Bank in New York was the Federal Reserve. There was no difference. But he went down to Washington and became the Undersecretary of the Treasury for Monetary Affairs. In that capacity Bob Roosa was responsible for anything that was international as well as domestic finance. I have a little hobbyhorse that I will give to you. It means something to me. It may not mean anything to anybody else. But Bob Roosa, when he was at the Treasury, when I was an assistant of his, was pretty occupied with international affairs, monetary affairs, central banks, American central banks, foreign central banks, and Treasury officials. His title was Undersecretary of the Treasury for Monetary Affairs. Monetary affairs meant monetary affairs without any distinction between domestic monetary affairs and foreign monetary affairs. I'm sure it's clear in this conference and elsewhere, but these days and in those days as well, there is no clear-cut distinction between domestic policy and monetary policy and international monetary policy. Back then he was the only person apart from the Secretary of the Treasury himself that inherently had the responsibility to reconcile in his own mind and in policy, international and domestic monetary affairs. Unfortunately, that title has been dropped and we now have an Undersecretary for Domestic Finance and an Undersecretary for International Institutions and an Undersecretary of International – we have more undersecretaries than you can shake a stick at. In those days, we only had two. We had one, the Administrative Undersecretary and the Undersecretary for Monetary Affairs. I'm really sorry that that still doesn't exist. I wish we could go back to that former pattern because it does recognize a connection between the international and domestic.

I'll tell you who Bob Roosa was. He was an imaginative man, and he devoted more time and more effort to maintain the stability of the dollar. In the early 1960s when it first came under pressure, the dollar was at the center of the international monetary system. It was very important at the time to keep the gold price at $35 an ounce.

RICHARD FISHER: So you mentioned gold. You were involved in the decision go off the gold standard in 1971 that ushered in the modern era of purely fiat money. So, I guess the question is, "Is there anything that could have been done differently in the run up to that decision?" There might have been a role for gold or some other commodity to continue to play some role – as some have advocated – in the global monetary system. Or, are we just well rid of what Keynes referred to as a barbaric relic?

PAUL VOLCKER: I don't think there is a really serious consideration of another commodity standard. Some people used to write about a basket of commodities. As a kind of preparation for this meeting, I went back and read a great debate – which was well-known at the time – between Bob Roosa defending fixed exchange rates and a fixed gold price, and Milton Friedman who was an articulate proponent of flexible exchange rates. Bob thought a lot about the importance of maintaining the dollar at the center of the system, and that this would require maintaining a fixed dollar price of gold. In that situation, other countries had more freedom to change the value of their own currencies and to change it in a way that was to their advantage by improving the competitiveness of their exports.

A key element in the push for international monetary reform, as we thought about it at that time, was: how do we maintain the position of the dollar and the gold price steady against the pressures that would inevitably exist to create an over valuation of the dollar as against under valuation of other currencies.

People worried endlessly about the trade deficit and the balance of payments in those days. When you look at these figures now, it's almost ludicrous. They would worry about the deficit and the balance of payments of $2 billion. Not $2 billion a day, $2 billion a week, $2 billion a month, but $2 billion a year. Most of that period, in fact, the United States ran a current account surplus.

The Federal Reserve did not have a 2 percent target for inflation in those days. Inflation was down towards zero and the economy was doing very well at that time. As the decade passed, with the Vietnam War we had some inflation. Our current account was not as strong as it had been a couple of years earlier. President Nixon took the decision in the summer of 1971 (August 15th, in my mind), to suspend gold payments for dollars, which left the dollar potentially floating and other currencies floating.

The decision was taken at Camp David. I remember wandering around Camp David. That night was a beautifully clear, the stars were still up there. They didn't seem to have moved. We were off gold. We're going to be off gold the next day and somehow the cosmos were still there. And it is still there, but it led to a very bumpy period thereafter.

There was no willingness by other countries to maintain the system. There was an effort to reconstruct a monetary system not quite like the old one but that would have maintained a fixed price for gold where we would have more flexibility in the exchange rates, but basically, a modification and reform of the previously existing system.

Now, I spent a year personally working on that. At the end of the day, we couldn't pull it off and we ended up with this kind of, I think, awkward floating system.

RICHARD FISHER: I guess the question is did the transition to a non-gold standard or the fiat money standard in the 1970s inevitably lead to inflation? Was that an inevitable outcome?

PAUL VOLCKER: Certainly, we had a lot of inflation. It's almost unbelievable how much inflation there was in commodity prices in the early 1970s when we went off gold, and there was the oil crisis and you had double-digit or more inflation and levels of commodity prices that we hadn't seen before. The argument was made that that would not have happened. Part of the argument of the oil producers was since we were losing our hold on the dollar, they were also losing on the price of oil, so they were justified in raising the price of oil. The result was a considerable inflation which continued to rise throughout the '70s.

Roosa's argument basically came down to the position that it's not beyond the capability of domestic policy changes to stabilize our external position. Milton Friedman said, "Enough! Forget about all of that." The loss of the dollar standard as a discipline was necessary to have effective domestic policy. If we don't have the discipline of the dollar, we don't need all the same domestic discipline. Obviously, he was not arguing for great inflation. But he did not believe the argument that you could submit the domestic economy to kind of continuing discipline to external demands and maintaining the value of the dollar. We could do better – we just let it float. That argument persisted to this day, and there we are.

RICHARD FISHER: I'll shift gears a little bit because you mentioned earlier the brief experiment with the new monetary system and people forgot about it. People have not forgotten about the Bretton Woods System. You've called recently for a new Bretton Woods System. I wonder if you could just sort of explain what do you want, what would you like to see.

PAUL VOLCKER: I'm back on the same argument. I'm sorry, I was educated by Mr. Roosa. I never forgot it. When you look back at this last crisis, a great crisis, the biggest crisis since the 1930s, and of course, it was a very complicated financial crisis. There were a lot of causes, a lot of things went wrong. Markets in housing went wild. I'm saying that perhaps the Federal Reserve was not quite as disciplined as it might have been. There were a lot of complex and new inventions of derivatives and all kinds of complicated things. We always had international capital flows, but international capital flows became much more complicated and much more complex. But the crisis originated in the mortgage market, into subprime mortgages.

I gave a speech in about 2005. I said, "We are on an unsustainable course. We're running a big balance-of-payments deficit." Everybody was happily lending money to us. China was growing like crazy by exporting. They were perfectly happy to hold dollars so long as they could export to us. Asia financed our deficits. They were financing our deficits with 2 percent interest or whatever it was. The funds could be used to build houses and buy a lot of other things, and there wasn't any real restraint. There was a lack of discipline in financial markets, generally, and in the American financial markets in particular. That was an awkward situation for the Federal Reserve to handle because it was more appropriate to get a stronger fiscal policy, which we didn't.

So we permitted all of these imbalances. I tried to say at the time that we could adjust to all these, we could take care of all these imbalances by intelligent policies but we won't, and it's all going to end up in a big financial crisis. I did not predict the nature of the crisis. I'd never heard of a subprime mortgage at that point. But in fact, I do think monetary policy was a contributing factor to the lack of discipline in financial markets that, indeed, led to a massive financial collapse in the United States and elsewhere in the world.

When I look at this, I haven't got any perfect answers, but I think we are missing two things. We are missing a sense of discipline. It stood to reason early in this century, I believe, that there's something wrong. We could not go on and continue borrowing four to five, six to seven percent of GDP from abroad without getting in trouble.

There needed to be some kind of an exchange rate adjustment, which nobody was making. So, we can redesign a financial system today. I'm not arguing it's easy, but we recognized that there is a desirability for some discipline in a financial system in terms of carrying out appropriately disciplined domestic policies and a way to get exchange rate adjustments when and if necessary without bringing down the house, so to speak. As in the early '70s, when exchange rates were going up and down by 25 percent, even 50 percent, it couldn't help anything without domestic discipline.

Can we define a new system? I don't think this can be very detailed, with every sentence argued about. We are going to have to use some judgment. I don't think the IMF is itself a strong enough institution to enforce it. I don't think any economy has a strong enough institution to do it alone. But we could set an institutional structure that, in fact, can provide warning signals when discipline is necessary in the collective interest. Everybody talks about the exorbitant privilege of the dollar, and I have a second thought of this because everyone is buying dollars today. We're not urging it upon them, but there's an exorbitant privilege that we can balance our payments so easily by the dollar. It's also an insidious temptation to keep doing and doing and doing that until we get in trouble.

So, I think the great privilege is also a great temptation. Put them both together, you haven't got a good monitoring system. "Oh, to be 80 again," I'd fix it up but I'm not going to do it.

RICHARD FISHER: When you speak about discipline, one of our speakers tomorrow, and by the way, one of the key advisers to this Bank is John Taylor. He's the father, of course, of the Taylor Rule. All of us should have rules named after us! But I'm curious, Paul, what are your views on a rules-based monetary policy.

PAUL VOLCKER: Well, I've always wanted to have discretion and we had quite a lot of discretion. A lot of discretion has been used in the last four or five years, and I think it would have been unfortunate to have been highly constrained by rules. No, I'm not an expert on the Taylor Rule and I'm sure it's kind of a sensible review of the way policy has reacted to ordinary recessions and inflations and so forth. But I would be very skeptical of trying to write into law or practice some very definite rule. The only rule I liked is the Federal Reserve's responsibility for price stability, and I started with that assumption.

RICHARD FISHER: Price stability.

PAUL VOLCKER: Yes. Obviously, when we are in a big recession and prices are pretty stable, monetary policy is going to offset the recession. There are other things you can do. But the basic responsibility of a central bank to me, I'm sorry, remains pretty simple – price stability.

RICHARD FISHER: I want to bring this to an end because we're going to have dinner and – I just want you to reflect, if you will, just a little bit personally. Here we are, one of the Banks of Federal Reserve System. You've had a lot of opportunity to reflect on your tenure. You did something great for our country in breaking the back of inflation. We've gone through a subsequent period of having a system nearly fall to its knees, and some of your successors have had to deal with these enormous difficulties.

The system is expanding, but if you could just share with us your overall feeling about the central bank, I mean, we're the third in American history. We've just turned 100. We, too, would like to be saying perhaps, "Oh, to be 80 again," because it was a lot less exciting perhaps at that time than it is now. So just share with us, if you will, just one or two personal vignettes of what makes us a precious institution.

PAUL VOLCKER: The Federal Reserve is a precious institution. A lot of people would like to get rid of it, but basically, it retains a respect and an independence that is really unique among regulatory agencies. You can argue about some others, the Centers for Disease Control, the FBI, and so on – all have a lot of respect. But the Federal Reserve is one of the few agencies that have general respect. It's got a lot of competent people, it's professional, it's professionally run. Now I have to admit, if you took a survey today, this would not be so strongly an expressed opinion today as it would have been 10 years ago because of the crisis. But I don't think you can have a strong regulatory system without the Federal Reserve being an important part of it.

I actually think that banking supervision and banking regulation have to be part of monetary policy because they are interrelated. You can't conduct monetary policy without worrying about the financial system. If you have a broken financial system, you're not going to have a sensible monetary policy.

One of the great things about the Federal Reserve has been this regional system that was the result of a political compromise 100 years ago. It worked out pretty well, and that's part of the strength of the Federal Reserve System. Things have changed, and nobody today would distribute Federal Reserve Banks the way they are currently distributed across the country. I don't know anybody on a campaign to change that, but the business role of the Federal Reserve has shrunk.

I will tell you from my own experience that the interest within the Federal Reserve itself in banking supervision has not been uniform. It has varied from time to time nationally, but also within the banks. The big question is: how can we utilize the resources that exist within the Federal Reserve System and a revised federal regulatory structure to take advantage of the respect of the Federal Reserve, the independence of the Federal Reserve, the regional strength and support of the Federal Reserve in a way that contributes to financial stability?

All are important assets that somehow we ought to combine in this new regulatory system.

RICHARD FISHER: Well, we will invite you back in six months. And again, we thank you for what you've done in serving our country. You had so many other options, and yet, you devoted yourself to the Federal Reserve, to economic stability, to quashing inflation.

PAUL VOLCKER: Bob Roosa, we will attribute it all to Bob Roosa. It's still there. It's still there in my mind.

RICHARD FISHER: Amazing that one man could have that much influence. I wanted to say transgenerational, but at least over his lifetime. I do want to remind people this is in honor of Robert Roosa, but the great honor for us is having Paul Volcker here tonight with such a distinguished audience. So, thank you, Paul, very much for being here this evening.

Index

Printed in the United States
By Bookmasters